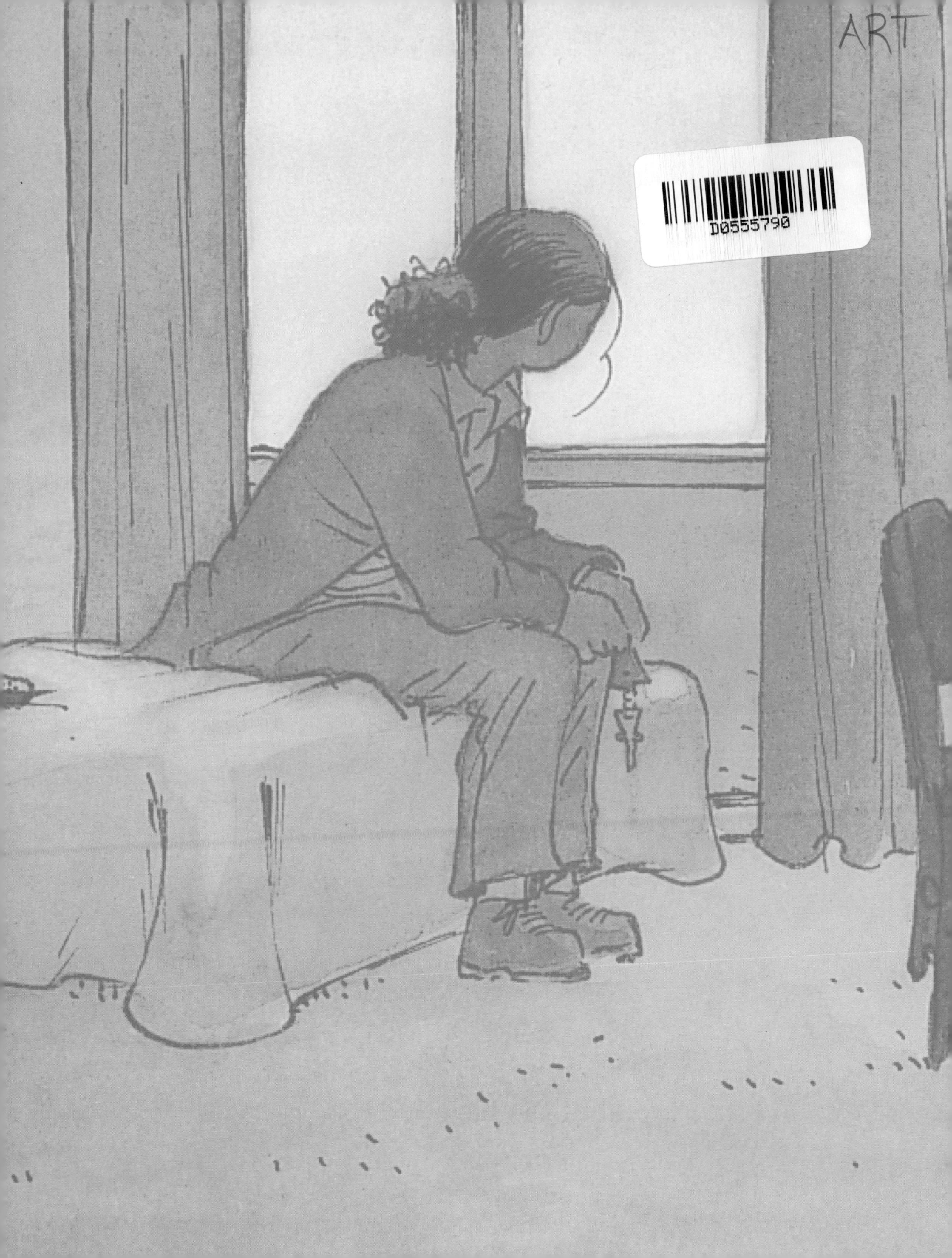

Lulu
Anew

ISBN 9781561639724
Library of Congress Control Number: 2014956688
© Futuropolis 2008, 2010
© NBM 2015 for the English translation
Translation by Joe Johnson
Lettering by Ortho
Printed in China
1st printing April 2015

This book is also available digitally wherever e-books are sold.

Comicslit is an imprint
and trademark of

NANTIER · BEALL · MINOUSTCHINE
Publishing inc.
new york

Étienne Davodeau

Lulu
Anew

This story is fiction. Any resemblance to events that may
have occurred in your life or those of your loved ones would
be purely by chance (which is one hell of a trickster).

É.D.

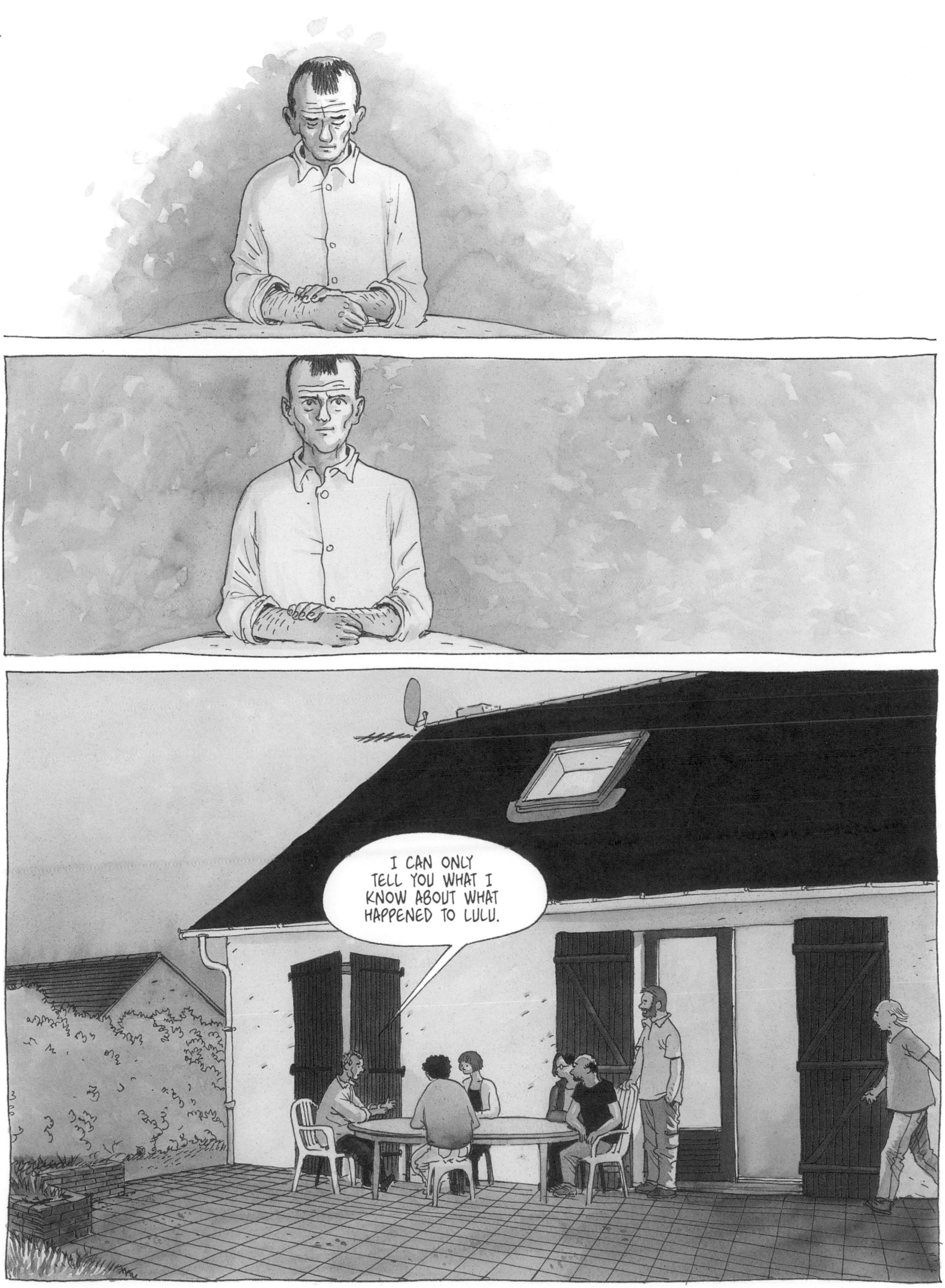
I CAN ONLY TELL YOU WHAT I KNOW ABOUT WHAT HAPPENED TO LULU.

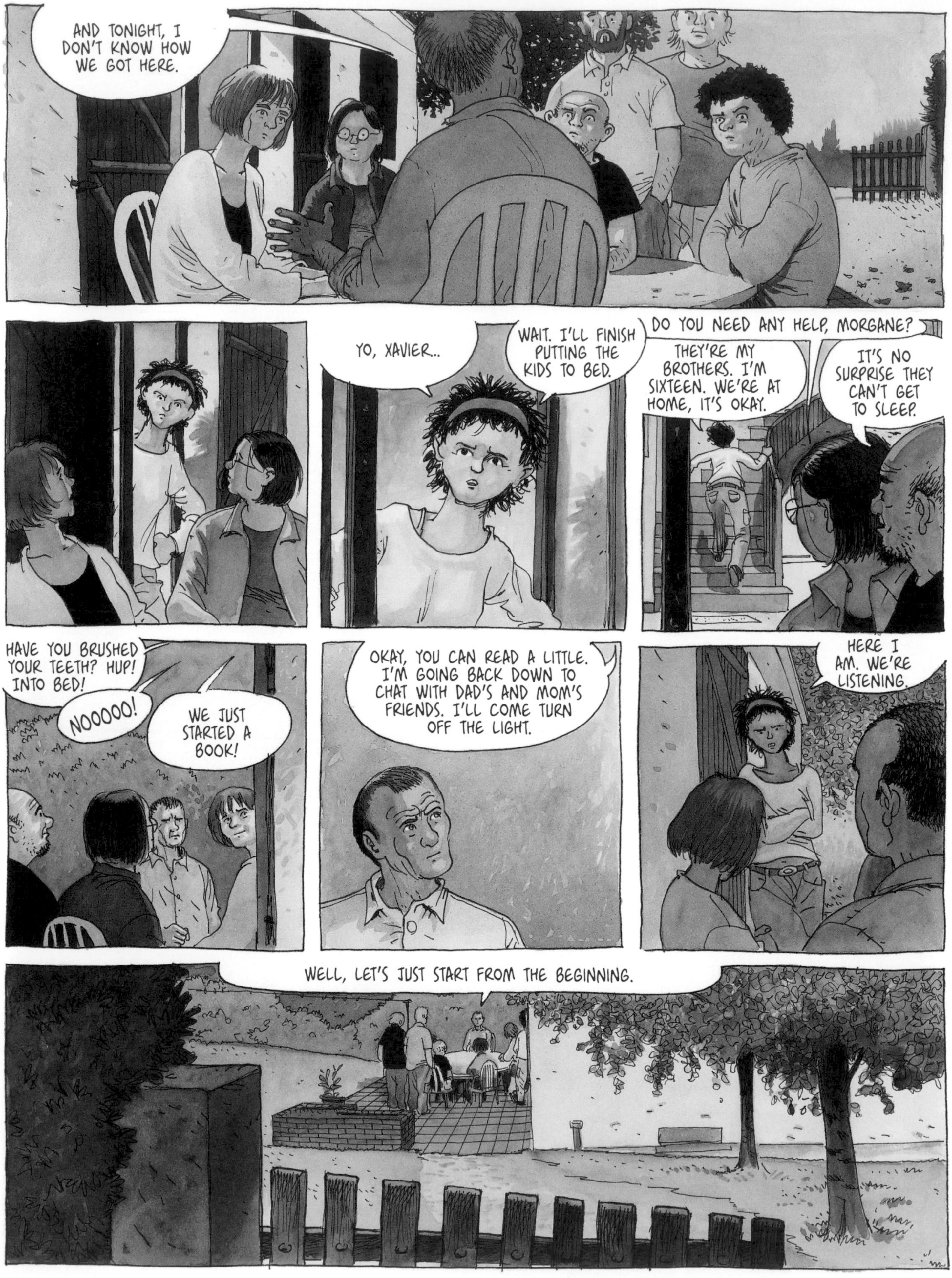
AND TONIGHT, I DON'T KNOW HOW WE GOT HERE.
YO, XAVIER...
WAIT. I'LL FINISH PUTTING THE KIDS TO BED.
DO YOU NEED ANY HELP, MORGANE?
THEY'RE MY BROTHERS. I'M SIXTEEN. WE'RE AT HOME, IT'S OKAY.
IT'S NO SURPRISE THEY CAN'T GET TO SLEEP.
HAVE YOU BRUSHED YOUR TEETH? HUP! INTO BED!
NOOOOO!
WE JUST STARTED A BOOK!
OKAY, YOU CAN READ A LITTLE. I'M GOING BACK DOWN TO CHAT WITH DAD'S AND MOM'S FRIENDS. I'LL COME TURN OFF THE LIGHT.
HERE I AM. WE'RE LISTENING.
WELL, LET'S JUST START FROM THE BEGINNING.

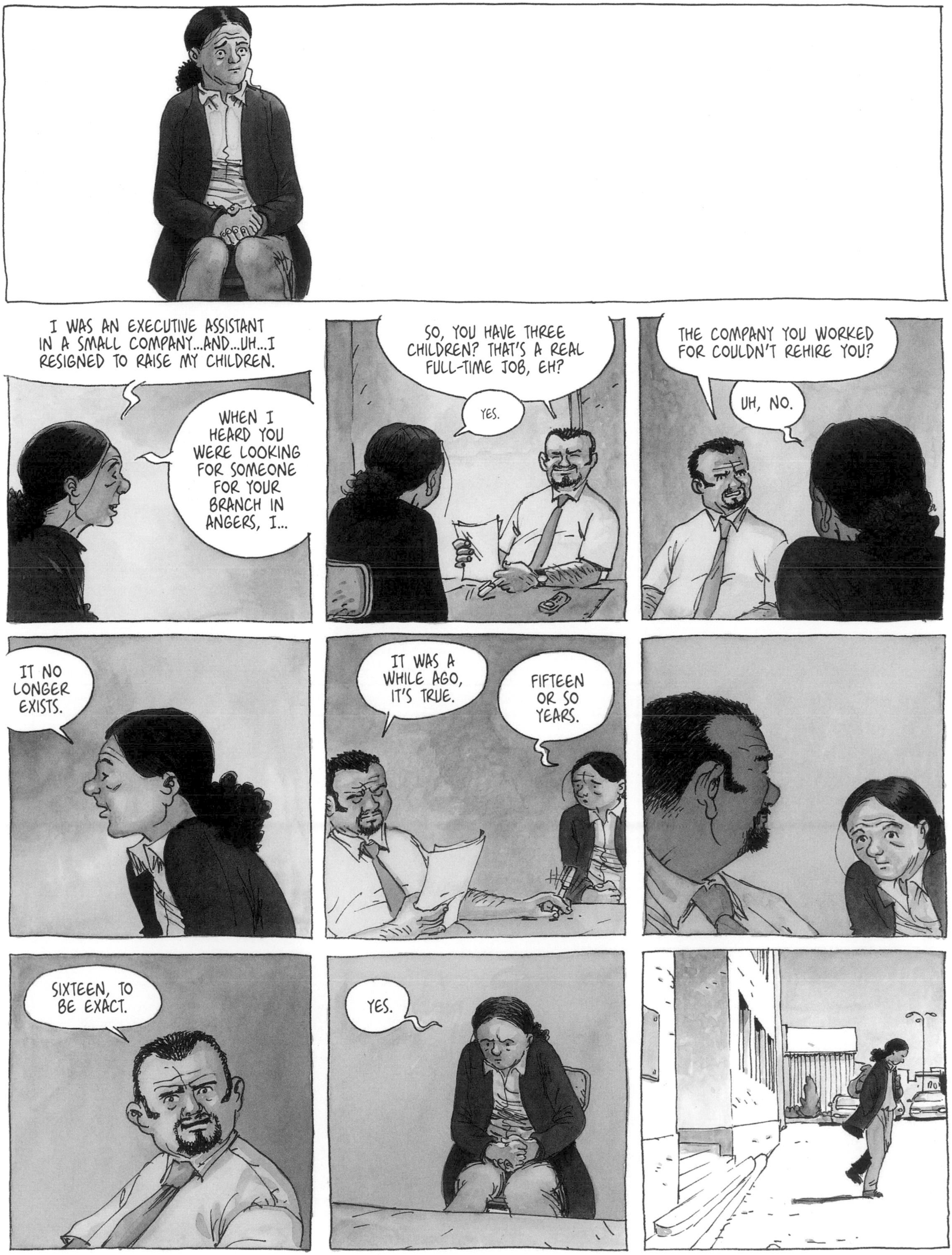
I WAS AN EXECUTIVE ASSISTANT IN A SMALL COMPANY...AND...UH...I RESIGNED TO RAISE MY CHILDREN.
WHEN I HEARD YOU WERE LOOKING FOR SOMEONE FOR YOUR BRANCH IN ANGERS, I...
SO, YOU HAVE THREE CHILDREN? THAT'S A REAL FULL-TIME JOB, EH?
YES.
THE COMPANY YOU WORKED FOR COULDN'T REHIRE YOU?
UH, NO.
IT NO LONGER EXISTS.
IT WAS A WHILE AGO, IT'S TRUE.
FIFTEEN OR SO YEARS.
SIXTEEN, TO BE EXACT.
YES.

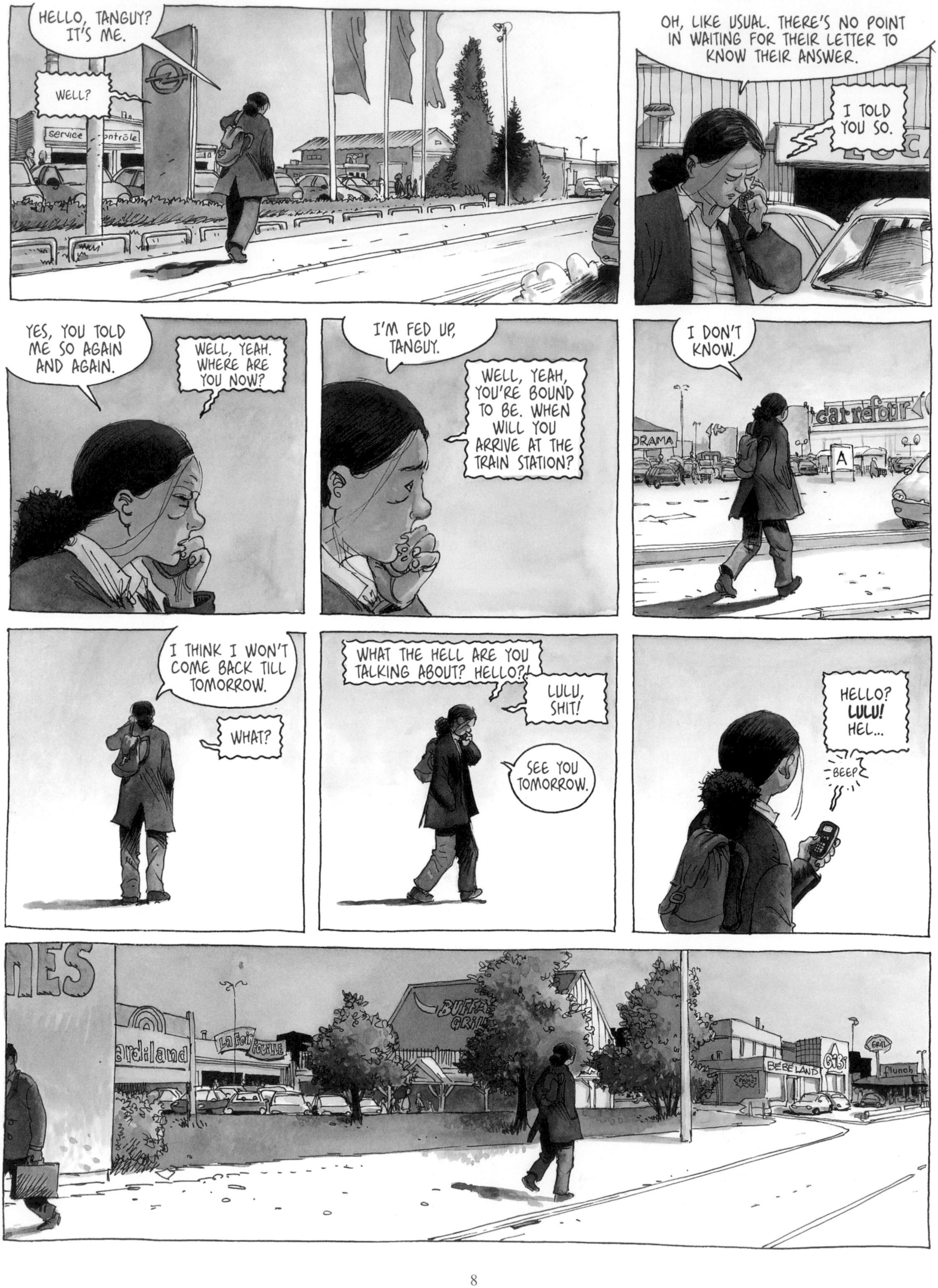

HELLO, TANGUY? IT'S ME.
WELL?
service
contrôle
OH, LIKE USUAL. THERE'S NO POINT IN WAITING FOR THEIR LETTER TO KNOW THEIR ANSWER.
I TOLD YOU SO.
YES, YOU TOLD ME SO AGAIN AND AGAIN.
WELL, YEAH. WHERE ARE YOU NOW?
I'M FED UP, TANGUY.
WELL, YEAH, YOU'RE BOUND TO BE. WHEN WILL YOU ARRIVE AT THE TRAIN STATION?
I DON'T KNOW.
carrefour
A
I THINK I WON'T COME BACK TILL TOMORROW.
WHAT?
WHAT THE HELL ARE YOU TALKING ABOUT? HELLO?!
LULU, SHIT!
SEE YOU TOMORROW.
HELLO? **LULU!** HEL...
BEEP
La Foir'Fouille
BUFFALO GRILL
BEBE LAND
GiFi
GRILL
flunch

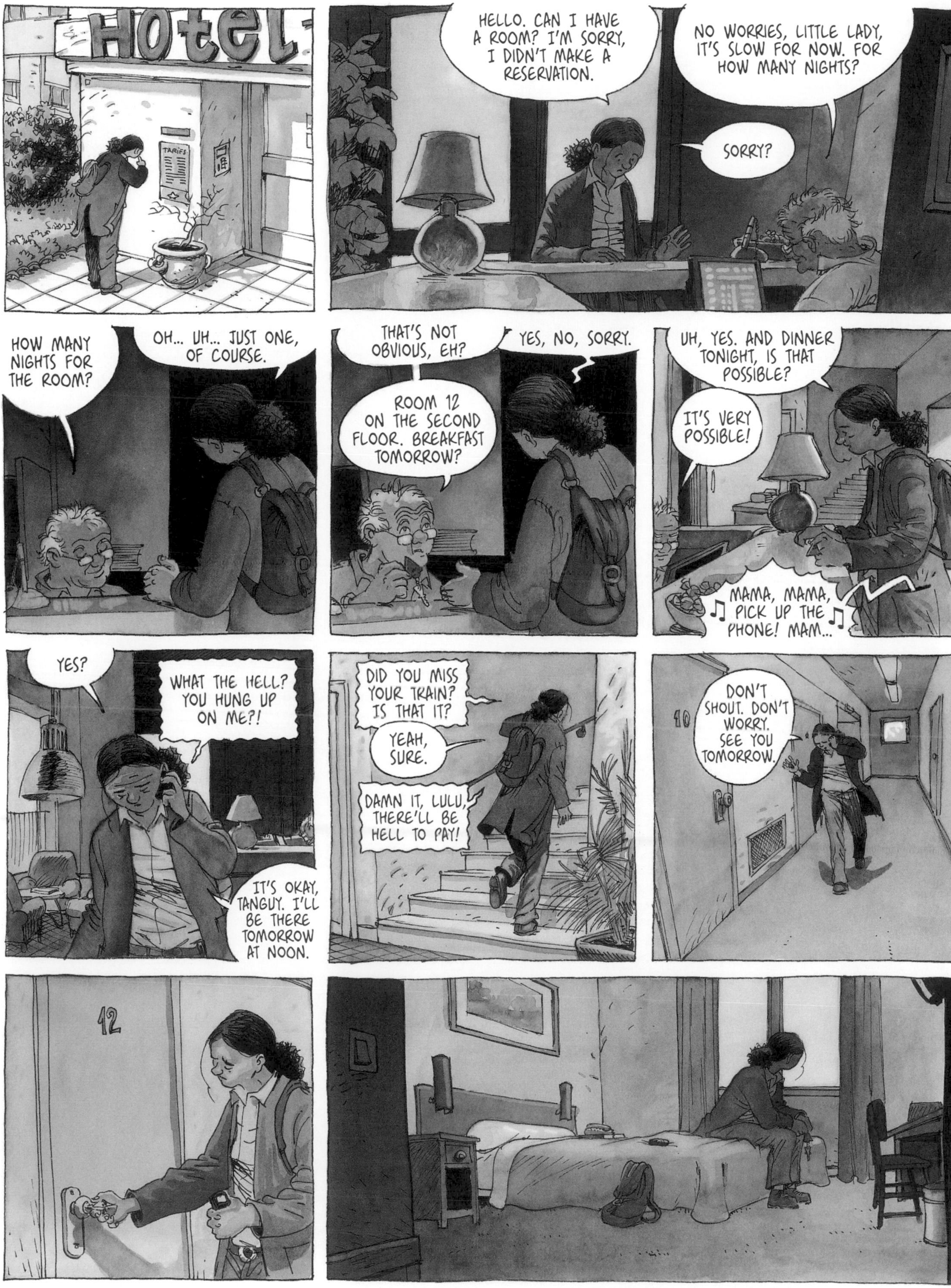
HELLO. CAN I HAVE A ROOM? I'M SORRY, I DIDN'T MAKE A RESERVATION.
NO WORRIES, LITTLE LADY, IT'S SLOW FOR NOW. FOR HOW MANY NIGHTS?
SORRY?
HOW MANY NIGHTS FOR THE ROOM?
OH... UH... JUST ONE, OF COURSE.
THAT'S NOT OBVIOUS, EH?
YES, NO, SORRY.
ROOM 12 ON THE SECOND FLOOR. BREAKFAST TOMORROW?
UH, YES. AND DINNER TONIGHT, IS THAT POSSIBLE?
IT'S VERY POSSIBLE!
MAMA, MAMA, PICK UP THE PHONE! MAM...
YES?
WHAT THE HELL? YOU HUNG UP ON ME?!
IT'S OKAY, TANGUY. I'LL BE THERE TOMORROW AT NOON.
DID YOU MISS YOUR TRAIN? IS THAT IT?
YEAH, SURE.
DAMN IT, LULU, THERE'LL BE HELL TO PAY!
DON'T SHOUT. DON'T WORRY. SEE YOU TOMORROW.

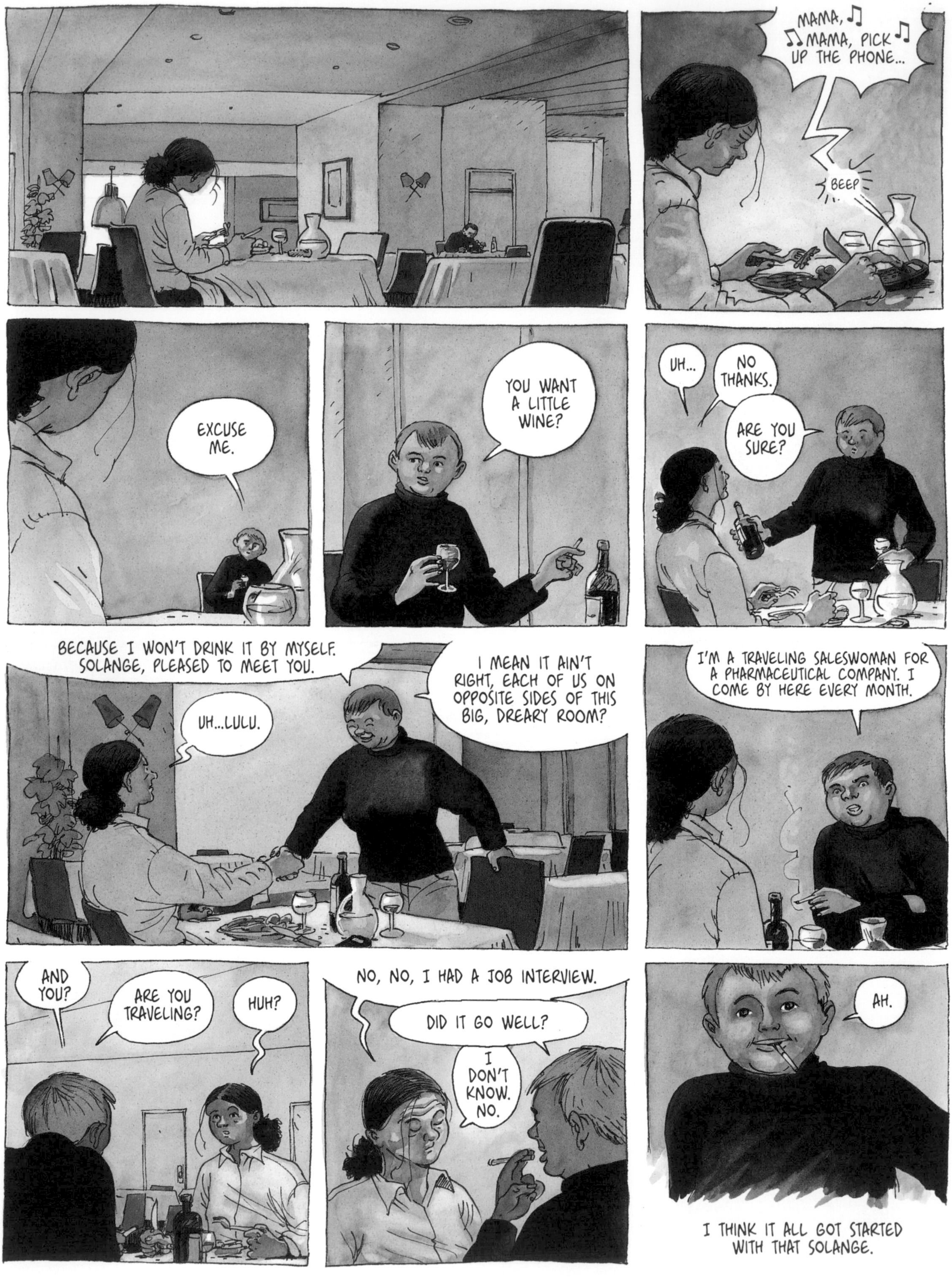

MAMA, ♫ ♫ MAMA, PICK ♫ UP THE PHONE...
BEEP
EXCUSE ME.
YOU WANT A LITTLE WINE?
UH...
NO THANKS.
ARE YOU SURE?
BECAUSE I WON'T DRINK IT BY MYSELF. SOLANGE, PLEASED TO MEET YOU.
UH...LULU.
I MEAN IT AIN'T RIGHT, EACH OF US ON OPPOSITE SIDES OF THIS BIG, DREARY ROOM?
I'M A TRAVELING SALESWOMAN FOR A PHARMACEUTICAL COMPANY. I COME BY HERE EVERY MONTH.
AND YOU?
ARE YOU TRAVELING?
HUH?
NO, NO, I HAD A JOB INTERVIEW.
DID IT GO WELL?
I DON'T KNOW. NO.
AH.
I THINK IT ALL GOT STARTED WITH THAT SOLANGE.

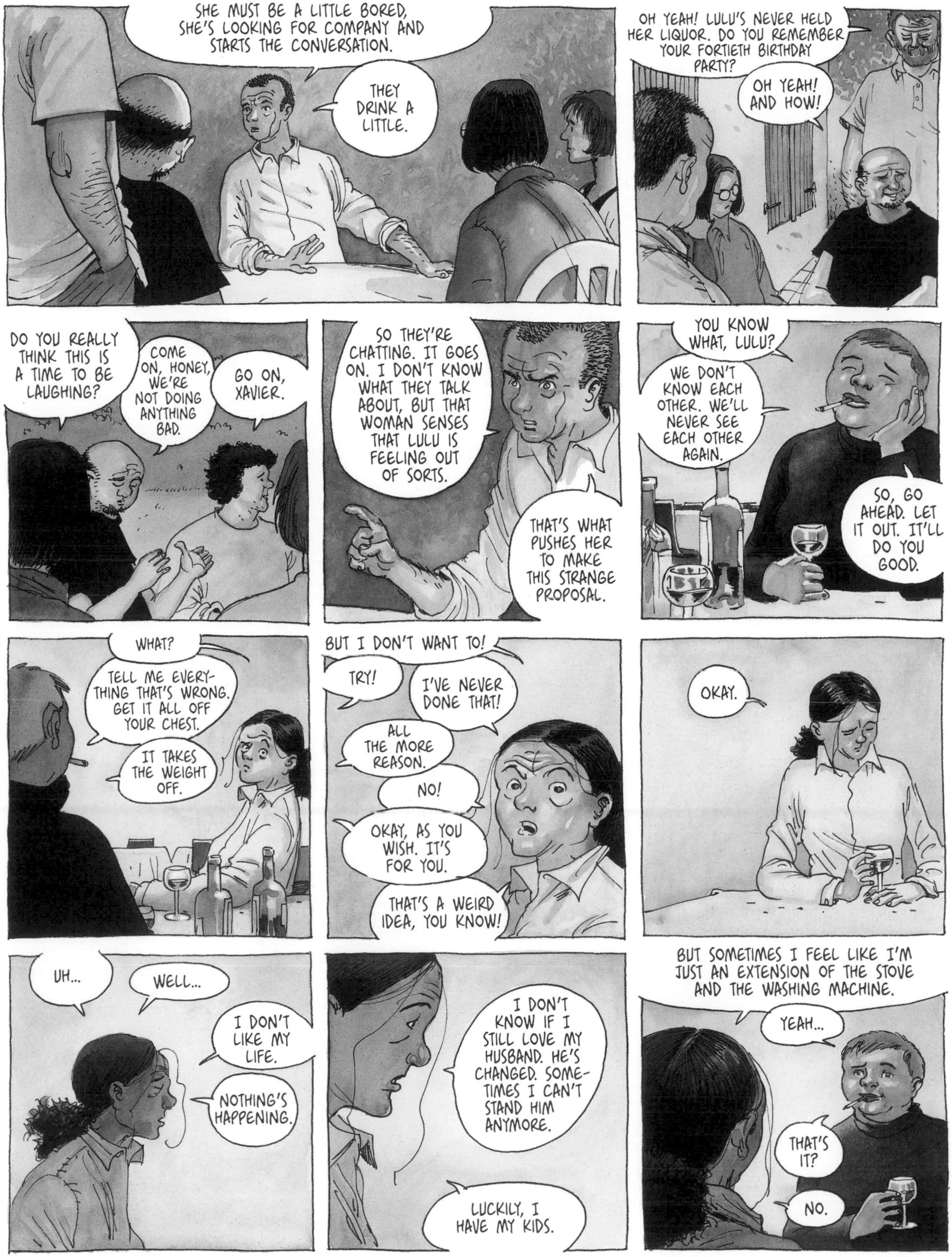
SHE MUST BE A LITTLE BORED, SHE'S LOOKING FOR COMPANY AND STARTS THE CONVERSATION.
THEY DRINK A LITTLE.
OH YEAH! LULU'S NEVER HELD HER LIQUOR. DO YOU REMEMBER YOUR FORTIETH BIRTHDAY PARTY?
OH YEAH! AND HOW!
DO YOU REALLY THINK THIS IS A TIME TO BE LAUGHING?
COME ON, HONEY, WE'RE NOT DOING ANYTHING BAD.
GO ON, XAVIER.
SO THEY'RE CHATTING. IT GOES ON. I DON'T KNOW WHAT THEY TALK ABOUT, BUT THAT WOMAN SENSES THAT LULU IS FEELING OUT OF SORTS.
THAT'S WHAT PUSHES HER TO MAKE THIS STRANGE PROPOSAL.
YOU KNOW WHAT, LULU?
WE DON'T KNOW EACH OTHER. WE'LL NEVER SEE EACH OTHER AGAIN.
SO, GO AHEAD. LET IT OUT. IT'LL DO YOU GOOD.
WHAT?
TELL ME EVERYTHING THAT'S WRONG. GET IT ALL OFF YOUR CHEST.
IT TAKES THE WEIGHT OFF.
BUT I DON'T WANT TO!
TRY!
I'VE NEVER DONE THAT!
ALL THE MORE REASON.
NO!
OKAY, AS YOU WISH. IT'S FOR YOU.
THAT'S A WEIRD IDEA, YOU KNOW!
OKAY.
UH...
WELL...
I DON'T LIKE MY LIFE.
NOTHING'S HAPPENING.
I DON'T KNOW IF I STILL LOVE MY HUSBAND. HE'S CHANGED. SOMETIMES I CAN'T STAND HIM ANYMORE.
LUCKILY, I HAVE MY KIDS.
BUT SOMETIMES I FEEL LIKE I'M JUST AN EXTENSION OF THE STOVE AND THE WASHING MACHINE.
YEAH...
THAT'S IT?
NO.

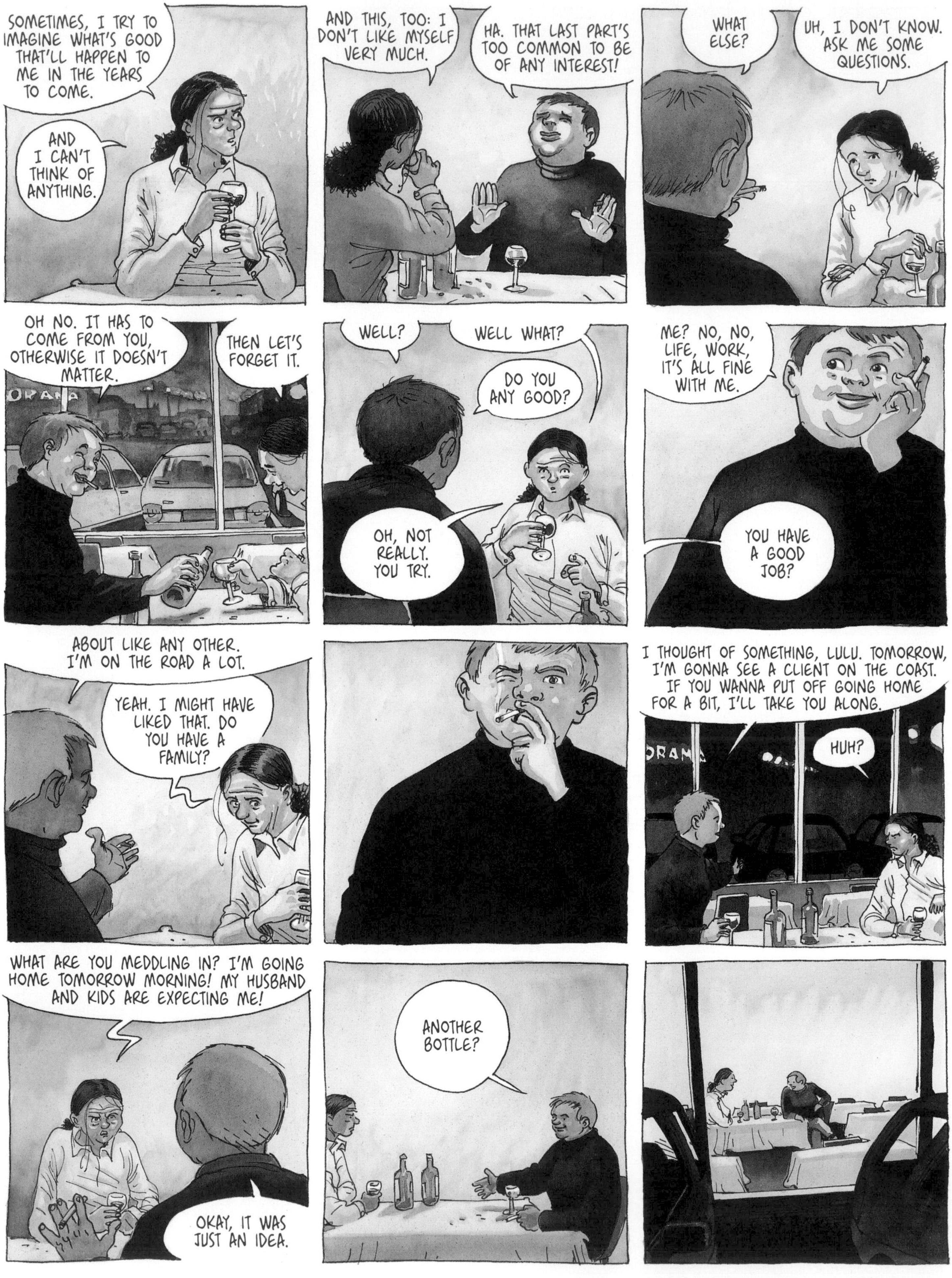
SOMETIMES, I TRY TO IMAGINE WHAT'S GOOD THAT'LL HAPPEN TO ME IN THE YEARS TO COME.
AND I CAN'T THINK OF ANYTHING.
AND THIS, TOO: I DON'T LIKE MYSELF VERY MUCH.
HA. THAT LAST PART'S TOO COMMON TO BE OF ANY INTEREST!
WHAT ELSE?
UH, I DON'T KNOW. ASK ME SOME QUESTIONS.
OH NO. IT HAS TO COME FROM YOU, OTHERWISE IT DOESN'T MATTER.
THEN LET'S FORGET IT.
WELL?
WELL WHAT?
DO YOU ANY GOOD?
OH, NOT REALLY. YOU TRY.
ME? NO, NO, LIFE, WORK, IT'S ALL FINE WITH ME.
YOU HAVE A GOOD JOB?
ABOUT LIKE ANY OTHER. I'M ON THE ROAD A LOT.
YEAH. I MIGHT HAVE LIKED THAT. DO YOU HAVE A FAMILY?
I THOUGHT OF SOMETHING, LULU. TOMORROW, I'M GONNA SEE A CLIENT ON THE COAST. IF YOU WANNA PUT OFF GOING HOME FOR A BIT, I'LL TAKE YOU ALONG.
HUH?
WHAT ARE YOU MEDDLING IN? I'M GOING HOME TOMORROW MORNING! MY HUSBAND AND KIDS ARE EXPECTING ME!
OKAY, IT WAS JUST AN IDEA.
ANOTHER BOTTLE?

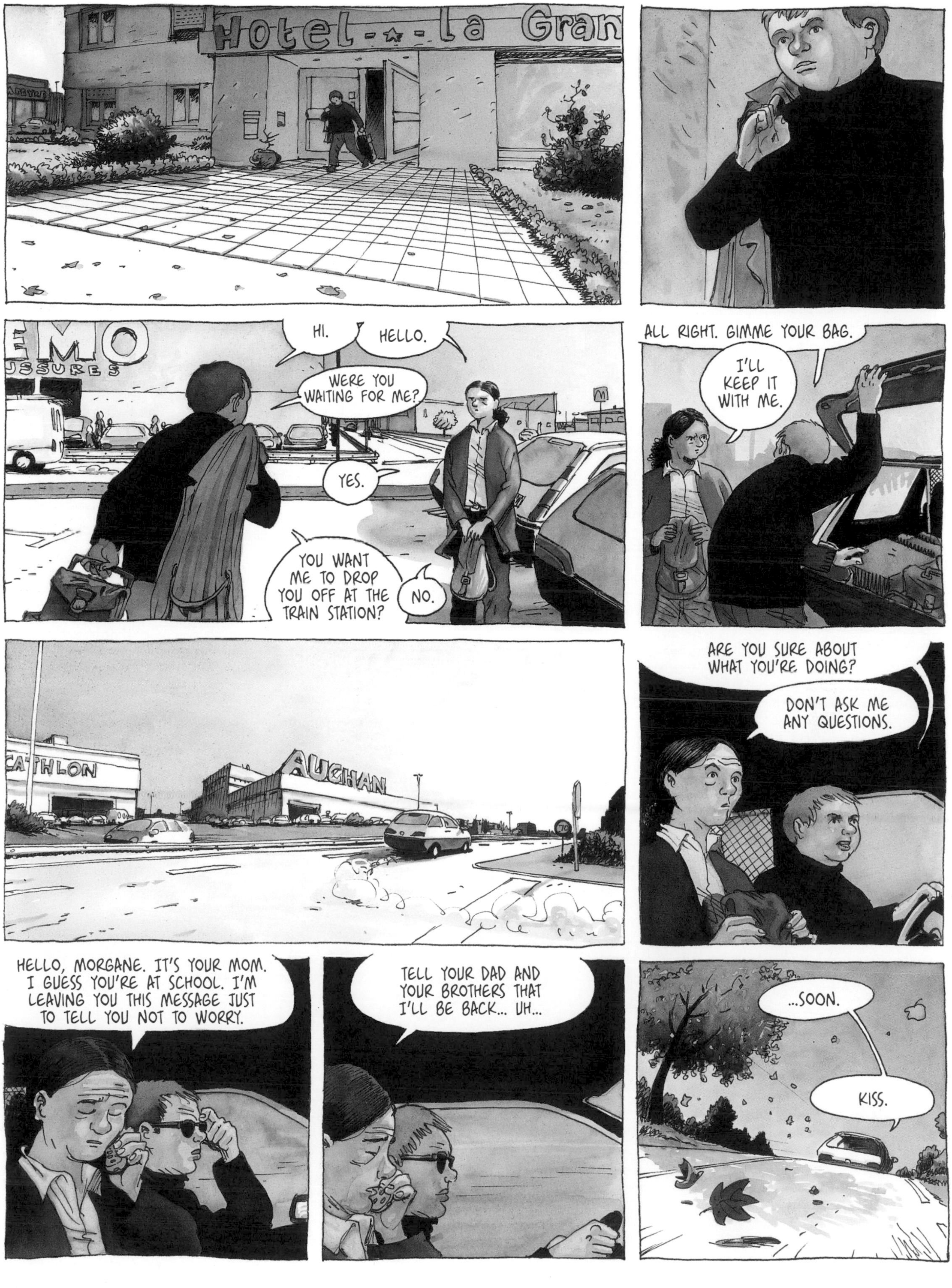
Hotel la Gran
HI.
HELLO.
WERE YOU WAITING FOR ME?
YES.
YOU WANT ME TO DROP YOU OFF AT THE TRAIN STATION?
NO.
ALL RIGHT. GIMME YOUR BAG.
I'LL KEEP IT WITH ME.
CATHLON
AUCHAN
ARE YOU SURE ABOUT WHAT YOU'RE DOING?
DON'T ASK ME ANY QUESTIONS.
HELLO, MORGANE. IT'S YOUR MOM. I GUESS YOU'RE AT SCHOOL. I'M LEAVING YOU THIS MESSAGE JUST TO TELL YOU NOT TO WORRY.
TELL YOUR DAD AND YOUR BROTHERS THAT I'LL BE BACK... UH...
...SOON.
KISS.

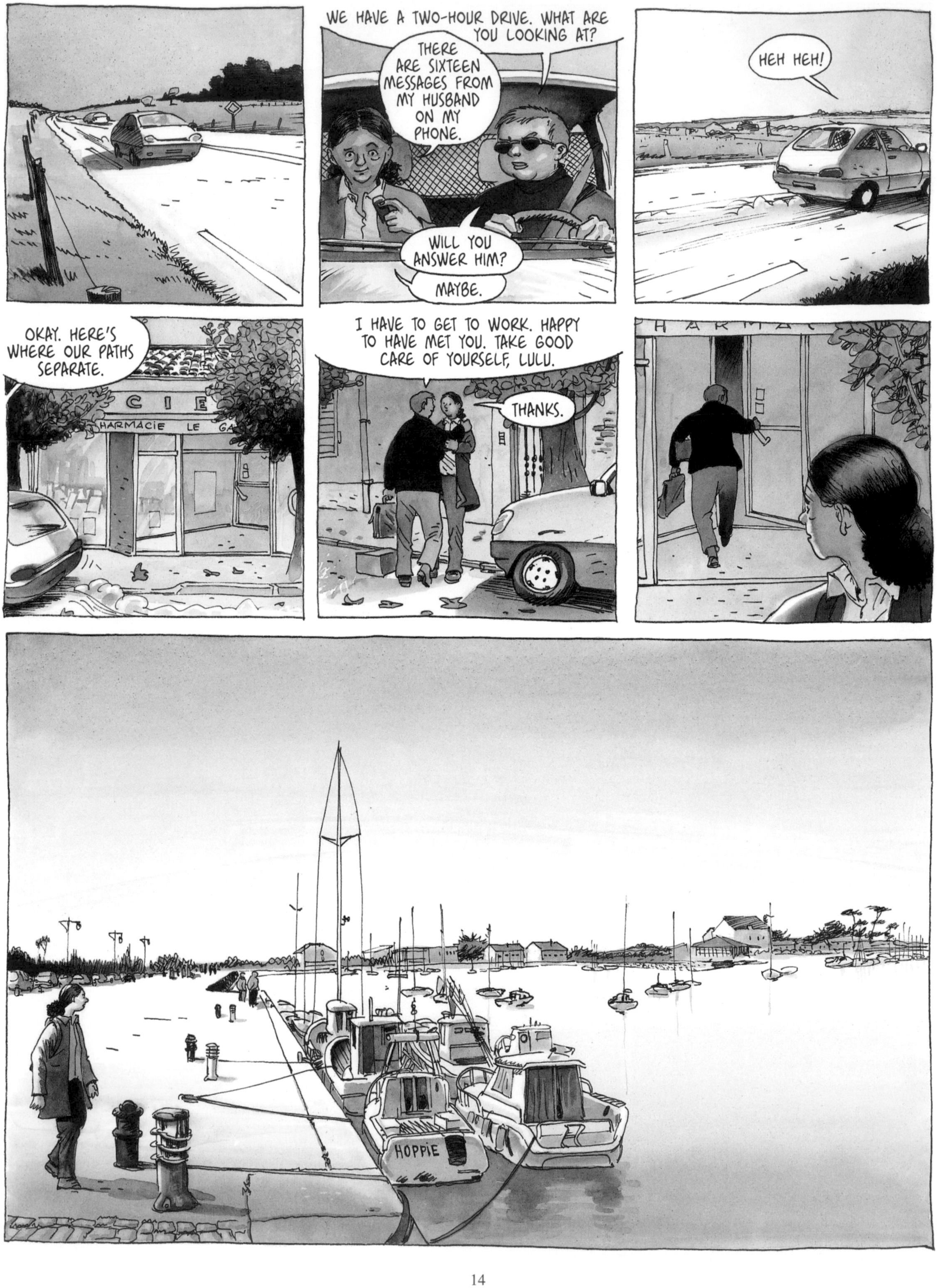
THERE ARE SIXTEEN MESSAGES FROM MY HUSBAND ON MY PHONE.
WE HAVE A TWO-HOUR DRIVE. WHAT ARE YOU LOOKING AT?
WILL YOU ANSWER HIM?
MAYBE.
HEH HEH!
OKAY. HERE'S WHERE OUR PATHS SEPARATE.
CIE
HARMACIE LE GA
I HAVE TO GET TO WORK. HAPPY TO HAVE MET YOU. TAKE GOOD CARE OF YOURSELF, LULU.
THANKS.
HOPPIE

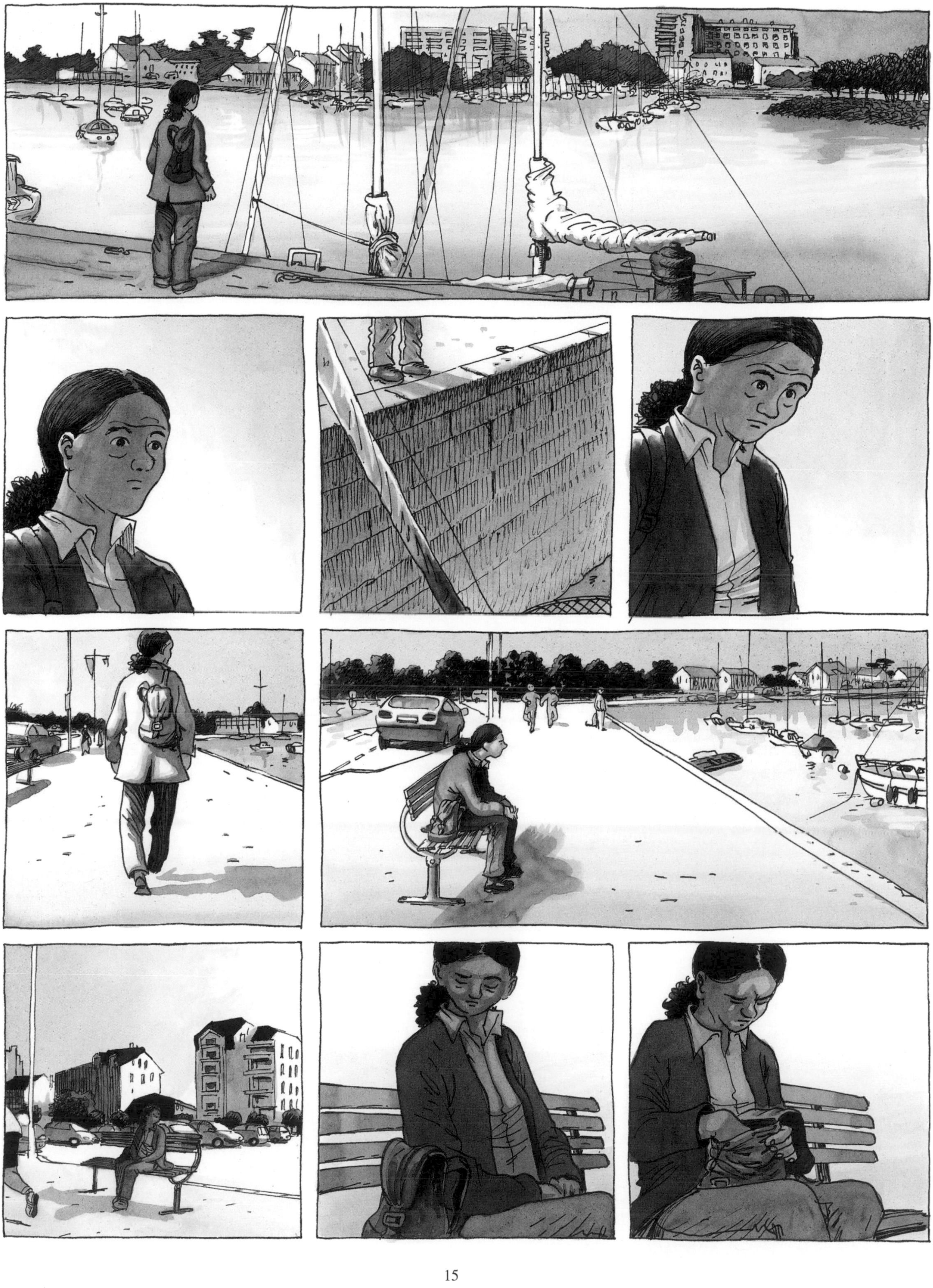

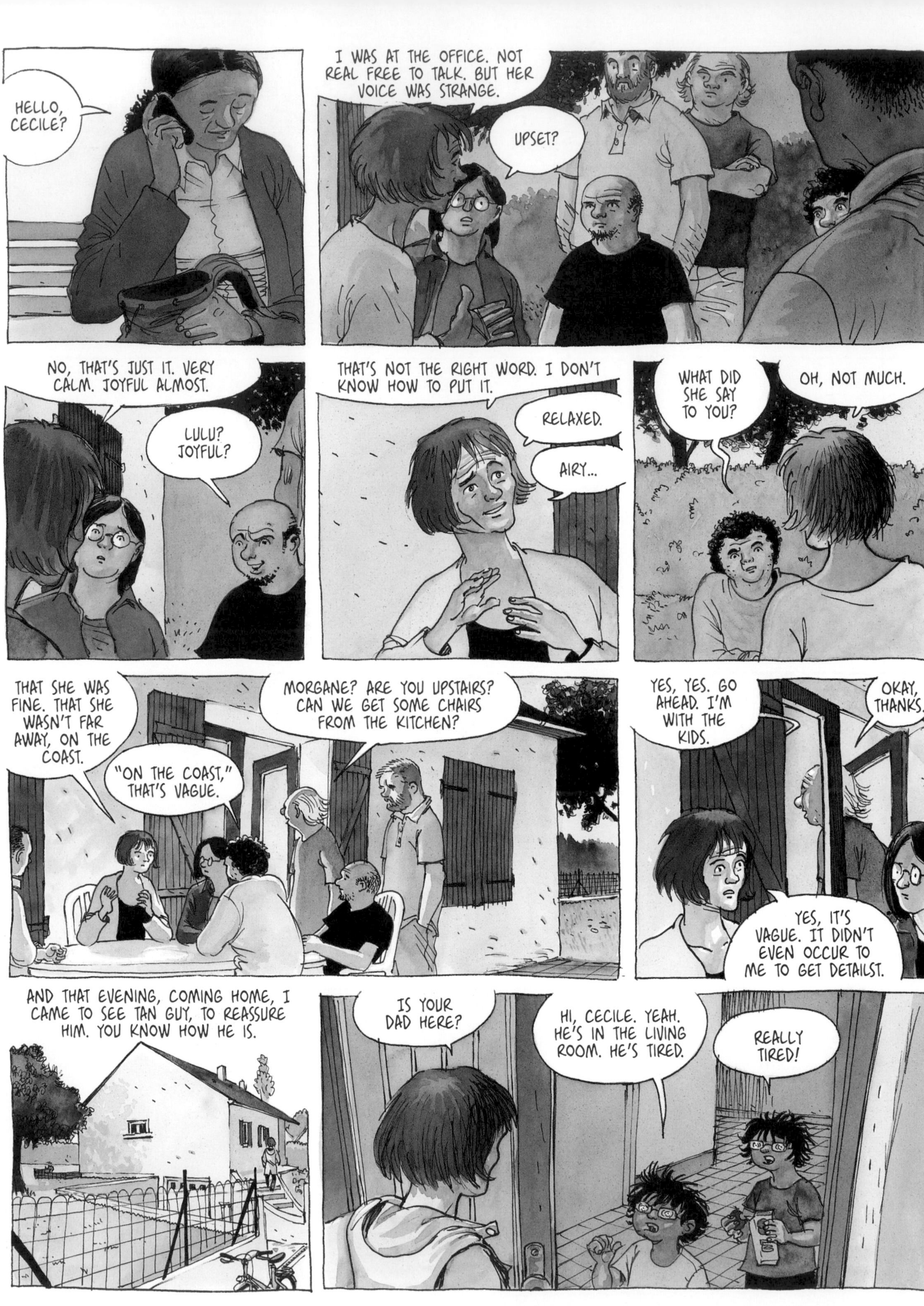
HELLO, CECILE?
I WAS AT THE OFFICE. NOT REAL FREE TO TALK. BUT HER VOICE WAS STRANGE.
UPSET?
NO, THAT'S JUST IT. VERY CALM. JOYFUL ALMOST.
LULU? JOYFUL?
THAT'S NOT THE RIGHT WORD. I DON'T KNOW HOW TO PUT IT.
RELAXED.
AIRY...
WHAT DID SHE SAY TO YOU?
OH, NOT MUCH.
THAT SHE WAS FINE. THAT SHE WASN'T FAR AWAY, ON THE COAST.
"ON THE COAST," THAT'S VAGUE.
MORGANE? ARE YOU UPSTAIRS? CAN WE GET SOME CHAIRS FROM THE KITCHEN?
YES, YES. GO AHEAD. I'M WITH THE KIDS.
OKAY, THANKS.
YES, IT'S VAGUE. IT DIDN'T EVEN OCCUR TO ME TO GET DETAILST.
AND THAT EVENING, COMING HOME, I CAME TO SEE TAN GUY, TO REASSURE HIM. YOU KNOW HOW HE IS.
IS YOUR DAD HERE?
HI, CECILE. YEAH. HE'S IN THE LIVING ROOM. HE'S TIRED.
REALLY TIRED!

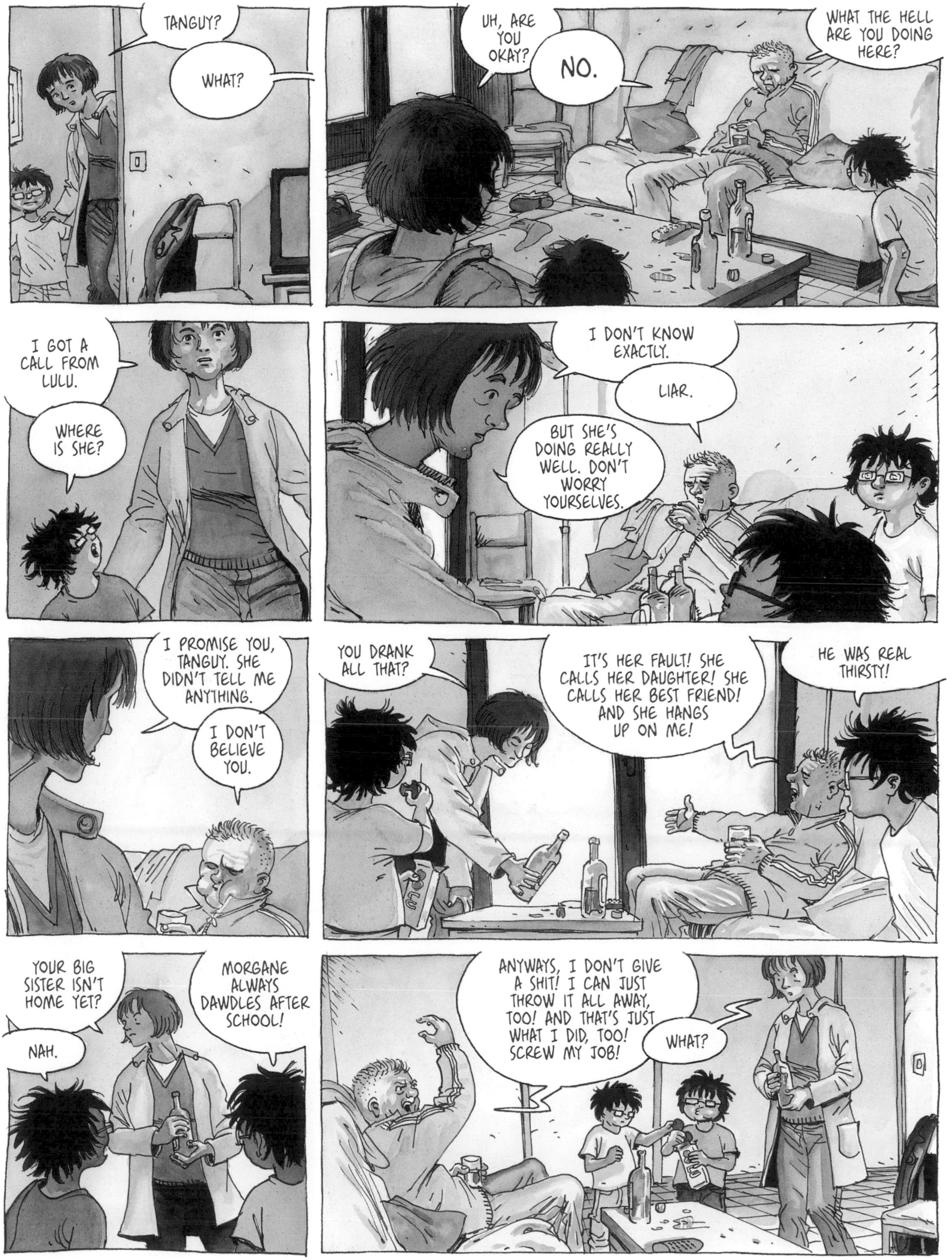
TANGUY?
WHAT?
UH, ARE YOU OKAY?
NO.
WHAT THE HELL ARE YOU DOING HERE?
I GOT A CALL FROM LULU.
WHERE IS SHE?
I DON'T KNOW EXACTLY.
LIAR.
BUT SHE'S DOING REALLY WELL. DON'T WORRY YOURSELVES.
I PROMISE YOU, TANGUY. SHE DIDN'T TELL ME ANYTHING.
I DON'T BELIEVE YOU.
YOU DRANK ALL THAT?
IT'S HER FAULT! SHE CALLS HER DAUGHTER! SHE CALLS HER BEST FRIEND! AND SHE HANGS UP ON ME!
HE WAS REAL THIRSTY!
YOUR BIG SISTER ISN'T HOME YET?
NAH.
MORGANE ALWAYS DAWDLES AFTER SCHOOL!
ANYWAYS, I DON'T GIVE A SHIT! I CAN JUST THROW IT ALL AWAY, TOO! AND THAT'S JUST WHAT I DID, TOO! SCREW MY JOB!
WHAT?

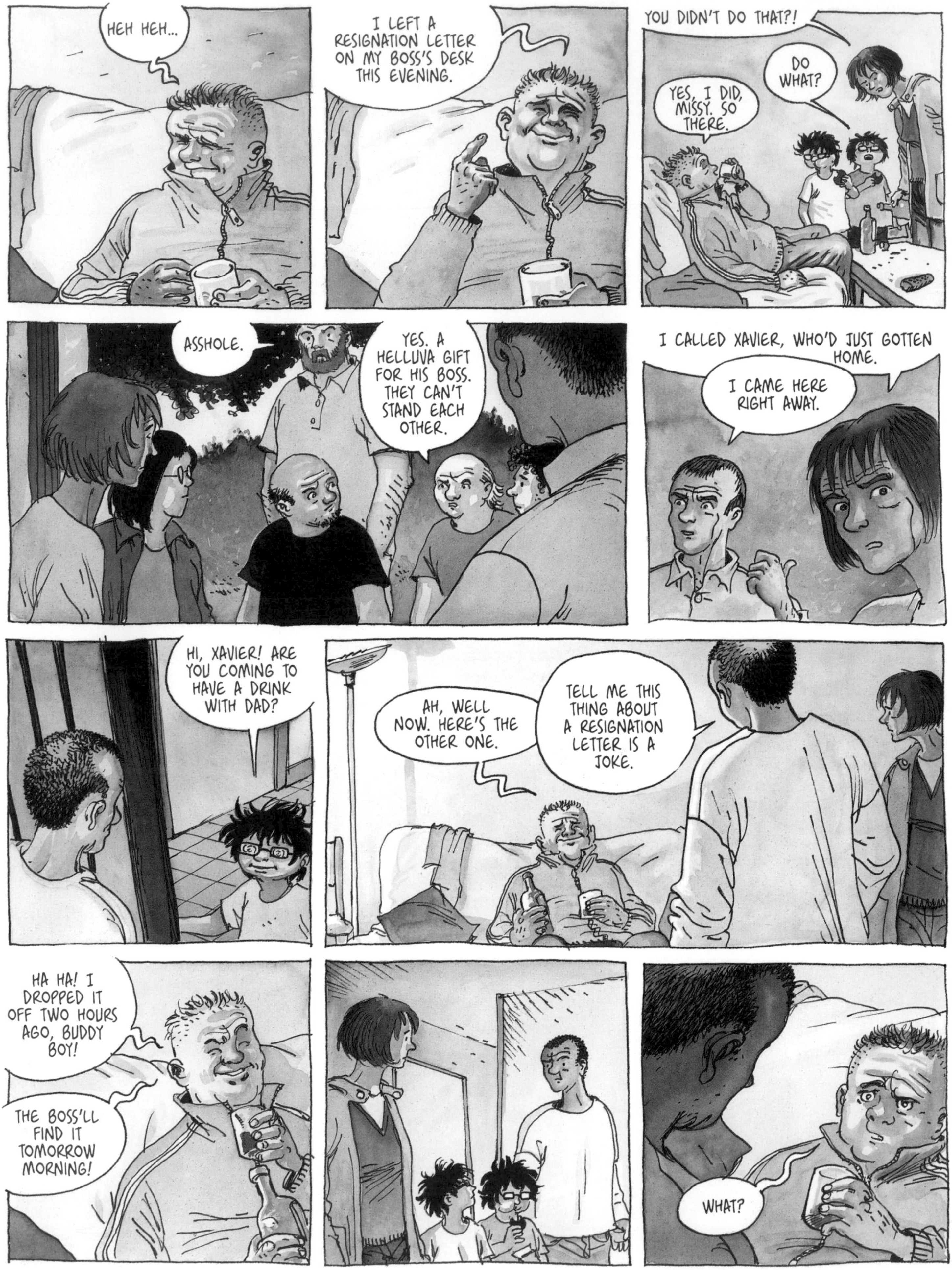
HEH HEH...
I LEFT A RESIGNATION LETTER ON MY BOSS'S DESK THIS EVENING.
YOU DIDN'T DO THAT?!
DO WHAT?
YES, I DID, MISSY. SO THERE.
ASSHOLE.
YES. A HELLUVA GIFT FOR HIS BOSS. THEY CAN'T STAND EACH OTHER.
I CALLED XAVIER, WHO'D JUST GOTTEN HOME.
I CAME HERE RIGHT AWAY.
HI, XAVIER! ARE YOU COMING TO HAVE A DRINK WITH DAD?
AH, WELL NOW. HERE'S THE OTHER ONE.
TELL ME THIS THING ABOUT A RESIGNATION LETTER IS A JOKE.
HA HA! I DROPPED IT OFF TWO HOURS AGO, BUDDY BOY!
THE BOSS'LL FIND IT TOMORROW MORNING!
WHAT?

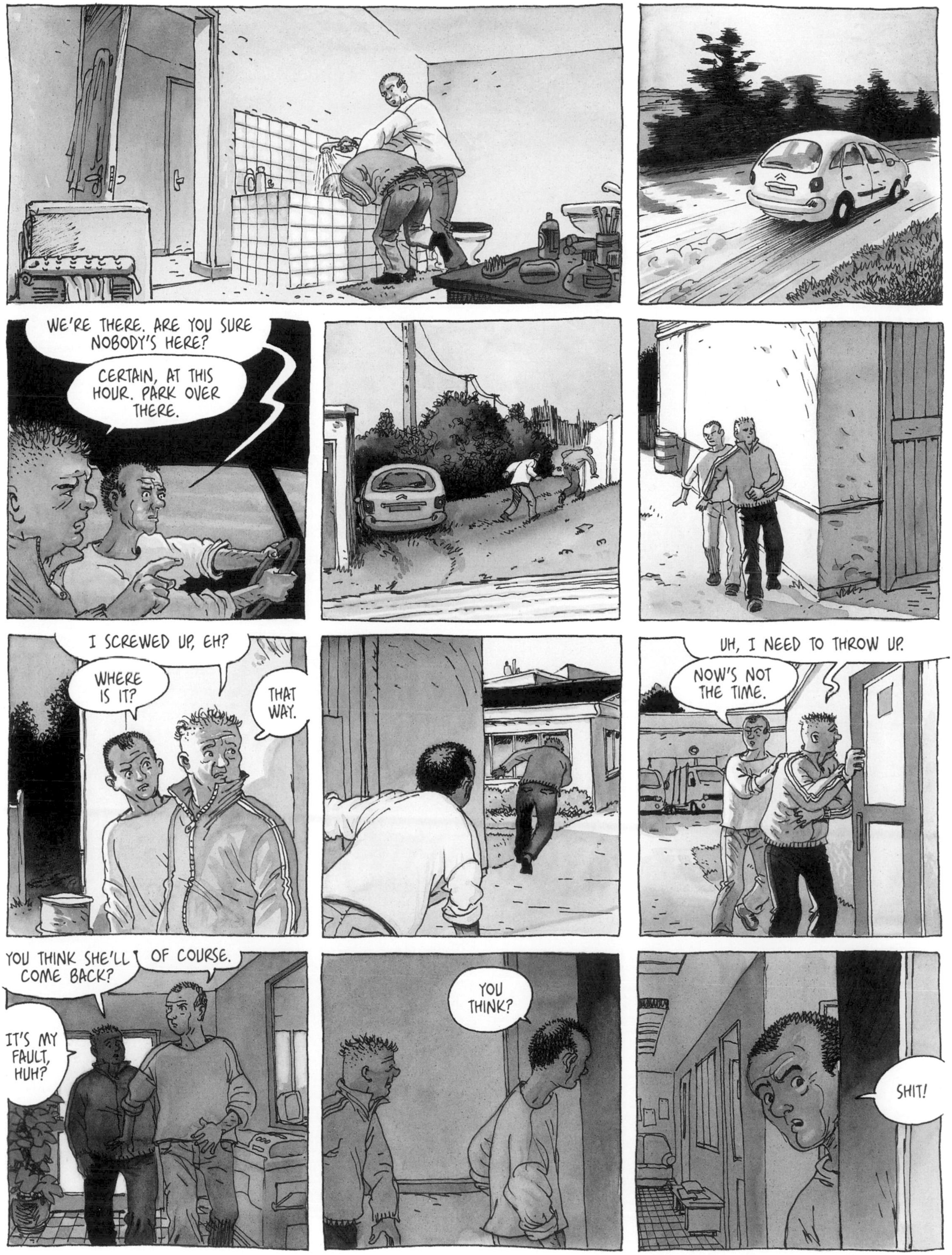
WE'RE THERE. ARE YOU SURE NOBODY'S HERE?
CERTAIN, AT THIS HOUR. PARK OVER THERE.
I SCREWED UP, EH?
WHERE IS IT?
THAT WAY.
UH, I NEED TO THROW UP.
NOW'S NOT THE TIME.
YOU THINK SHE'LL COME BACK?
OF COURSE.
IT'S MY FAULT, HUH?
YOU THINK?
SHIT!

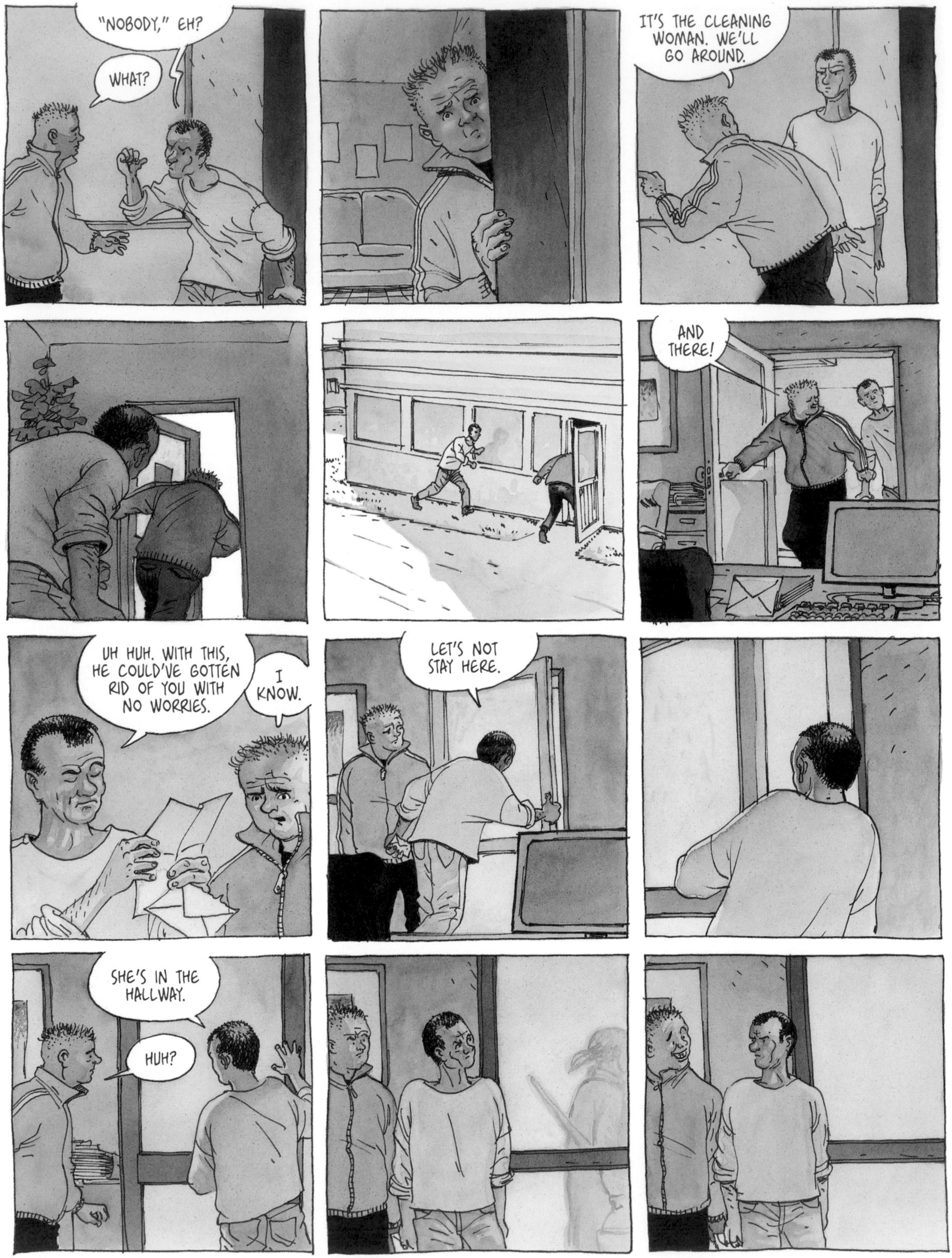
"NOBODY," EH?
WHAT?
IT'S THE CLEANING WOMAN. WE'LL GO AROUND.
AND THERE!
UH HUH. WITH THIS, HE COULD'VE GOTTEN RID OF YOU WITH NO WORRIES.
I KNOW.
LET'S NOT STAY HERE.
SHE'S IN THE HALLWAY.
HUH?

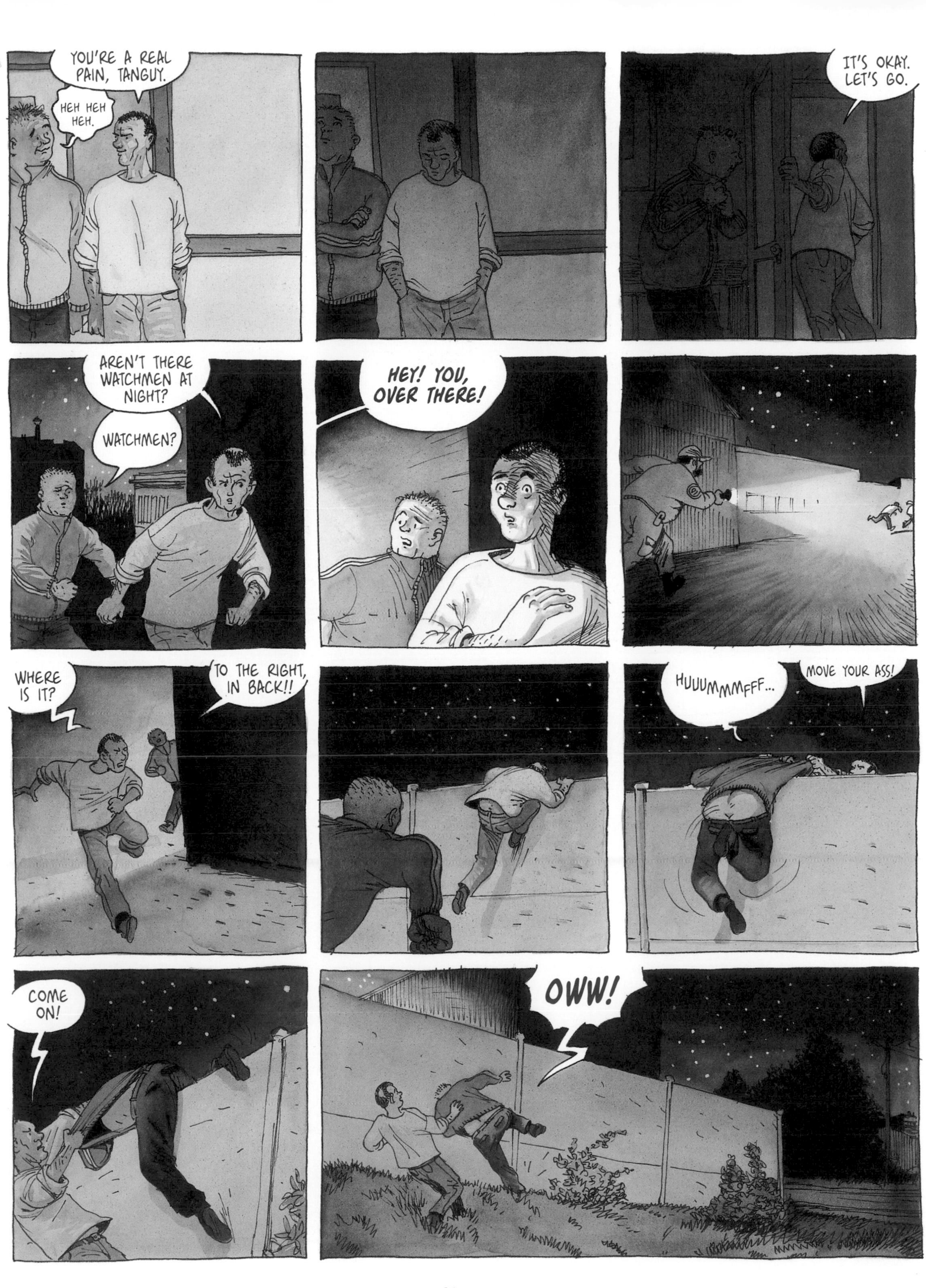

YOU'RE A REAL PAIN, TANGUY.
HEH HEH HEH.
IT'S OKAY. LET'S GO.
AREN'T THERE WATCHMEN AT NIGHT?
WATCHMEN?
HEY! YOU, OVER THERE!
WHERE IS IT?
TO THE RIGHT, IN BACK!!
HUUUMMMFFF...
MOVE YOUR ASS!
COME ON!
OWW!

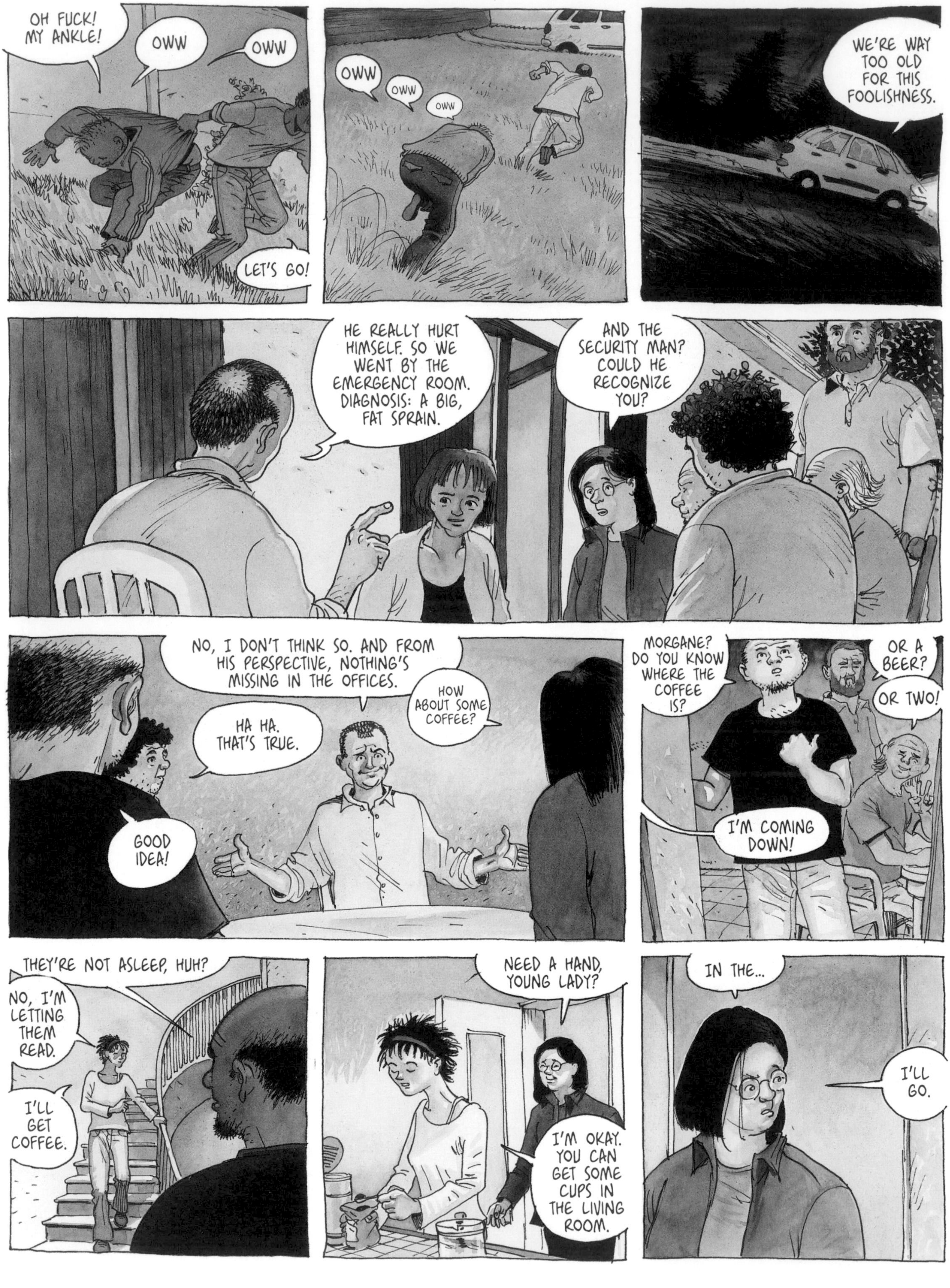
OH FUCK! MY ANKLE!
OWW
OWW
LET'S GO!
OWW
OWW
OWW
WE'RE WAY TOO OLD FOR THIS FOOLISHNESS.
HE REALLY HURT HIMSELF. SO WE WENT BY THE EMERGENCY ROOM. DIAGNOSIS: A BIG, FAT SPRAIN.
AND THE SECURITY MAN? COULD HE RECOGNIZE YOU?
NO, I DON'T THINK SO. AND FROM HIS PERSPECTIVE, NOTHING'S MISSING IN THE OFFICES.
HA HA. THAT'S TRUE.
HOW ABOUT SOME COFFEE?
GOOD IDEA!
MORGANE? DO YOU KNOW WHERE THE COFFEE IS?
OR A BEER?
OR TWO!
I'M COMING DOWN!
THEY'RE NOT ASLEEP, HUH?
NO, I'M LETTING THEM READ.
I'LL GET COFFEE.
NEED A HAND, YOUNG LADY?
I'M OKAY. YOU CAN GET SOME CUPS IN THE LIVING ROOM.
IN THE...
I'LL GO.

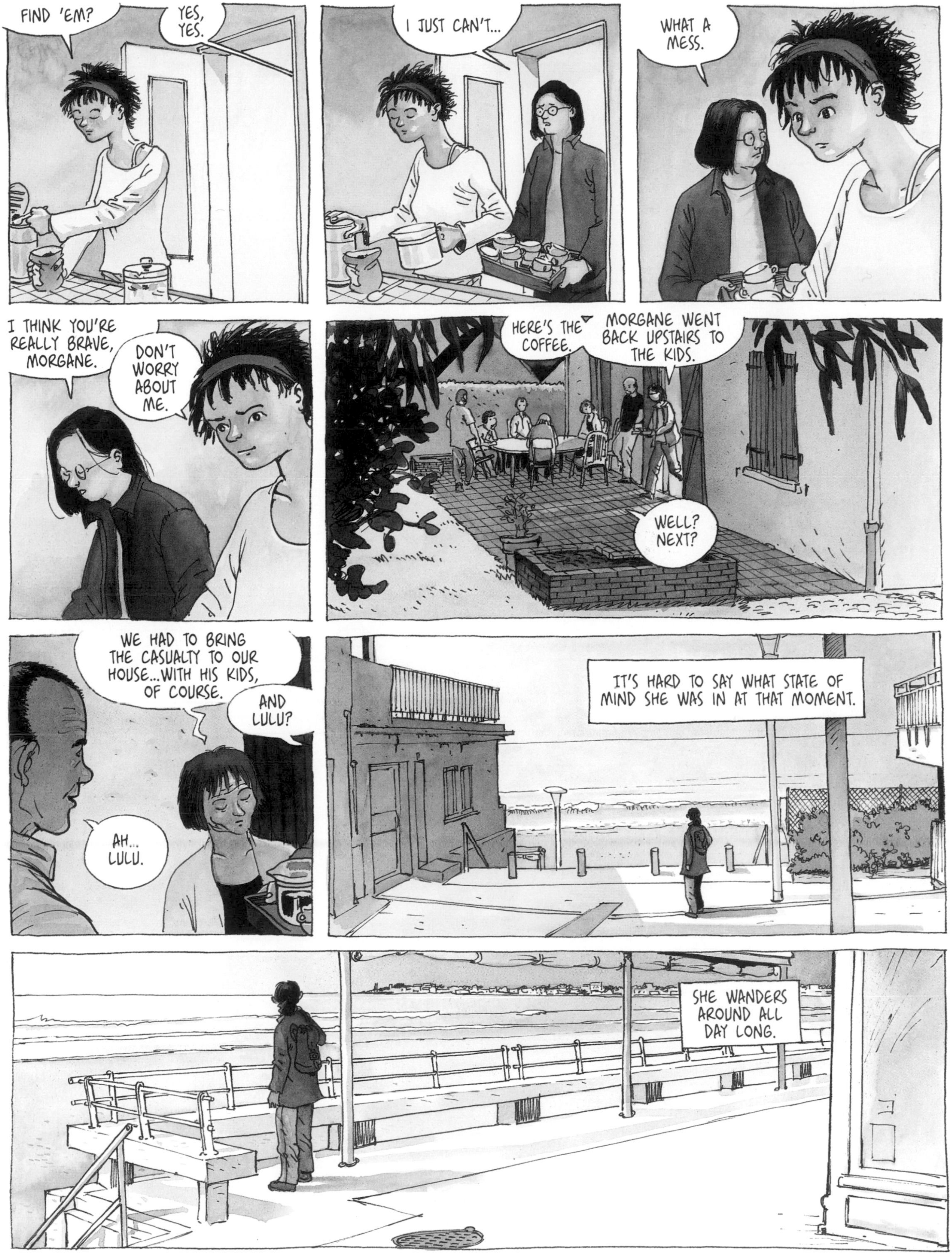
FIND 'EM?
YES, YES.
I JUST CAN'T...
WHAT A MESS.
I THINK YOU'RE REALLY BRAVE, MORGANE.
DON'T WORRY ABOUT ME.
HERE'S THE COFFEE.
MORGANE WENT BACK UPSTAIRS TO THE KIDS.
WELL? NEXT?
WE HAD TO BRING THE CASUALTY TO OUR HOUSE...WITH HIS KIDS, OF COURSE.
AND LULU?
AH... LULU.
IT'S HARD TO SAY WHAT STATE OF MIND SHE WAS IN AT THAT MOMENT.
SHE WANDERS AROUND ALL DAY LONG.

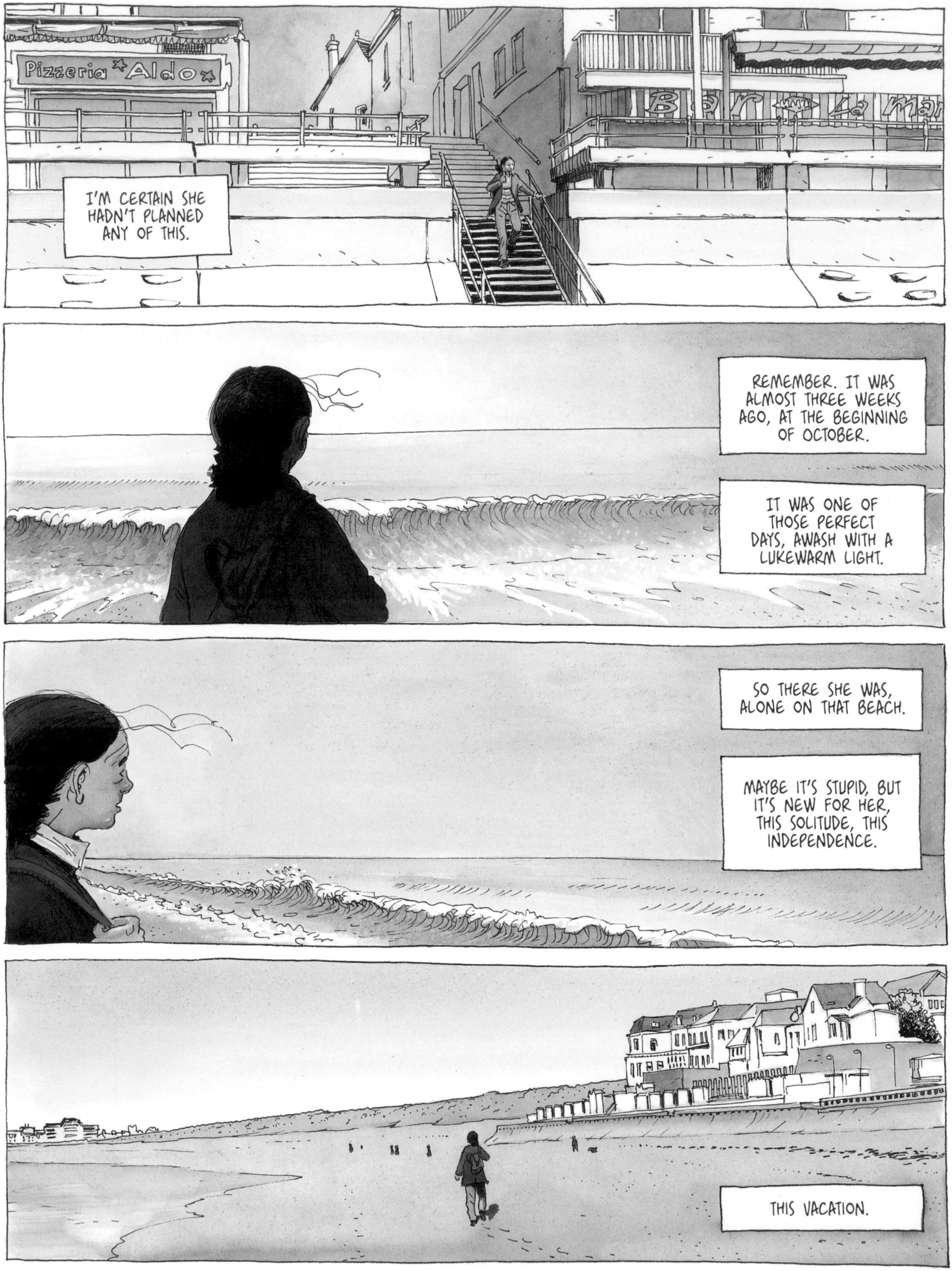
Pizzeria Aldo
I'M CERTAIN SHE HADN'T PLANNED ANY OF THIS.
REMEMBER. IT WAS ALMOST THREE WEEKS AGO, AT THE BEGINNING OF OCTOBER.
IT WAS ONE OF THOSE PERFECT DAYS, AWASH WITH A LUKEWARM LIGHT.
SO THERE SHE WAS, ALONE ON THAT BEACH.
MAYBE IT'S STUPID, BUT IT'S NEW FOR HER, THIS SOLITUDE, THIS INDEPENDENCE.
THIS VACATION.

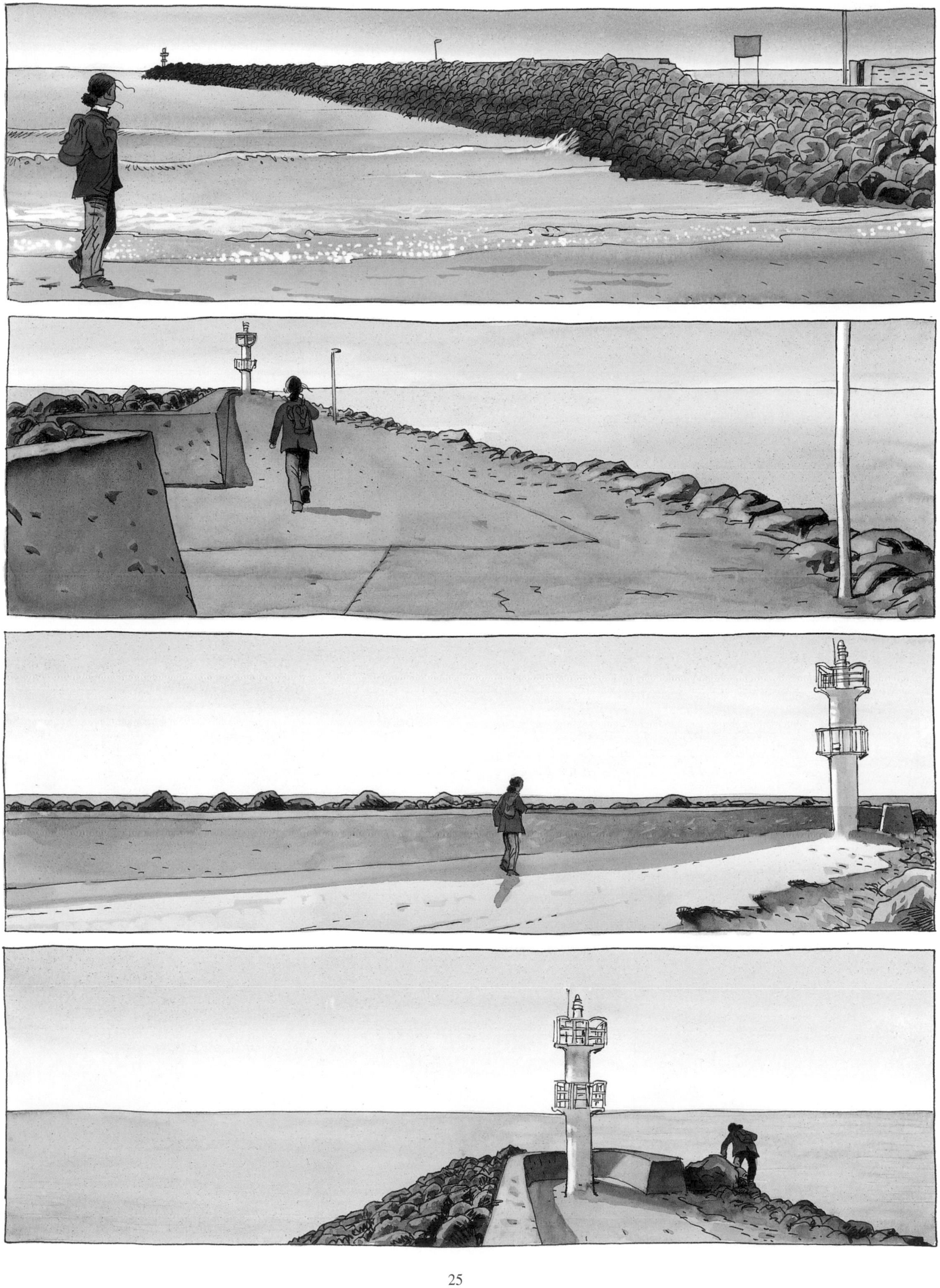

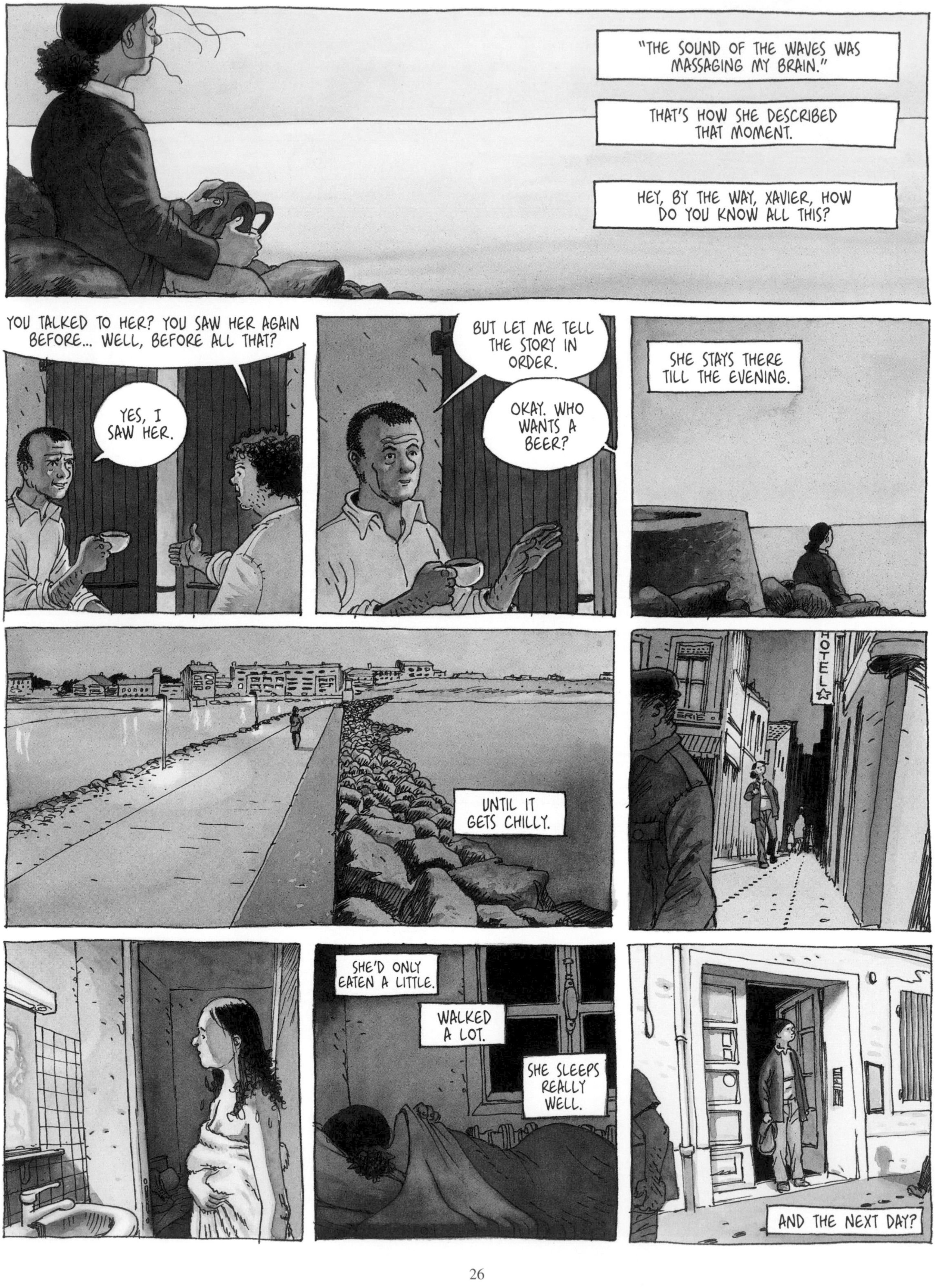

"THE SOUND OF THE WAVES WAS MASSAGING MY BRAIN."
THAT'S HOW SHE DESCRIBED THAT MOMENT.
HEY, BY THE WAY, XAVIER, HOW DO YOU KNOW ALL THIS?
YOU TALKED TO HER? YOU SAW HER AGAIN BEFORE... WELL, BEFORE ALL THAT?
YES, I SAW HER.
BUT LET ME TELL THE STORY IN ORDER.
OKAY. WHO WANTS A BEER?
SHE STAYS THERE TILL THE EVENING.
UNTIL IT GETS CHILLY.
HOTEL
SHE'D ONLY EATEN A LITTLE.
WALKED A LOT.
SHE SLEEPS REALLY WELL.
AND THE NEXT DAY?

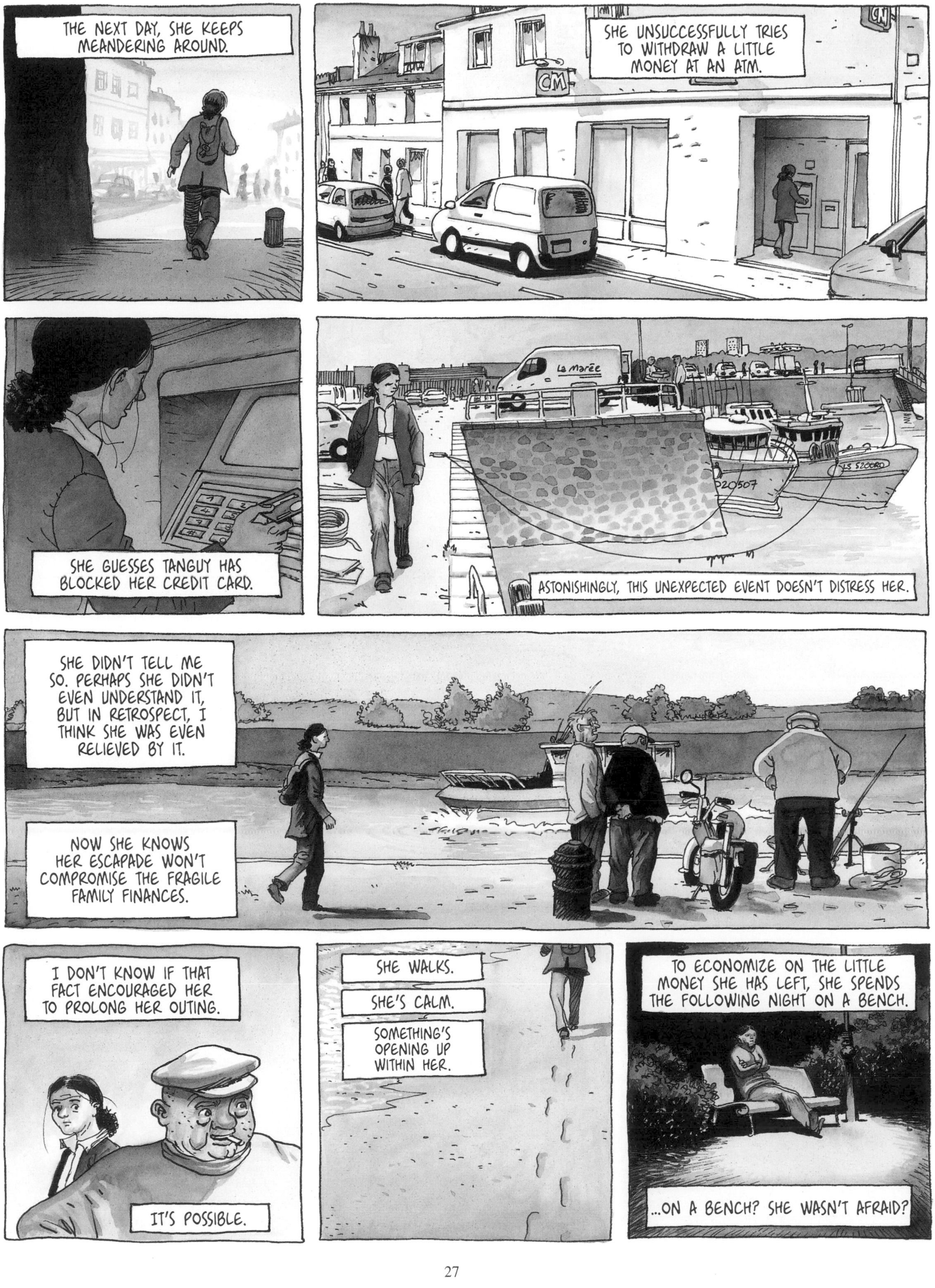
THE NEXT DAY, SHE KEEPS MEANDERING AROUND.
SHE UNSUCCESSFULLY TRIES TO WITHDRAW A LITTLE MONEY AT AN ATM.
SHE GUESSES TANGUY HAS BLOCKED HER CREDIT CARD.
ASTONISHINGLY, THIS UNEXPECTED EVENT DOESN'T DISTRESS HER.
SHE DIDN'T TELL ME SO. PERHAPS SHE DIDN'T EVEN UNDERSTAND IT, BUT IN RETROSPECT, I THINK SHE WAS EVEN RELIEVED BY IT.
NOW SHE KNOWS HER ESCAPADE WON'T COMPROMISE THE FRAGILE FAMILY FINANCES.
I DON'T KNOW IF THAT FACT ENCOURAGED HER TO PROLONG HER OUTING.
IT'S POSSIBLE.
SHE WALKS.
SHE'S CALM.
SOMETHING'S OPENING UP WITHIN HER.
TO ECONOMIZE ON THE LITTLE MONEY SHE HAS LEFT, SHE SPENDS THE FOLLOWING NIGHT ON A BENCH.
...ON A BENCH? SHE WASN'T AFRAID?

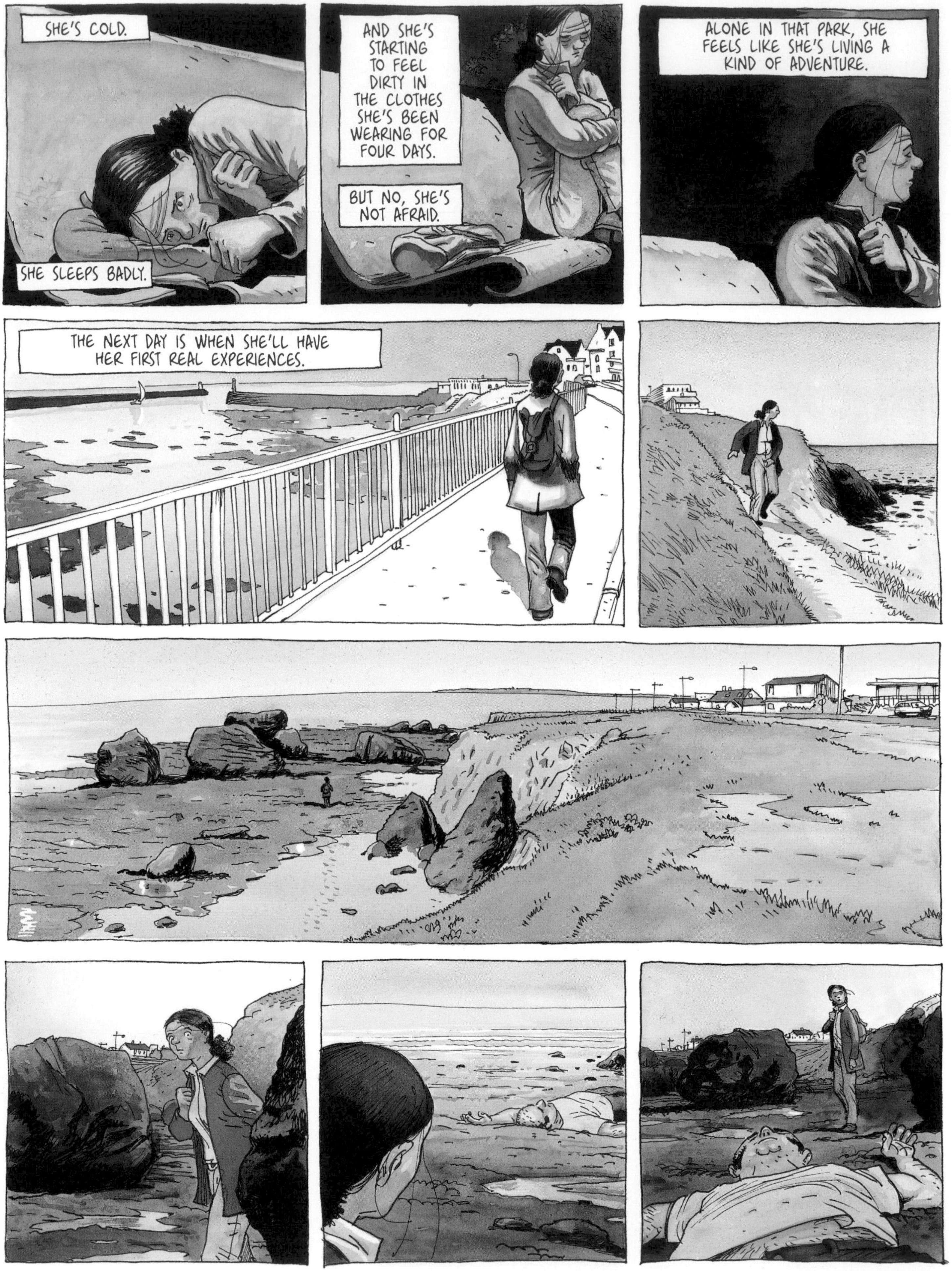
SHE'S COLD.
SHE SLEEPS BADLY.
AND SHE'S STARTING TO FEEL DIRTY IN THE CLOTHES SHE'S BEEN WEARING FOR FOUR DAYS.
BUT NO, SHE'S NOT AFRAID.
ALONE IN THAT PARK, SHE FEELS LIKE SHE'S LIVING A KIND OF ADVENTURE.
THE NEXT DAY IS WHEN SHE'LL HAVE HER FIRST REAL EXPERIENCES.

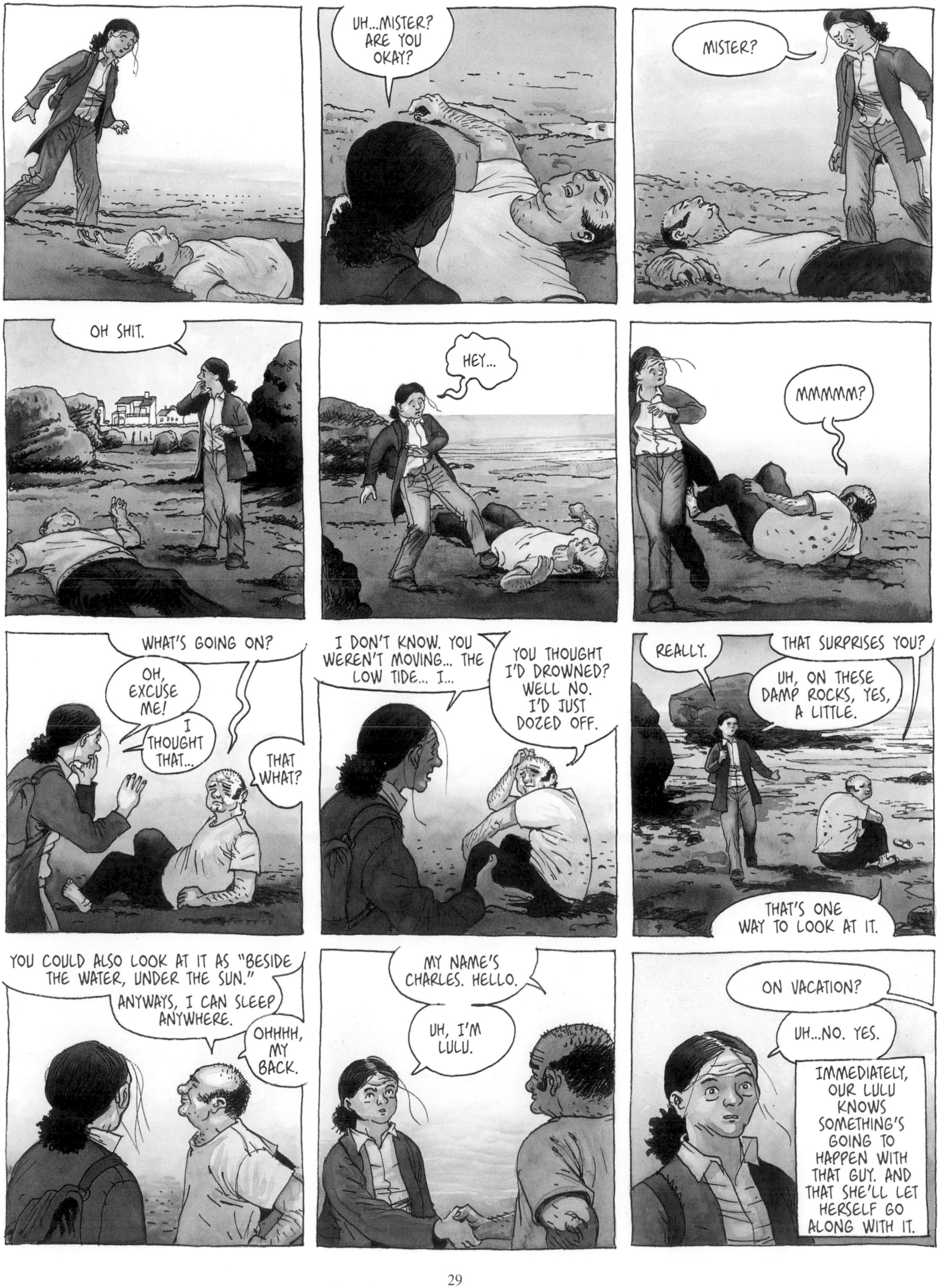
UH...MISTER? ARE YOU OKAY?
MISTER?
OH SHIT.
HEY...
MMMMM?
WHAT'S GOING ON?
OH, EXCUSE ME!
I THOUGHT THAT...
THAT WHAT?
I DON'T KNOW. YOU WEREN'T MOVING... THE LOW TIDE... I...
YOU THOUGHT I'D DROWNED? WELL NO. I'D JUST DOZED OFF.
REALLY.
THAT SURPRISES YOU?
UH, ON THESE DAMP ROCKS, YES, A LITTLE.
THAT'S ONE WAY TO LOOK AT IT.
YOU COULD ALSO LOOK AT IT AS "BESIDE THE WATER, UNDER THE SUN."
ANYWAYS, I CAN SLEEP ANYWHERE.
OHHHH, MY BACK.
MY NAME'S CHARLES. HELLO.
UH, I'M LULU.
ON VACATION?
UH...NO. YES.
IMMEDIATELY, OUR LULU KNOWS SOMETHING'S GOING TO HAPPEN WITH THAT GUY. AND THAT SHE'LL LET HERSELF GO ALONG WITH IT.

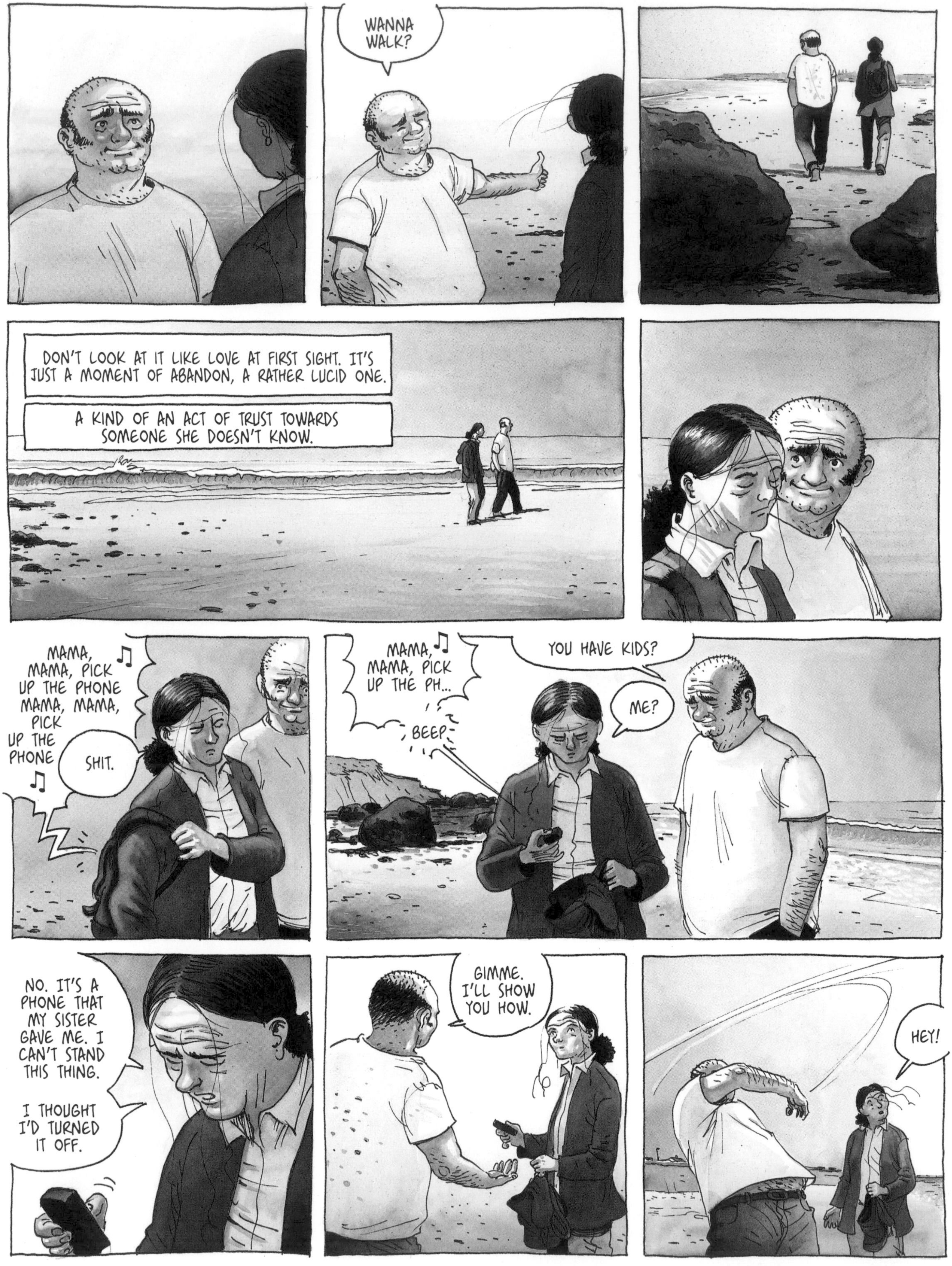
WANNA WALK?
DON'T LOOK AT IT LIKE LOVE AT FIRST SIGHT. IT'S JUST A MOMENT OF ABANDON, A RATHER LUCID ONE.
A KIND OF AN ACT OF TRUST TOWARDS SOMEONE SHE DOESN'T KNOW.
MAMA, MAMA, PICK UP THE PHONE MAMA, MAMA, PICK UP THE PHONE
SHIT.
MAMA, MAMA, PICK UP THE PH...
BEEP
YOU HAVE KIDS?
ME?
NO. IT'S A PHONE THAT MY SISTER GAVE ME. I CAN'T STAND THIS THING.
I THOUGHT I'D TURNED IT OFF.
GIMME. I'LL SHOW YOU HOW.
HEY!

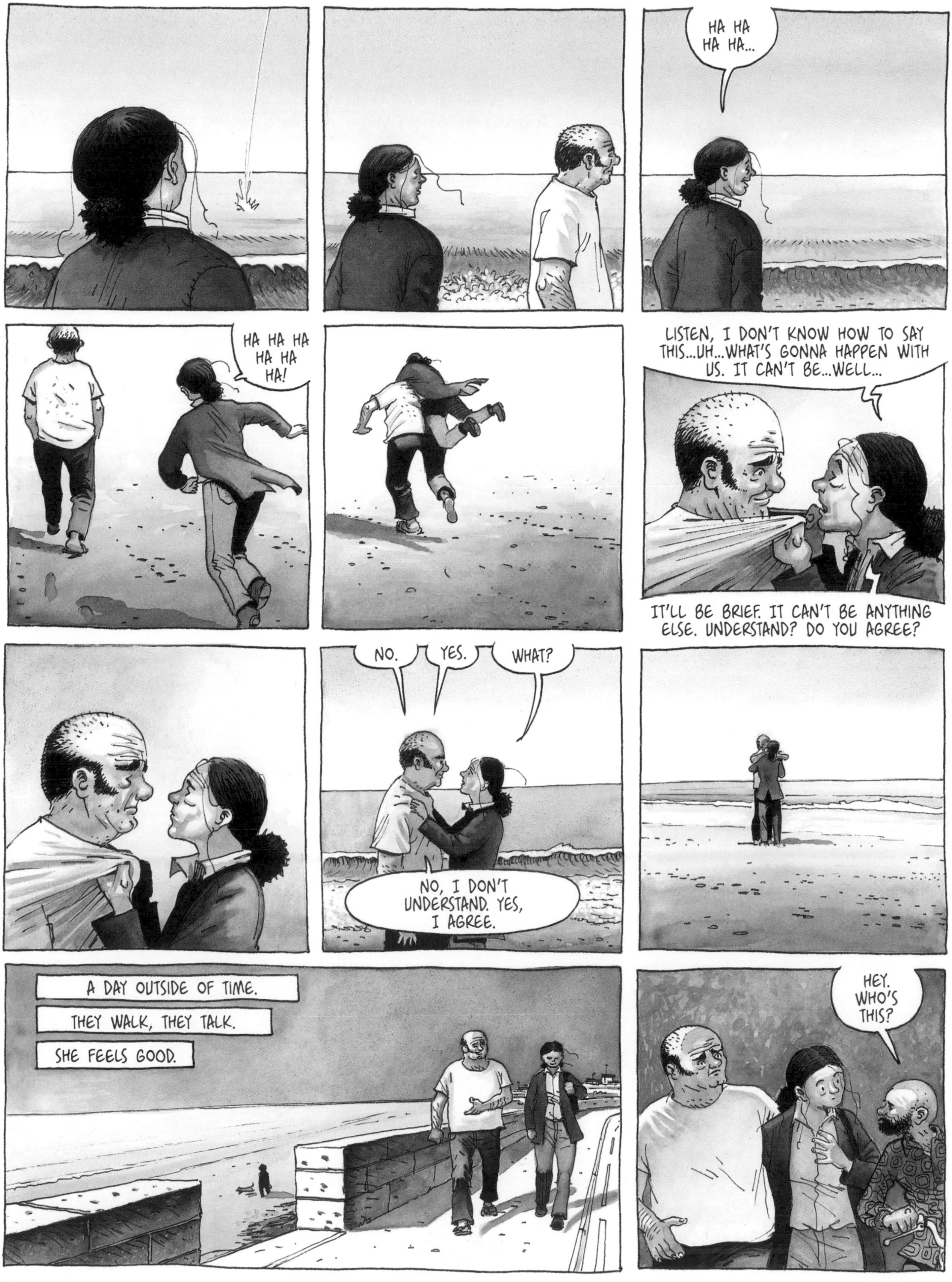
HA HA
HA HA...
HA HA HA
HA HA
HA!
LISTEN, I DON'T KNOW HOW TO SAY THIS...UH...WHAT'S GONNA HAPPEN WITH US. IT CAN'T BE...WELL...
IT'LL BE BRIEF. IT CAN'T BE ANYTHING ELSE. UNDERSTAND? DO YOU AGREE?
NO.
YES.
WHAT?
NO, I DON'T UNDERSTAND. YES, I AGREE.
A DAY OUTSIDE OF TIME.
THEY WALK, THEY TALK.
SHE FEELS GOOD.
HEY. WHO'S THIS?

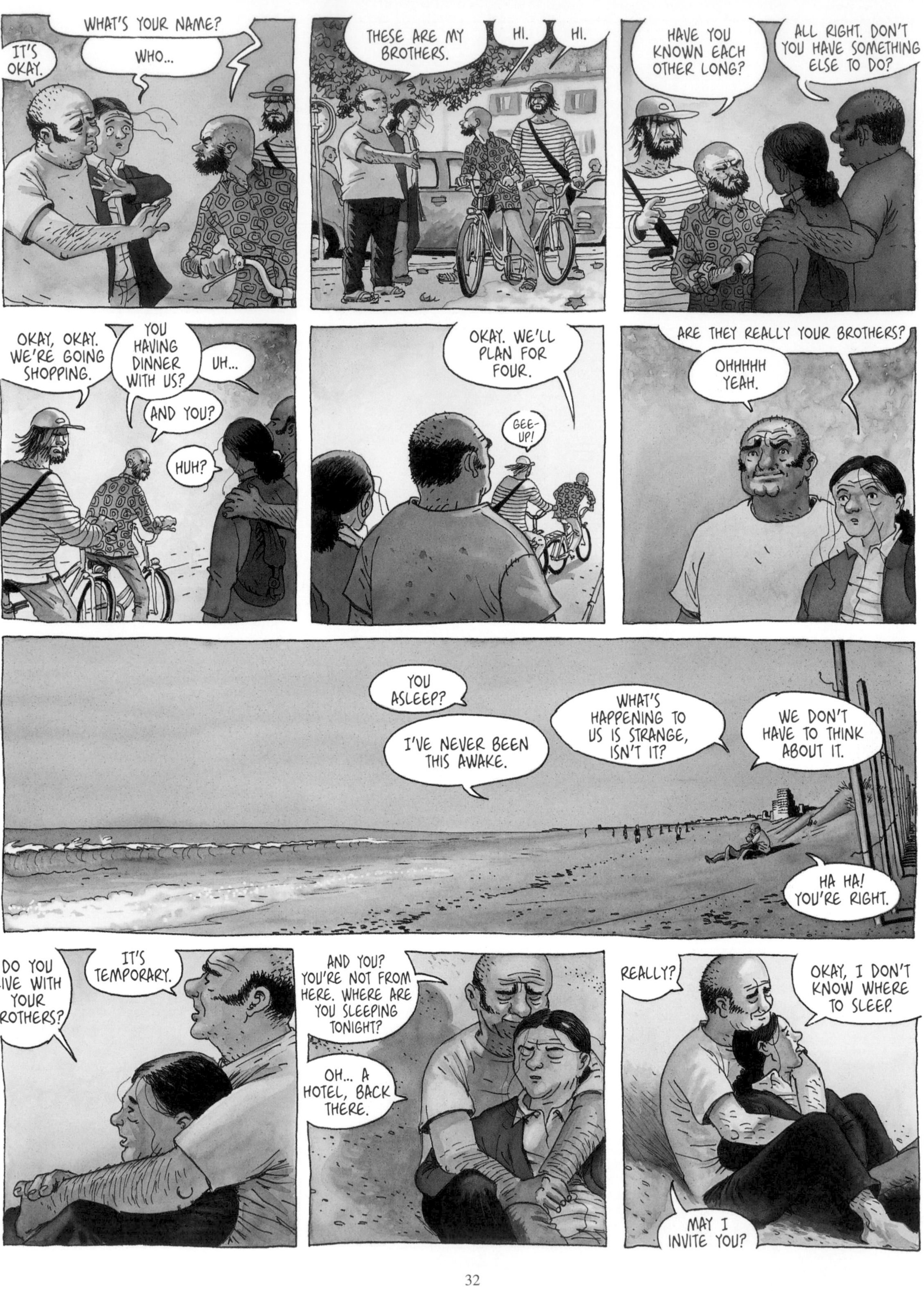
WHAT'S YOUR NAME?
IT'S OKAY.
WHO...
THESE ARE MY BROTHERS.
HI.
HI.
HAVE YOU KNOWN EACH OTHER LONG?
ALL RIGHT. DON'T YOU HAVE SOMETHING ELSE TO DO?
OKAY, OKAY. WE'RE GOING SHOPPING.
YOU HAVING DINNER WITH US?
UH...
AND YOU?
HUH?
OKAY. WE'LL PLAN FOR FOUR.
GEE-UP!
ARE THEY REALLY YOUR BROTHERS?
OHHHHH YEAH.
YOU ASLEEP?
I'VE NEVER BEEN THIS AWAKE.
WHAT'S HAPPENING TO US IS STRANGE, ISN'T IT?
WE DON'T HAVE TO THINK ABOUT IT.
HA HA! YOU'RE RIGHT.
DO YOU LIVE WITH YOUR BROTHERS?
IT'S TEMPORARY.
AND YOU? YOU'RE NOT FROM HERE. WHERE ARE YOU SLEEPING TONIGHT?
OH... A HOTEL, BACK THERE.
REALLY?
OKAY, I DON'T KNOW WHERE TO SLEEP.
MAY I INVITE YOU?

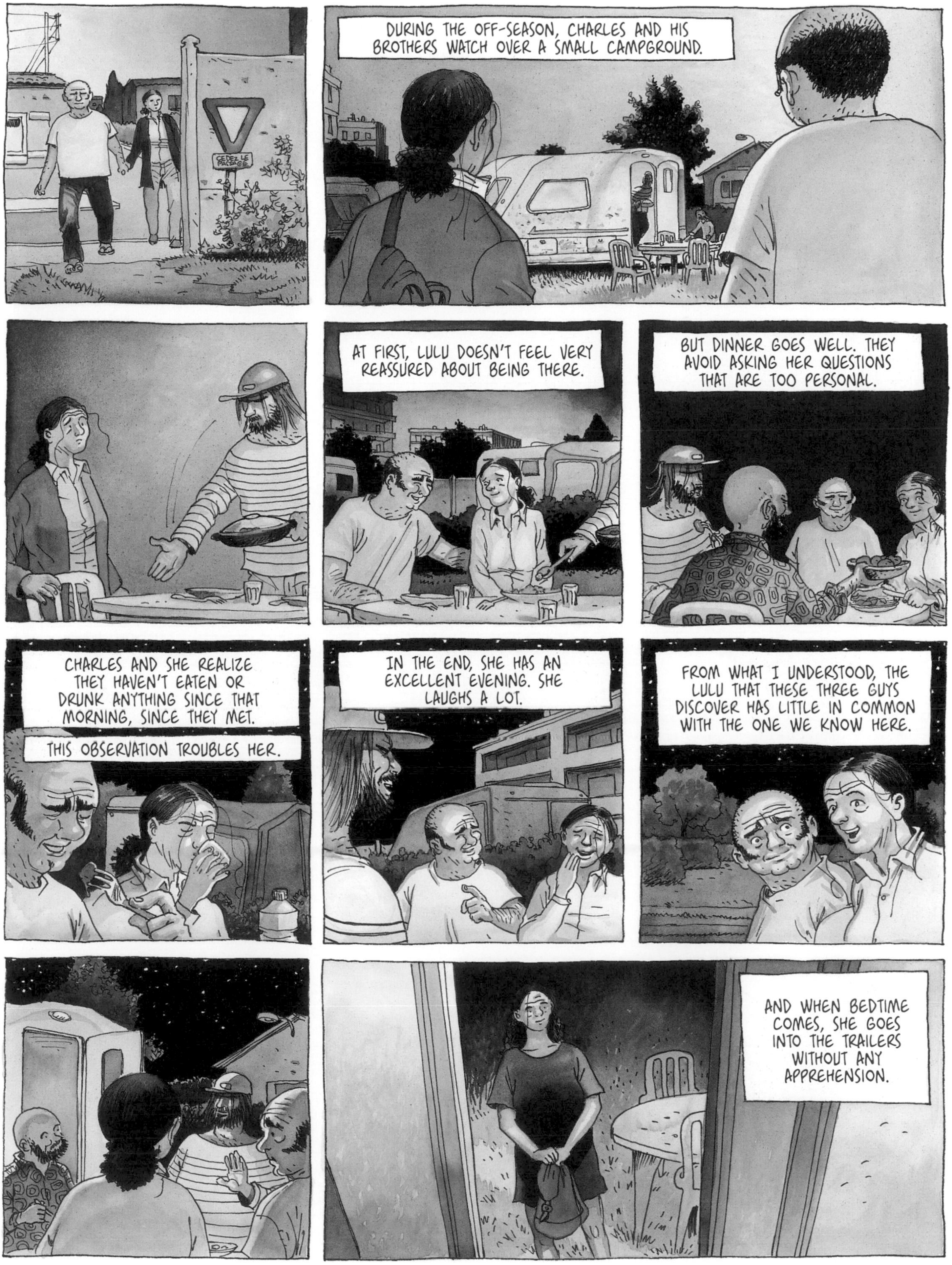
DURING THE OFF-SEASON, CHARLES AND HIS BROTHERS WATCH OVER A SMALL CAMPGROUND.
AT FIRST, LULU DOESN'T FEEL VERY REASSURED ABOUT BEING THERE.
BUT DINNER GOES WELL. THEY AVOID ASKING HER QUESTIONS THAT ARE TOO PERSONAL.
CHARLES AND SHE REALIZE THEY HAVEN'T EATEN OR DRUNK ANYTHING SINCE THAT MORNING, SINCE THEY MET.
THIS OBSERVATION TROUBLES HER.
IN THE END, SHE HAS AN EXCELLENT EVENING. SHE LAUGHS A LOT.
FROM WHAT I UNDERSTOOD, THE LULU THAT THESE THREE GUYS DISCOVER HAS LITTLE IN COMMON WITH THE ONE WE KNOW HERE.
AND WHEN BEDTIME COMES, SHE GOES INTO THE TRAILERS WITHOUT ANY APPREHENSION.

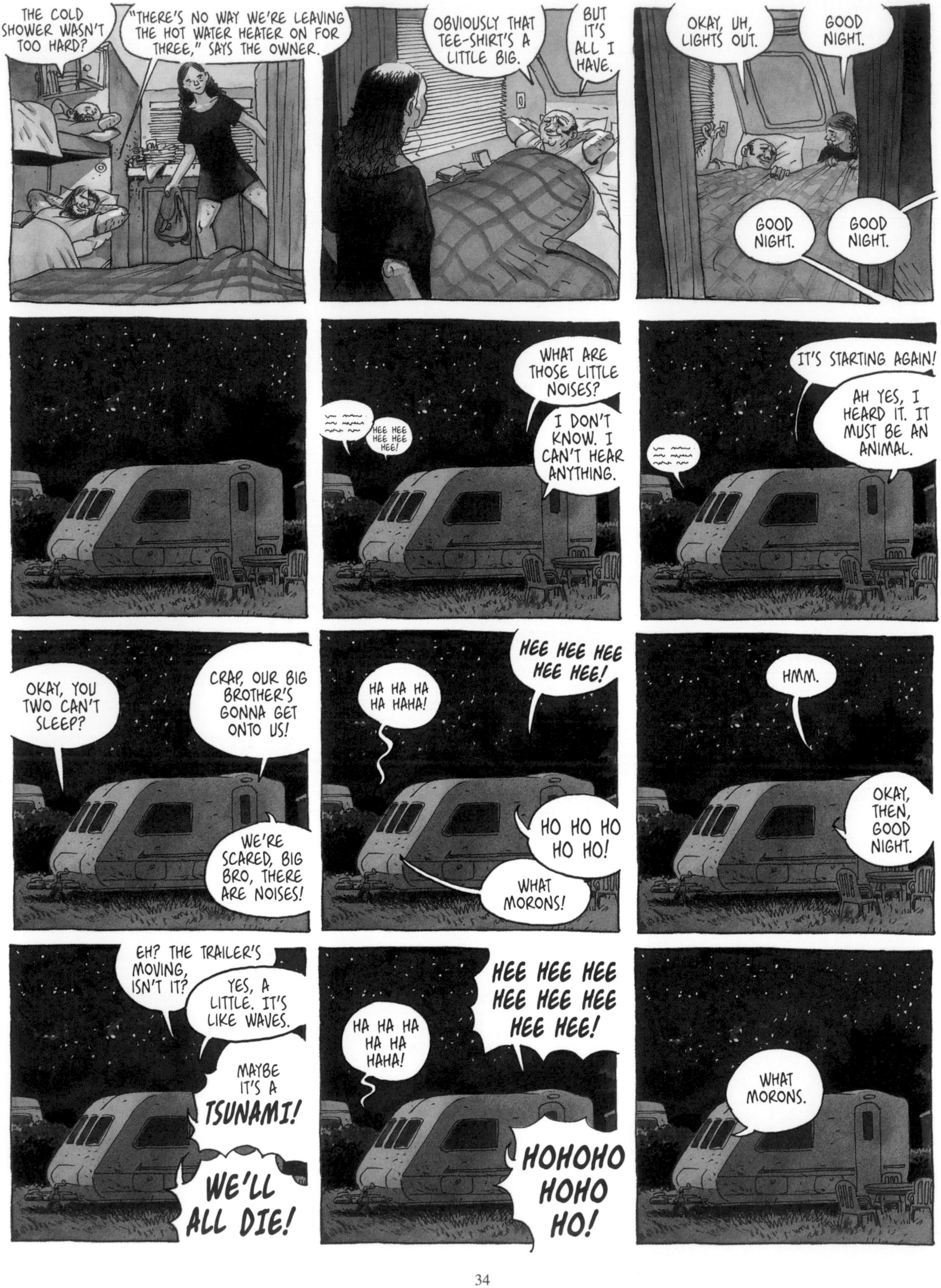
THE COLD SHOWER WASN'T TOO HARD?
"THERE'S NO WAY WE'RE LEAVING THE HOT WATER HEATER ON FOR THREE," SAYS THE OWNER.
OBVIOUSLY THAT TEE-SHIRT'S A LITTLE BIG.
BUT IT'S ALL I HAVE.
OKAY, UH, LIGHTS OUT.
GOOD NIGHT.
GOOD NIGHT.
GOOD NIGHT.
HEE HEE HEE HEE HEE!
WHAT ARE THOSE LITTLE NOISES?
I DON'T KNOW. I CAN'T HEAR ANYTHING.
IT'S STARTING AGAIN!
AH YES, I HEARD IT. IT MUST BE AN ANIMAL.
OKAY, YOU TWO CAN'T SLEEP?
CRAP, OUR BIG BROTHER'S GONNA GET ONTO US!
WE'RE SCARED, BIG BRO, THERE ARE NOISES!
HA HA HA HA HAHA!
HEE HEE HEE HEE HEE!
HO HO HO HO HO!
WHAT MORONS!
HMM.
OKAY, THEN, GOOD NIGHT.
EH? THE TRAILER'S MOVING, ISN'T IT?
YES, A LITTLE. IT'S LIKE WAVES.
MAYBE IT'S A TSUNAMI!
WE'LL ALL DIE!
HA HA HA HA HA HAHA!
HEE HEE HEE HEE HEE HEE HEE HEE!
HOHOHO HOHO HO!
WHAT MORONS.

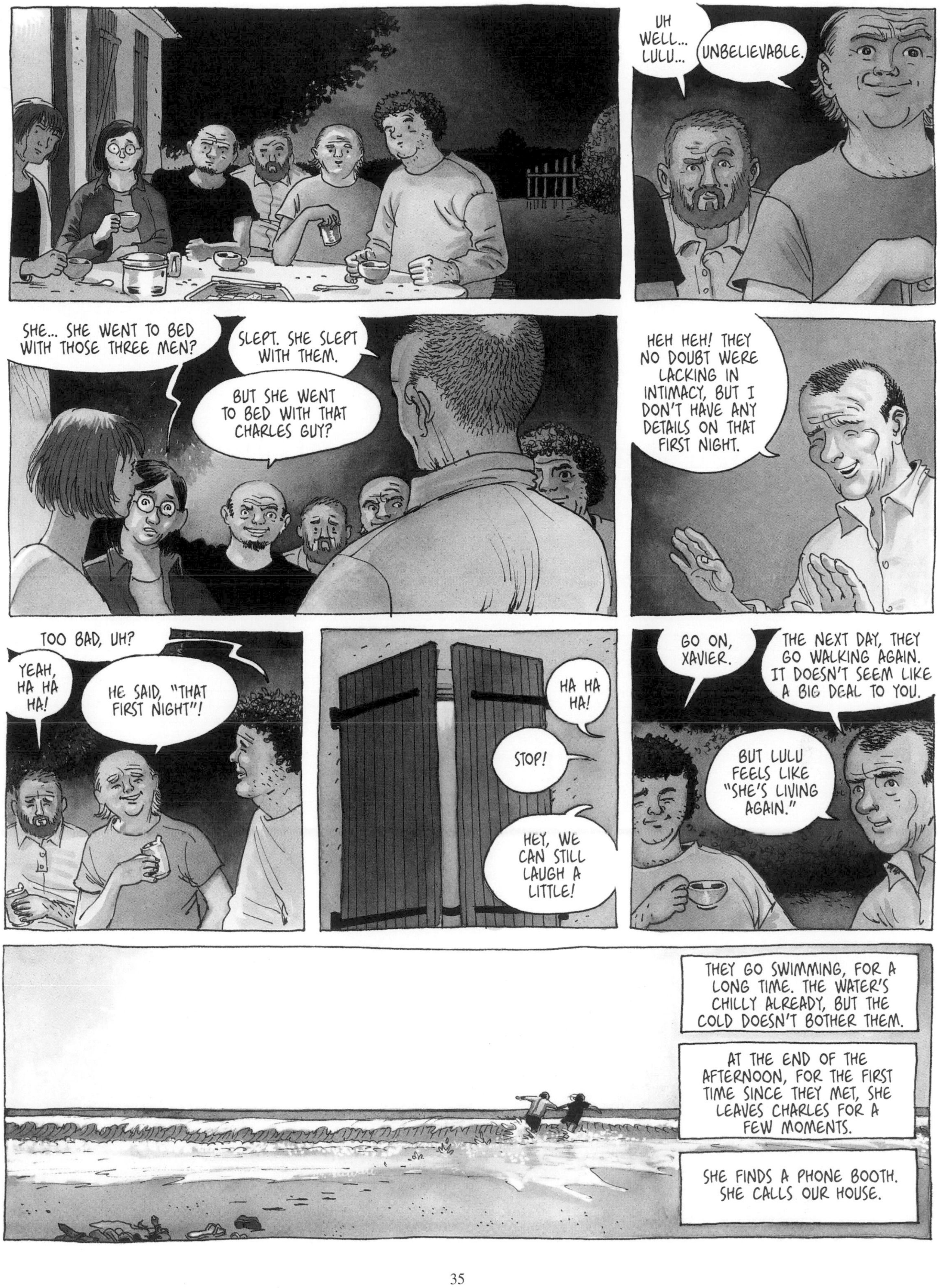

UH WELL... LULU...
UNBELIEVABLE.
SHE... SHE WENT TO BED WITH THOSE THREE MEN?
SLEPT. SHE SLEPT WITH THEM.
BUT SHE WENT TO BED WITH THAT CHARLES GUY?
HEH HEH! THEY NO DOUBT WERE LACKING IN INTIMACY, BUT I DON'T HAVE ANY DETAILS ON THAT FIRST NIGHT.
TOO BAD, UH?
YEAH, HA HA HA!
HE SAID, "THAT FIRST NIGHT"!
HA HA HA!
STOP!
HEY, WE CAN STILL LAUGH A LITTLE!
GO ON, XAVIER.
THE NEXT DAY, THEY GO WALKING AGAIN. IT DOESN'T SEEM LIKE A BIG DEAL TO YOU.
BUT LULU FEELS LIKE "SHE'S LIVING AGAIN."
THEY GO SWIMMING, FOR A LONG TIME. THE WATER'S CHILLY ALREADY, BUT THE COLD DOESN'T BOTHER THEM.
AT THE END OF THE AFTERNOON, FOR THE FIRST TIME SINCE THEY MET, SHE LEAVES CHARLES FOR A FEW MOMENTS.
SHE FINDS A PHONE BOOTH. SHE CALLS OUR HOUSE.

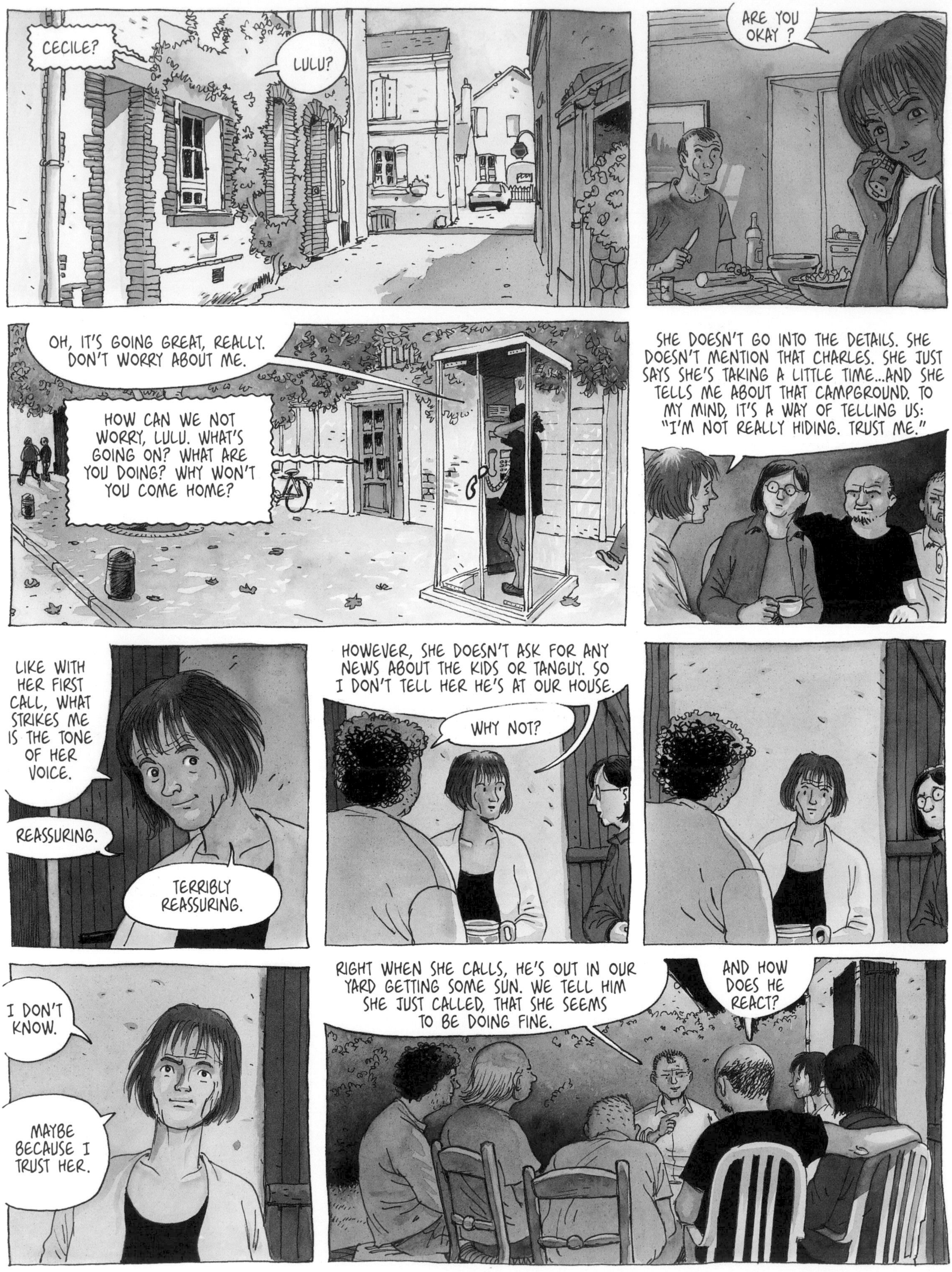

CECILE?
LULU?
ARE YOU OKAY ?
OH, IT'S GOING GREAT, REALLY. DON'T WORRY ABOUT ME.
HOW CAN WE NOT WORRY, LULU. WHAT'S GOING ON? WHAT ARE YOU DOING? WHY WON'T YOU COME HOME?
SHE DOESN'T GO INTO THE DETAILS. SHE DOESN'T MENTION THAT CHARLES. SHE JUST SAYS SHE'S TAKING A LITTLE TIME...AND SHE TELLS ME ABOUT THAT CAMPGROUND. TO MY MIND, IT'S A WAY OF TELLING US: "I'M NOT REALLY HIDING. TRUST ME."
LIKE WITH HER FIRST CALL, WHAT STRIKES ME IS THE TONE OF HER VOICE.
REASSURING.
TERRIBLY REASSURING.
HOWEVER, SHE DOESN'T ASK FOR ANY NEWS ABOUT THE KIDS OR TANGUY. SO I DON'T TELL HER HE'S AT OUR HOUSE.
WHY NOT?
I DON'T KNOW.
MAYBE BECAUSE I TRUST HER.
RIGHT WHEN SHE CALLS, HE'S OUT IN OUR YARD GETTING SOME SUN. WE TELL HIM SHE JUST CALLED, THAT SHE SEEMS TO BE DOING FINE.
AND HOW DOES HE REACT?

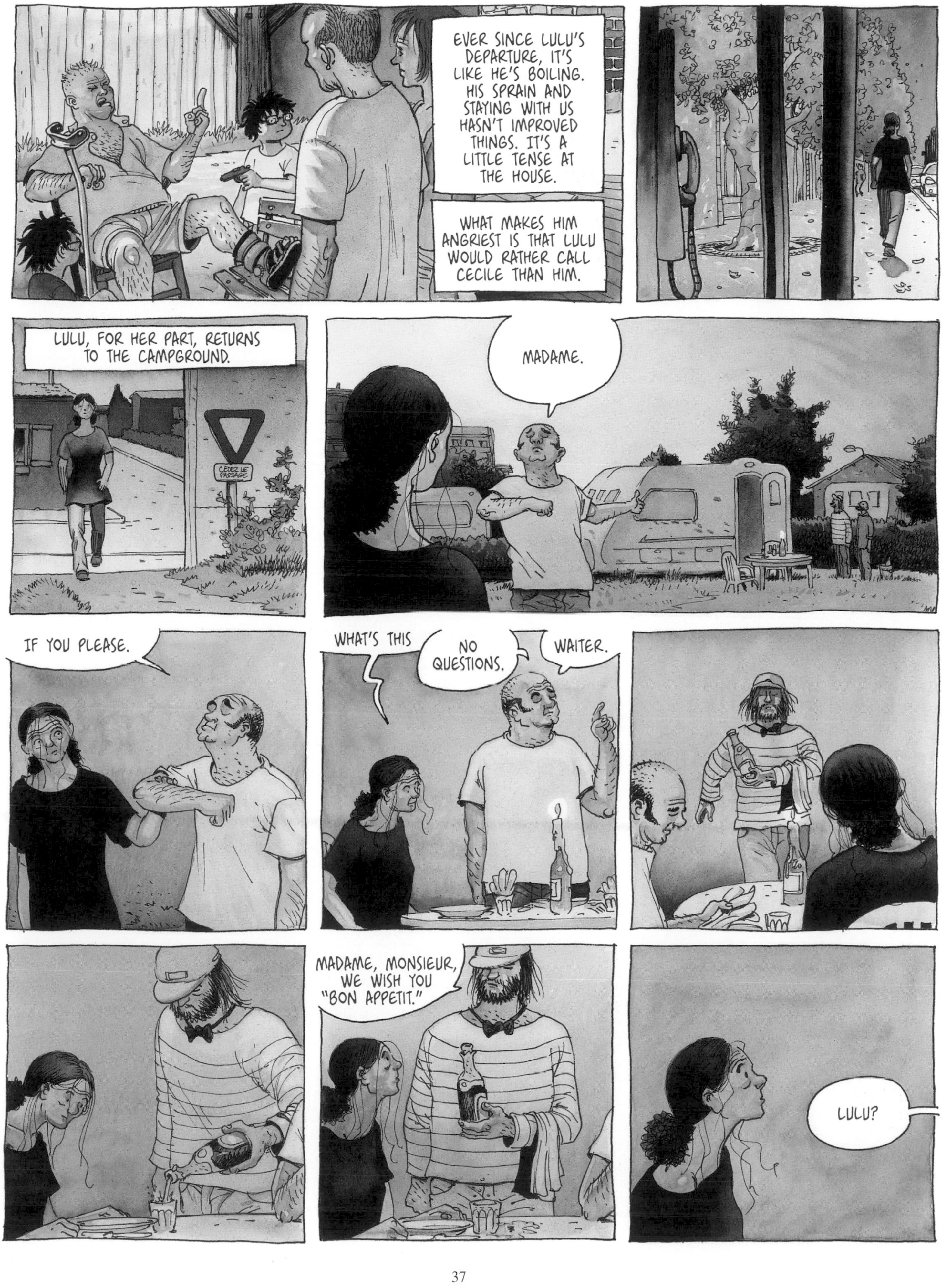
EVER SINCE LULU'S DEPARTURE, IT'S LIKE HE'S BOILING. HIS SPRAIN AND STAYING WITH US HASN'T IMPROVED THINGS. IT'S A LITTLE TENSE AT THE HOUSE.
WHAT MAKES HIM ANGRIEST IS THAT LULU WOULD RATHER CALL CECILE THAN HIM.
LULU, FOR HER PART, RETURNS TO THE CAMPGROUND.
CEDEZ LE PASSAGE
MADAME.
IF YOU PLEASE.
WHAT'S THIS
NO QUESTIONS.
WAITER.
MADAME, MONSIEUR, WE WISH YOU "BON APPETIT."
LULU?

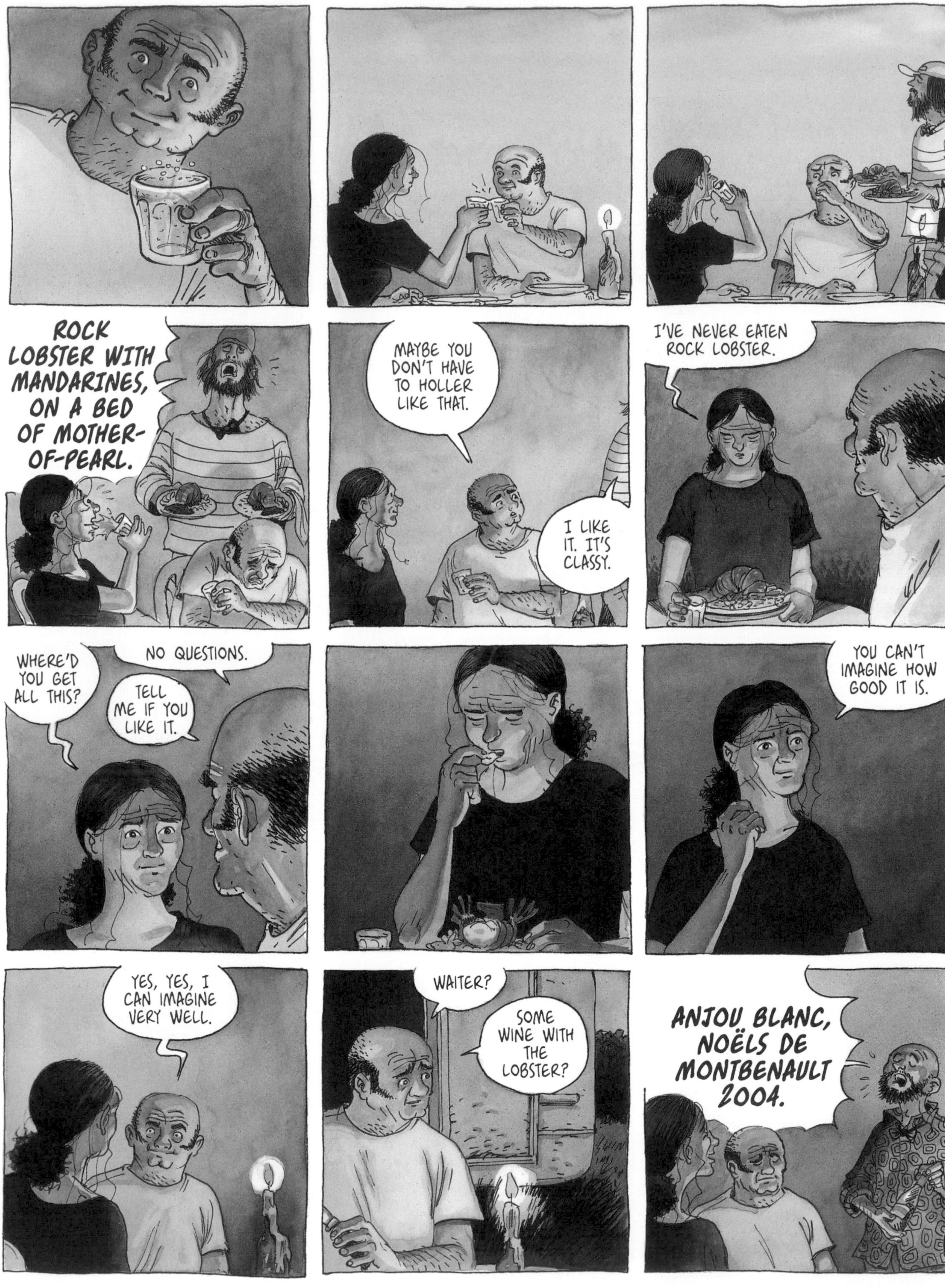

ROCK LOBSTER WITH MANDARINES, ON A BED OF MOTHER-OF-PEARL.
MAYBE YOU DON'T HAVE TO HOLLER LIKE THAT.
I LIKE IT. IT'S CLASSY.
I'VE NEVER EATEN ROCK LOBSTER.
WHERE'D YOU GET ALL THIS?
NO QUESTIONS.
TELL ME IF YOU LIKE IT.
YOU CAN'T IMAGINE HOW GOOD IT IS.
YES, YES, I CAN IMAGINE VERY WELL.
WAITER?
SOME WINE WITH THE LOBSTER?
ANJOU BLANC, NOËLS DE MONTBENAULT 2004.

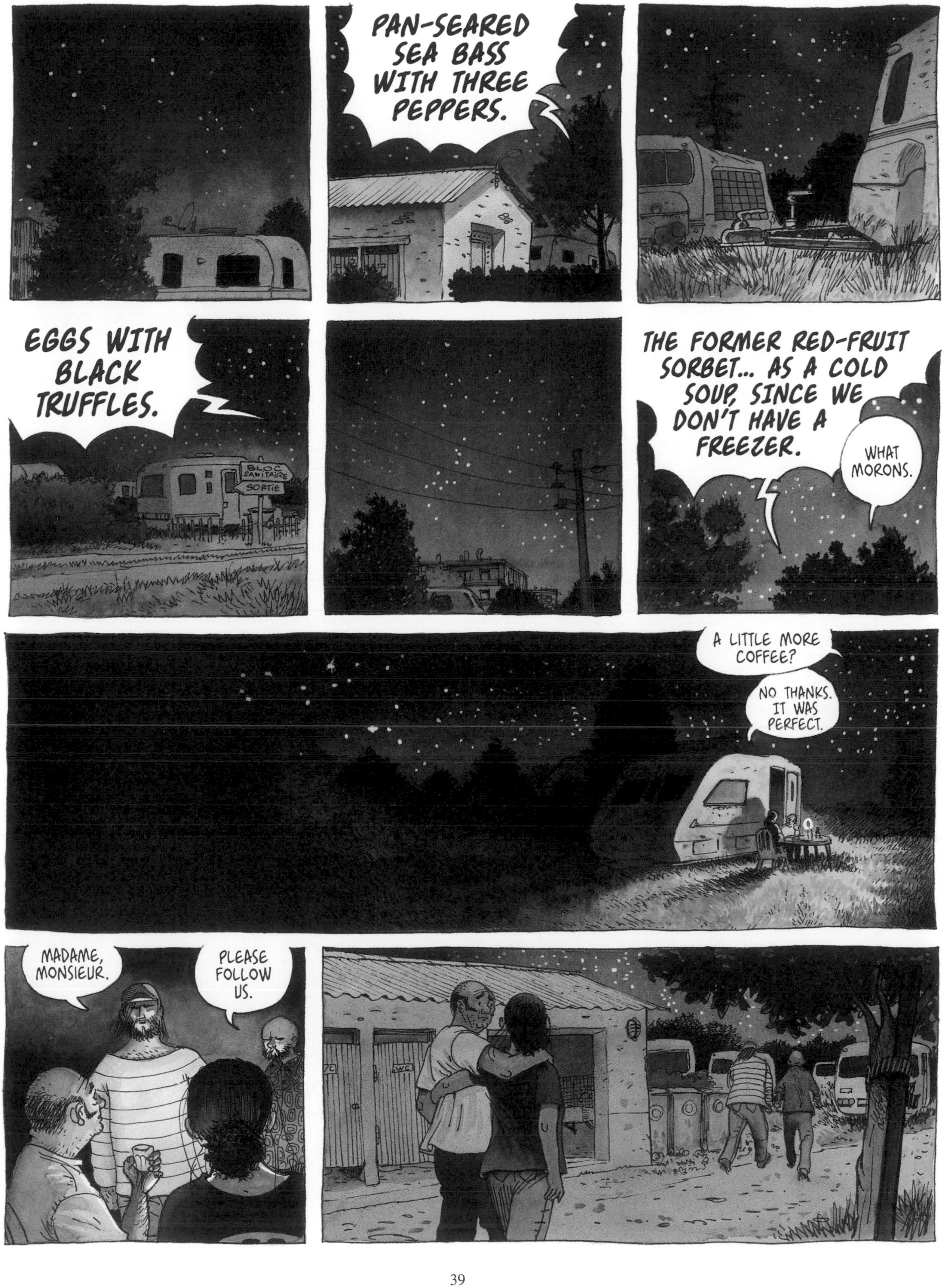
PAN-SEARED SEA BASS WITH THREE PEPPERS.
EGGS WITH BLACK TRUFFLES.
BLOC SANITAIRE
SORTIE
THE FORMER RED-FRUIT SORBET... AS A COLD SOUP, SINCE WE DON'T HAVE A FREEZER.
WHAT MORONS.
A LITTLE MORE COFFEE?
NO THANKS. IT WAS PERFECT.
MADAME, MONSIEUR.
PLEASE FOLLOW US.
WC

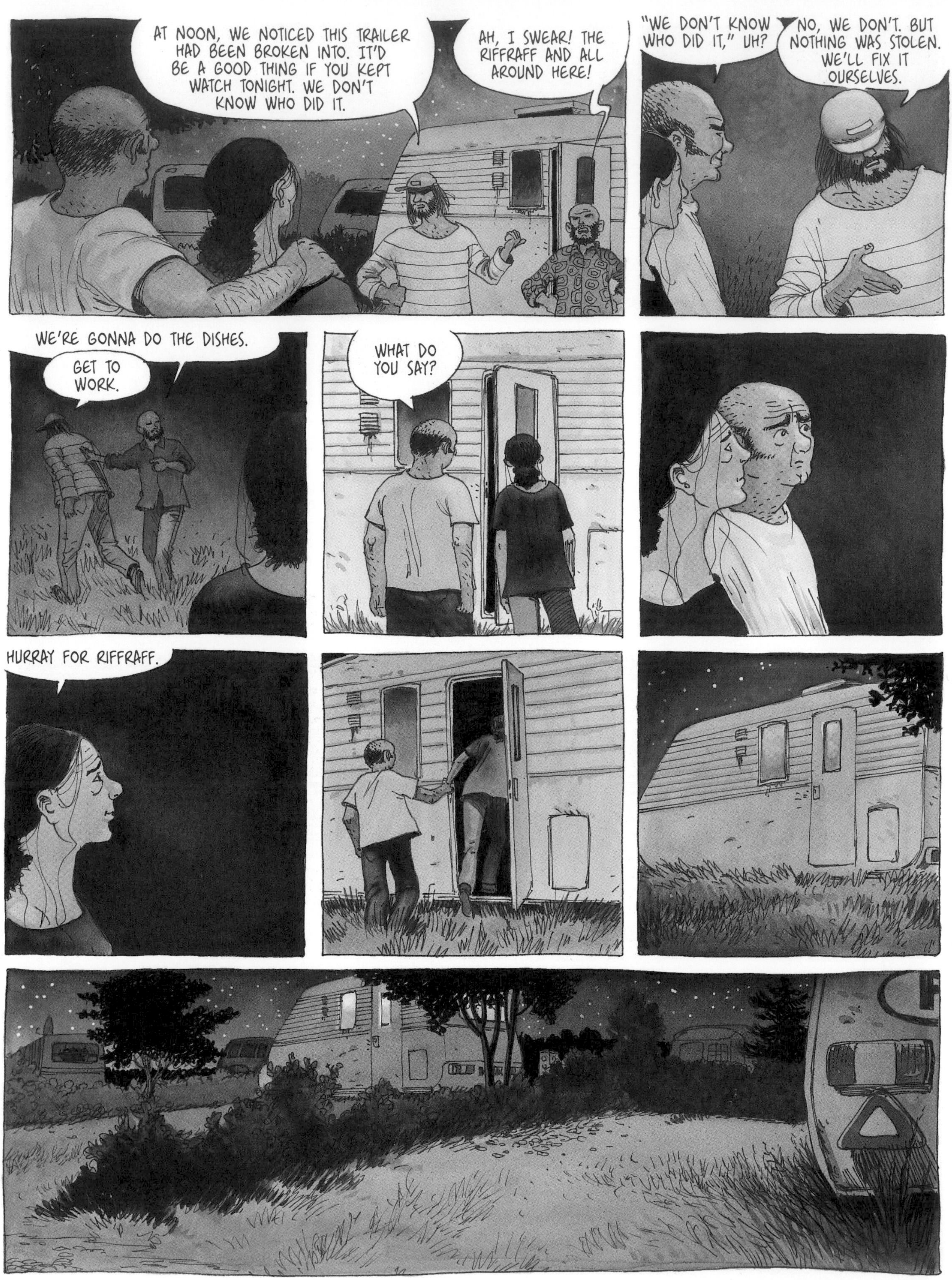
AT NOON, WE NOTICED THIS TRAILER HAD BEEN BROKEN INTO. IT'D BE A GOOD THING IF YOU KEPT WATCH TONIGHT. WE DON'T KNOW WHO DID IT.
AH, I SWEAR! THE RIFFRAFF AND ALL AROUND HERE!
"WE DON'T KNOW WHO DID IT," UH?
NO, WE DON'T. BUT NOTHING WAS STOLEN. WE'LL FIX IT OURSELVES.
WE'RE GONNA DO THE DISHES.
GET TO WORK.
WHAT DO YOU SAY?
HURRAY FOR RIFFRAFF.

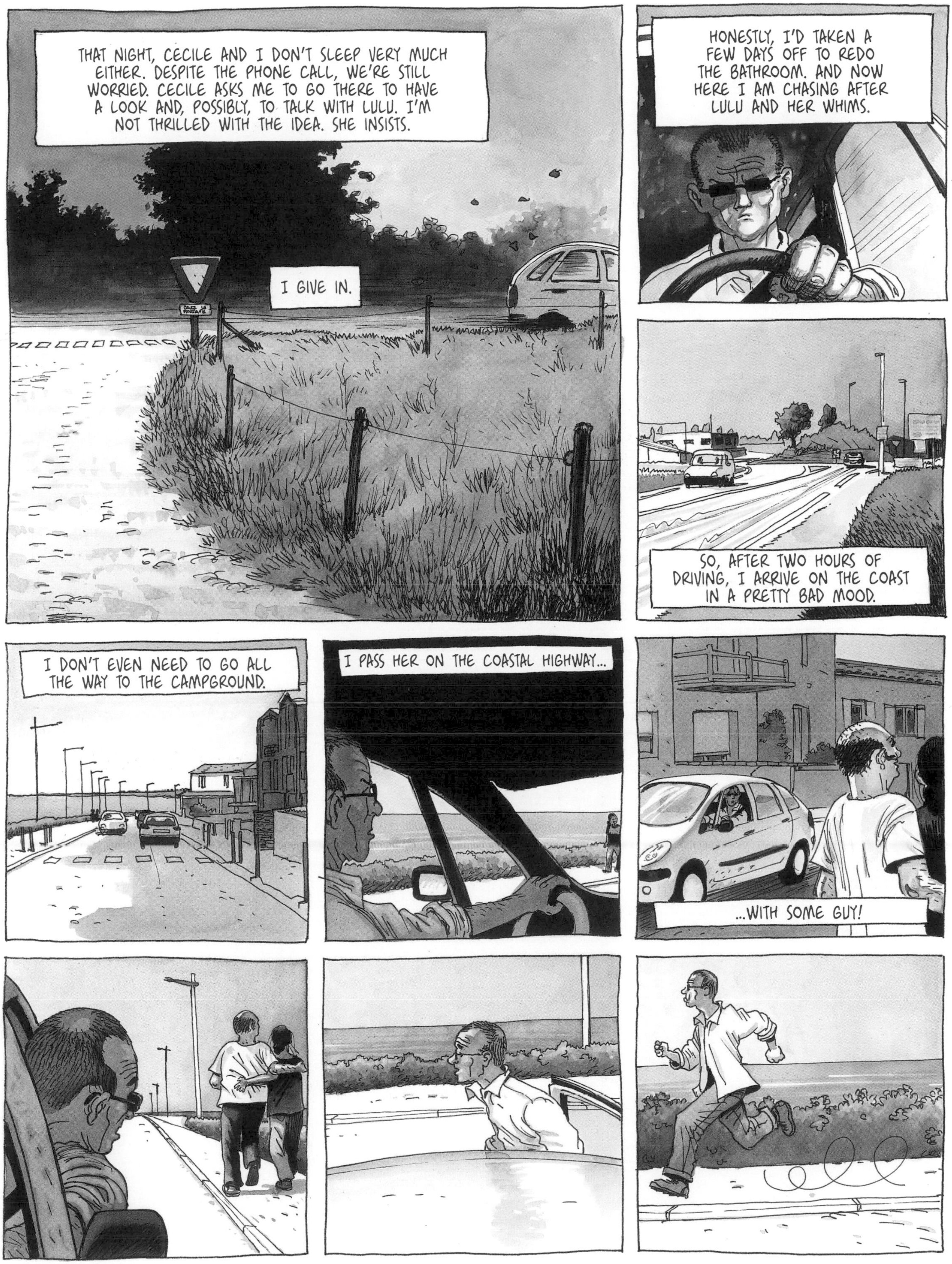
THAT NIGHT, CECILE AND I DON'T SLEEP VERY MUCH EITHER. DESPITE THE PHONE CALL, WE'RE STILL WORRIED. CECILE ASKS ME TO GO THERE TO HAVE A LOOK AND, POSSIBLY, TO TALK WITH LULU. I'M NOT THRILLED WITH THE IDEA. SHE INSISTS.
I GIVE IN.
HONESTLY, I'D TAKEN A FEW DAYS OFF TO REDO THE BATHROOM. AND NOW HERE I AM CHASING AFTER LULU AND HER WHIMS.
SO, AFTER TWO HOURS OF DRIVING, I ARRIVE ON THE COAST IN A PRETTY BAD MOOD.
I DON'T EVEN NEED TO GO ALL THE WAY TO THE CAMPGROUND.
I PASS HER ON THE COASTAL HIGHWAY...
...WITH SOME GUY!

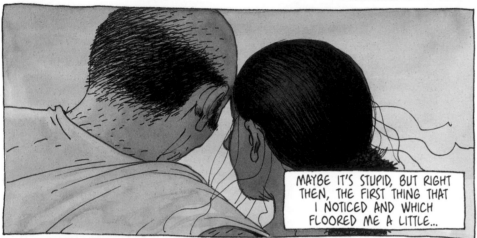

MAYBE IT'S STUPID, BUT RIGHT THEN, THE FIRST THING THAT I NOTICED AND WHICH FLOORED ME A LITTLE...

...IS THAT I'D RARELY EVER SEEN LULU LAUGHING.

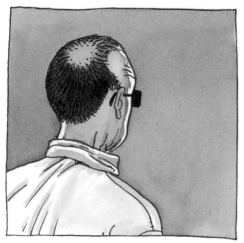

WHAT DO I DO?

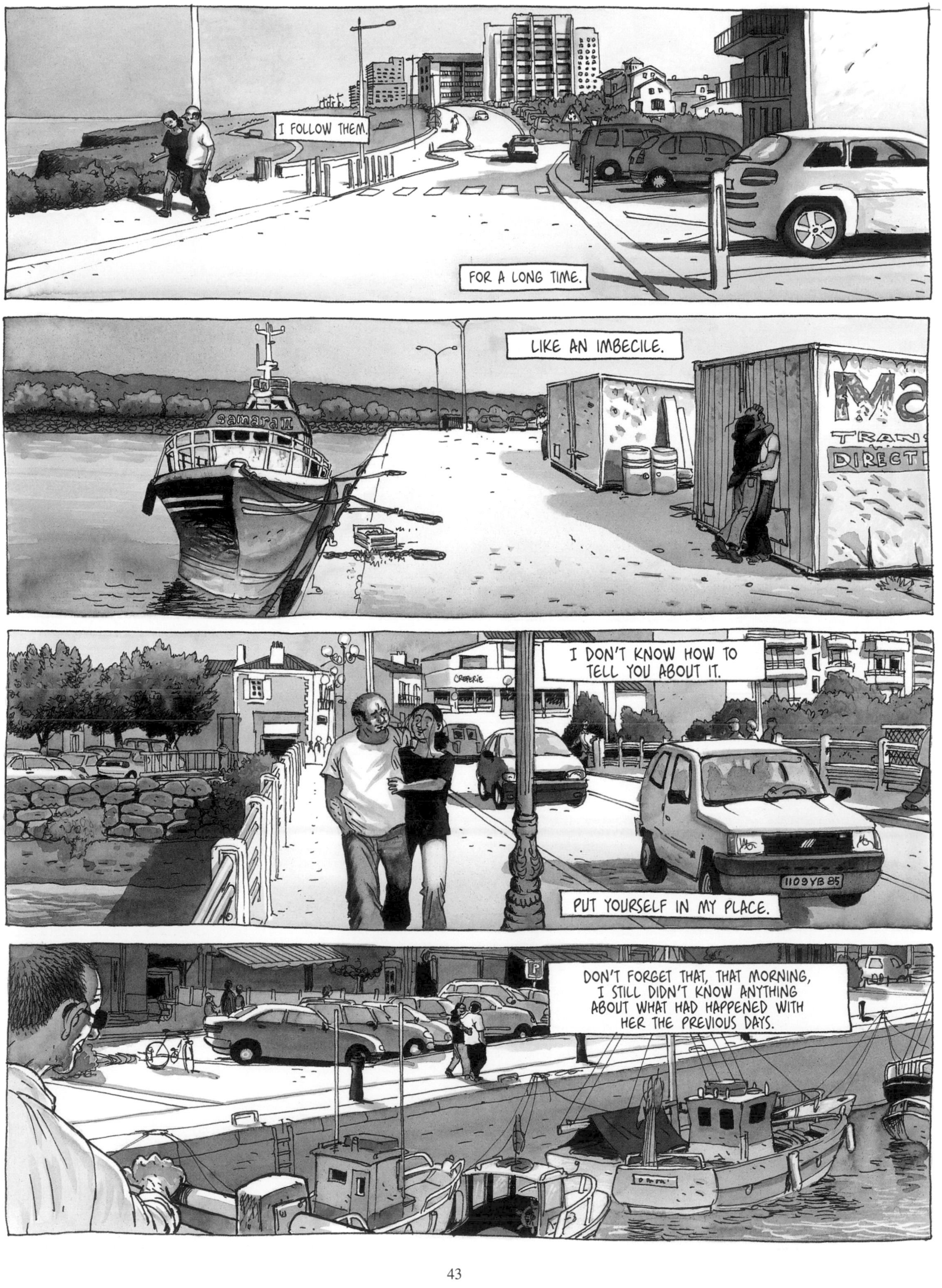
I FOLLOW THEM.
FOR A LONG TIME.
LIKE AN IMBECILE.
I DON'T KNOW HOW TO TELL YOU ABOUT IT.
PUT YOURSELF IN MY PLACE.
DON'T FORGET THAT, THAT MORNING, I STILL DIDN'T KNOW ANYTHING ABOUT WHAT HAD HAPPENED WITH HER THE PREVIOUS DAYS.

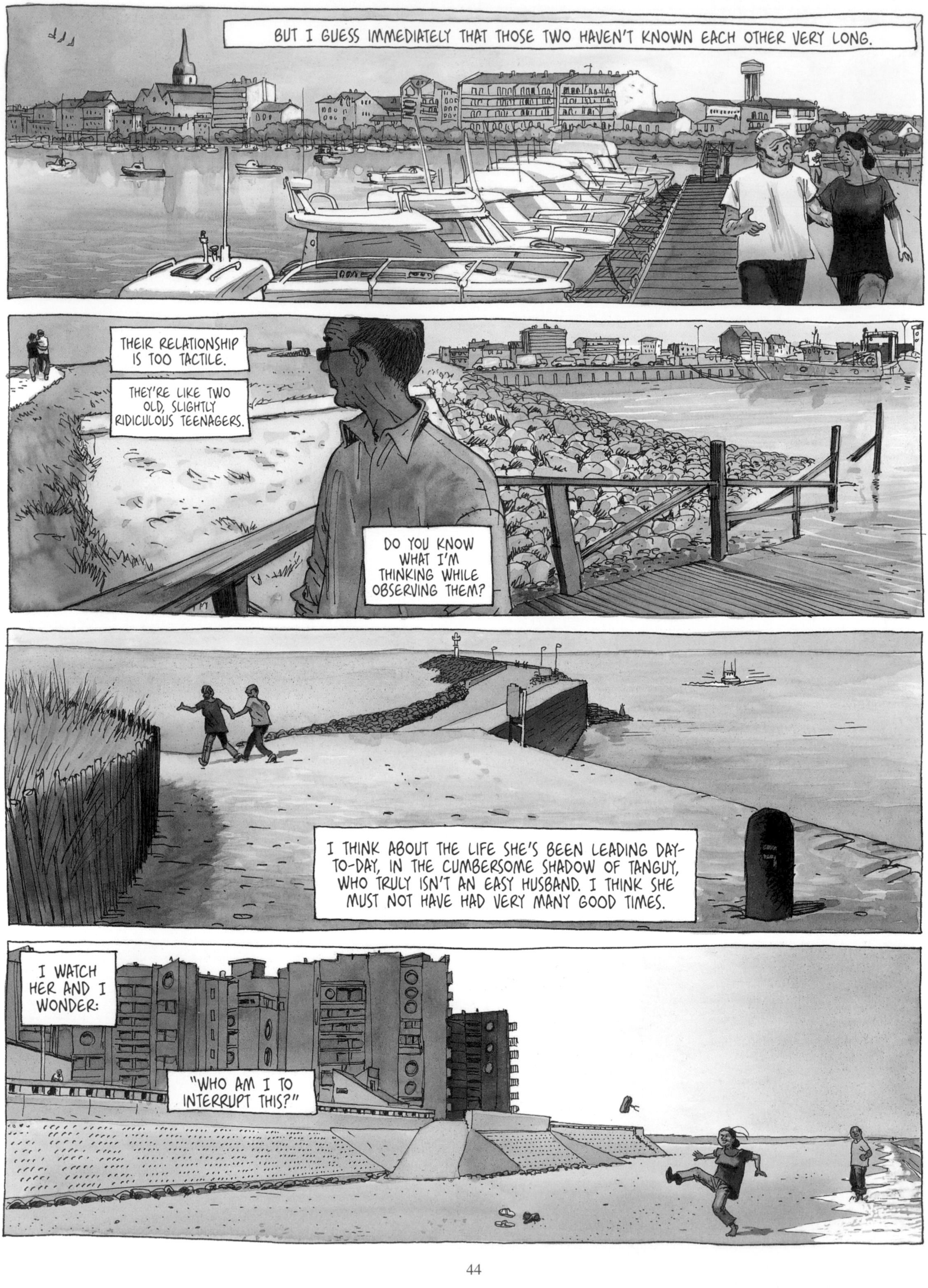
BUT I GUESS IMMEDIATELY THAT THOSE TWO HAVEN'T KNOWN EACH OTHER VERY LONG.
THEIR RELATIONSHIP IS TOO TACTILE.
THEY'RE LIKE TWO OLD, SLIGHTLY RIDICULOUS TEENAGERS.
DO YOU KNOW WHAT I'M THINKING WHILE OBSERVING THEM?
I THINK ABOUT THE LIFE SHE'S BEEN LEADING DAY-TO-DAY, IN THE CUMBERSOME SHADOW OF TANGUY, WHO TRULY ISN'T AN EASY HUSBAND. I THINK SHE MUST NOT HAVE HAD VERY MANY GOOD TIMES.
I WATCH HER AND I WONDER:
"WHO AM I TO INTERRUPT THIS?"

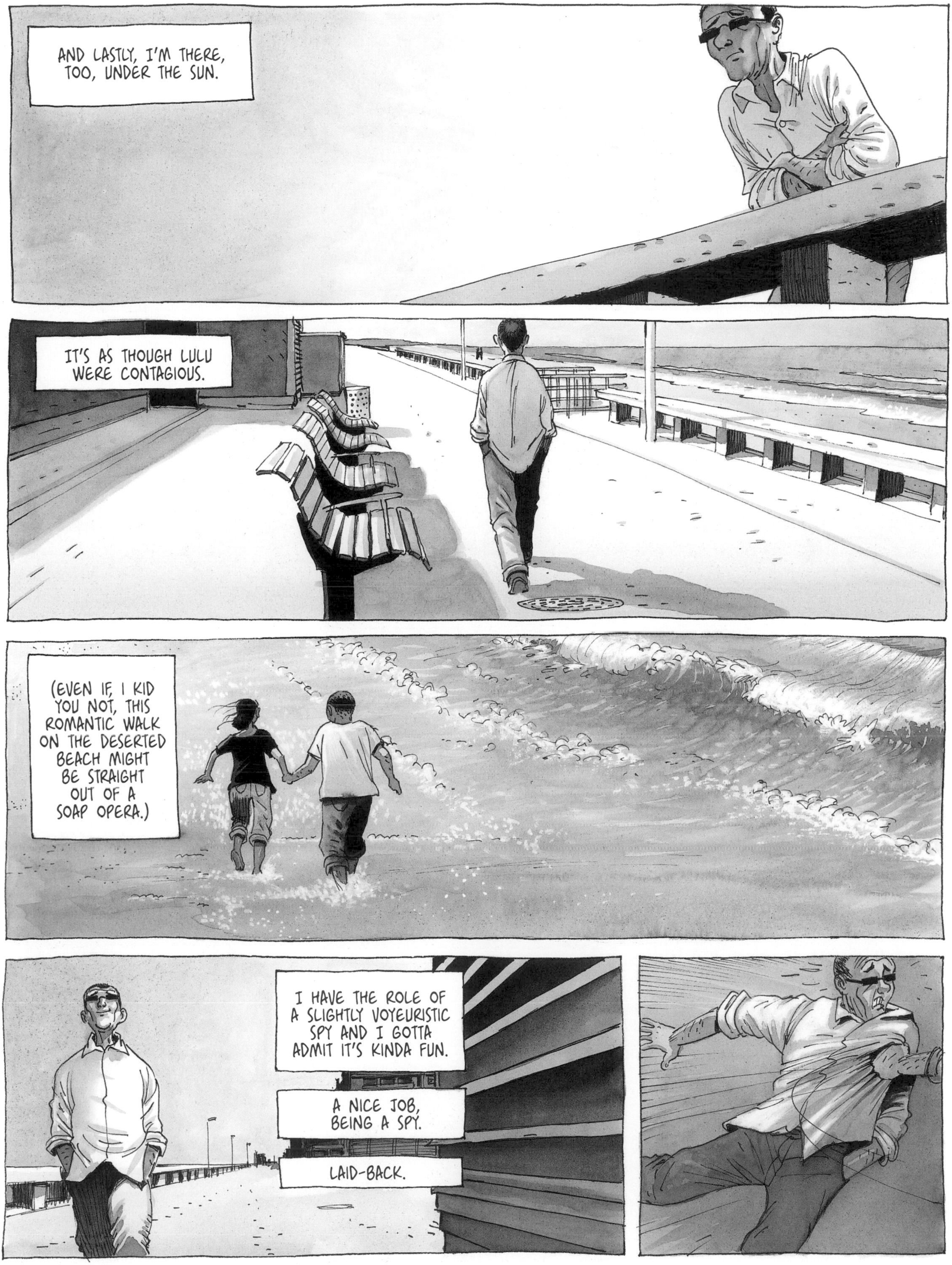
AND LASTLY, I'M THERE, TOO, UNDER THE SUN.
IT'S AS THOUGH LULU WERE CONTAGIOUS.
(EVEN IF, I KID YOU NOT, THIS ROMANTIC WALK ON THE DESERTED BEACH MIGHT BE STRAIGHT OUT OF A SOAP OPERA.)
I HAVE THE ROLE OF A SLIGHTLY VOYEURISTIC SPY AND I GOTTA ADMIT IT'S KINDA FUN.
A NICE JOB, BEING A SPY.
LAID-BACK.

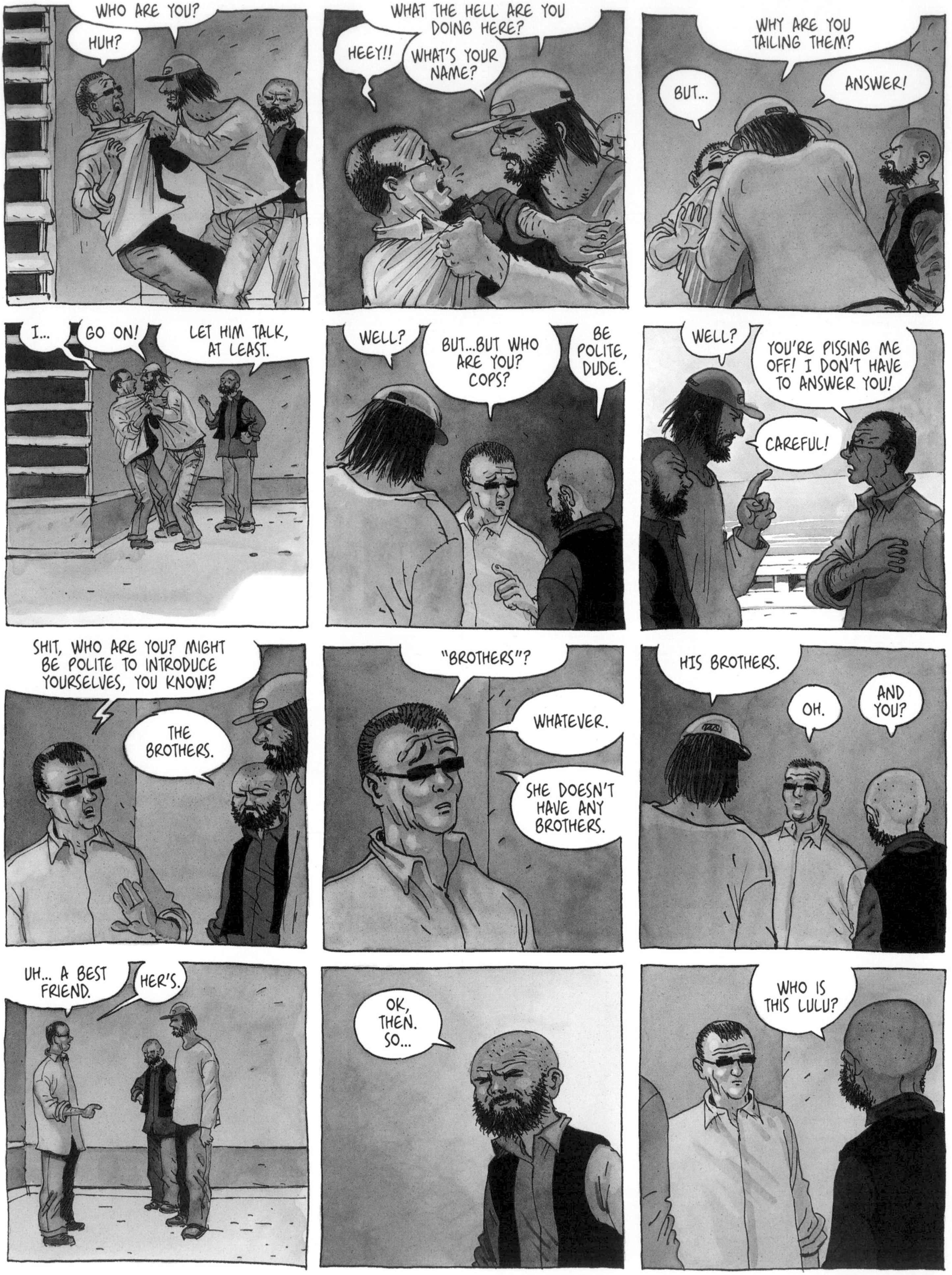
WHO ARE YOU?
HUH?
WHAT THE HELL ARE YOU DOING HERE?
HEEY!!
WHAT'S YOUR NAME?
WHY ARE YOU TAILING THEM?
BUT...
ANSWER!
I...
GO ON!
LET HIM TALK, AT LEAST.
WELL?
BUT...BUT WHO ARE YOU? COPS?
BE POLITE, DUDE.
WELL?
YOU'RE PISSING ME OFF! I DON'T HAVE TO ANSWER YOU!
CAREFUL!
SHIT, WHO ARE YOU? MIGHT BE POLITE TO INTRODUCE YOURSELVES, YOU KNOW?
THE BROTHERS.
"BROTHERS"?
WHATEVER.
SHE DOESN'T HAVE ANY BROTHERS.
HIS BROTHERS.
OH.
AND YOU?
UH... A BEST FRIEND.
HER'S.
OK, THEN. SO...
WHO IS THIS LULU?

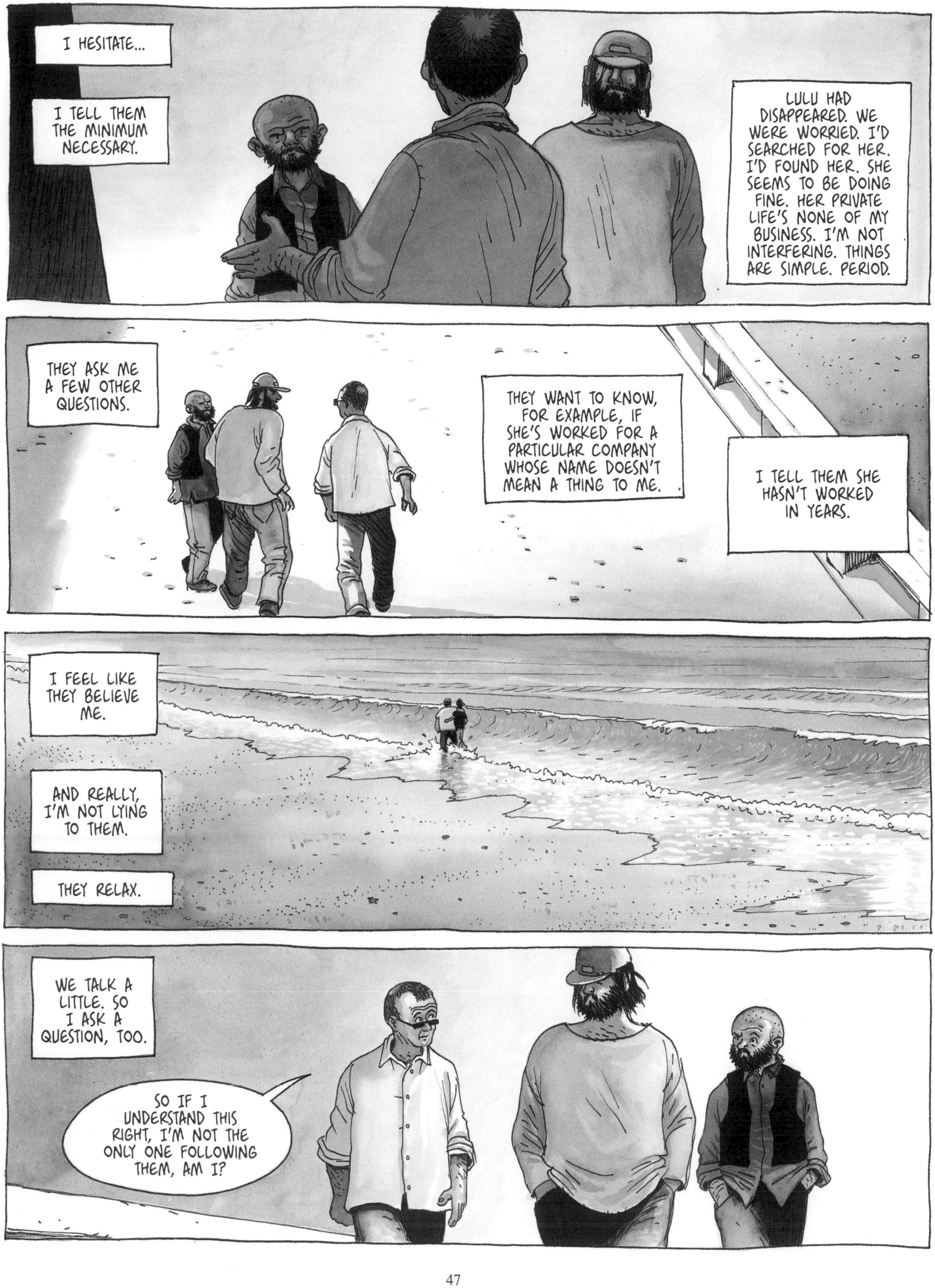
I HESITATE...
I TELL THEM THE MINIMUM NECESSARY.
LULU HAD DISAPPEARED. WE WERE WORRIED. I'D SEARCHED FOR HER. I'D FOUND HER. SHE SEEMS TO BE DOING FINE. HER PRIVATE LIFE'S NONE OF MY BUSINESS. I'M NOT INTERFERING. THINGS ARE SIMPLE. PERIOD.
THEY ASK ME A FEW OTHER QUESTIONS.
THEY WANT TO KNOW, FOR EXAMPLE, IF SHE'S WORKED FOR A PARTICULAR COMPANY WHOSE NAME DOESN'T MEAN A THING TO ME.
I TELL THEM SHE HASN'T WORKED IN YEARS.
I FEEL LIKE THEY BELIEVE ME.
AND REALLY, I'M NOT LYING TO THEM.
THEY RELAX.
WE TALK A LITTLE. SO I ASK A QUESTION, TOO.
SO IF I UNDERSTAND THIS RIGHT, I'M NOT THE ONLY ONE FOLLOWING THEM, AM I?

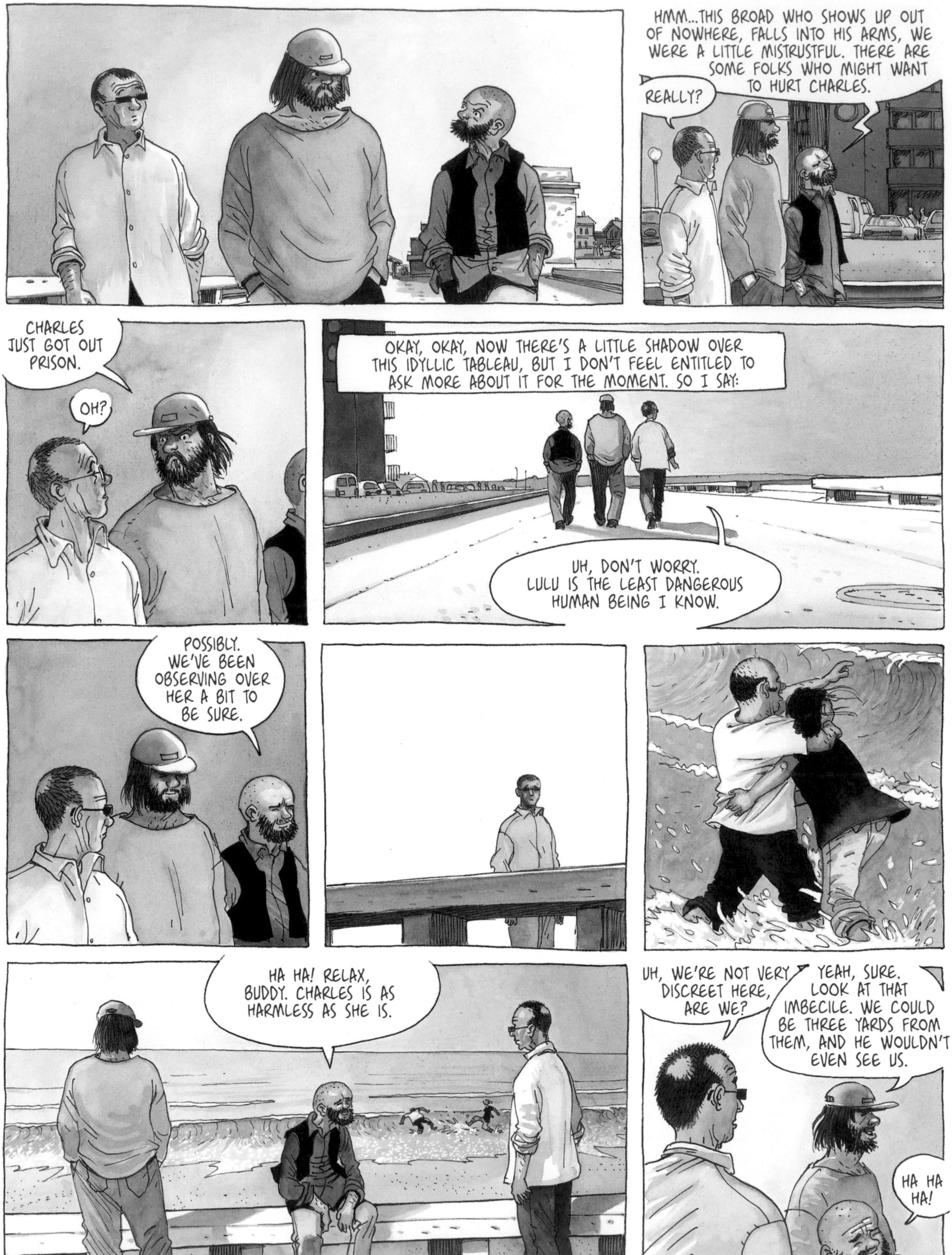
HMM...THIS BROAD WHO SHOWS UP OUT OF NOWHERE, FALLS INTO HIS ARMS, WE WERE A LITTLE MISTRUSTFUL. THERE ARE SOME FOLKS WHO MIGHT WANT TO HURT CHARLES.
REALLY?
CHARLES JUST GOT OUT PRISON.
OH?
OKAY, OKAY, NOW THERE'S A LITTLE SHADOW OVER THIS IDYLLIC TABLEAU, BUT I DON'T FEEL ENTITLED TO ASK MORE ABOUT IT FOR THE MOMENT. SO I SAY:
UH, DON'T WORRY. LULU IS THE LEAST DANGEROUS HUMAN BEING I KNOW.
POSSIBLY. WE'VE BEEN OBSERVING OVER HER A BIT TO BE SURE.
HA HA! RELAX, BUDDY. CHARLES IS AS HARMLESS AS SHE IS.
UH, WE'RE NOT VERY DISCREET HERE, ARE WE?
YEAH, SURE. LOOK AT THAT IMBECILE. WE COULD BE THREE YARDS FROM THEM, AND HE WOULDN'T EVEN SEE US.
HA HA HA!

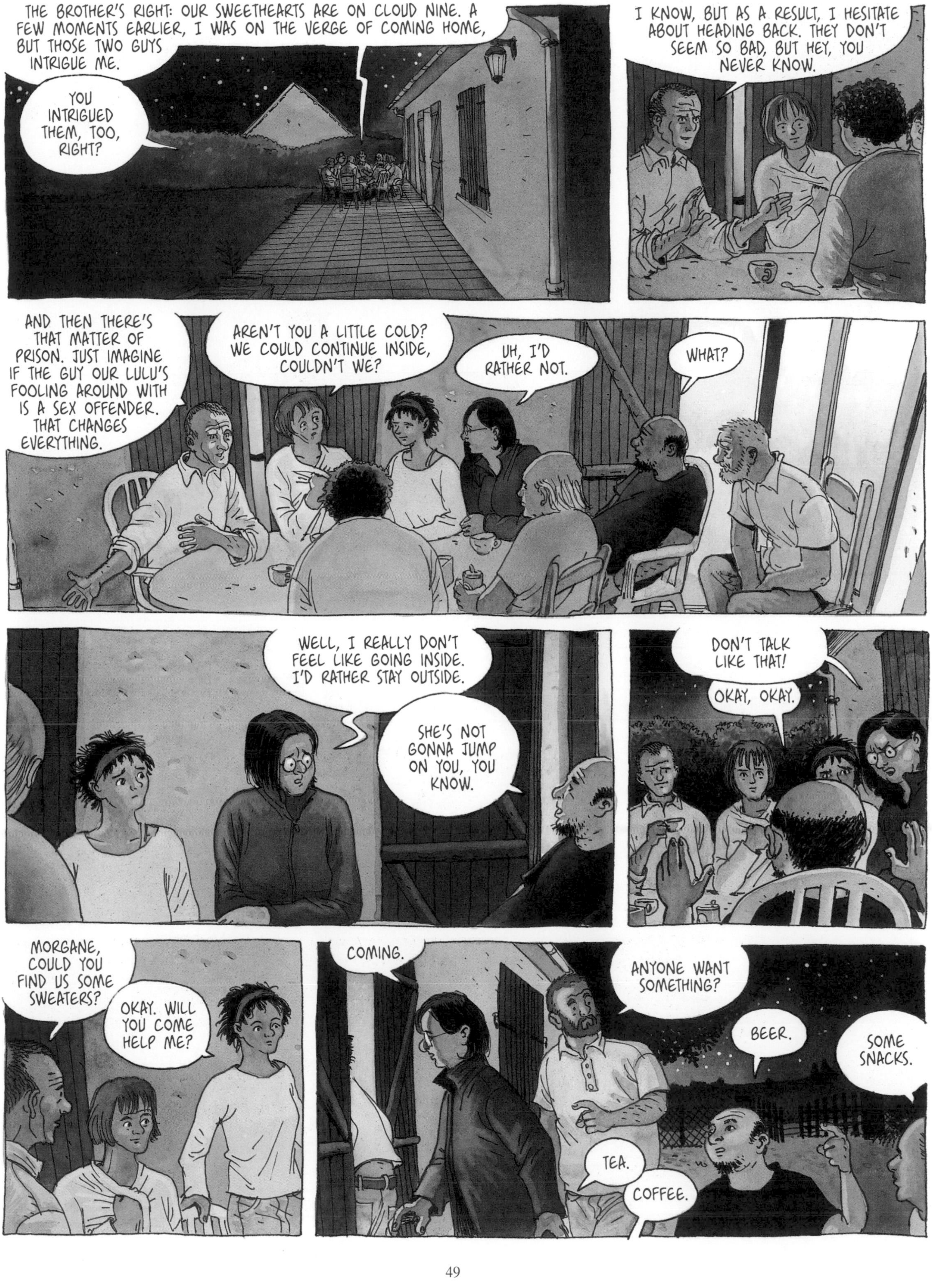
THE BROTHER'S RIGHT: OUR SWEETHEARTS ARE ON CLOUD NINE. A FEW MOMENTS EARLIER, I WAS ON THE VERGE OF COMING HOME, BUT THOSE TWO GUYS INTRIGUE ME.
YOU INTRIGUED THEM, TOO, RIGHT?
I KNOW, BUT AS A RESULT, I HESITATE ABOUT HEADING BACK. THEY DON'T SEEM SO BAD, BUT HEY, YOU NEVER KNOW.
AND THEN THERE'S THAT MATTER OF PRISON. JUST IMAGINE IF THE GUY OUR LULU'S FOOLING AROUND WITH IS A SEX OFFENDER. THAT CHANGES EVERYTHING.
AREN'T YOU A LITTLE COLD? WE COULD CONTINUE INSIDE, COULDN'T WE?
UH, I'D RATHER NOT.
WHAT?
WELL, I REALLY DON'T FEEL LIKE GOING INSIDE. I'D RATHER STAY OUTSIDE.
SHE'S NOT GONNA JUMP ON YOU, YOU KNOW.
DON'T TALK LIKE THAT!
OKAY, OKAY.
MORGANE, COULD YOU FIND US SOME SWEATERS?
OKAY. WILL YOU COME HELP ME?
COMING.
ANYONE WANT SOMETHING?
BEER.
SOME SNACKS.
TEA.
COFFEE.

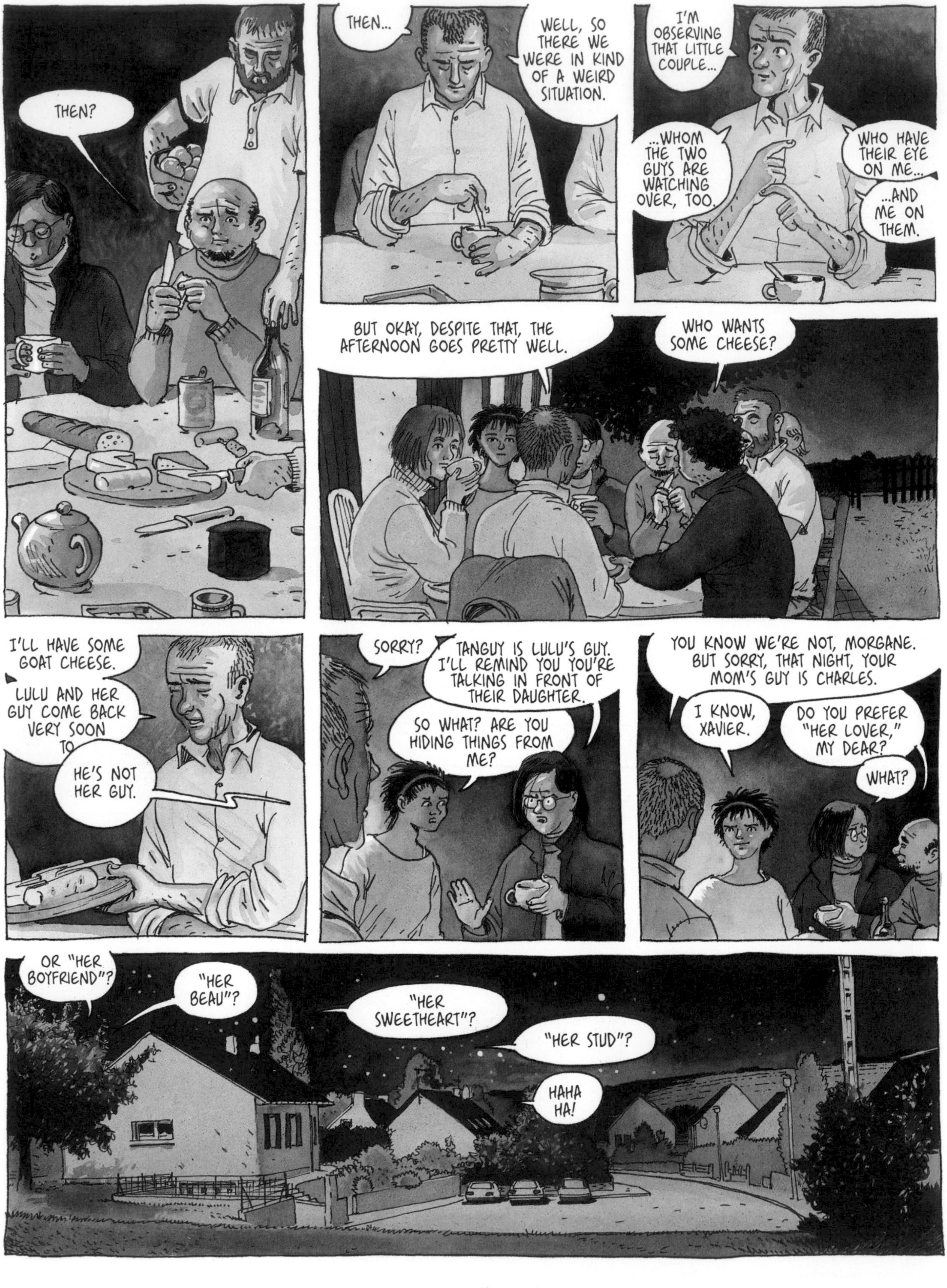
THEN?
THEN...
WELL, SO THERE WE WERE IN KIND OF A WEIRD SITUATION.
I'M OBSERVING THAT LITTLE COUPLE...
...WHOM THE TWO GUYS ARE WATCHING OVER, TOO.
WHO HAVE THEIR EYE ON ME...
...AND ME ON THEM.
BUT OKAY, DESPITE THAT, THE AFTERNOON GOES PRETTY WELL.
WHO WANTS SOME CHEESE?
I'LL HAVE SOME GOAT CHEESE.
LULU AND HER GUY COME BACK VERY SOON TO
HE'S NOT HER GUY.
SORRY?
TANGUY IS LULU'S GUY. I'LL REMIND YOU YOU'RE TALKING IN FRONT OF THEIR DAUGHTER.
SO WHAT? ARE YOU HIDING THINGS FROM ME?
YOU KNOW WE'RE NOT, MORGANE. BUT SORRY, THAT NIGHT, YOUR MOM'S GUY IS CHARLES.
I KNOW, XAVIER.
DO YOU PREFER "HER LOVER," MY DEAR?
WHAT?
OR "HER BOYFRIEND"?
"HER BEAU"?
"HER SWEETHEART"?
"HER STUD"?
HAHA HA!

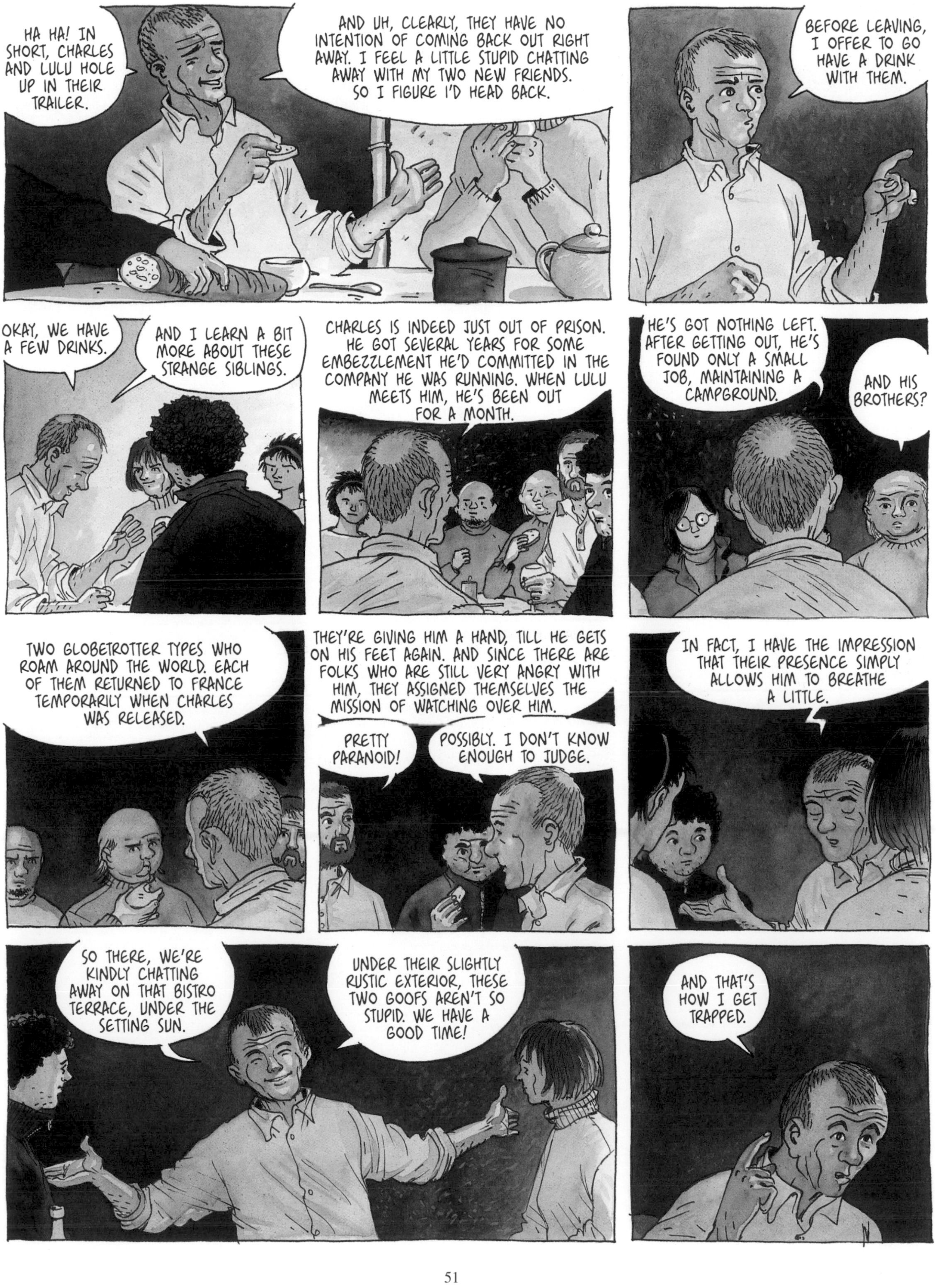
HA HA! IN SHORT, CHARLES AND LULU HOLE UP IN THEIR TRAILER.
AND UH, CLEARLY, THEY HAVE NO INTENTION OF COMING BACK OUT RIGHT AWAY. I FEEL A LITTLE STUPID CHATTING AWAY WITH MY TWO NEW FRIENDS. SO I FIGURE I'D HEAD BACK.
BEFORE LEAVING, I OFFER TO GO HAVE A DRINK WITH THEM.
OKAY, WE HAVE A FEW DRINKS.
AND I LEARN A BIT MORE ABOUT THESE STRANGE SIBLINGS.
CHARLES IS INDEED JUST OUT OF PRISON. HE GOT SEVERAL YEARS FOR SOME EMBEZZLEMENT HE'D COMMITTED IN THE COMPANY HE WAS RUNNING. WHEN LULU MEETS HIM, HE'S BEEN OUT FOR A MONTH.
HE'S GOT NOTHING LEFT. AFTER GETTING OUT, HE'S FOUND ONLY A SMALL JOB, MAINTAINING A CAMPGROUND.
AND HIS BROTHERS?
TWO GLOBETROTTER TYPES WHO ROAM AROUND THE WORLD. EACH OF THEM RETURNED TO FRANCE TEMPORARILY WHEN CHARLES WAS RELEASED.
THEY'RE GIVING HIM A HAND, TILL HE GETS ON HIS FEET AGAIN. AND SINCE THERE ARE FOLKS WHO ARE STILL VERY ANGRY WITH HIM, THEY ASSIGNED THEMSELVES THE MISSION OF WATCHING OVER HIM.
PRETTY PARANOID!
POSSIBLY. I DON'T KNOW ENOUGH TO JUDGE.
IN FACT, I HAVE THE IMPRESSION THAT THEIR PRESENCE SIMPLY ALLOWS HIM TO BREATHE A LITTLE.
SO THERE, WE'RE KINDLY CHATTING AWAY ON THAT BISTRO TERRACE, UNDER THE SETTING SUN.
UNDER THEIR SLIGHTLY RUSTIC EXTERIOR, THESE TWO GOOFS AREN'T SO STUPID. WE HAVE A GOOD TIME!
AND THAT'S HOW I GET TRAPPED.

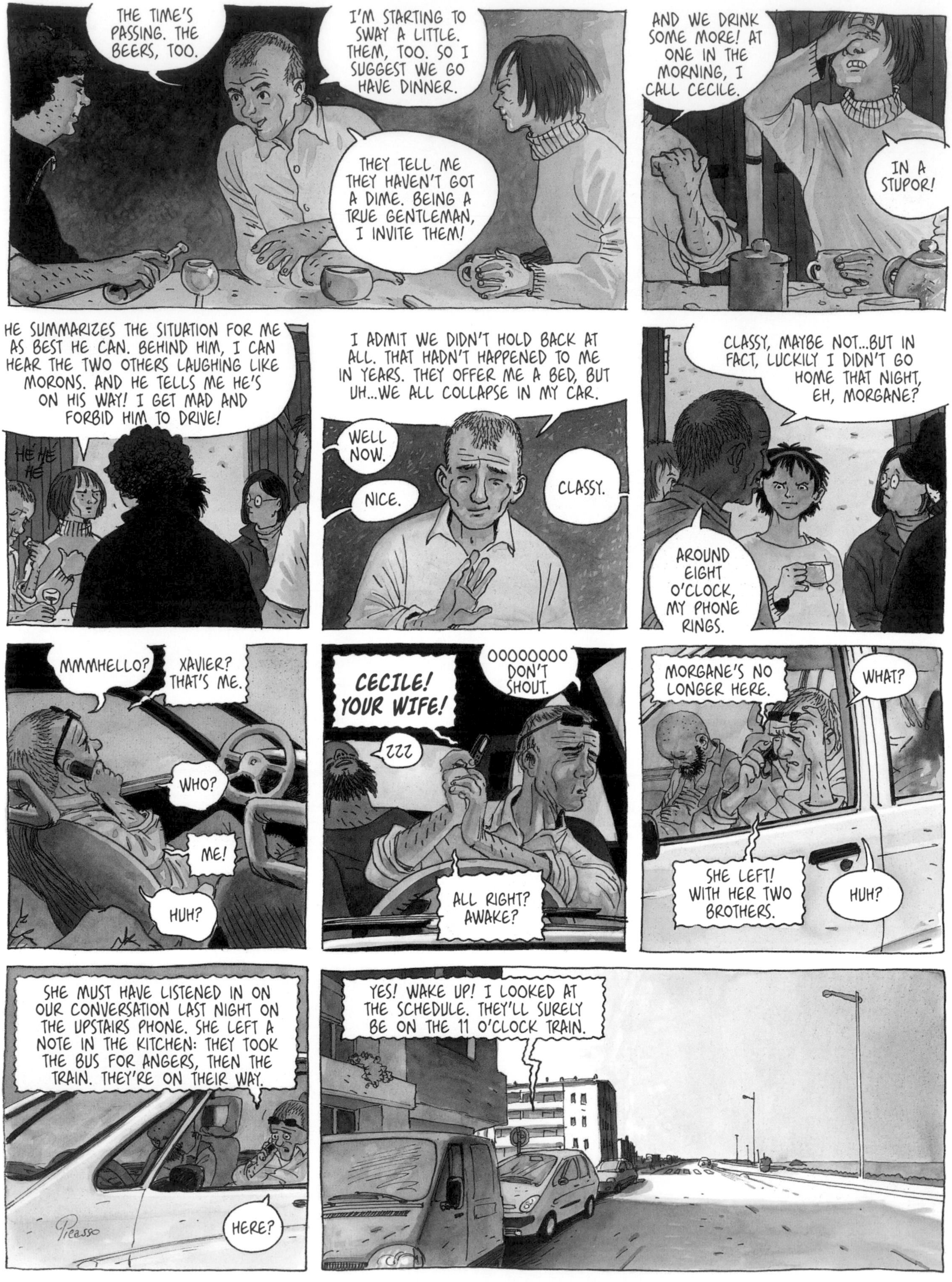
THE TIME'S PASSING. THE BEERS, TOO.
I'M STARTING TO SWAY A LITTLE. THEM, TOO. SO I SUGGEST WE GO HAVE DINNER.
THEY TELL ME THEY HAVEN'T GOT A DIME. BEING A TRUE GENTLEMAN, I INVITE THEM!
AND WE DRINK SOME MORE! AT ONE IN THE MORNING, I CALL CECILE.
IN A STUPOR!
HE SUMMARIZES THE SITUATION FOR ME AS BEST HE CAN. BEHIND HIM, I CAN HEAR THE TWO OTHERS LAUGHING LIKE MORONS. AND HE TELLS ME HE'S ON HIS WAY! I GET MAD AND FORBID HIM TO DRIVE!
HÉ HÉ HÉ
I ADMIT WE DIDN'T HOLD BACK AT ALL. THAT HADN'T HAPPENED TO ME IN YEARS. THEY OFFER ME A BED, BUT UH...WE ALL COLLAPSE IN MY CAR.
WELL NOW.
NICE.
CLASSY.
CLASSY, MAYBE NOT...BUT IN FACT, LUCKILY I DIDN'T GO HOME THAT NIGHT, EH, MORGANE?
AROUND EIGHT O'CLOCK, MY PHONE RINGS.
MMMHELLO?
XAVIER? THAT'S ME.
WHO?
ME!
HUH?
CECILE! YOUR WIFE!
OOOOOOOO DON'T SHOUT.
ZZZ
ALL RIGHT? AWAKE?
MORGANE'S NO LONGER HERE.
WHAT?
SHE LEFT! WITH HER TWO BROTHERS.
HUH?
SHE MUST HAVE LISTENED IN ON OUR CONVERSATION LAST NIGHT ON THE UPSTAIRS PHONE. SHE LEFT A NOTE IN THE KITCHEN: THEY TOOK THE BUS FOR ANGERS, THEN THE TRAIN. THEY'RE ON THEIR WAY.
Picasso
HERE?
YES! WAKE UP! I LOOKED AT THE SCHEDULE. THEY'LL SURELY BE ON THE 11 O'CLOCK TRAIN.

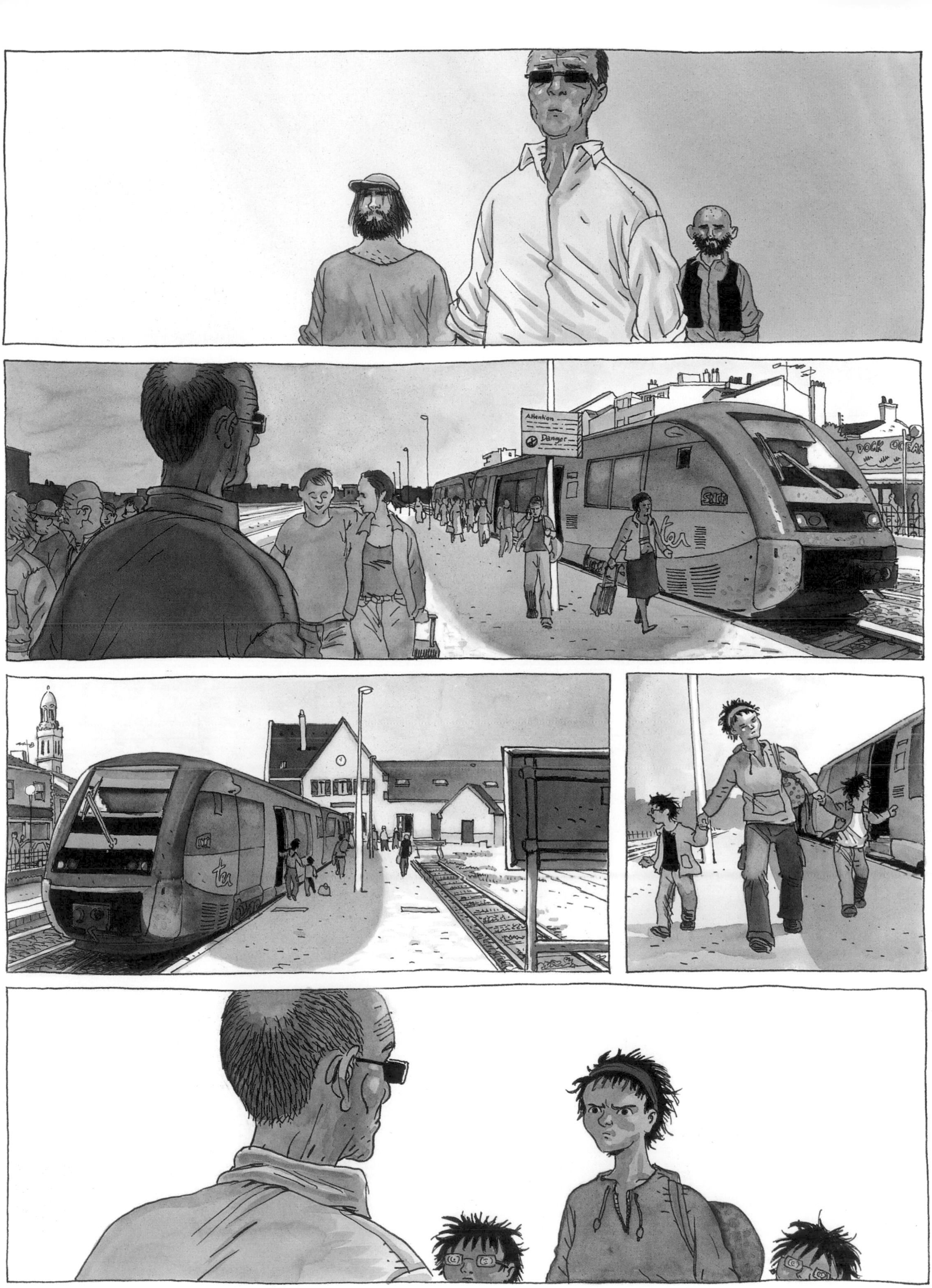
Attention
Danger

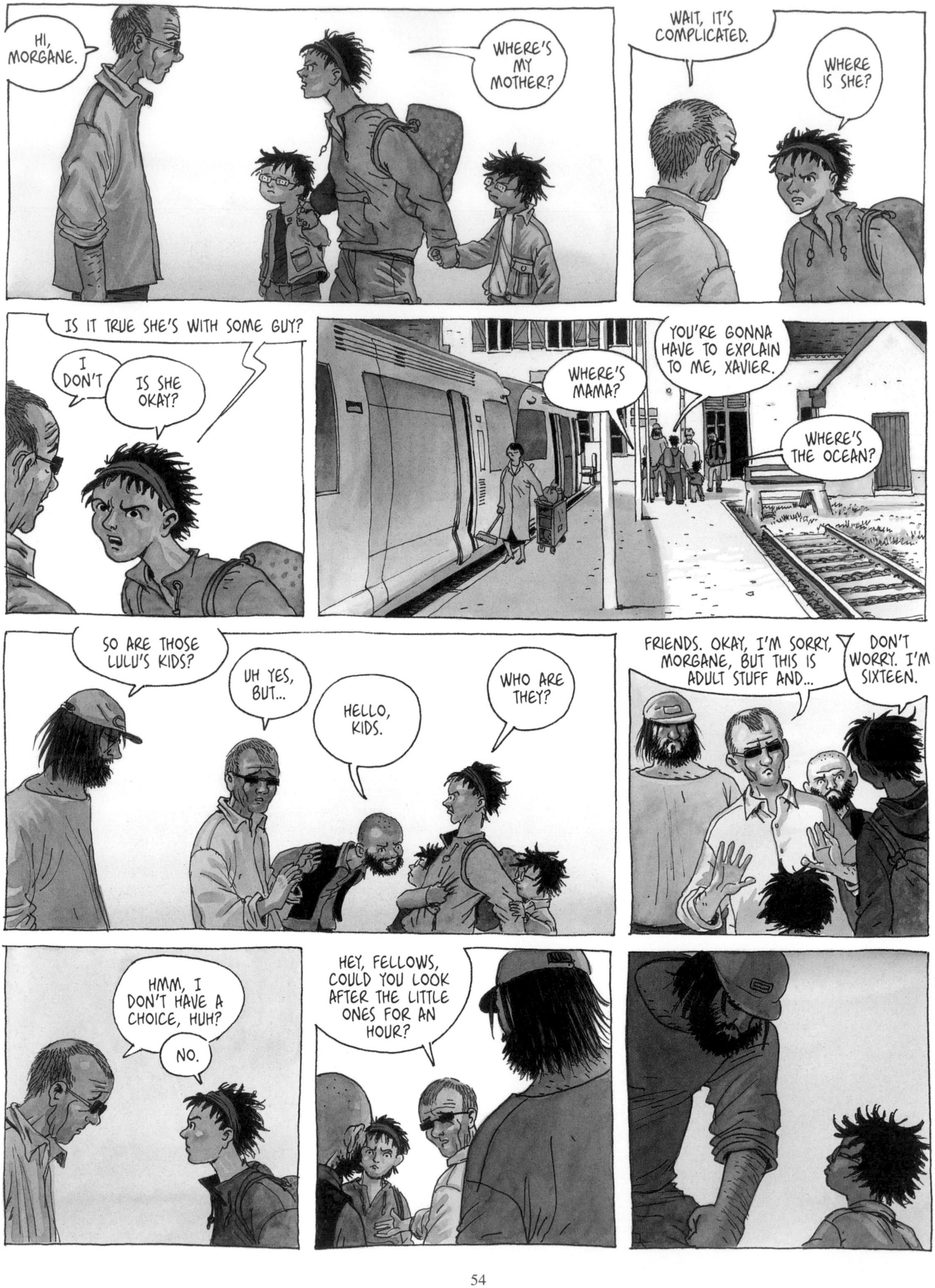
HI, MORGANE.
WHERE'S MY MOTHER?
WAIT, IT'S COMPLICATED.
WHERE IS SHE?
IS IT TRUE SHE'S WITH SOME GUY?
I DON'T
IS SHE OKAY?
WHERE'S MAMA?
YOU'RE GONNA HAVE TO EXPLAIN TO ME, XAVIER.
WHERE'S THE OCEAN?
SO ARE THOSE LULU'S KIDS?
UH YES, BUT...
HELLO, KIDS.
WHO ARE THEY?
FRIENDS. OKAY, I'M SORRY, MORGANE, BUT THIS IS ADULT STUFF AND...
DON'T WORRY. I'M SIXTEEN.
HMM, I DON'T HAVE A CHOICE, HUH?
NO.
HEY, FELLOWS, COULD YOU LOOK AFTER THE LITTLE ONES FOR AN HOUR?

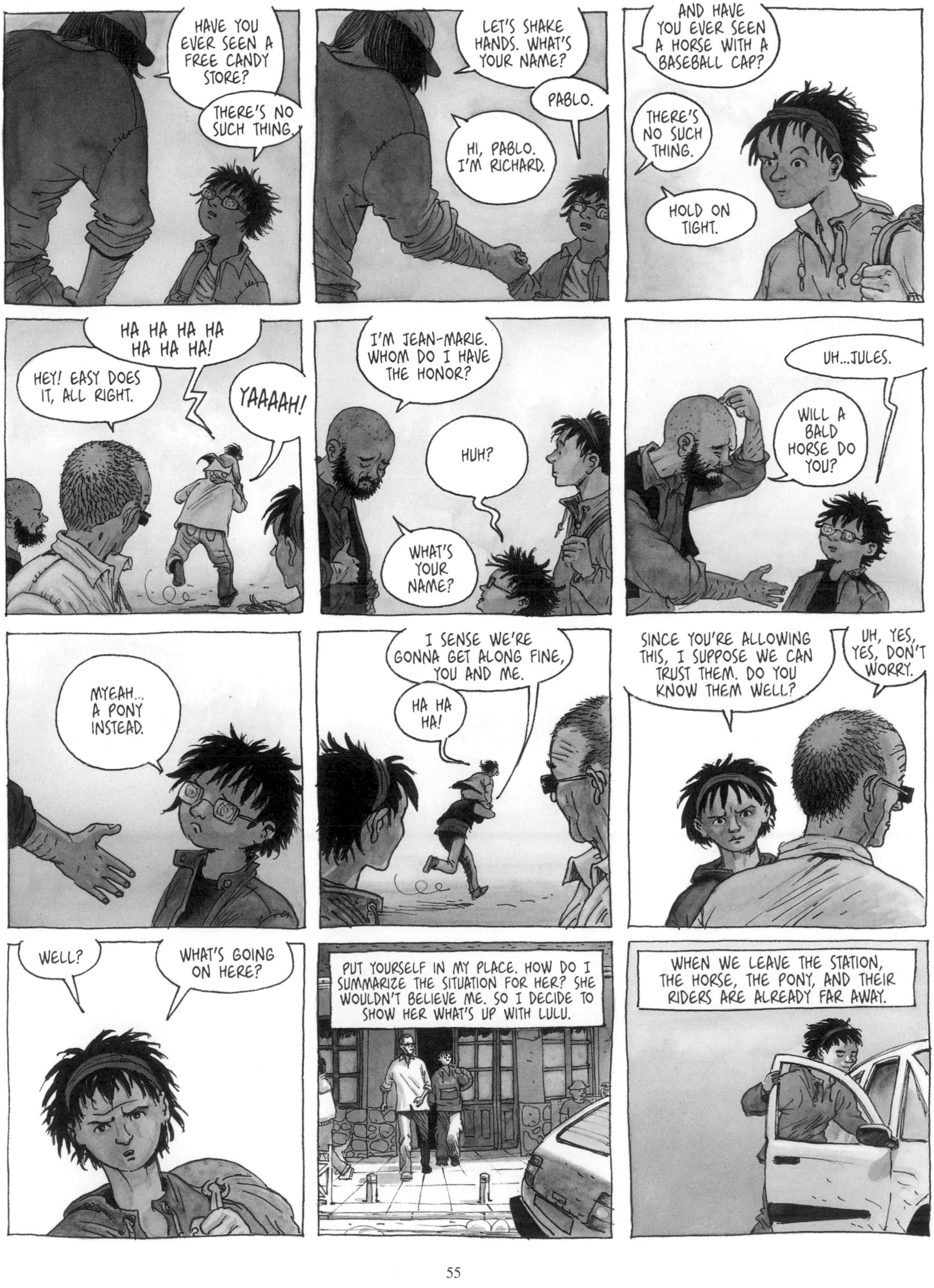

HAVE YOU EVER SEEN A FREE CANDY STORE?
THERE'S NO SUCH THING.
LET'S SHAKE HANDS. WHAT'S YOUR NAME?
PABLO.
HI, PABLO. I'M RICHARD.
AND HAVE YOU EVER SEEN A HORSE WITH A BASEBALL CAP?
THERE'S NO SUCH THING.
HOLD ON TIGHT.
HA HA HA HA HA HA HA!
HEY! EASY DOES IT, ALL RIGHT.
YAAAAH!
I'M JEAN-MARIE. WHOM DO I HAVE THE HONOR?
HUH?
WHAT'S YOUR NAME?
UH...JULES.
WILL A BALD HORSE DO YOU?
MYEAH... A PONY INSTEAD.
I SENSE WE'RE GONNA GET ALONG FINE, YOU AND ME.
HA HA HA!
SINCE YOU'RE ALLOWING THIS, I SUPPOSE WE CAN TRUST THEM. DO YOU KNOW THEM WELL?
UH, YES, YES, DON'T WORRY.
WELL?
WHAT'S GOING ON HERE?
PUT YOURSELF IN MY PLACE. HOW DO I SUMMARIZE THE SITUATION FOR HER? SHE WOULDN'T BELIEVE ME. SO I DECIDE TO SHOW HER WHAT'S UP WITH LULU.
WHEN WE LEAVE THE STATION, THE HORSE, THE PONY, AND THEIR RIDERS ARE ALREADY FAR AWAY.

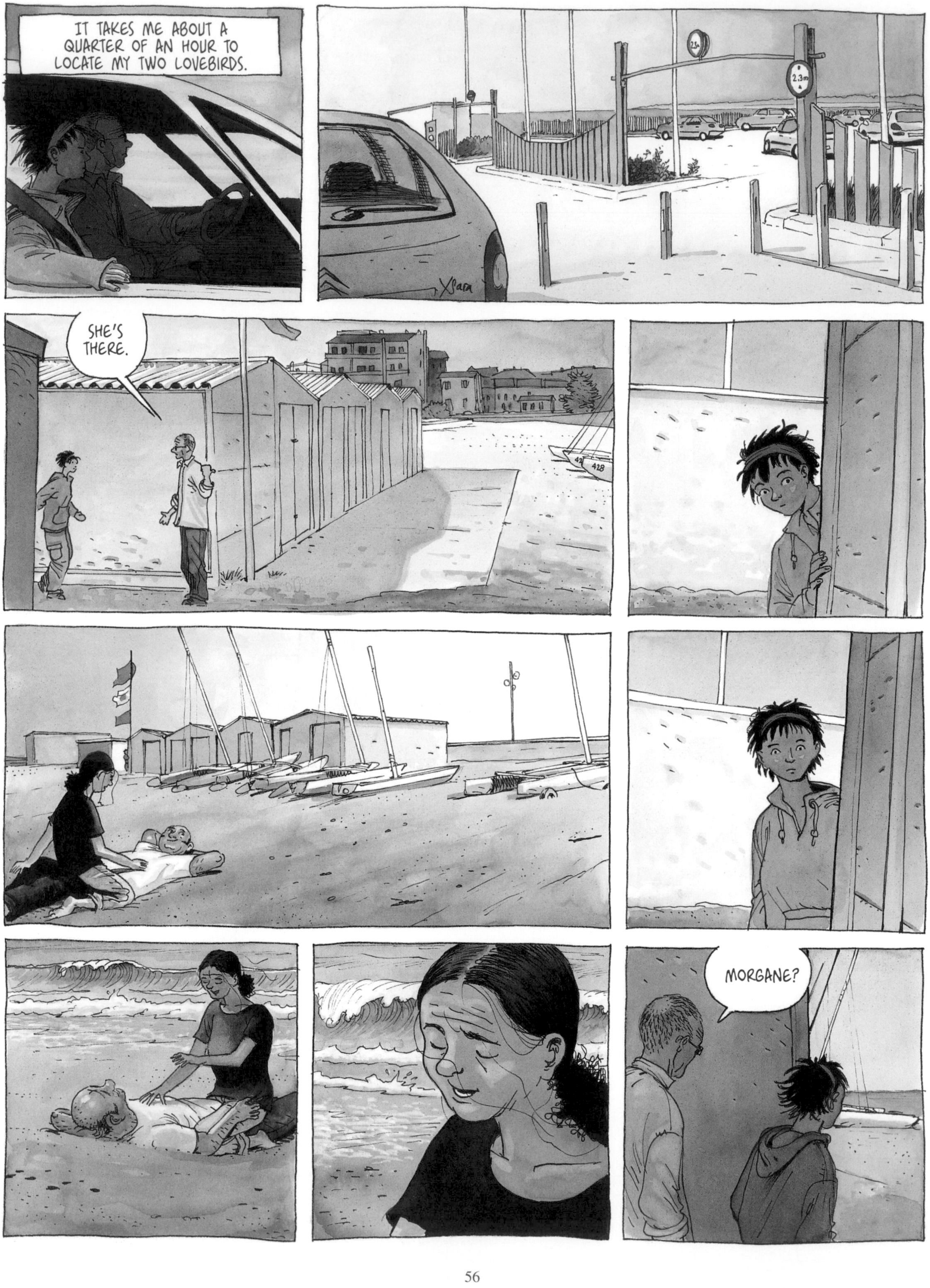
IT TAKES ME ABOUT A QUARTER OF AN HOUR TO LOCATE MY TWO LOVEBIRDS.
SHE'S THERE.
MORGANE?

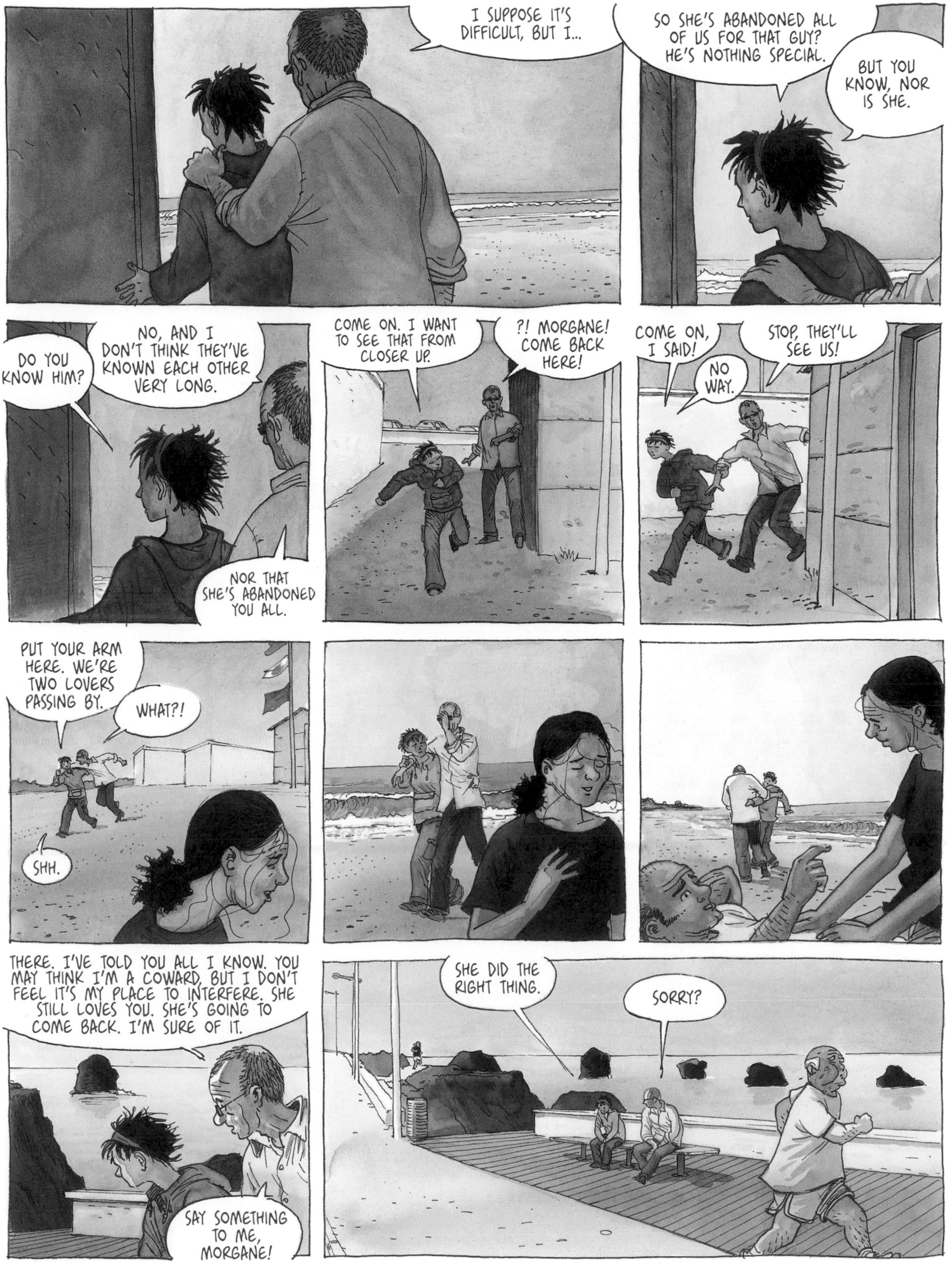

I SUPPOSE IT'S DIFFICULT, BUT I...
SO SHE'S ABANDONED ALL OF US FOR THAT GUY? HE'S NOTHING SPECIAL.
BUT YOU KNOW, NOR IS SHE.
DO YOU KNOW HIM?
NO, AND I DON'T THINK THEY'VE KNOWN EACH OTHER VERY LONG.
NOR THAT SHE'S ABANDONED YOU ALL.
COME ON. I WANT TO SEE THAT FROM CLOSER UP.
?! MORGANE! COME BACK HERE!
COME ON, I SAID!
NO WAY.
STOP, THEY'LL SEE US!
PUT YOUR ARM HERE. WE'RE TWO LOVERS PASSING BY.
WHAT?!
SHH.
THERE. I'VE TOLD YOU ALL I KNOW. YOU MAY THINK I'M A COWARD, BUT I DON'T FEEL IT'S MY PLACE TO INTERFERE. SHE STILL LOVES YOU. SHE'S GOING TO COME BACK. I'M SURE OF IT.
SAY SOMETHING TO ME, MORGANE!
SHE DID THE RIGHT THING.
SORRY?

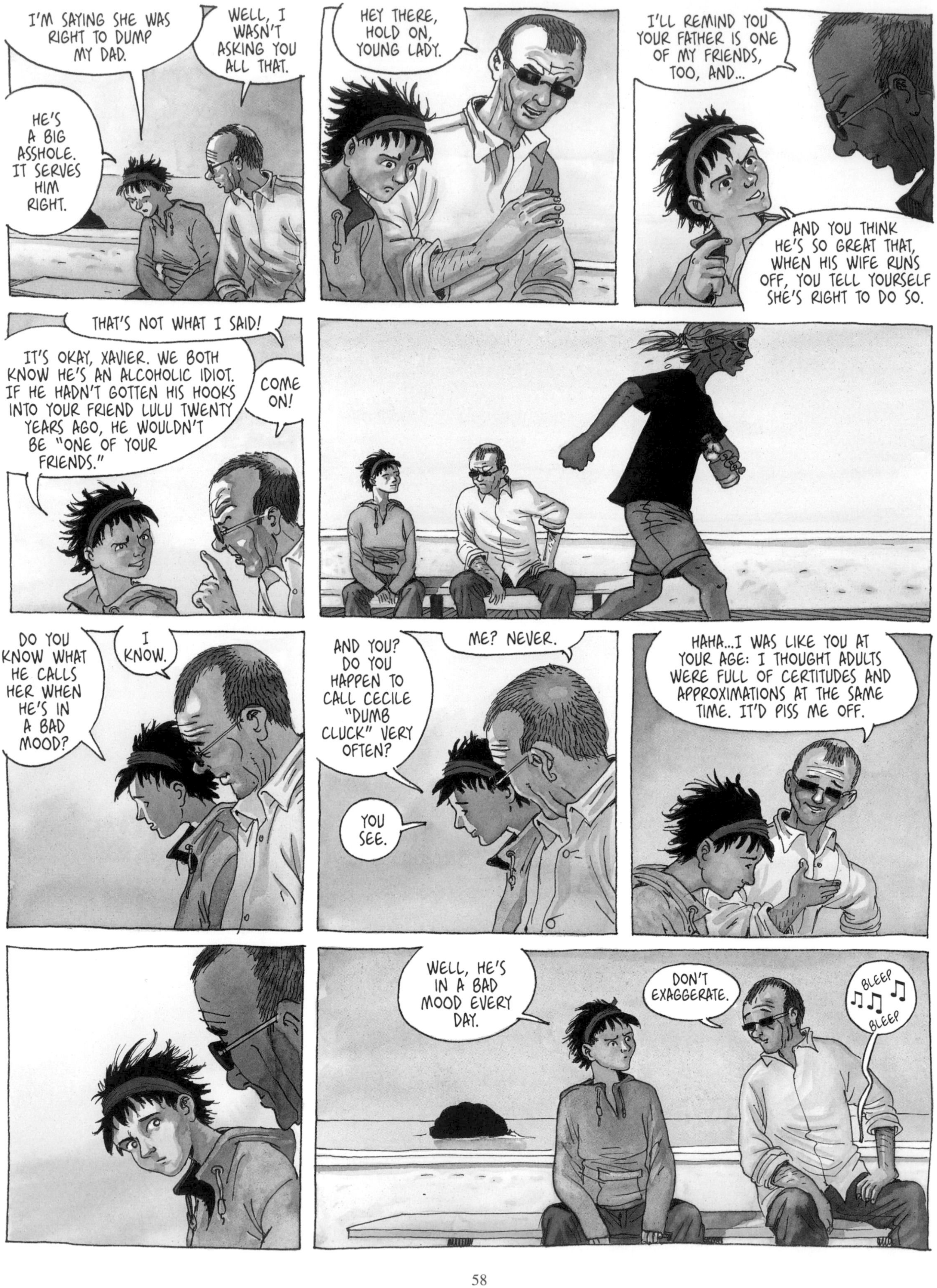
I'M SAYING SHE WAS RIGHT TO DUMP MY DAD.
WELL, I WASN'T ASKING YOU ALL THAT.
HE'S A BIG ASSHOLE. IT SERVES HIM RIGHT.
HEY THERE, HOLD ON, YOUNG LADY.
I'LL REMIND YOU YOUR FATHER IS ONE OF MY FRIENDS, TOO, AND...
AND YOU THINK HE'S SO GREAT THAT, WHEN HIS WIFE RUNS OFF, YOU TELL YOURSELF SHE'S RIGHT TO DO SO.
THAT'S NOT WHAT I SAID!
IT'S OKAY, XAVIER. WE BOTH KNOW HE'S AN ALCOHOLIC IDIOT. IF HE HADN'T GOTTEN HIS HOOKS INTO YOUR FRIEND LULU TWENTY YEARS AGO, HE WOULDN'T BE "ONE OF YOUR FRIENDS."
COME ON!
DO YOU KNOW WHAT HE CALLS HER WHEN HE'S IN A BAD MOOD?
I KNOW.
AND YOU? DO YOU HAPPEN TO CALL CECILE "DUMB CLUCK" VERY OFTEN?
ME? NEVER.
YOU SEE.
HAHA...I WAS LIKE YOU AT YOUR AGE: I THOUGHT ADULTS WERE FULL OF CERTITUDES AND APPROXIMATIONS AT THE SAME TIME. IT'D PISS ME OFF.
WELL, HE'S IN A BAD MOOD EVERY DAY.
DON'T EXAGGERATE.
BLEEP BLEEP

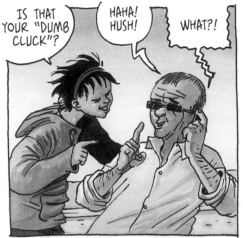

HELLO?

IT'S ME, CECILE, YOUR WIFE. DO YOU REMEMBER?

YES. WHAT?

ARE THE CHILDREN WITH YOU?

YES, YES, I HAVEN'T HAD TIME TO CALL YOU BACK.

IS THAT YOUR "DUMB CLUCK"?

HAHA! HUSH!

WHAT?!

NOTHING. IT'S MORGANE BESIDE ME, FOOLING AROUND.

DID YOU EXPLAIN TO HER?

UH YES. SHE'S UNDERSTOOD THE SITUATION.

NO KIDDING.

HOW'S SHE REACTING?

PRETTY WELL.

AND THE KIDS?

THE KIDS? WHAT K...? OH, FINE, TOO. WE DIDN'T TELL THEM EVERYTHING.

OKAY. WHAT NOW?

I'LL BRING BACK THE KIDS.

WITHOUT TALKING TO LULU?

UH, I DON'T KNOW. YOU THINK I SHOULD?

YES.

TO TELL HER WHAT? "ENOUGH WITH THE FOOLISHNESS. COME HOME"?

YES. IF YOU HAD A MORE DIPLOMATIC VERSION, THAT'D BE PERFECT.

HMM, I'LL SEE.

AND YOU? HOW'S IT GOING WITH TANGUY?

GUESS.

WELL?

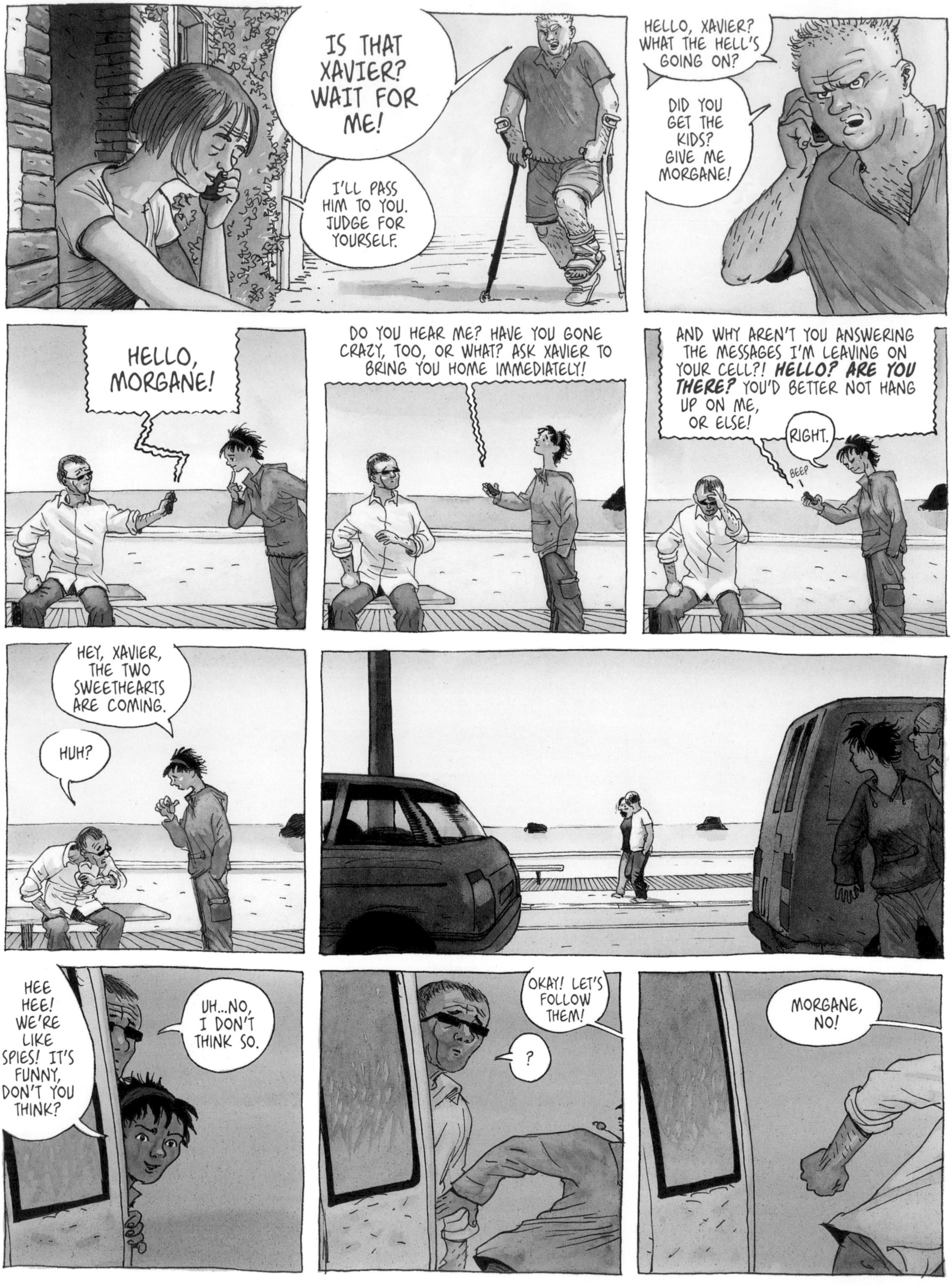
IS THAT XAVIER? WAIT FOR ME!
I'LL PASS HIM TO YOU. JUDGE FOR YOURSELF.
HELLO, XAVIER? WHAT THE HELL'S GOING ON?
DID YOU GET THE KIDS? GIVE ME MORGANE!
HELLO, MORGANE!
DO YOU HEAR ME? HAVE YOU GONE CRAZY, TOO, OR WHAT? ASK XAVIER TO BRING YOU HOME IMMEDIATELY!
AND WHY AREN'T YOU ANSWERING THE MESSAGES I'M LEAVING ON YOUR CELL?! **HELLO? ARE YOU THERE?** YOU'D BETTER NOT HANG UP ON ME, OR ELSE!
RIGHT.
BEEP
HEY, XAVIER, THE TWO SWEETHEARTS ARE COMING.
HUH?
HEE HEE! WE'RE LIKE SPIES! IT'S FUNNY, DON'T YOU THINK?
UH...NO, I DON'T THINK SO.
OKAY! LET'S FOLLOW THEM!
?
MORGANE, NO!

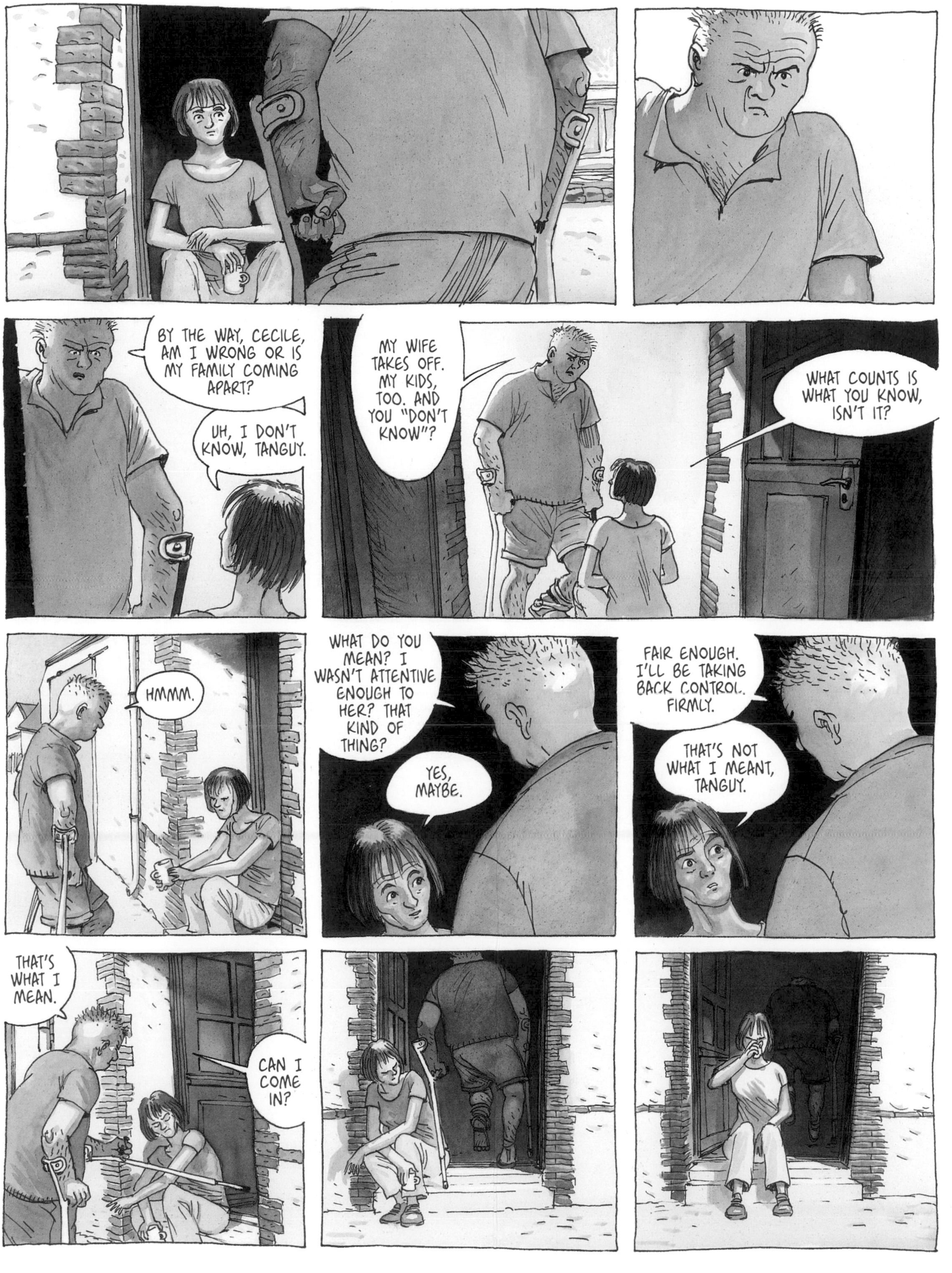
BY THE WAY, CECILE, AM I WRONG OR IS MY FAMILY COMING APART?
UH, I DON'T KNOW, TANGUY.
MY WIFE TAKES OFF. MY KIDS, TOO. AND YOU "DON'T KNOW"?
WHAT COUNTS IS WHAT YOU KNOW, ISN'T IT?
HMMM.
WHAT DO YOU MEAN? I WASN'T ATTENTIVE ENOUGH TO HER? THAT KIND OF THING?
YES, MAYBE.
FAIR ENOUGH. I'LL BE TAKING BACK CONTROL. FIRMLY.
THAT'S NOT WHAT I MEANT, TANGUY.
THAT'S WHAT I MEAN.
CAN I COME IN?

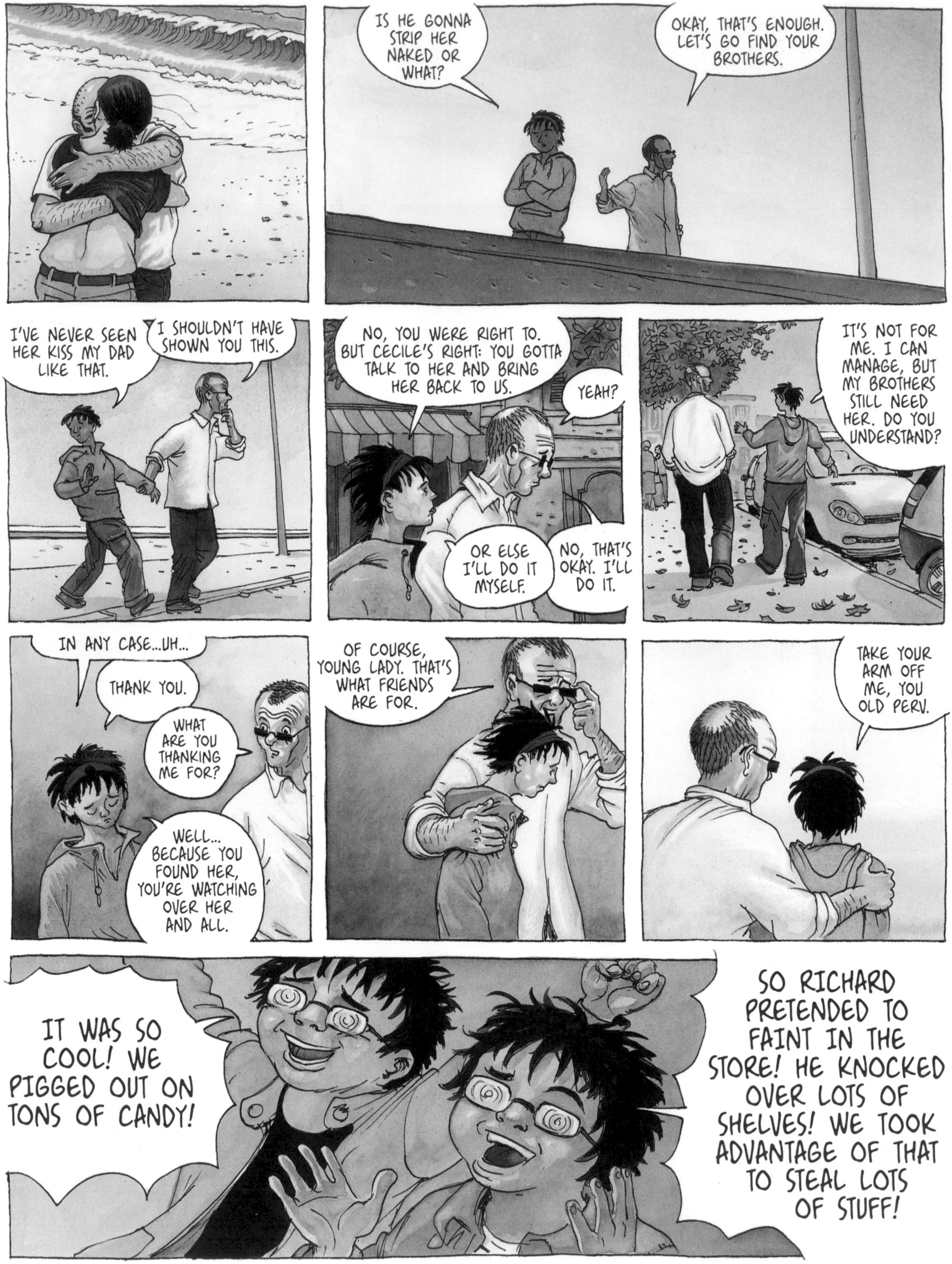
IS HE GONNA STRIP HER NAKED OR WHAT?
OKAY, THAT'S ENOUGH. LET'S GO FIND YOUR BROTHERS.
I'VE NEVER SEEN HER KISS MY DAD LIKE THAT.
I SHOULDN'T HAVE SHOWN YOU THIS.
NO, YOU WERE RIGHT TO. BUT CECILE'S RIGHT: YOU GOTTA TALK TO HER AND BRING HER BACK TO US.
YEAH?
OR ELSE I'LL DO IT MYSELF.
NO, THAT'S OKAY. I'LL DO IT.
IT'S NOT FOR ME. I CAN MANAGE, BUT MY BROTHERS STILL NEED HER. DO YOU UNDERSTAND?
IN ANY CASE...UH...
THANK YOU.
WHAT ARE YOU THANKING ME FOR?
WELL... BECAUSE YOU FOUND HER, YOU'RE WATCHING OVER HER AND ALL.
OF COURSE, YOUNG LADY. THAT'S WHAT FRIENDS ARE FOR.
TAKE YOUR ARM OFF ME, YOU OLD PERV.
IT WAS SO COOL! WE PIGGED OUT ON TONS OF CANDY!
SO RICHARD PRETENDED TO FAINT IN THE STORE! HE KNOCKED OVER LOTS OF SHELVES! WE TOOK ADVANTAGE OF THAT TO STEAL LOTS OF STUFF!

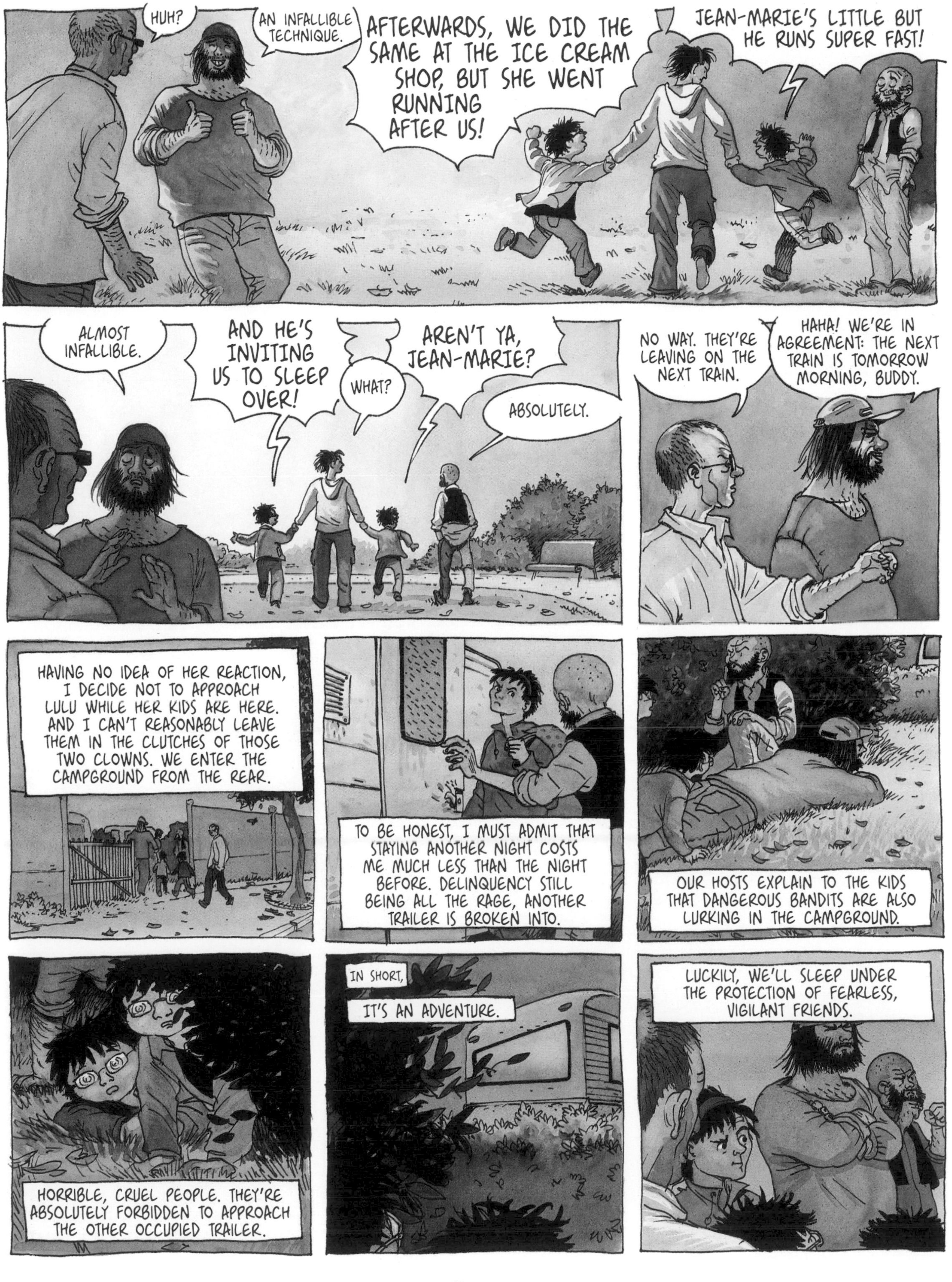
HUH?
AN INFALLIBLE TECHNIQUE.
AFTERWARDS, WE DID THE SAME AT THE ICE CREAM SHOP, BUT SHE WENT RUNNING AFTER US!
JEAN-MARIE'S LITTLE BUT HE RUNS SUPER FAST!
ALMOST INFALLIBLE.
AND HE'S INVITING US TO SLEEP OVER!
WHAT?
AREN'T YA, JEAN-MARIE?
ABSOLUTELY.
NO WAY. THEY'RE LEAVING ON THE NEXT TRAIN.
HAHA! WE'RE IN AGREEMENT: THE NEXT TRAIN IS TOMORROW MORNING, BUDDY.
HAVING NO IDEA OF HER REACTION, I DECIDE NOT TO APPROACH LULU WHILE HER KIDS ARE HERE. AND I CAN'T REASONABLY LEAVE THEM IN THE CLUTCHES OF THOSE TWO CLOWNS. WE ENTER THE CAMPGROUND FROM THE REAR.
TO BE HONEST, I MUST ADMIT THAT STAYING ANOTHER NIGHT COSTS ME MUCH LESS THAN THE NIGHT BEFORE. DELINQUENCY STILL BEING ALL THE RAGE, ANOTHER TRAILER IS BROKEN INTO.
OUR HOSTS EXPLAIN TO THE KIDS THAT DANGEROUS BANDITS ARE ALSO LURKING IN THE CAMPGROUND.
HORRIBLE, CRUEL PEOPLE. THEY'RE ABSOLUTELY FORBIDDEN TO APPROACH THE OTHER OCCUPIED TRAILER.
IN SHORT,
IT'S AN ADVENTURE.
LUCKILY, WE'LL SLEEP UNDER THE PROTECTION OF FEARLESS, VIGILANT FRIENDS.

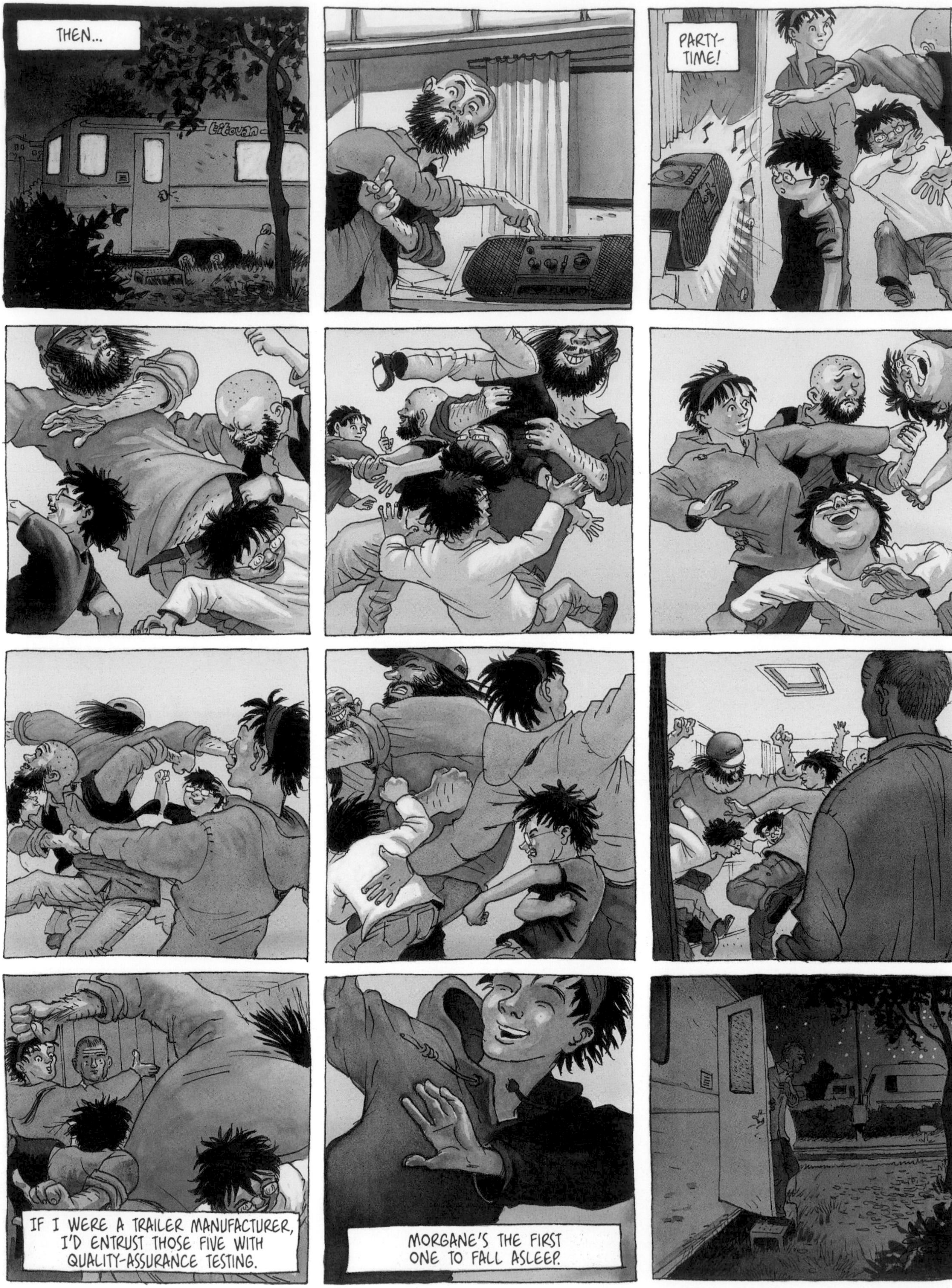
THEN...
PARTY-TIME!
IF I WERE A TRAILER MANUFACTURER, I'D ENTRUST THOSE FIVE WITH QUALITY-ASSURANCE TESTING.
MORGANE'S THE FIRST ONE TO FALL ASLEEP.

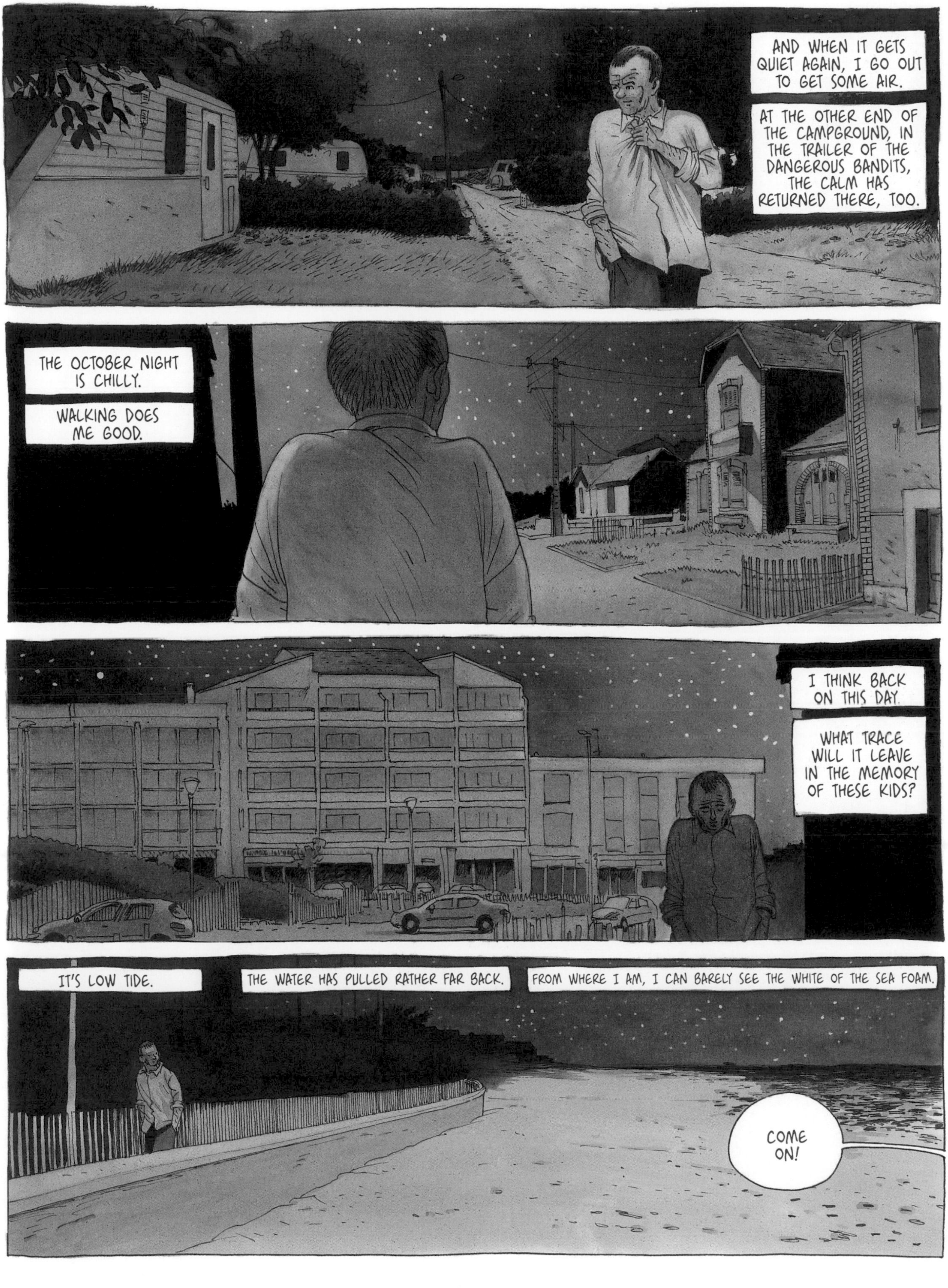

AND WHEN IT GETS QUIET AGAIN, I GO OUT TO GET SOME AIR.
AT THE OTHER END OF THE CAMPGROUND, IN THE TRAILER OF THE DANGEROUS BANDITS, THE CALM HAS RETURNED THERE, TOO.
THE OCTOBER NIGHT IS CHILLY.
WALKING DOES ME GOOD.
I THINK BACK ON THIS DAY.
WHAT TRACE WILL IT LEAVE IN THE MEMORY OF THESE KIDS?
IT'S LOW TIDE.
THE WATER HAS PULLED RATHER FAR BACK.
FROM WHERE I AM, I CAN BARELY SEE THE WHITE OF THE SEA FOAM.
COME ON!

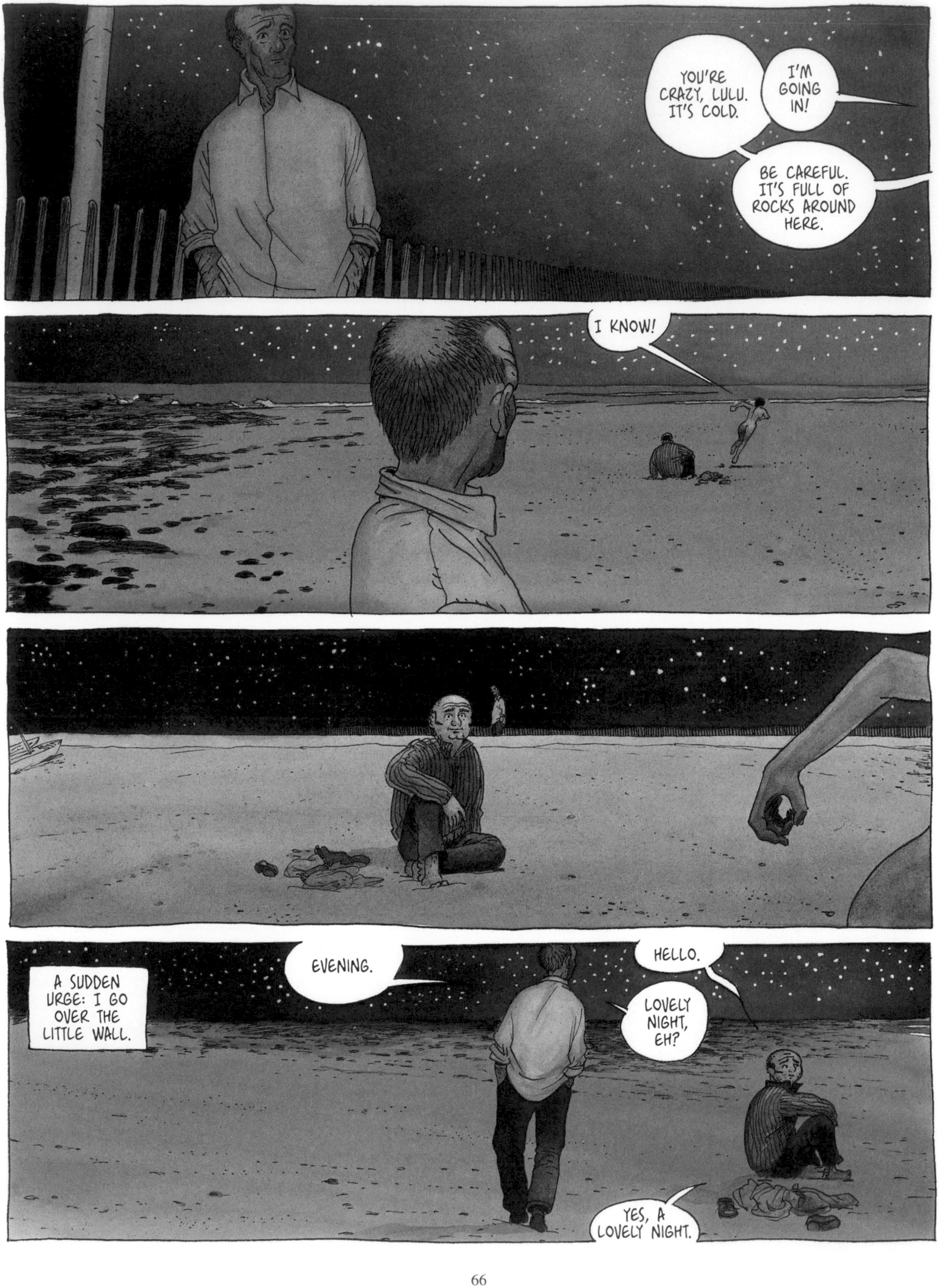
YOU'RE CRAZY, LULU. IT'S COLD.
I'M GOING IN!
BE CAREFUL. IT'S FULL OF ROCKS AROUND HERE.
I KNOW!
A SUDDEN URGE: I GO OVER THE LITTLE WALL.
EVENING.
HELLO.
LOVELY NIGHT, EH?
YES, A LOVELY NIGHT.

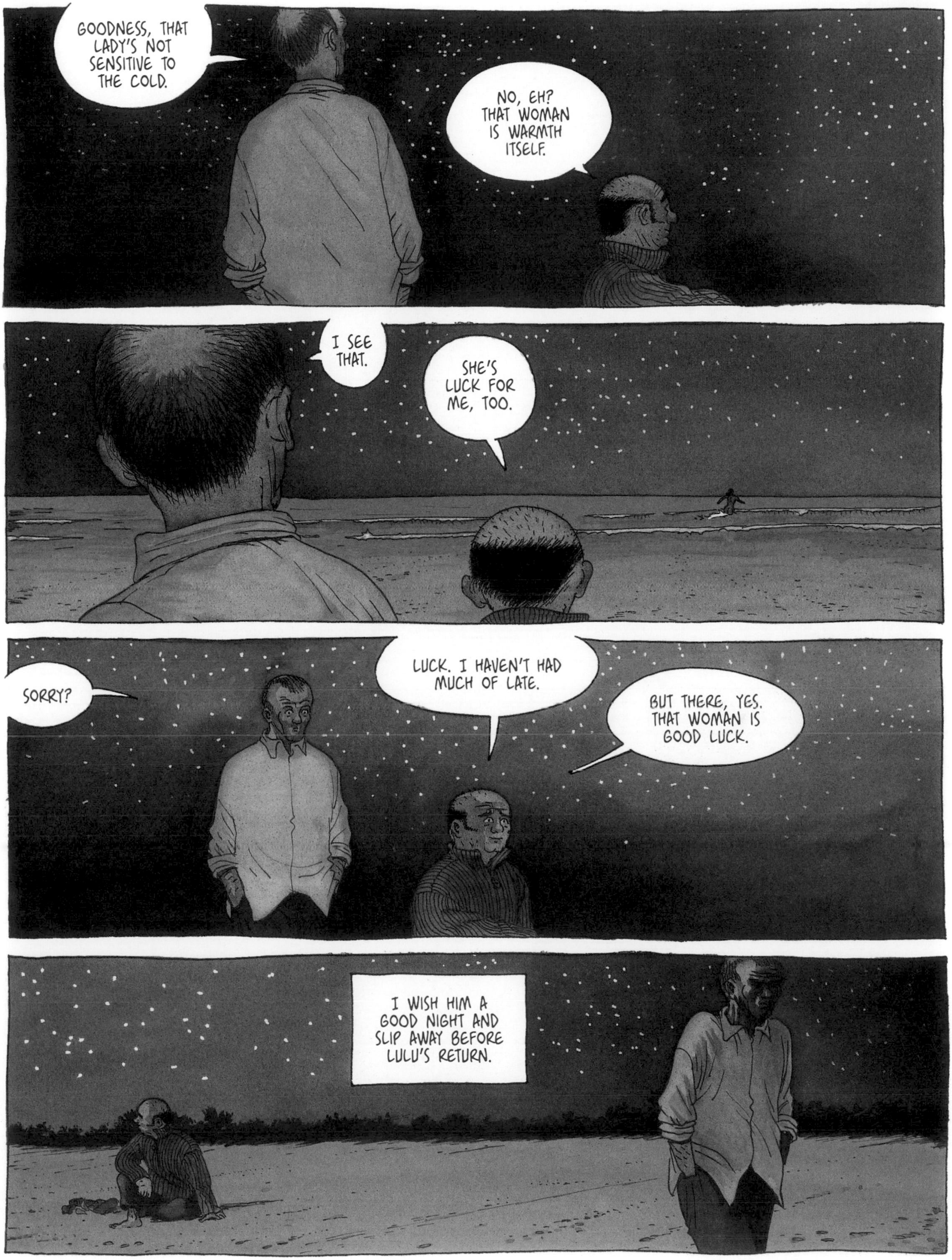

GOODNESS, THAT LADY'S NOT SENSITIVE TO THE COLD.
NO, EH? THAT WOMAN IS WARMTH ITSELF.
I SEE THAT.
SHE'S LUCK FOR ME, TOO.
SORRY?
LUCK. I HAVEN'T HAD MUCH OF LATE.
BUT THERE, YES. THAT WOMAN IS GOOD LUCK.
I WISH HIM A GOOD NIGHT AND SLIP AWAY BEFORE LULU'S RETURN.

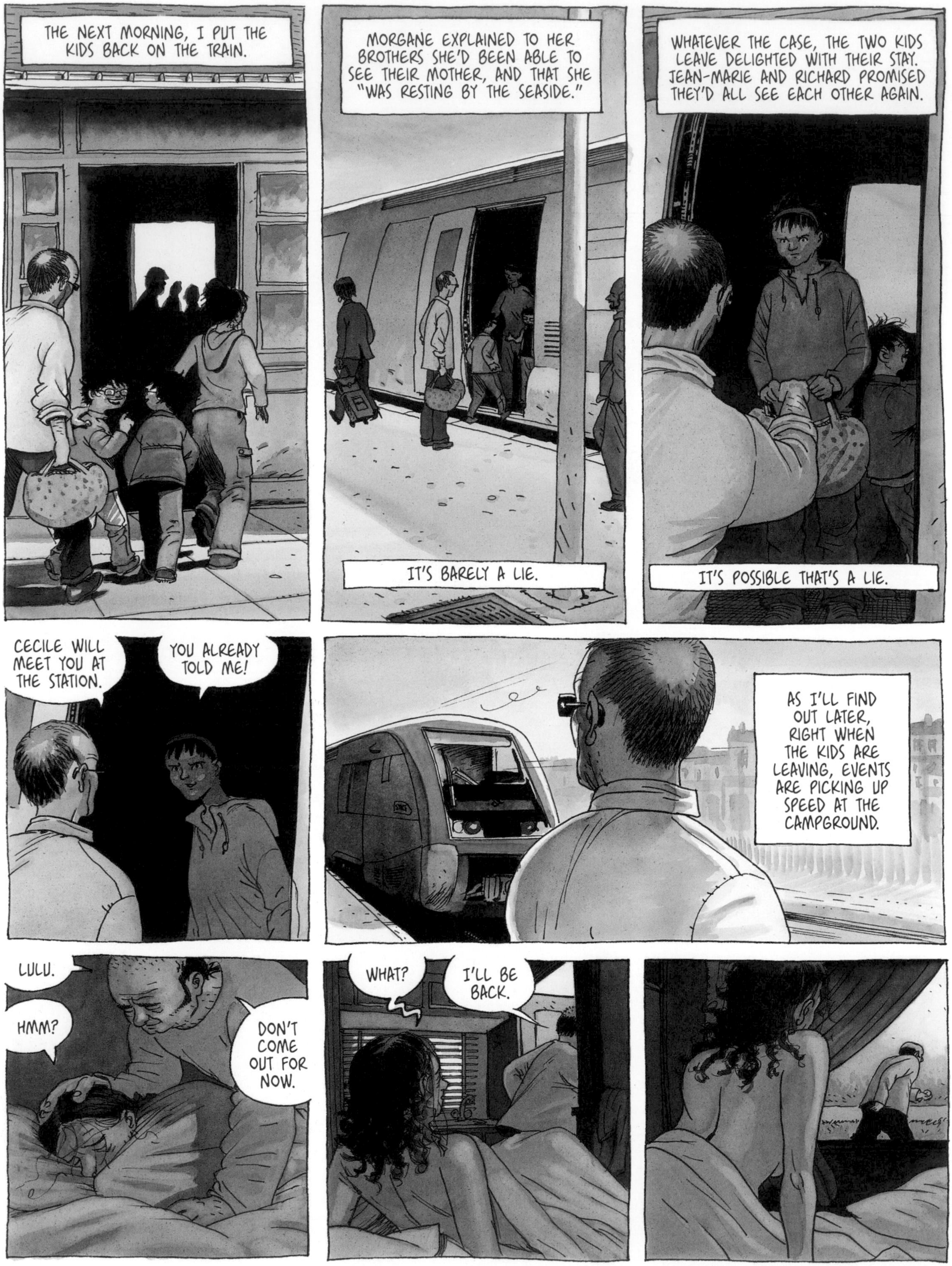
THE NEXT MORNING, I PUT THE KIDS BACK ON THE TRAIN.
MORGANE EXPLAINED TO HER BROTHERS SHE'D BEEN ABLE TO SEE THEIR MOTHER, AND THAT SHE "WAS RESTING BY THE SEASIDE."
IT'S BARELY A LIE.
WHATEVER THE CASE, THE TWO KIDS LEAVE DELIGHTED WITH THEIR STAY. JEAN-MARIE AND RICHARD PROMISED THEY'D ALL SEE EACH OTHER AGAIN.
IT'S POSSIBLE THAT'S A LIE.
CECILE WILL MEET YOU AT THE STATION.
YOU ALREADY TOLD ME!
AS I'LL FIND OUT LATER, RIGHT WHEN THE KIDS ARE LEAVING, EVENTS ARE PICKING UP SPEED AT THE CAMPGROUND.
LULU.
HMM?
DON'T COME OUT FOR NOW.
WHAT?
I'LL BE BACK.

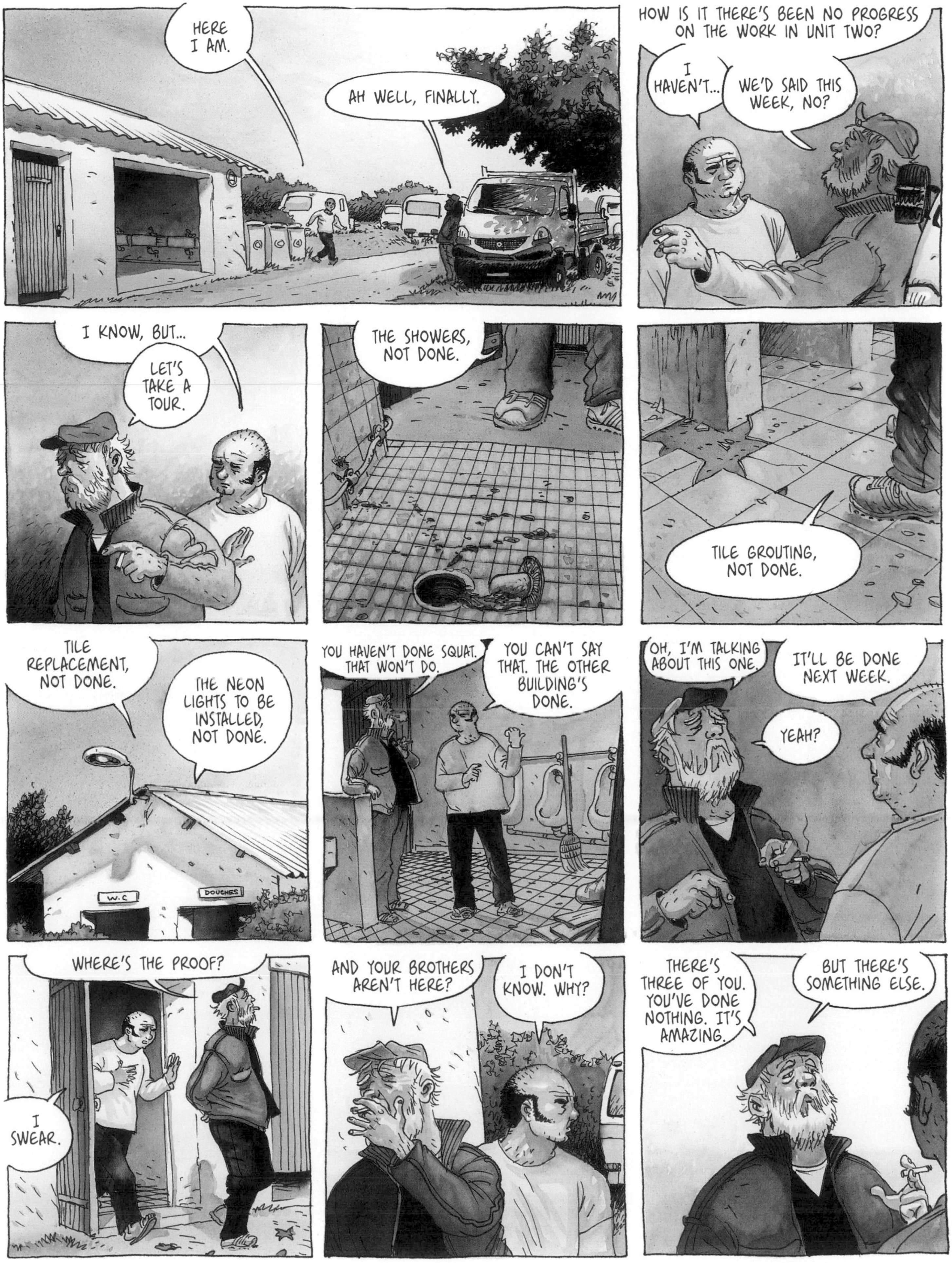
HERE I AM.
AH WELL, FINALLY.
HOW IS IT THERE'S BEEN NO PROGRESS ON THE WORK IN UNIT TWO?
I HAVEN'T...
WE'D SAID THIS WEEK, NO?
I KNOW, BUT...
LET'S TAKE A TOUR.
THE SHOWERS, NOT DONE.
TILE GROUTING, NOT DONE.
TILE REPLACEMENT, NOT DONE.
THE NEON LIGHTS TO BE INSTALLED, NOT DONE.
W.C
DOUCHES
YOU HAVEN'T DONE SQUAT. THAT WON'T DO.
YOU CAN'T SAY THAT. THE OTHER BUILDING'S DONE.
OH, I'M TALKING ABOUT THIS ONE.
IT'LL BE DONE NEXT WEEK.
YEAH?
WHERE'S THE PROOF?
I SWEAR.
AND YOUR BROTHERS AREN'T HERE?
I DON'T KNOW. WHY?
THERE'S THREE OF YOU. YOU'VE DONE NOTHING. IT'S AMAZING.
BUT THERE'S SOMETHING ELSE.

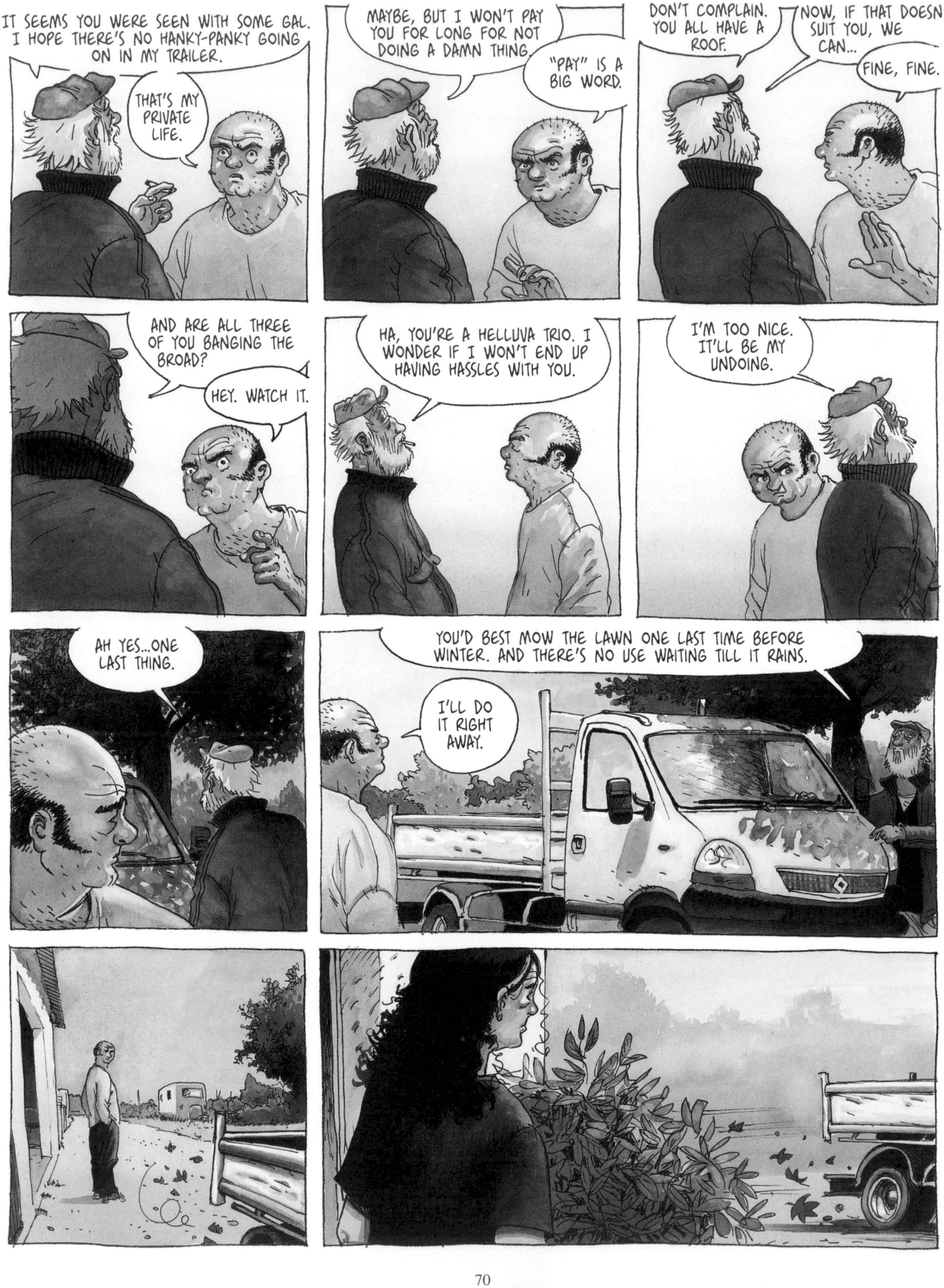
IT SEEMS YOU WERE SEEN WITH SOME GAL. I HOPE THERE'S NO HANKY-PANKY GOING ON IN MY TRAILER.
THAT'S MY PRIVATE LIFE.
MAYBE, BUT I WON'T PAY YOU FOR LONG FOR NOT DOING A DAMN THING.
"PAY" IS A BIG WORD.
DON'T COMPLAIN. YOU ALL HAVE A ROOF.
NOW, IF THAT DOESN'T SUIT YOU, WE CAN...
FINE, FINE.
AND ARE ALL THREE OF YOU BANGING THE BROAD?
HEY. WATCH IT.
HA, YOU'RE A HELLUVA TRIO. I WONDER IF I WON'T END UP HAVING HASSLES WITH YOU.
I'M TOO NICE. IT'LL BE MY UNDOING.
AH YES...ONE LAST THING.
YOU'D BEST MOW THE LAWN ONE LAST TIME BEFORE WINTER. AND THERE'S NO USE WAITING TILL IT RAINS.
I'LL DO IT RIGHT AWAY.

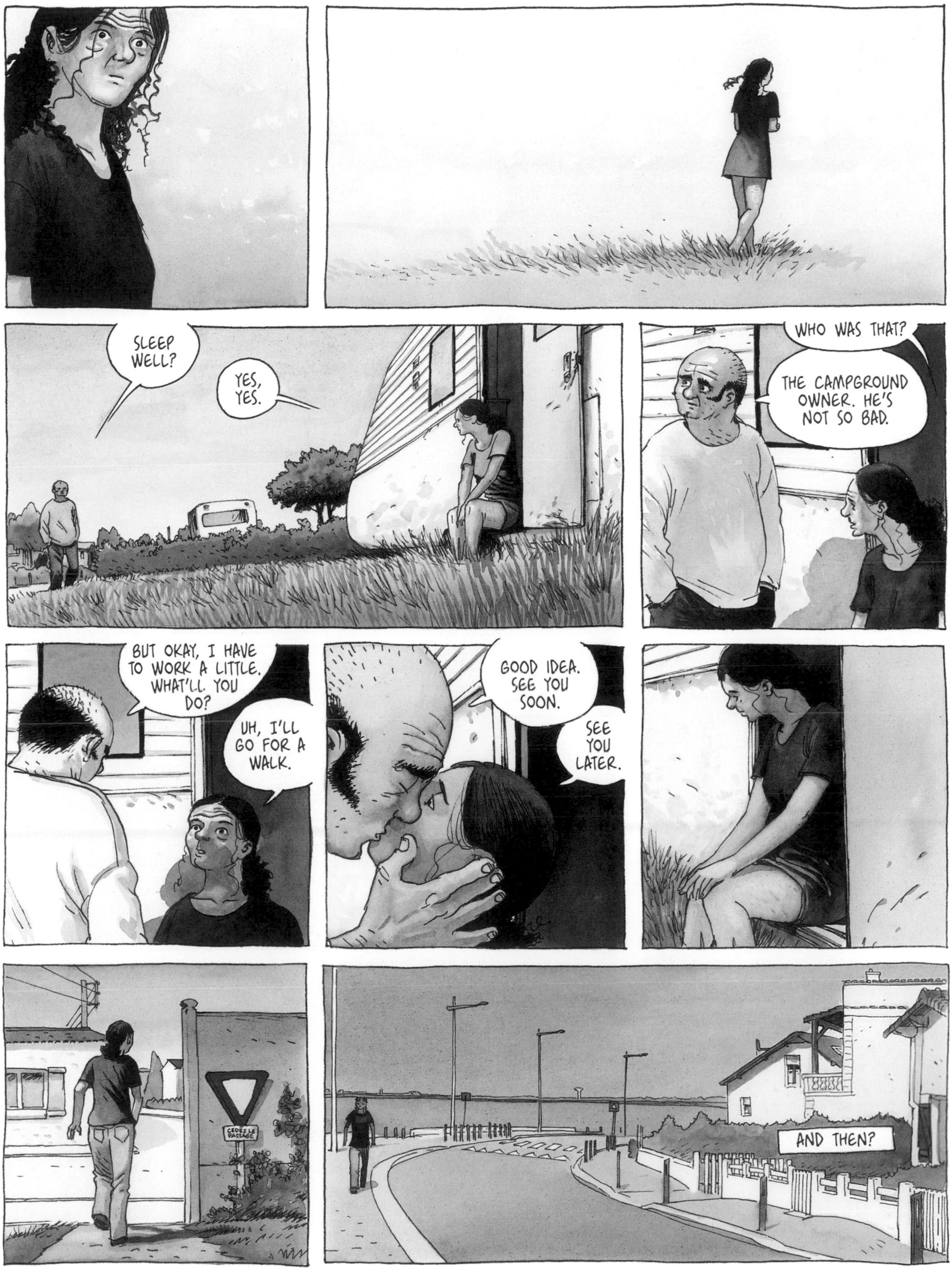
SLEEP WELL?
YES, YES.
WHO WAS THAT?
THE CAMPGROUND OWNER. HE'S NOT SO BAD.
BUT OKAY, I HAVE TO WORK A LITTLE. WHAT'LL YOU DO?
UH, I'LL GO FOR A WALK.
GOOD IDEA. SEE YOU SOON.
SEE YOU LATER.
AND THEN?

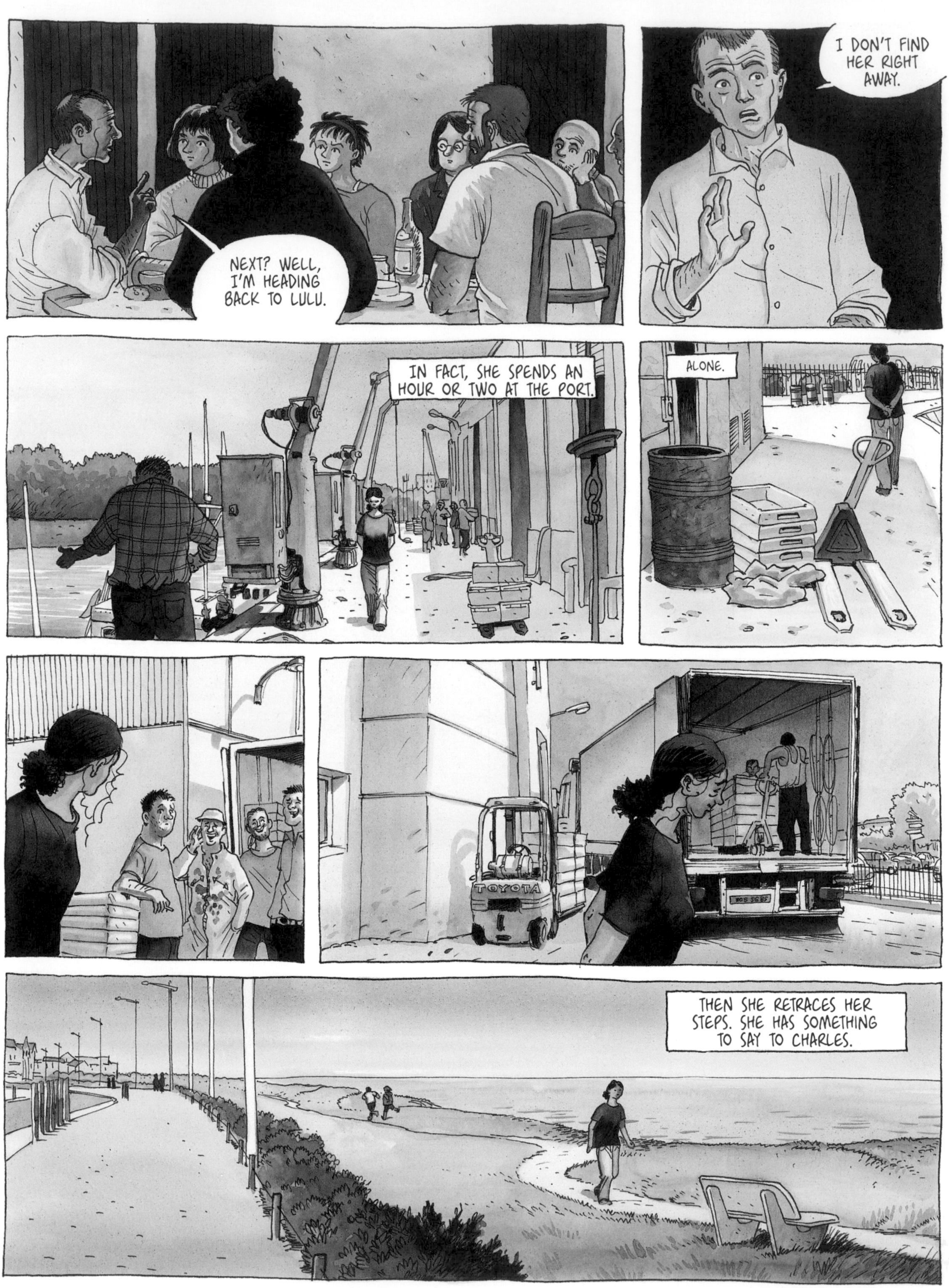
NEXT? WELL, I'M HEADING BACK TO LULU.
I DON'T FIND HER RIGHT AWAY.
IN FACT, SHE SPENDS AN HOUR OR TWO AT THE PORT.
ALONE.
THEN SHE RETRACES HER STEPS. SHE HAS SOMETHING TO SAY TO CHARLES.

HE UNDERSTANDS IMMEDIATELY.

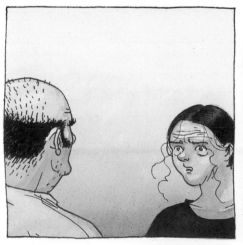

SHE JUST TELLS HIM IT'S TIME.

SHE'S GOING TO LEAVE.

HE ABSORBS IT.

HE MANAGES ONLY TO ASK:

"FOR FOREVER?"

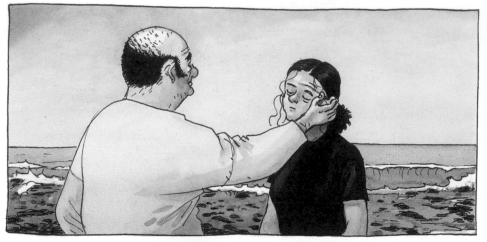

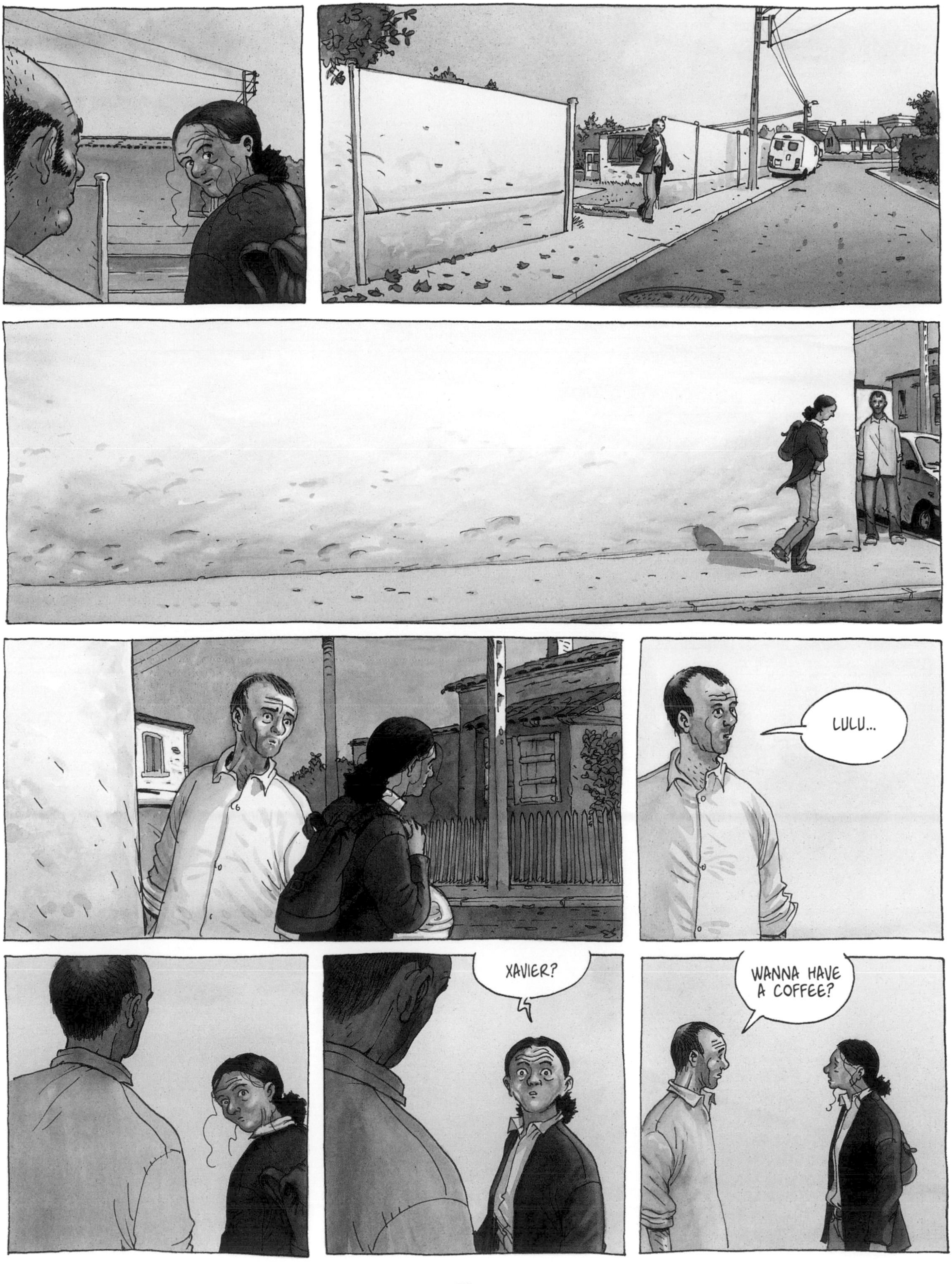
LULU...
XAVIER?
WANNA HAVE A COFFEE?

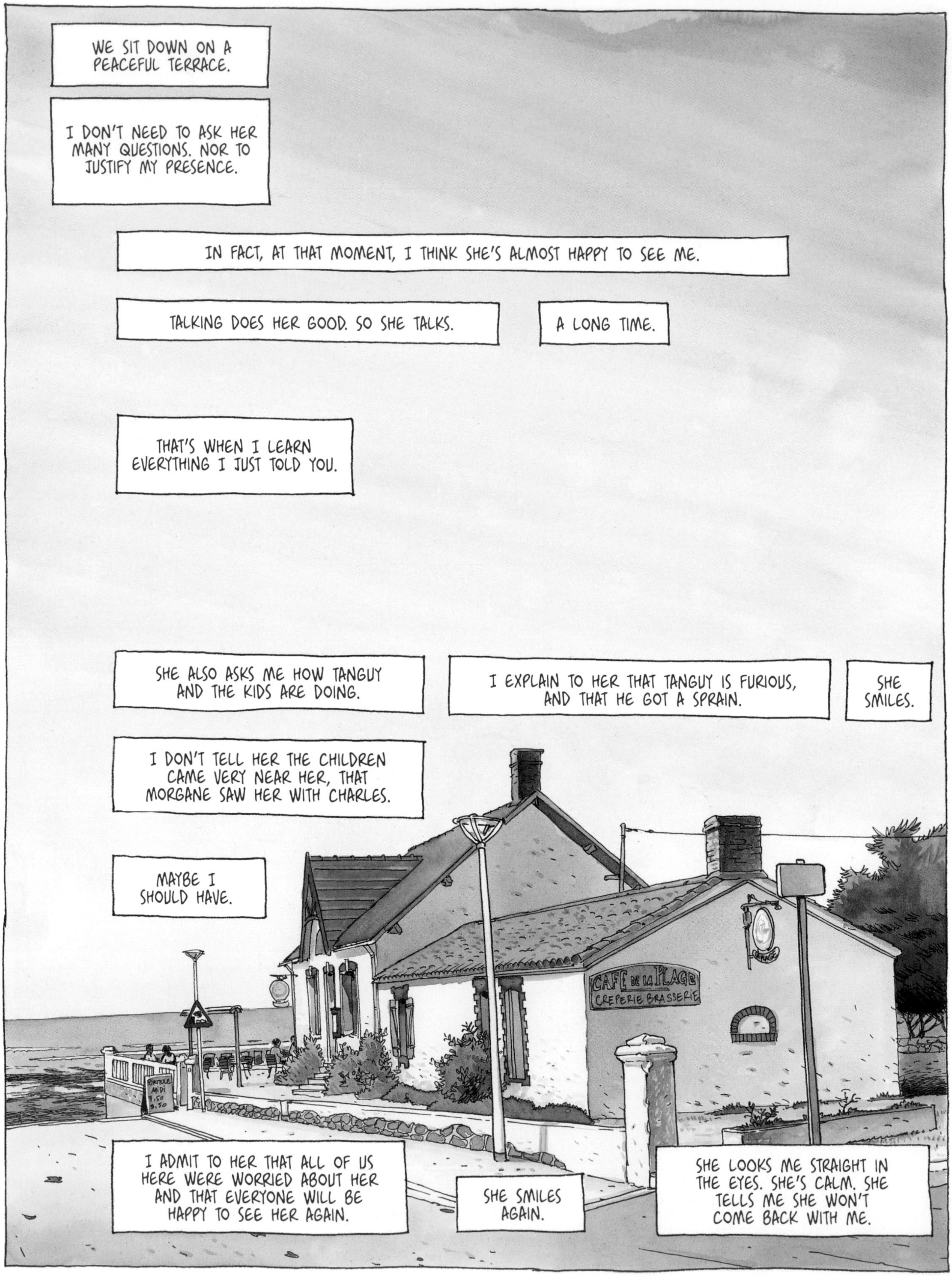
WE SIT DOWN ON A PEACEFUL TERRACE.
I DON'T NEED TO ASK HER MANY QUESTIONS. NOR TO JUSTIFY MY PRESENCE.
IN FACT, AT THAT MOMENT, I THINK SHE'S ALMOST HAPPY TO SEE ME.
TALKING DOES HER GOOD. SO SHE TALKS.
A LONG TIME.
THAT'S WHEN I LEARN EVERYTHING I JUST TOLD YOU.
SHE ALSO ASKS ME HOW TANGUY AND THE KIDS ARE DOING.
I EXPLAIN TO HER THAT TANGUY IS FURIOUS, AND THAT HE GOT A SPRAIN.
SHE SMILES.
I DON'T TELL HER THE CHILDREN CAME VERY NEAR HER, THAT MORGANE SAW HER WITH CHARLES.
MAYBE I SHOULD HAVE.
CAFE DE LA PLAGE
CREPERIE BRASSERIE
I ADMIT TO HER THAT ALL OF US HERE WERE WORRIED ABOUT HER AND THAT EVERYONE WILL BE HAPPY TO SEE HER AGAIN.
SHE SMILES AGAIN.
SHE LOOKS ME STRAIGHT IN THE EYES. SHE'S CALM. SHE TELLS ME SHE WON'T COME BACK WITH ME.

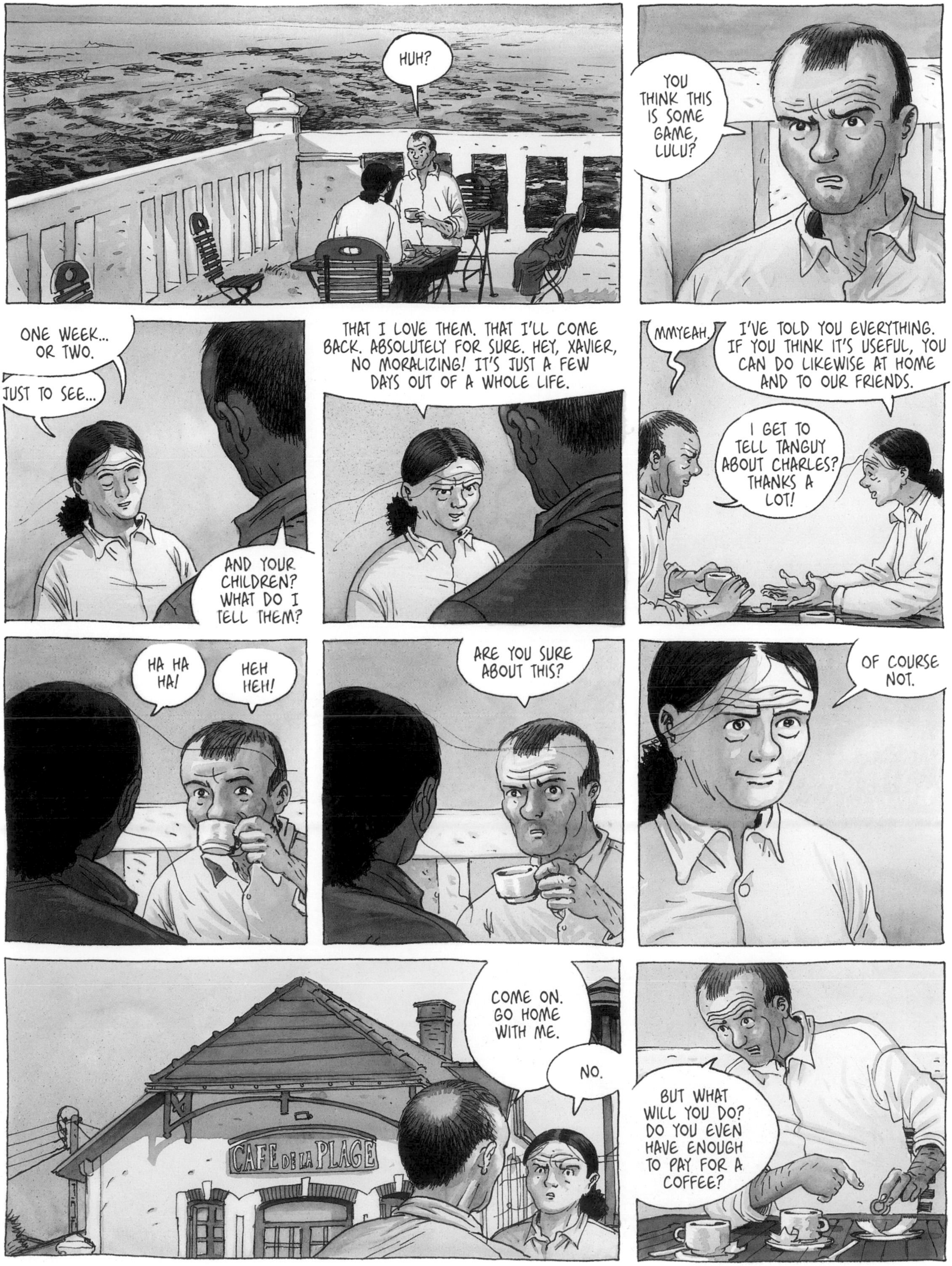
HUH?
YOU THINK THIS IS SOME GAME, LULU?
ONE WEEK... OR TWO.
JUST TO SEE...
AND YOUR CHILDREN? WHAT DO I TELL THEM?
THAT I LOVE THEM. THAT I'LL COME BACK. ABSOLUTELY FOR SURE. HEY, XAVIER, NO MORALIZING! IT'S JUST A FEW DAYS OUT OF A WHOLE LIFE.
MMYEAH.
I'VE TOLD YOU EVERYTHING. IF YOU THINK IT'S USEFUL, YOU CAN DO LIKEWISE AT HOME AND TO OUR FRIENDS.
I GET TO TELL TANGUY ABOUT CHARLES? THANKS A LOT!
HA HA HA!
HEH HEH!
ARE YOU SURE ABOUT THIS?
OF COURSE NOT.
COME ON. GO HOME WITH ME.
NO.
CAFE DE LA PLAGE
BUT WHAT WILL YOU DO? DO YOU EVEN HAVE ENOUGH TO PAY FOR A COFFEE?

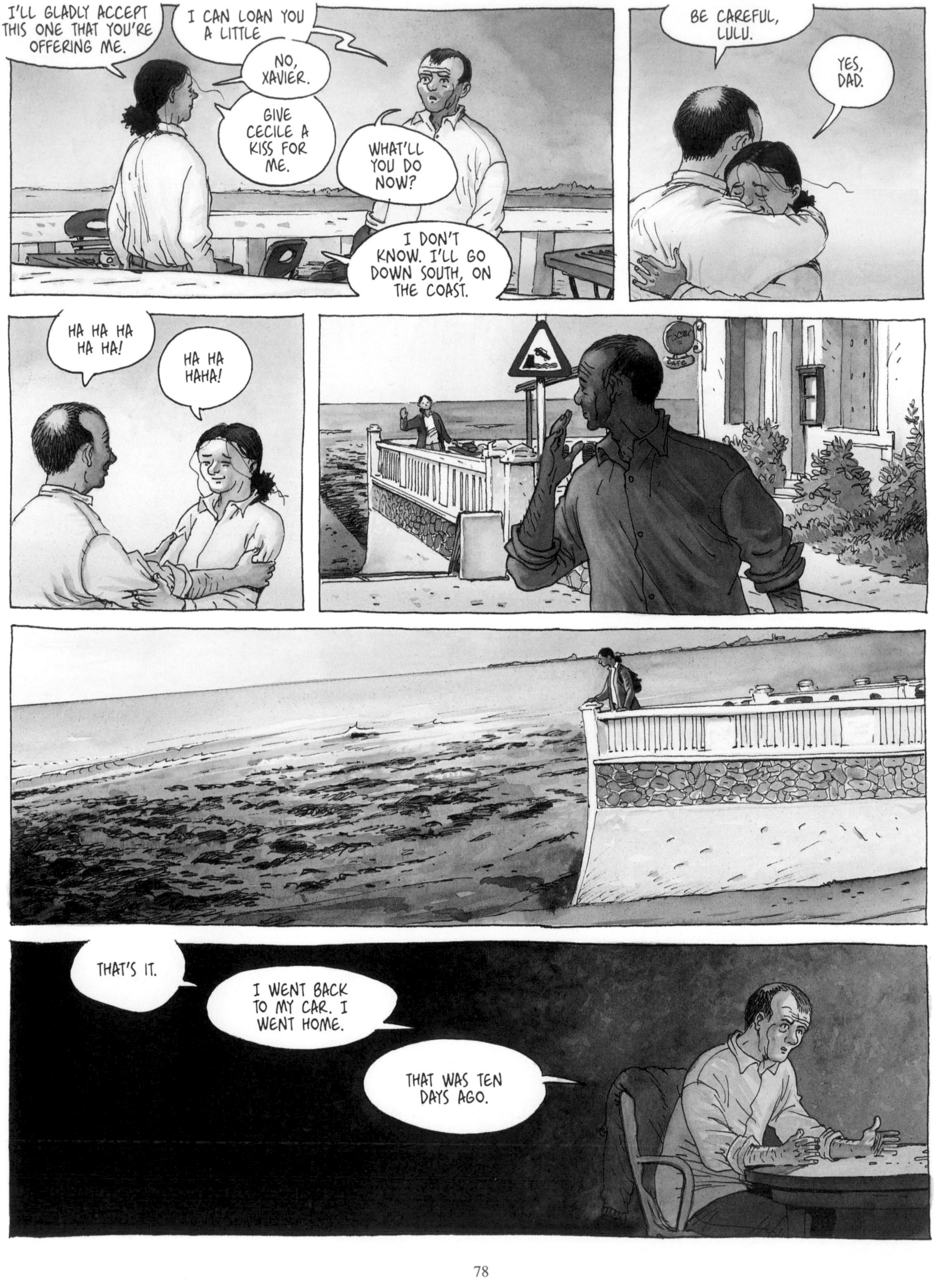
I'LL GLADLY ACCEPT THIS ONE THAT YOU'RE OFFERING ME.
I CAN LOAN YOU A LITTLE
NO, XAVIER.
GIVE CECILE A KISS FOR ME.
WHAT'LL YOU DO NOW?
I DON'T KNOW. I'LL GO DOWN SOUTH, ON THE COAST.
BE CAREFUL, LULU.
YES, DAD.
HA HA HA HA HA!
HA HA HAHA!
THAT'S IT.
I WENT BACK TO MY CAR. I WENT HOME.
THAT WAS TEN DAYS AGO.

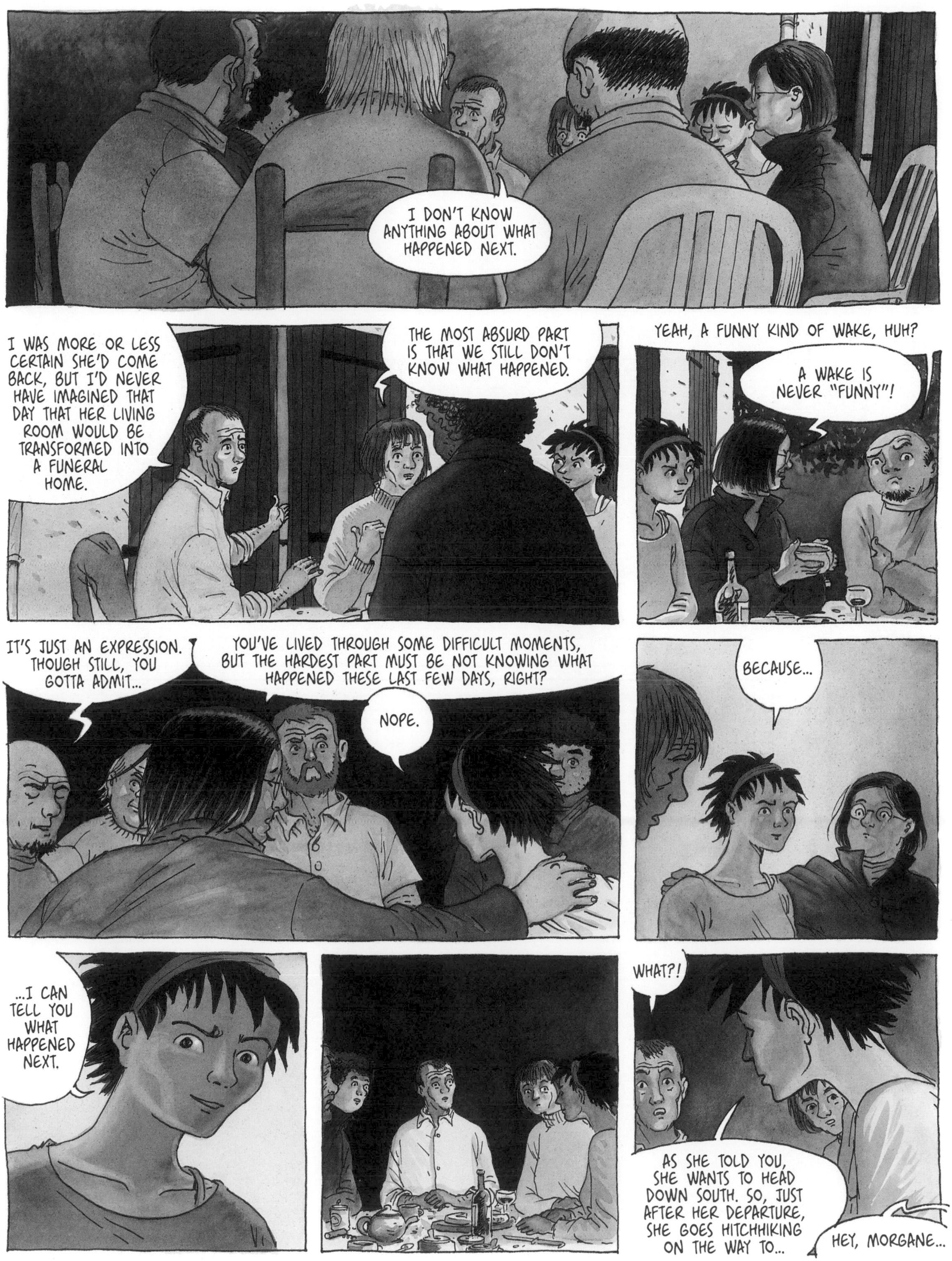
I DON'T KNOW ANYTHING ABOUT WHAT HAPPENED NEXT.
I WAS MORE OR LESS CERTAIN SHE'D COME BACK, BUT I'D NEVER HAVE IMAGINED THAT DAY THAT HER LIVING ROOM WOULD BE TRANSFORMED INTO A FUNERAL HOME.
THE MOST ABSURD PART IS THAT WE STILL DON'T KNOW WHAT HAPPENED.
YEAH, A FUNNY KIND OF WAKE, HUH?
A WAKE IS NEVER "FUNNY"!
IT'S JUST AN EXPRESSION. THOUGH STILL, YOU GOTTA ADMIT...
YOU'VE LIVED THROUGH SOME DIFFICULT MOMENTS, BUT THE HARDEST PART MUST BE NOT KNOWING WHAT HAPPENED THESE LAST FEW DAYS, RIGHT?
NOPE.
BECAUSE...
...I CAN TELL YOU WHAT HAPPENED NEXT.
WHAT?!
AS SHE TOLD YOU, SHE WANTS TO HEAD DOWN SOUTH. SO, JUST AFTER HER DEPARTURE, SHE GOES HITCHHIKING ON THE WAY TO...
HEY, MORGANE...

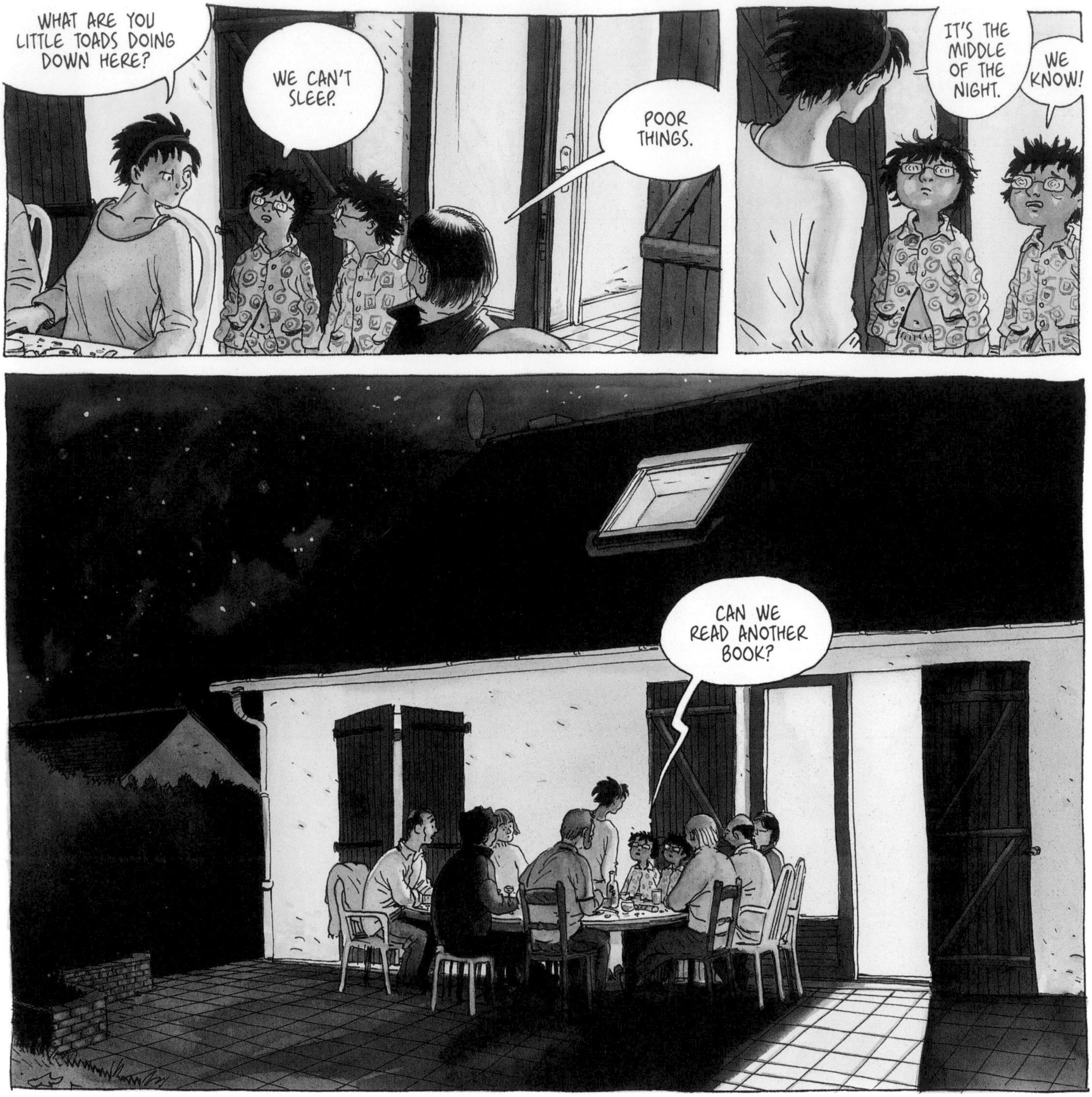
WHAT ARE YOU LITTLE TOADS DOING DOWN HERE?
WE CAN'T SLEEP.
POOR THINGS.
IT'S THE MIDDLE OF THE NIGHT.
WE KNOW!
CAN WE READ ANOTHER BOOK?

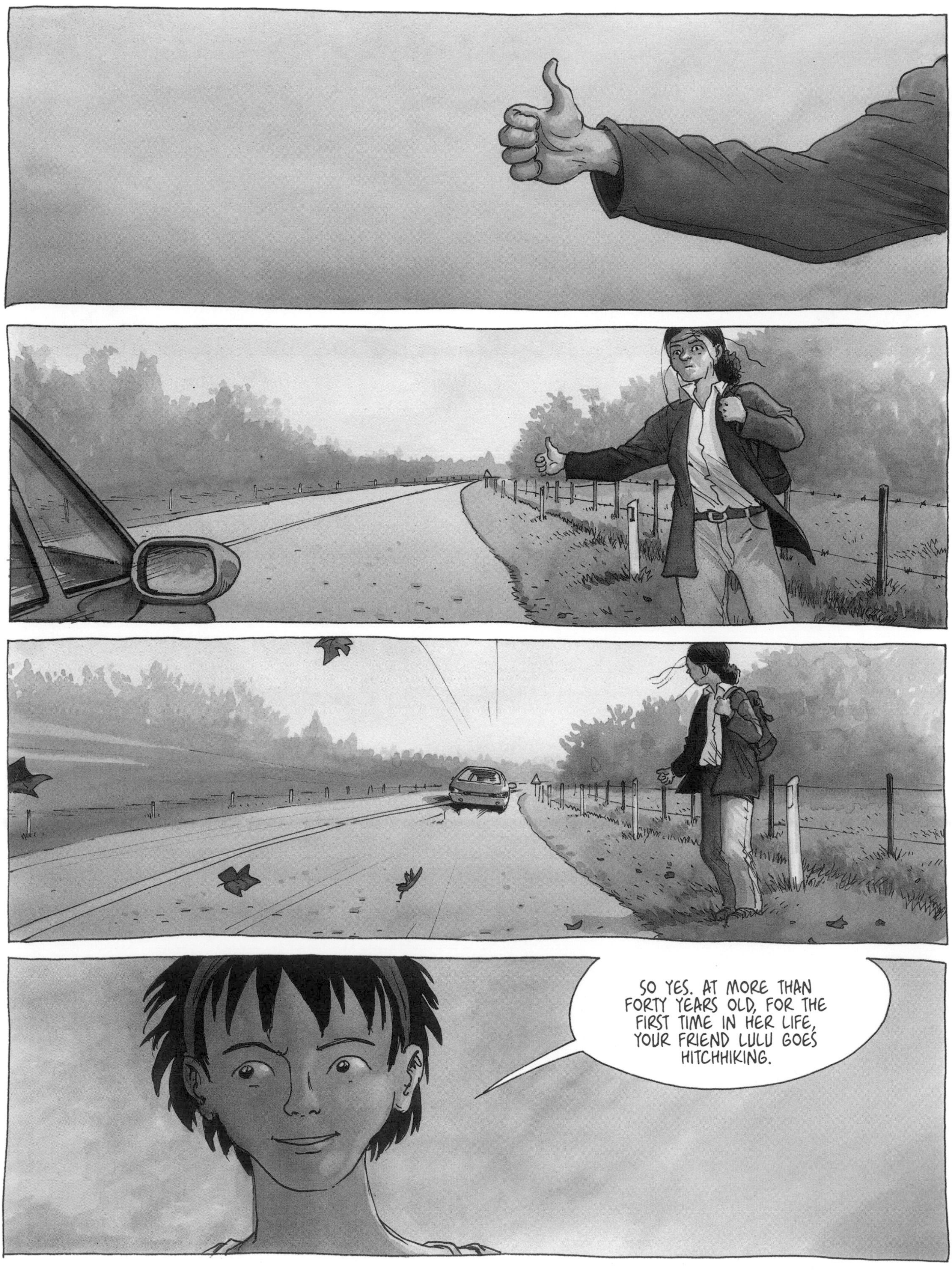
SO YES. AT MORE THAN FORTY YEARS OLD, FOR THE FIRST TIME IN HER LIFE, YOUR FRIEND LULU GOES HITCHHIKING.

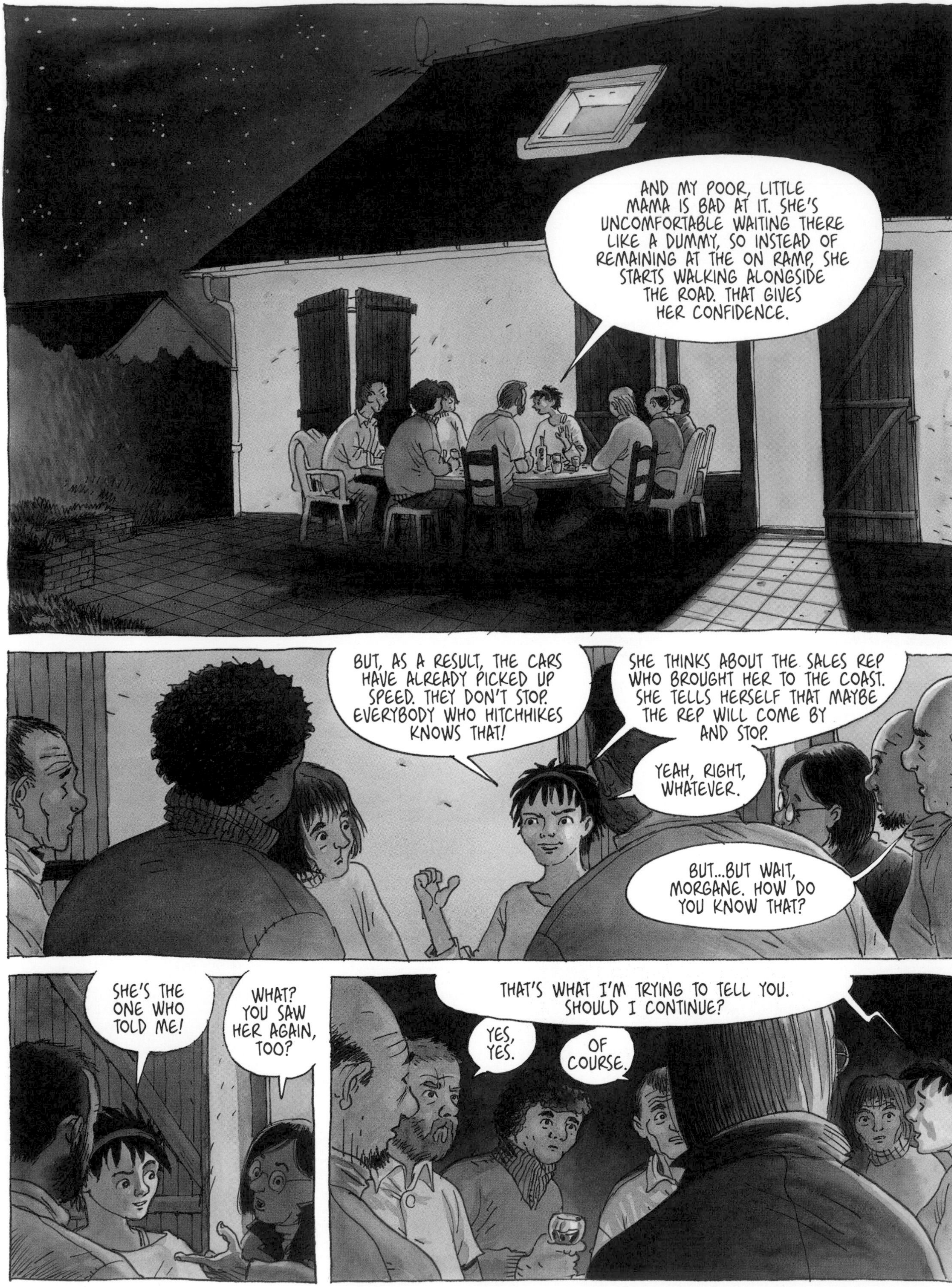
AND MY POOR, LITTLE MAMA IS BAD AT IT. SHE'S UNCOMFORTABLE WAITING THERE LIKE A DUMMY, SO INSTEAD OF REMAINING AT THE ON RAMP, SHE STARTS WALKING ALONGSIDE THE ROAD. THAT GIVES HER CONFIDENCE.
BUT, AS A RESULT, THE CARS HAVE ALREADY PICKED UP SPEED. THEY DON'T STOP. EVERYBODY WHO HITCHHIKES KNOWS THAT!
SHE THINKS ABOUT THE SALES REP WHO BROUGHT HER TO THE COAST. SHE TELLS HERSELF THAT MAYBE THE REP WILL COME BY AND STOP.
YEAH, RIGHT, WHATEVER.
BUT...BUT WAIT, MORGANE. HOW DO YOU KNOW THAT?
SHE'S THE ONE WHO TOLD ME!
WHAT? YOU SAW HER AGAIN, TOO?
THAT'S WHAT I'M TRYING TO TELL YOU. SHOULD I CONTINUE?
YES, YES.
OF COURSE.

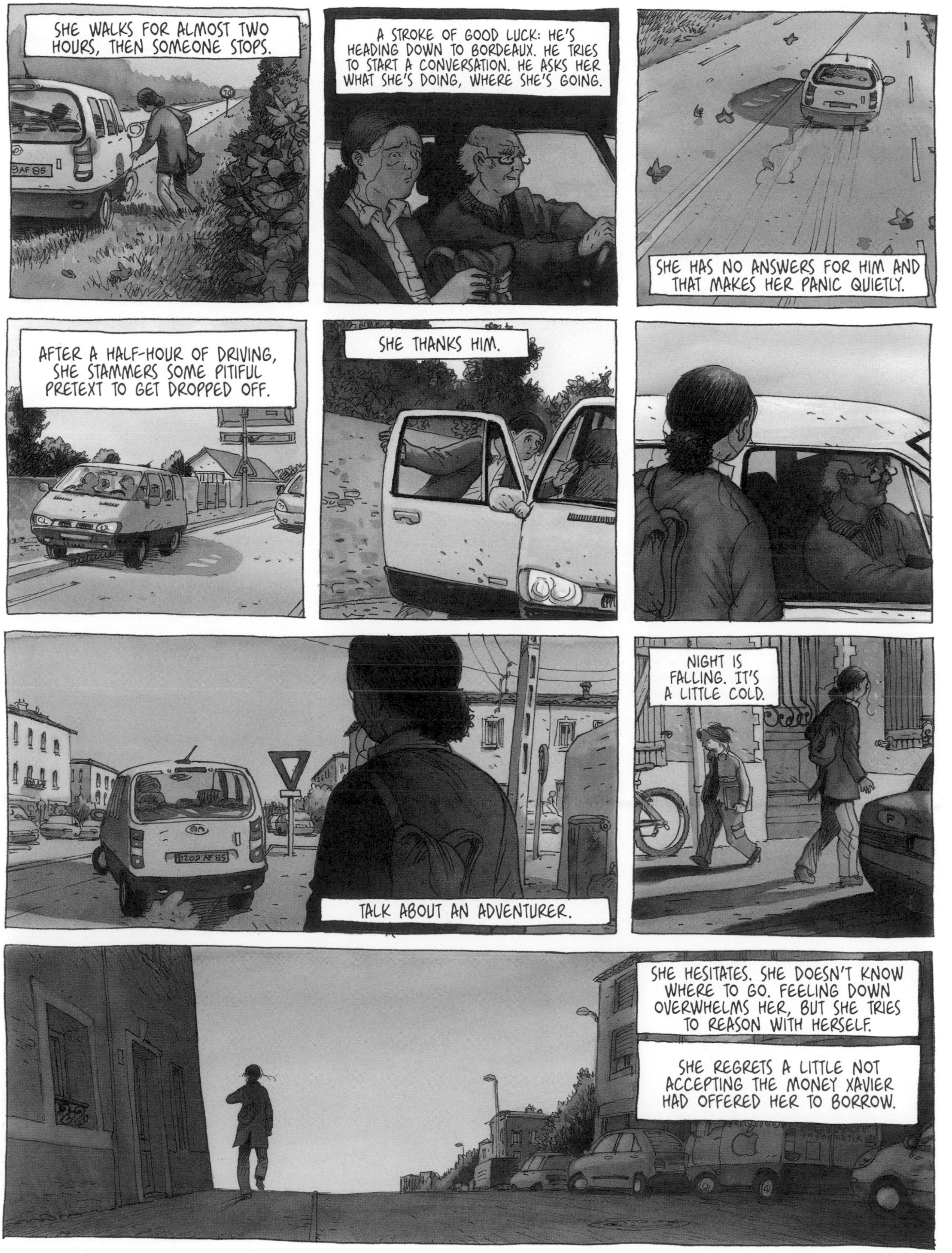
SHE WALKS FOR ALMOST TWO HOURS, THEN SOMEONE STOPS.
A STROKE OF GOOD LUCK: HE'S HEADING DOWN TO BORDEAUX. HE TRIES TO START A CONVERSATION. HE ASKS HER WHAT SHE'S DOING, WHERE SHE'S GOING.
SHE HAS NO ANSWERS FOR HIM AND THAT MAKES HER PANIC QUIETLY.
AFTER A HALF-HOUR OF DRIVING, SHE STAMMERS SOME PITIFUL PRETEXT TO GET DROPPED OFF.
SHE THANKS HIM.
TALK ABOUT AN ADVENTURER.
NIGHT IS FALLING. IT'S A LITTLE COLD.
SHE HESITATES. SHE DOESN'T KNOW WHERE TO GO. FEELING DOWN OVERWHELMS HER, BUT SHE TRIES TO REASON WITH HERSELF.
SHE REGRETS A LITTLE NOT ACCEPTING THE MONEY XAVIER HAD OFFERED HER TO BORROW.

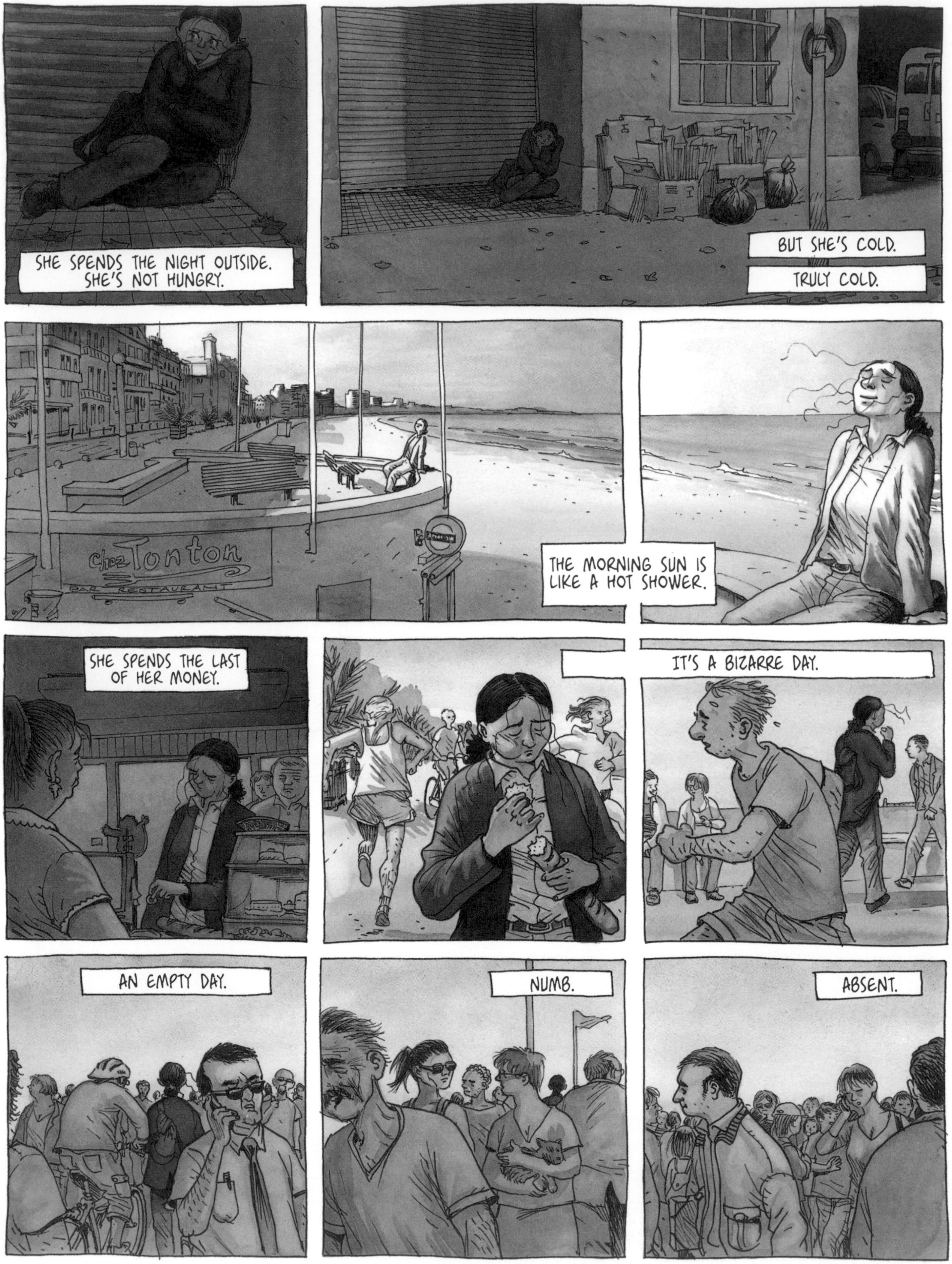
SHE SPENDS THE NIGHT OUTSIDE. SHE'S NOT HUNGRY.
BUT SHE'S COLD.
TRULY COLD.
Chez Tonton
BAR RESTAURANT
THE MORNING SUN IS LIKE A HOT SHOWER.
SHE SPENDS THE LAST OF HER MONEY.
IT'S A BIZARRE DAY.
AN EMPTY DAY.
NUMB.
ABSENT.

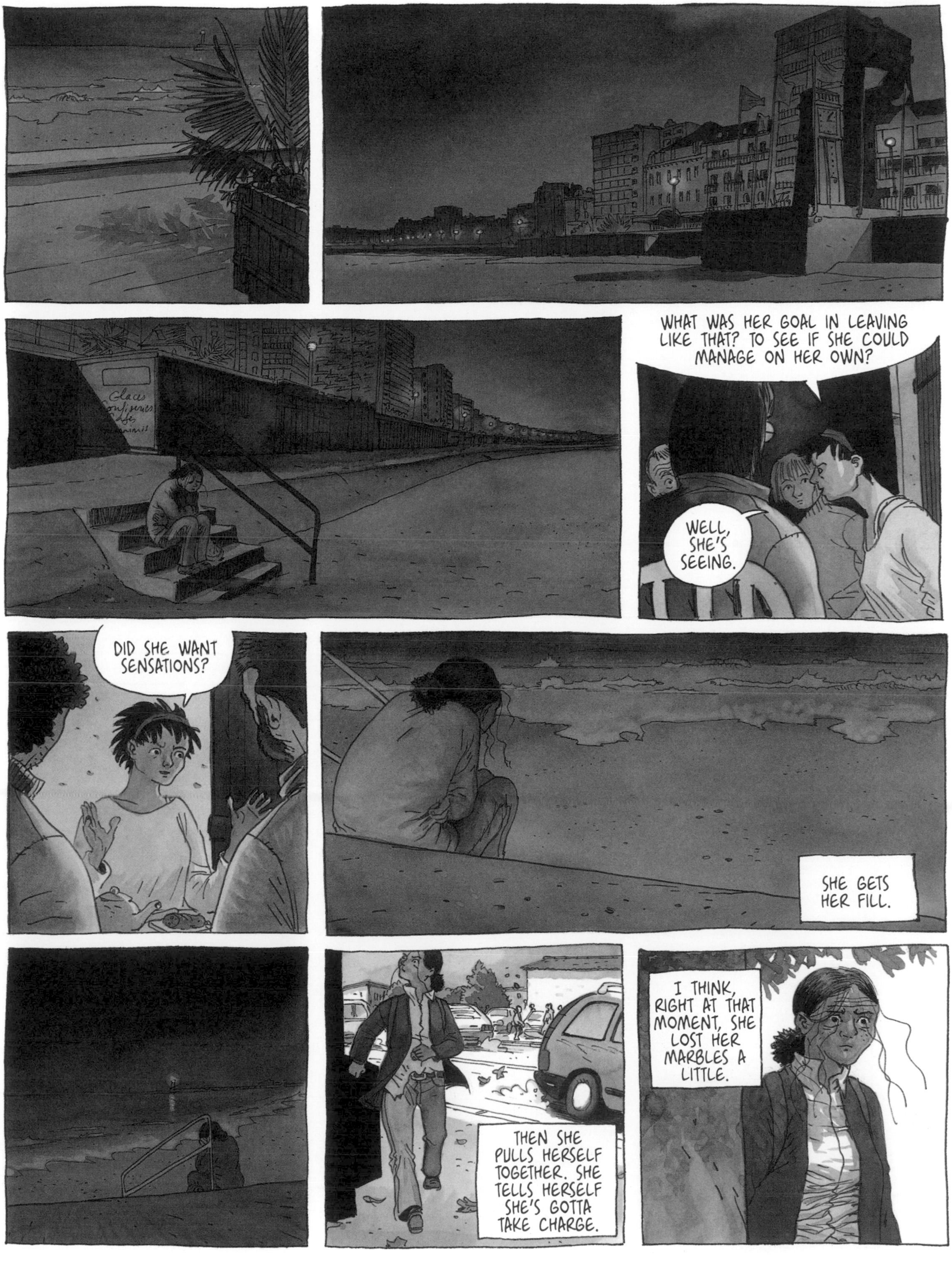
WHAT WAS HER GOAL IN LEAVING LIKE THAT? TO SEE IF SHE COULD MANAGE ON HER OWN?
WELL, SHE'S SEEING.
DID SHE WANT SENSATIONS?
SHE GETS HER FILL.
THEN SHE PULLS HERSELF TOGETHER. SHE TELLS HERSELF SHE'S GOTTA TAKE CHARGE.
I THINK, RIGHT AT THAT MOMENT, SHE LOST HER MARBLES A LITTLE.

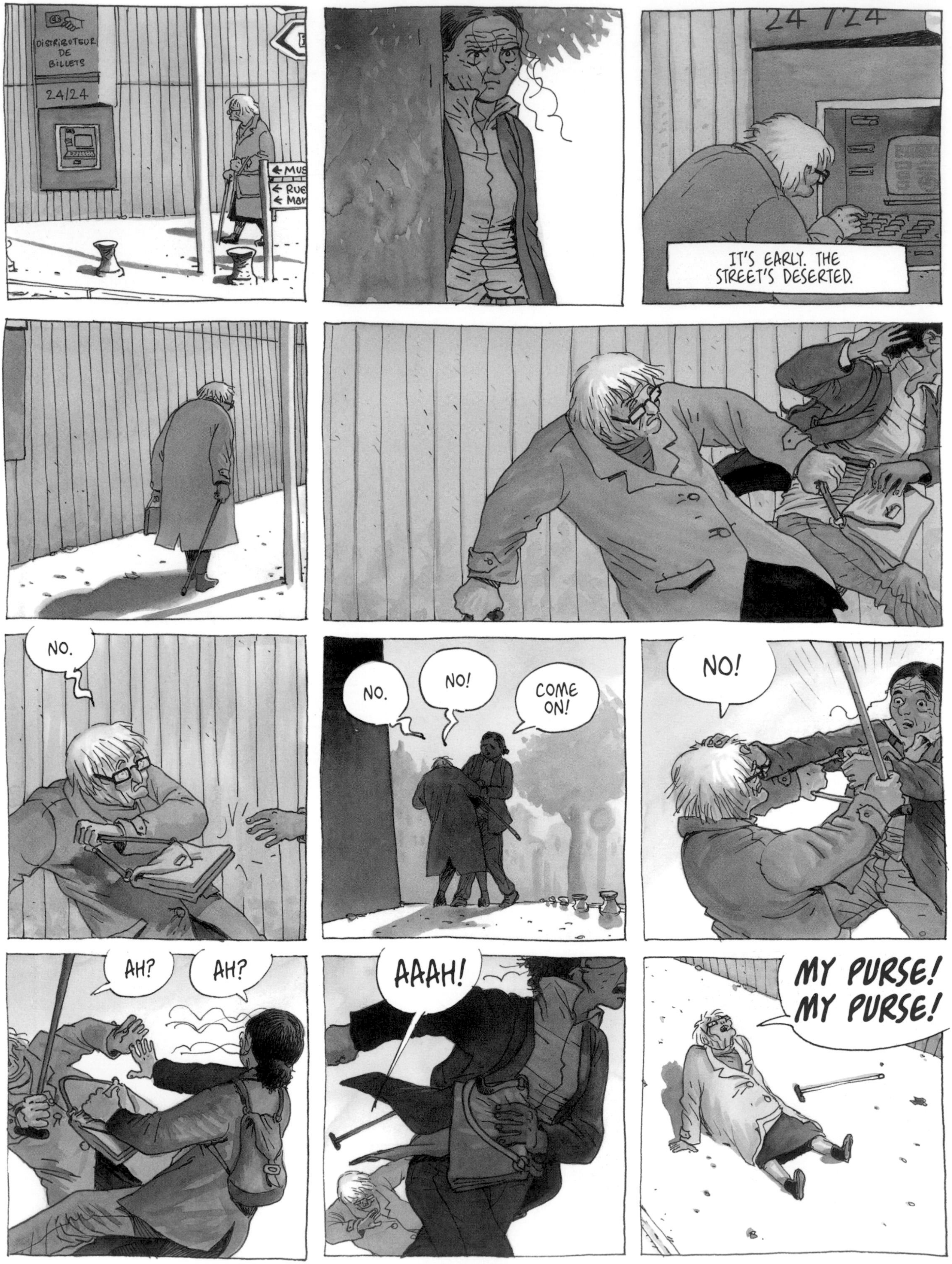
DISTRIBUTEUR DE BILLETS
24/24
24/24
IT'S EARLY. THE STREET'S DESERTED.
NO.
NO.
NO!
COME ON!
NO!
AH?
AH?
AAAH!
MY PURSE! MY PURSE!

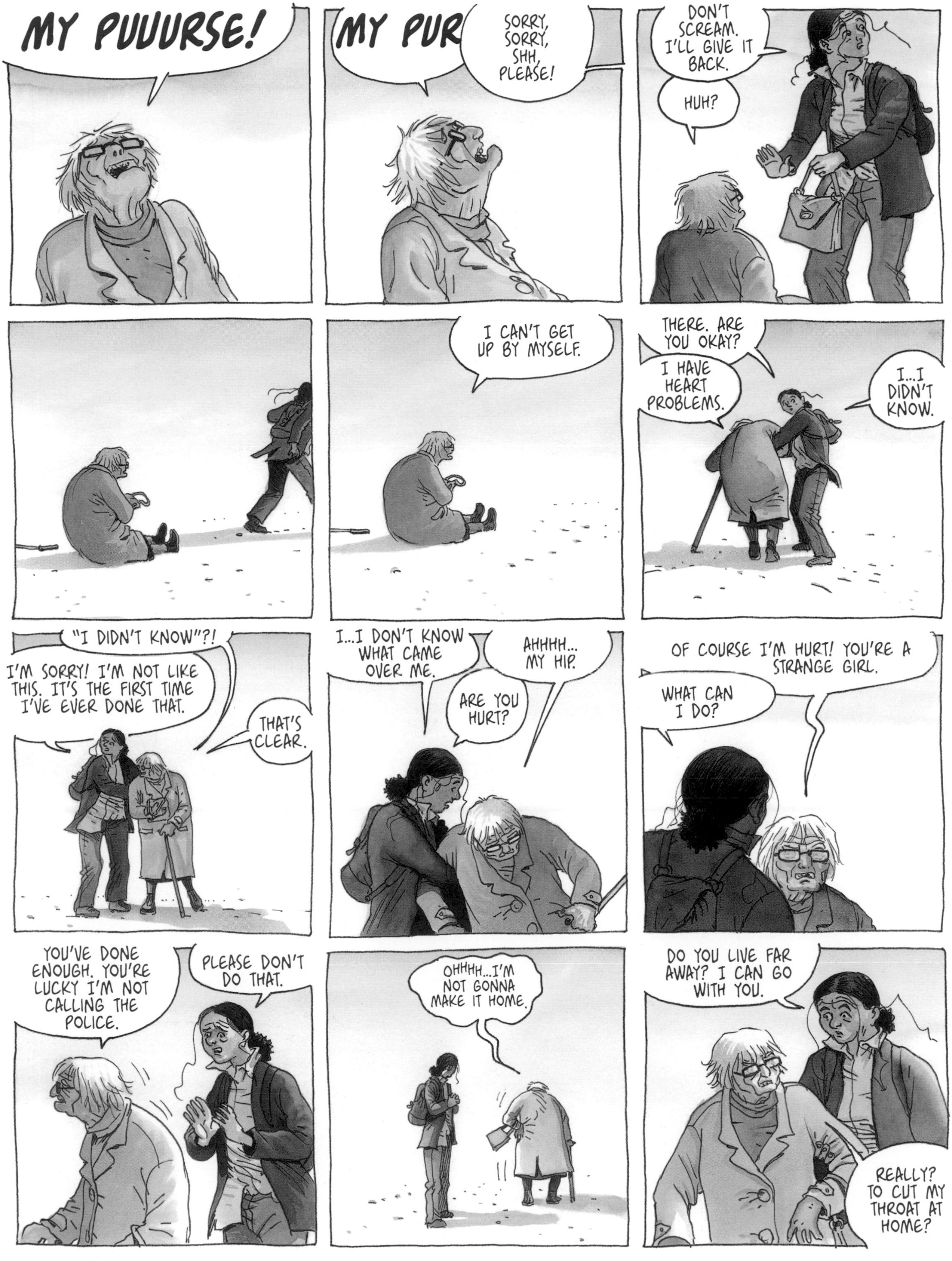
MY PUUURSE!
MY PUR
SORRY, SORRY, SHH, PLEASE!
DON'T SCREAM. I'LL GIVE IT BACK.
HUH?
I CAN'T GET UP BY MYSELF.
THERE. ARE YOU OKAY?
I HAVE HEART PROBLEMS.
I...I DIDN'T KNOW.
"I DIDN'T KNOW"?!
I'M SORRY! I'M NOT LIKE THIS. IT'S THE FIRST TIME I'VE EVER DONE THAT.
THAT'S CLEAR.
I...I DON'T KNOW WHAT CAME OVER ME.
AHHHH... MY HIP.
ARE YOU HURT?
OF COURSE I'M HURT! YOU'RE A STRANGE GIRL.
WHAT CAN I DO?
YOU'VE DONE ENOUGH. YOU'RE LUCKY I'M NOT CALLING THE POLICE.
PLEASE DON'T DO THAT.
OHHHH...I'M NOT GONNA MAKE IT HOME.
DO YOU LIVE FAR AWAY? I CAN GO WITH YOU.
REALLY? TO CUT MY THROAT AT HOME?

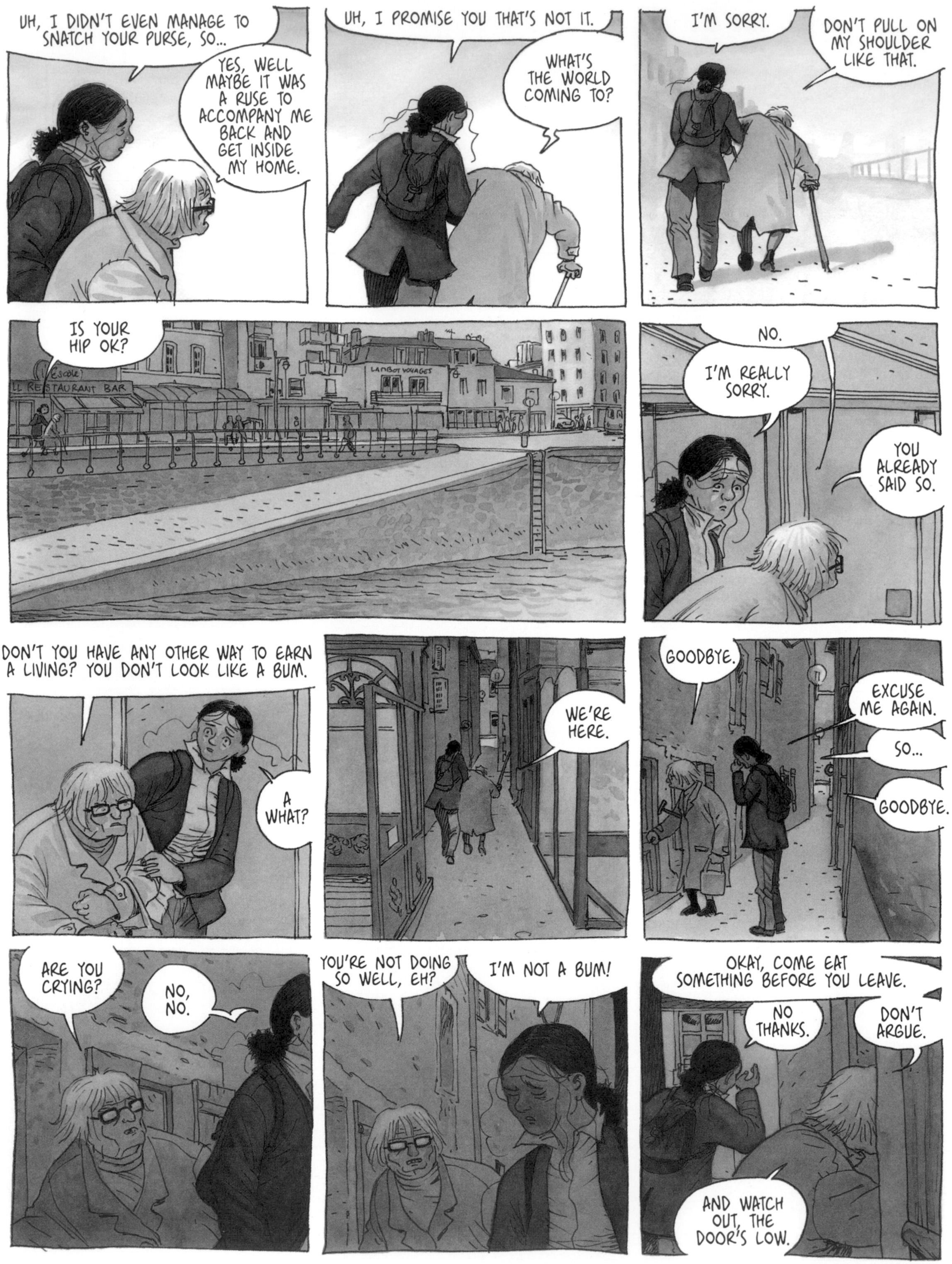
UH, I DIDN'T EVEN MANAGE TO SNATCH YOUR PURSE, SO...
YES, WELL MAYBE IT WAS A RUSE TO ACCOMPANY ME BACK AND GET INSIDE MY HOME.
UH, I PROMISE YOU THAT'S NOT IT.
WHAT'S THE WORLD COMING TO?
I'M SORRY.
DON'T PULL ON MY SHOULDER LIKE THAT.
IS YOUR HIP OK?
RESTAURANT BAR
LAMBOT VOYAGES
NO.
I'M REALLY SORRY.
YOU ALREADY SAID SO.
DON'T YOU HAVE ANY OTHER WAY TO EARN A LIVING? YOU DON'T LOOK LIKE A BUM.
A WHAT?
WE'RE HERE.
GOODBYE.
EXCUSE ME AGAIN.
SO...
GOODBYE.
ARE YOU CRYING?
NO, NO.
YOU'RE NOT DOING SO WELL, EH?
I'M NOT A BUM!
OKAY, COME EAT SOMETHING BEFORE YOU LEAVE.
NO THANKS.
DON'T ARGUE.
AND WATCH OUT, THE DOOR'S LOW.

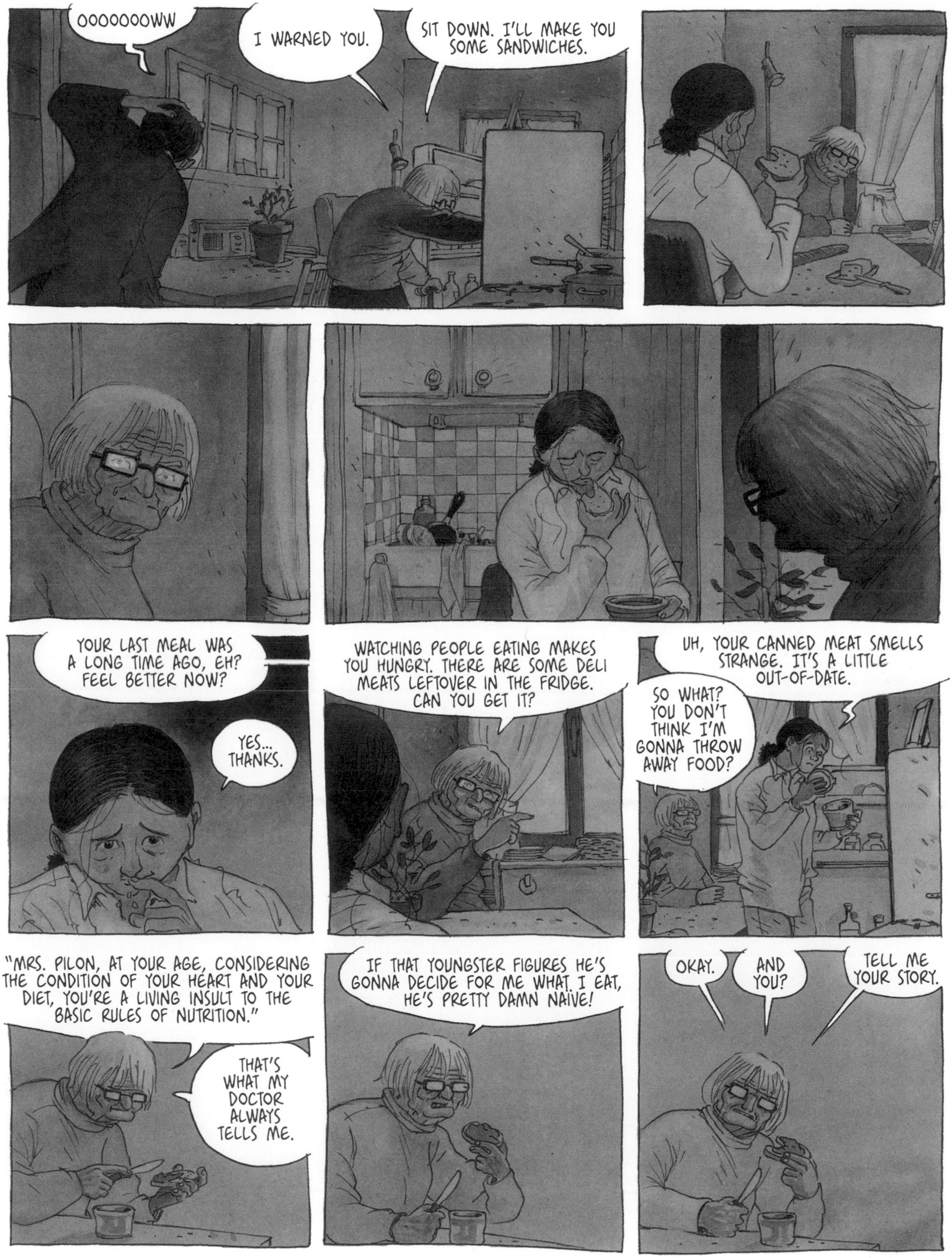
OOOOOOOWW
I WARNED YOU.
SIT DOWN. I'LL MAKE YOU SOME SANDWICHES.
YOUR LAST MEAL WAS A LONG TIME AGO, EH? FEEL BETTER NOW?
YES... THANKS.
WATCHING PEOPLE EATING MAKES YOU HUNGRY. THERE ARE SOME DELI MEATS LEFTOVER IN THE FRIDGE. CAN YOU GET IT?
UH, YOUR CANNED MEAT SMELLS STRANGE. IT'S A LITTLE OUT-OF-DATE.
SO WHAT? YOU DON'T THINK I'M GONNA THROW AWAY FOOD?
"MRS. PILON, AT YOUR AGE, CONSIDERING THE CONDITION OF YOUR HEART AND YOUR DIET, YOU'RE A LIVING INSULT TO THE BASIC RULES OF NUTRITION."
THAT'S WHAT MY DOCTOR ALWAYS TELLS ME.
IF THAT YOUNGSTER FIGURES HE'S GONNA DECIDE FOR ME WHAT I EAT, HE'S PRETTY DAMN NAÏVE!
OKAY.
AND YOU?
TELL ME YOUR STORY.

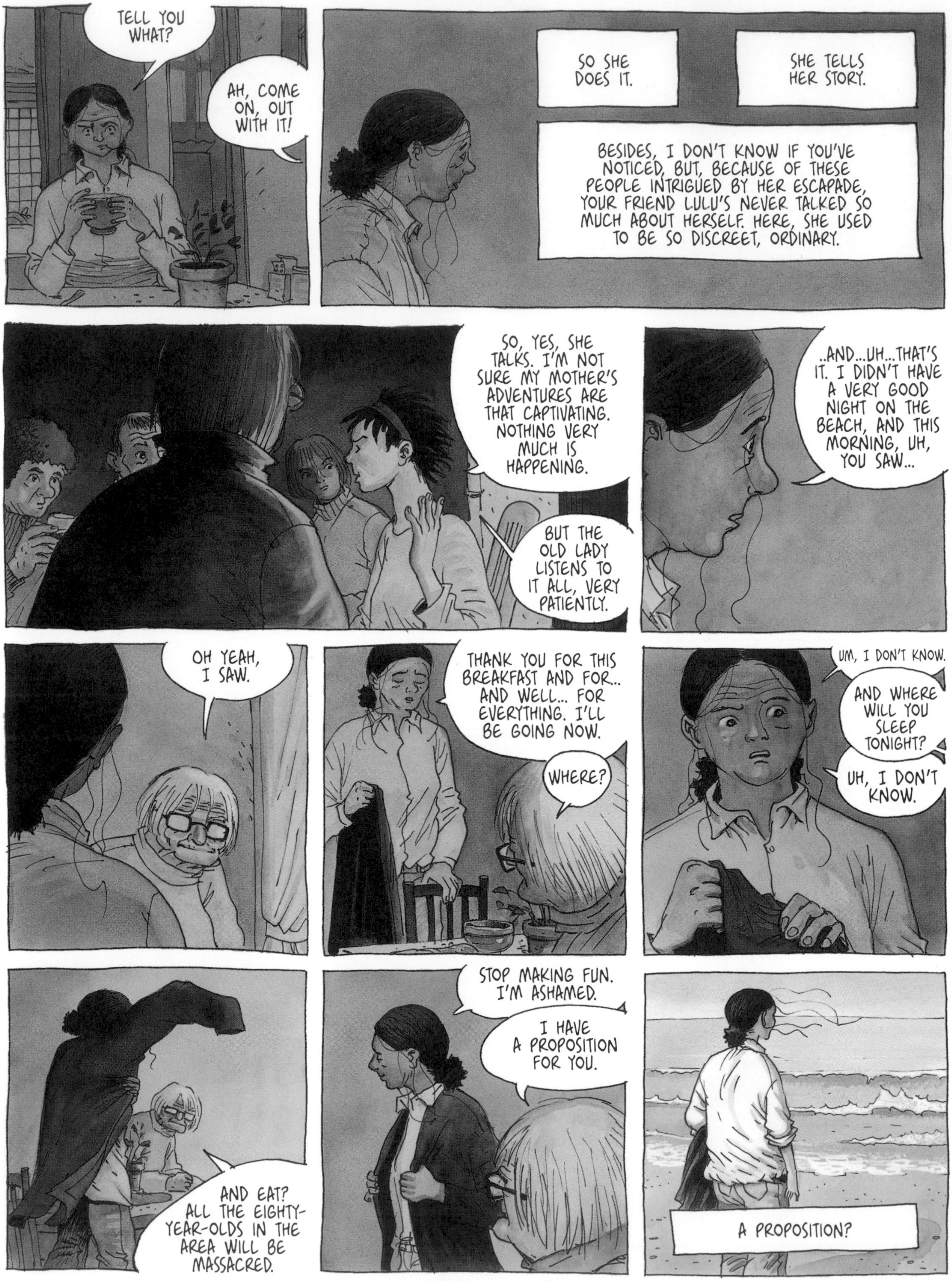
TELL YOU WHAT?
AH, COME ON, OUT WITH IT!
SO SHE DOES IT.
SHE TELLS HER STORY.
BESIDES, I DON'T KNOW IF YOU'VE NOTICED, BUT, BECAUSE OF THESE PEOPLE INTRIGUED BY HER ESCAPADE, YOUR FRIEND LULU'S NEVER TALKED SO MUCH ABOUT HERSELF. HERE, SHE USED TO BE SO DISCREET, ORDINARY.
SO, YES, SHE TALKS. I'M NOT SURE MY MOTHER'S ADVENTURES ARE THAT CAPTIVATING. NOTHING VERY MUCH IS HAPPENING.
BUT THE OLD LADY LISTENS TO IT ALL, VERY PATIENTLY.
..AND...UH...THAT'S IT. I DIDN'T HAVE A VERY GOOD NIGHT ON THE BEACH, AND THIS MORNING, UH, YOU SAW...
OH YEAH, I SAW.
THANK YOU FOR THIS BREAKFAST AND FOR.. AND WELL... FOR EVERYTHING. I'LL BE GOING NOW.
WHERE?
UM, I DON'T KNOW.
AND WHERE WILL YOU SLEEP TONIGHT?
UH, I DON'T KNOW.
AND EAT? ALL THE EIGHTY-YEAR-OLDS IN THE AREA WILL BE MASSACRED.
STOP MAKING FUN. I'M ASHAMED.
I HAVE A PROPOSITION FOR YOU.
A PROPOSITION?

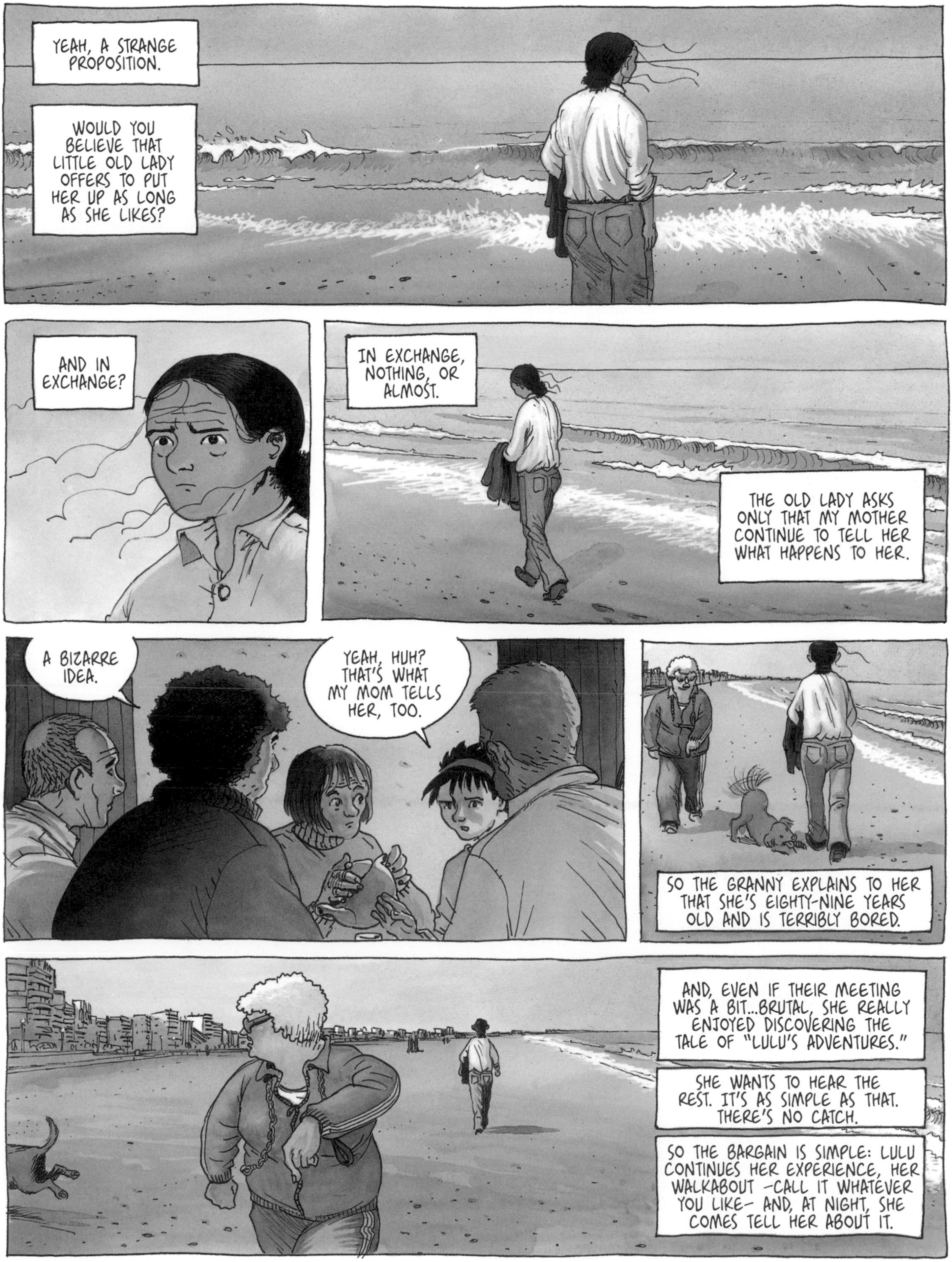
YEAH, A STRANGE PROPOSITION.
WOULD YOU BELIEVE THAT LITTLE OLD LADY OFFERS TO PUT HER UP AS LONG AS SHE LIKES?
AND IN EXCHANGE?
IN EXCHANGE, NOTHING, OR ALMOST.
THE OLD LADY ASKS ONLY THAT MY MOTHER CONTINUE TO TELL HER WHAT HAPPENS TO HER.
A BIZARRE IDEA.
YEAH, HUH? THAT'S WHAT MY MOM TELLS HER, TOO.
SO THE GRANNY EXPLAINS TO HER THAT SHE'S EIGHTY-NINE YEARS OLD AND IS TERRIBLY BORED.
AND, EVEN IF THEIR MEETING WAS A BIT...BRUTAL, SHE REALLY ENJOYED DISCOVERING THE TALE OF "LULU'S ADVENTURES."
SHE WANTS TO HEAR THE REST. IT'S AS SIMPLE AS THAT. THERE'S NO CATCH.
SO THE BARGAIN IS SIMPLE: LULU CONTINUES HER EXPERIENCE, HER WALKABOUT –CALL IT WHATEVER YOU LIKE– AND, AT NIGHT, SHE COMES TELL HER ABOUT IT.

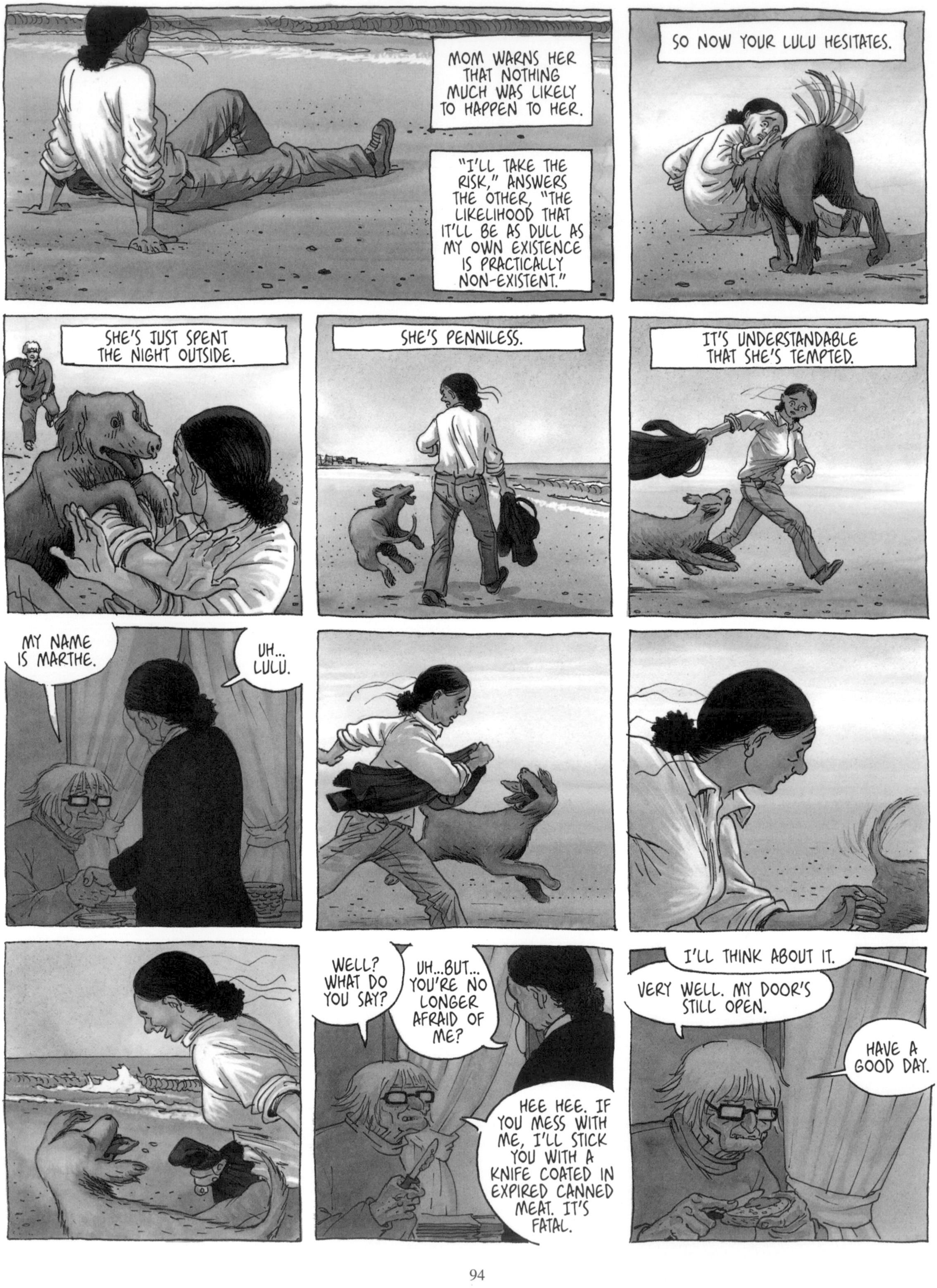
MOM WARNS HER THAT NOTHING MUCH WAS LIKELY TO HAPPEN TO HER.
"I'LL TAKE THE RISK," ANSWERS THE OTHER, "THE LIKELIHOOD THAT IT'LL BE AS DULL AS MY OWN EXISTENCE IS PRACTICALLY NON-EXISTENT."
SO NOW YOUR LULU HESITATES.
SHE'S JUST SPENT THE NIGHT OUTSIDE.
SHE'S PENNILESS.
IT'S UNDERSTANDABLE THAT SHE'S TEMPTED.
MY NAME IS MARTHE.
UH... LULU.
WELL? WHAT DO YOU SAY?
UH...BUT... YOU'RE NO LONGER AFRAID OF ME?
HEE HEE. IF YOU MESS WITH ME, I'LL STICK YOU WITH A KNIFE COATED IN EXPIRED CANNED MEAT. IT'S FATAL.
I'LL THINK ABOUT IT.
VERY WELL. MY DOOR'S STILL OPEN.
HAVE A GOOD DAY.

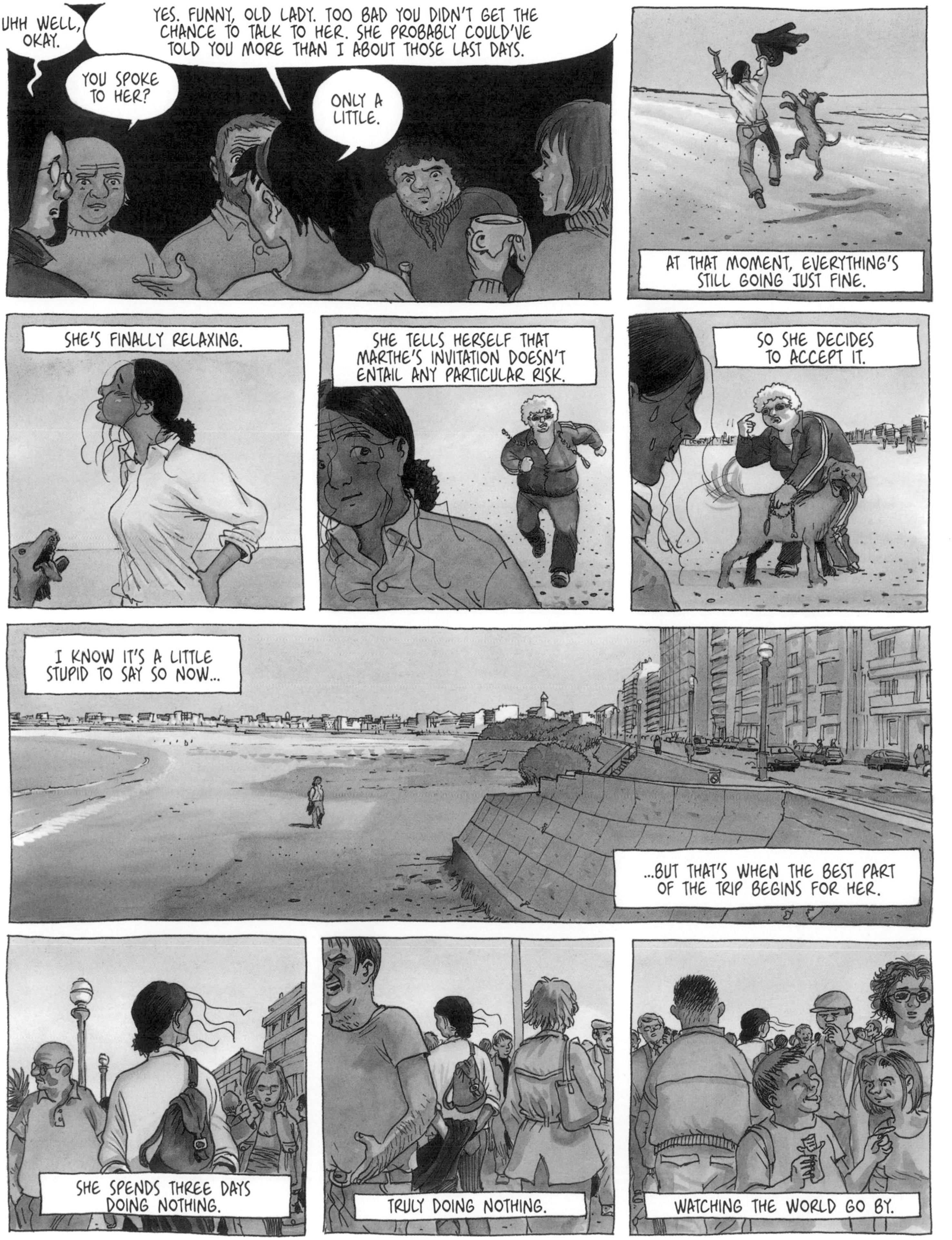
UHH WELL, OKAY.
YES. FUNNY, OLD LADY. TOO BAD YOU DIDN'T GET THE CHANCE TO TALK TO HER. SHE PROBABLY COULD'VE TOLD YOU MORE THAN I ABOUT THOSE LAST DAYS.
YOU SPOKE TO HER?
ONLY A LITTLE.
AT THAT MOMENT, EVERYTHING'S STILL GOING JUST FINE.
SHE'S FINALLY RELAXING.
SHE TELLS HERSELF THAT MARTHE'S INVITATION DOESN'T ENTAIL ANY PARTICULAR RISK.
SO SHE DECIDES TO ACCEPT IT.
I KNOW IT'S A LITTLE STUPID TO SAY SO NOW...
...BUT THAT'S WHEN THE BEST PART OF THE TRIP BEGINS FOR HER.
SHE SPENDS THREE DAYS DOING NOTHING.
TRULY DOING NOTHING.
WATCHING THE WORLD GO BY.

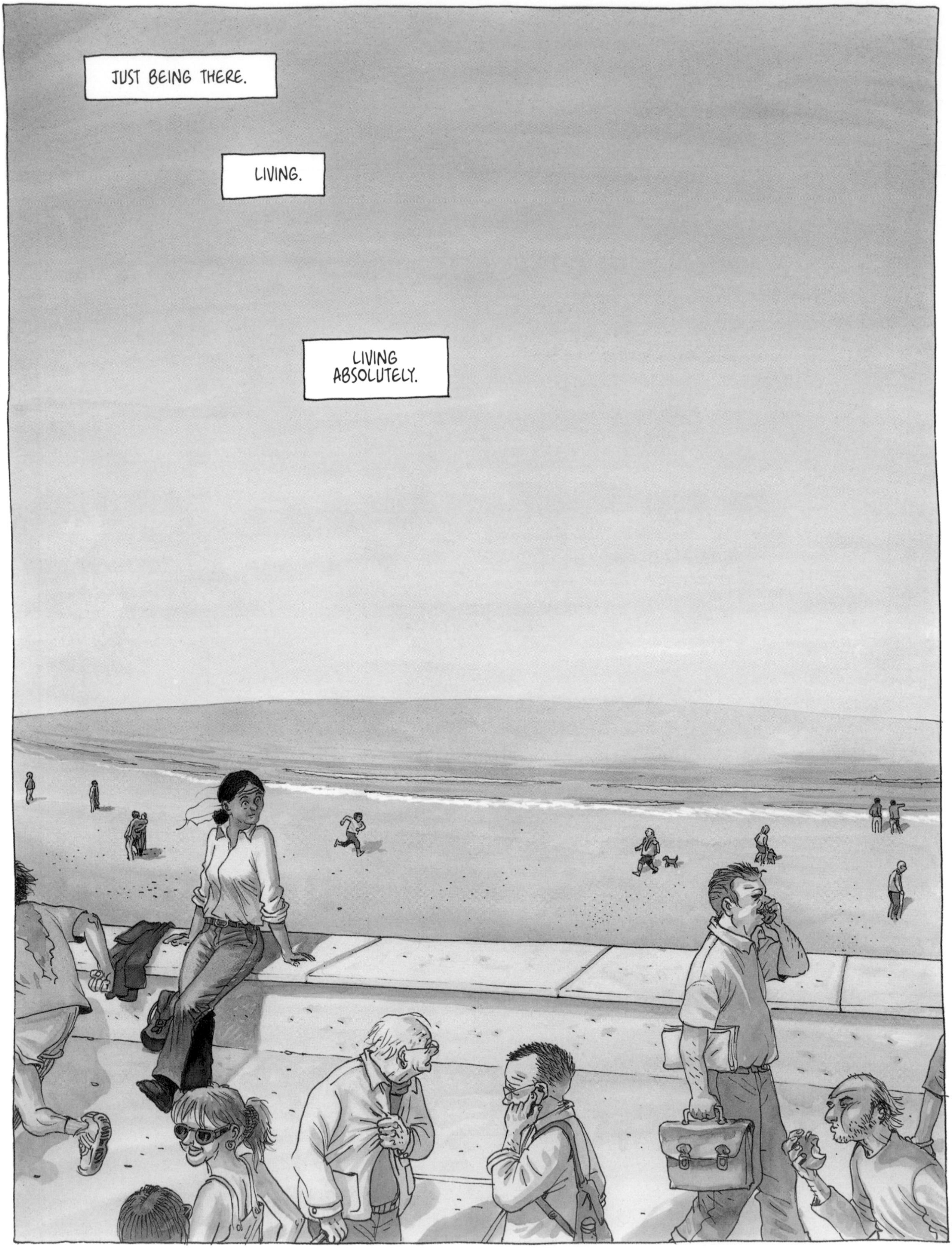
JUST BEING THERE.
LIVING.
LIVING ABSOLUTELY.

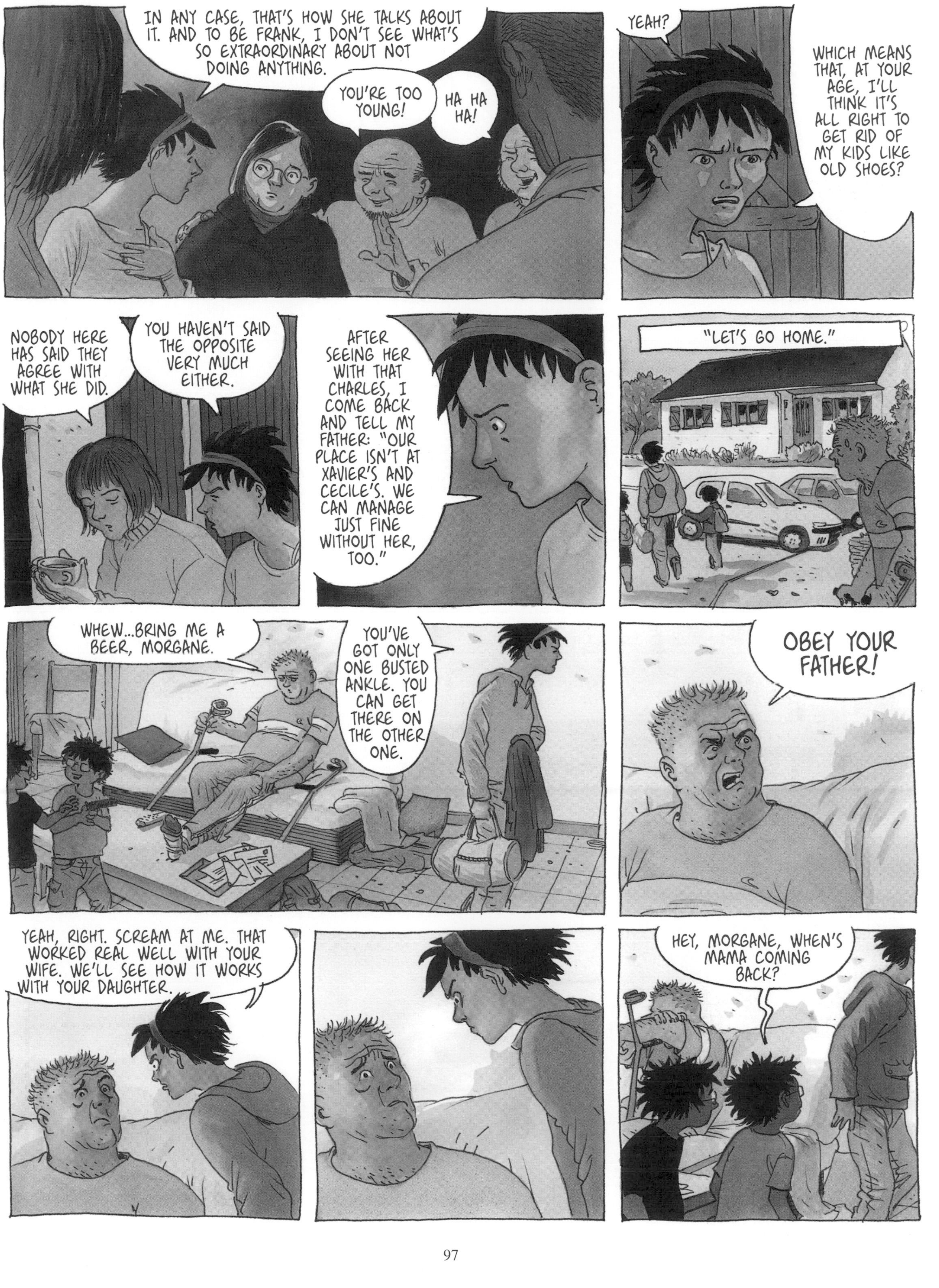
IN ANY CASE, THAT'S HOW SHE TALKS ABOUT IT. AND TO BE FRANK, I DON'T SEE WHAT'S SO EXTRAORDINARY ABOUT NOT DOING ANYTHING.
YOU'RE TOO YOUNG!
HA HA HA!
YEAH?
WHICH MEANS THAT, AT YOUR AGE, I'LL THINK IT'S ALL RIGHT TO GET RID OF MY KIDS LIKE OLD SHOES?
NOBODY HERE HAS SAID THEY AGREE WITH WHAT SHE DID.
YOU HAVEN'T SAID THE OPPOSITE VERY MUCH EITHER.
AFTER SEEING HER WITH THAT CHARLES, I COME BACK AND TELL MY FATHER: "OUR PLACE ISN'T AT XAVIER'S AND CECILE'S. WE CAN MANAGE JUST FINE WITHOUT HER, TOO."
"LET'S GO HOME."
WHEW...BRING ME A BEER, MORGANE.
YOU'VE GOT ONLY ONE BUSTED ANKLE. YOU CAN GET THERE ON THE OTHER ONE.
OBEY YOUR FATHER!
YEAH, RIGHT. SCREAM AT ME. THAT WORKED REAL WELL WITH YOUR WIFE. WE'LL SEE HOW IT WORKS WITH YOUR DAUGHTER.
HEY, MORGANE, WHEN'S MAMA COMING BACK?

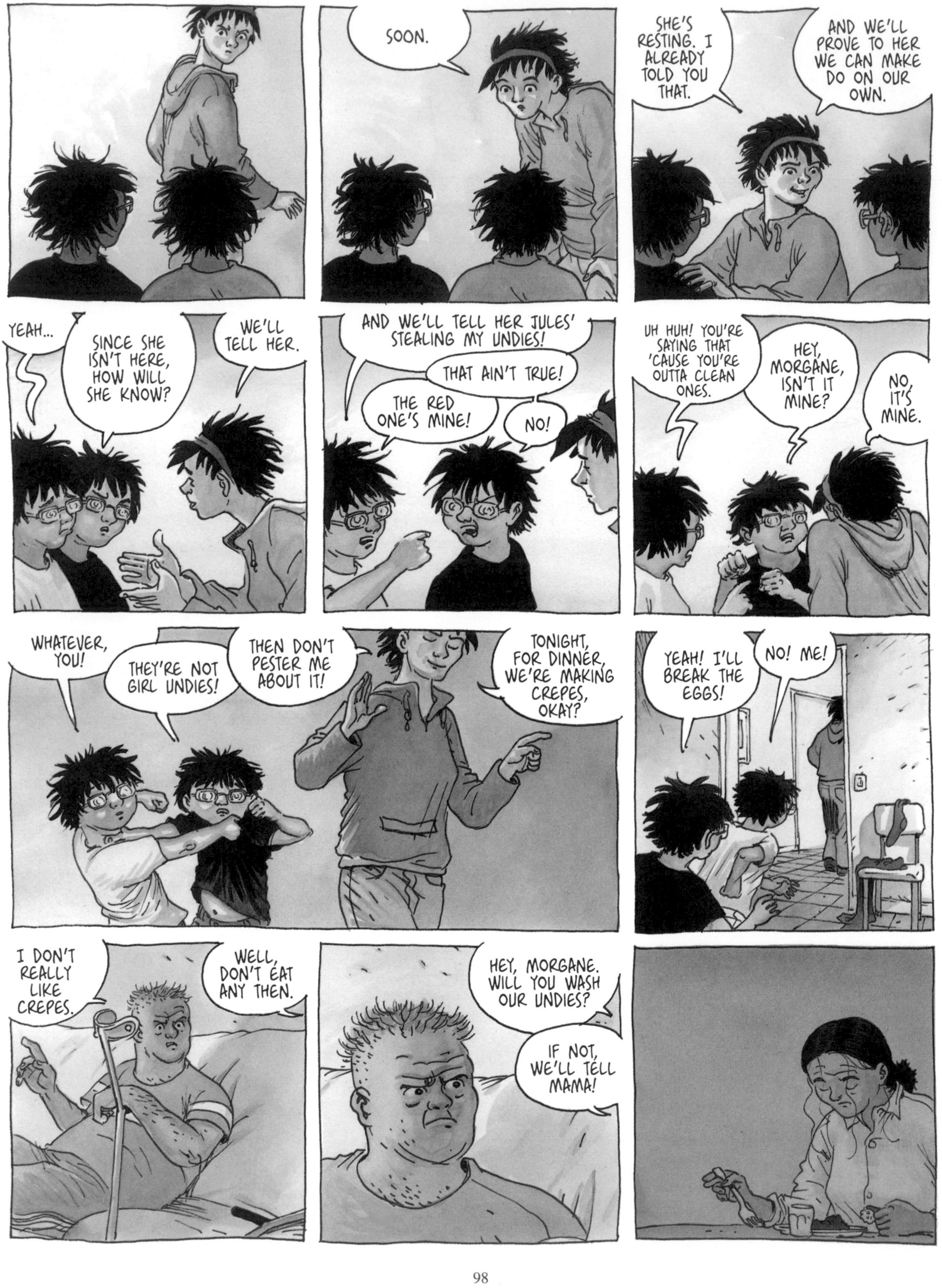
SOON.
SHE'S RESTING. I ALREADY TOLD YOU THAT.
AND WE'LL PROVE TO HER WE CAN MAKE DO ON OUR OWN.
YEAH...
SINCE SHE ISN'T HERE, HOW WILL SHE KNOW?
WE'LL TELL HER.
AND WE'LL TELL HER JULES' STEALING MY UNDIES!
THAT AIN'T TRUE!
THE RED ONE'S MINE!
NO!
UH HUH! YOU'RE SAYING THAT 'CAUSE YOU'RE OUTTA CLEAN ONES.
HEY, MORGANE, ISN'T IT MINE?
NO, IT'S MINE.
WHATEVER, YOU!
THEY'RE NOT GIRL UNDIES!
THEN DON'T PESTER ME ABOUT IT!
TONIGHT, FOR DINNER, WE'RE MAKING CREPES, OKAY?
YEAH! I'LL BREAK THE EGGS!
NO! ME!
I DON'T REALLY LIKE CREPES.
WELL, DON'T EAT ANY THEN.
HEY, MORGANE. WILL YOU WASH OUR UNDIES?
IF NOT, WE'LL TELL MAMA!

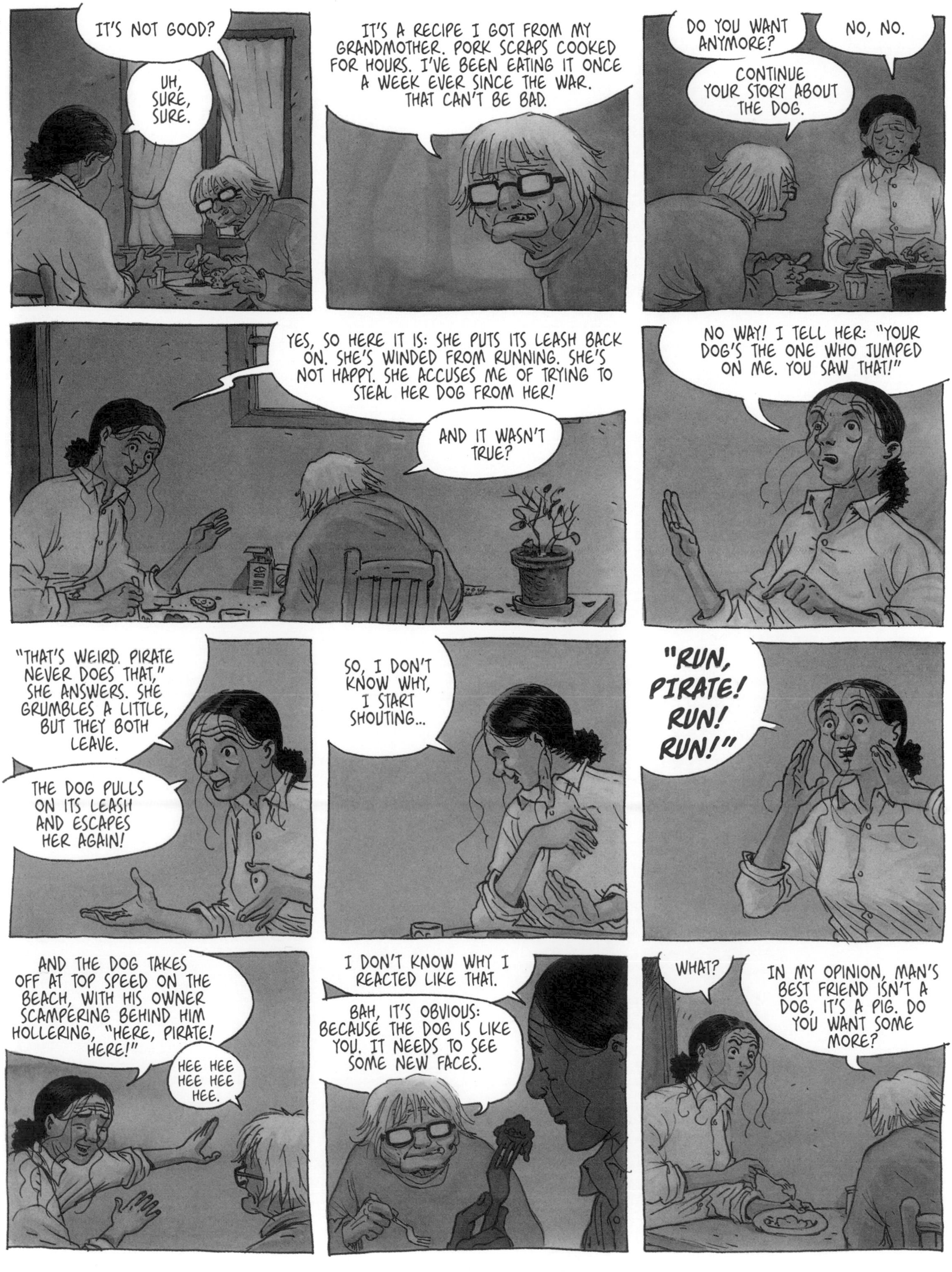
IT'S NOT GOOD?
UH, SURE, SURE.
IT'S A RECIPE I GOT FROM MY GRANDMOTHER. PORK SCRAPS COOKED FOR HOURS. I'VE BEEN EATING IT ONCE A WEEK EVER SINCE THE WAR. THAT CAN'T BE BAD.
DO YOU WANT ANYMORE?
NO, NO.
CONTINUE YOUR STORY ABOUT THE DOG.
YES, SO HERE IT IS: SHE PUTS ITS LEASH BACK ON. SHE'S WINDED FROM RUNNING. SHE'S NOT HAPPY. SHE ACCUSES ME OF TRYING TO STEAL HER DOG FROM HER!
AND IT WASN'T TRUE?
NO WAY! I TELL HER: "YOUR DOG'S THE ONE WHO JUMPED ON ME. YOU SAW THAT!"
"THAT'S WEIRD. PIRATE NEVER DOES THAT," SHE ANSWERS. SHE GRUMBLES A LITTLE, BUT THEY BOTH LEAVE.
THE DOG PULLS ON ITS LEASH AND ESCAPES HER AGAIN!
SO, I DON'T KNOW WHY, I START SHOUTING...
"RUN, PIRATE! RUN! RUN!"
AND THE DOG TAKES OFF AT TOP SPEED ON THE BEACH, WITH HIS OWNER SCAMPERING BEHIND HIM HOLLERING, "HERE, PIRATE! HERE!"
HEE HEE HEE HEE HEE.
I DON'T KNOW WHY I REACTED LIKE THAT.
BAH, IT'S OBVIOUS: BECAUSE THE DOG IS LIKE YOU. IT NEEDS TO SEE SOME NEW FACES.
WHAT?
IN MY OPINION, MAN'S BEST FRIEND ISN'T A DOG, IT'S A PIG. DO YOU WANT SOME MORE?

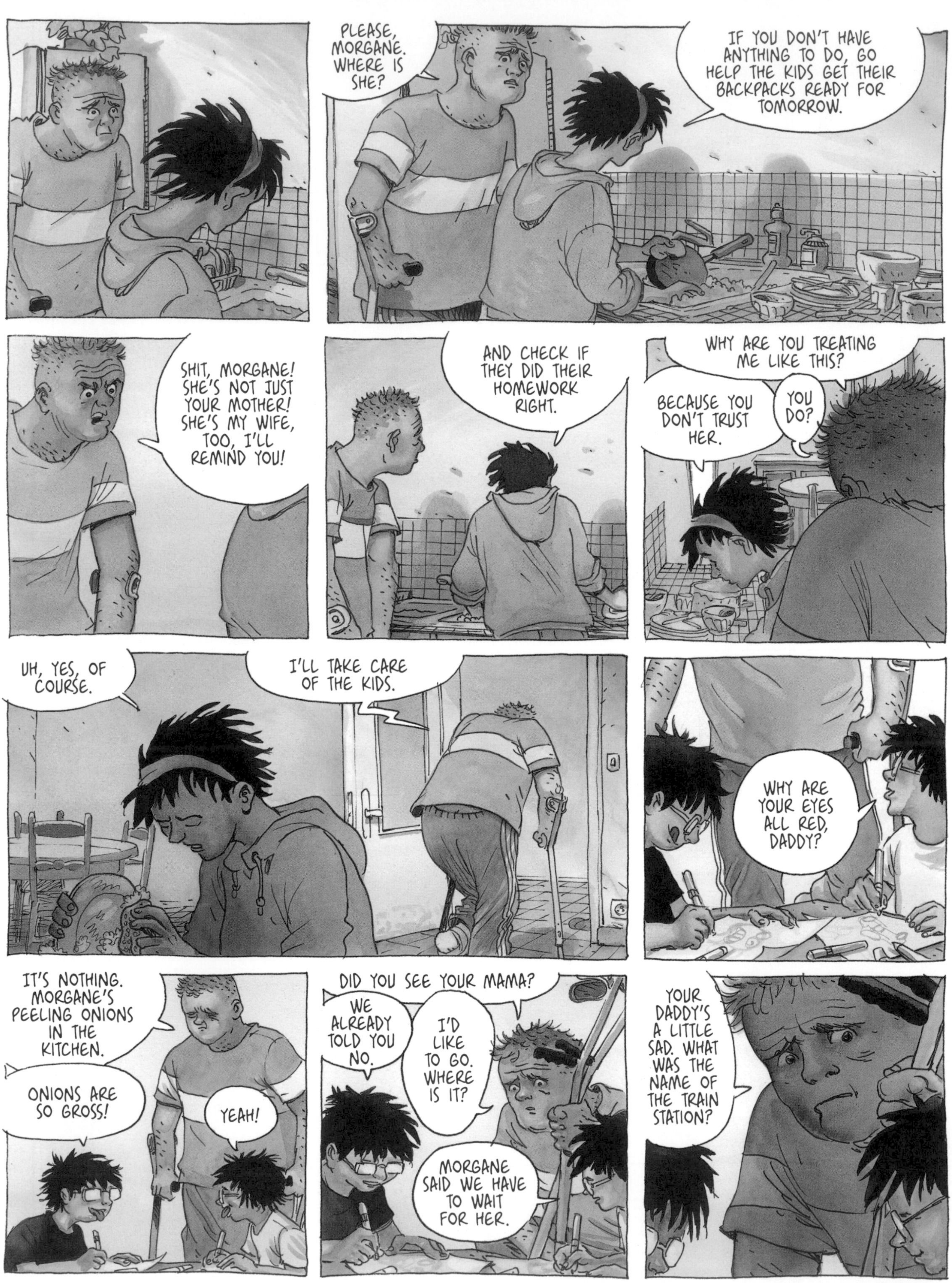
PLEASE, MORGANE. WHERE IS SHE?
IF YOU DON'T HAVE ANYTHING TO DO, GO HELP THE KIDS GET THEIR BACKPACKS READY FOR TOMORROW.
SHIT, MORGANE! SHE'S NOT JUST YOUR MOTHER! SHE'S MY WIFE, TOO, I'LL REMIND YOU!
AND CHECK IF THEY DID THEIR HOMEWORK RIGHT.
WHY ARE YOU TREATING ME LIKE THIS?
BECAUSE YOU DON'T TRUST HER.
YOU DO?
UH, YES, OF COURSE.
I'LL TAKE CARE OF THE KIDS.
WHY ARE YOUR EYES ALL RED, DADDY?
IT'S NOTHING. MORGANE'S PEELING ONIONS IN THE KITCHEN.
ONIONS ARE SO GROSS!
YEAH!
DID YOU SEE YOUR MAMA?
WE ALREADY TOLD YOU NO.
I'D LIKE TO GO. WHERE IS IT?
MORGANE SAID WE HAVE TO WAIT FOR HER.
YOUR DADDY'S A LITTLE SAD. WHAT WAS THE NAME OF THE TRAIN STATION?

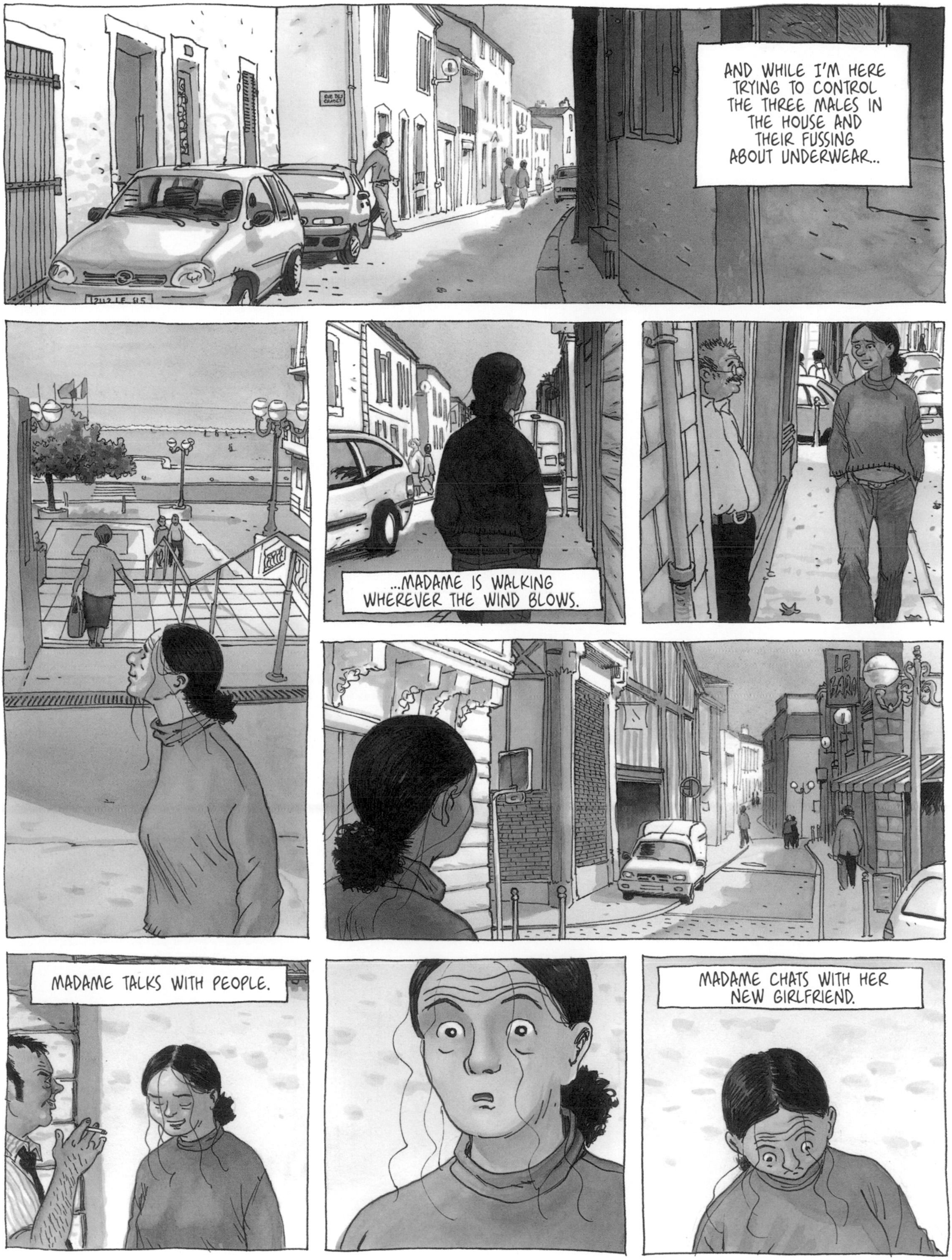
AND WHILE I'M HERE TRYING TO CONTROL THE THREE MALES IN THE HOUSE AND THEIR FUSSING ABOUT UNDERWEAR...
...MADAME IS WALKING WHEREVER THE WIND BLOWS.
MADAME TALKS WITH PEOPLE.
MADAME CHATS WITH HER NEW GIRLFRIEND.

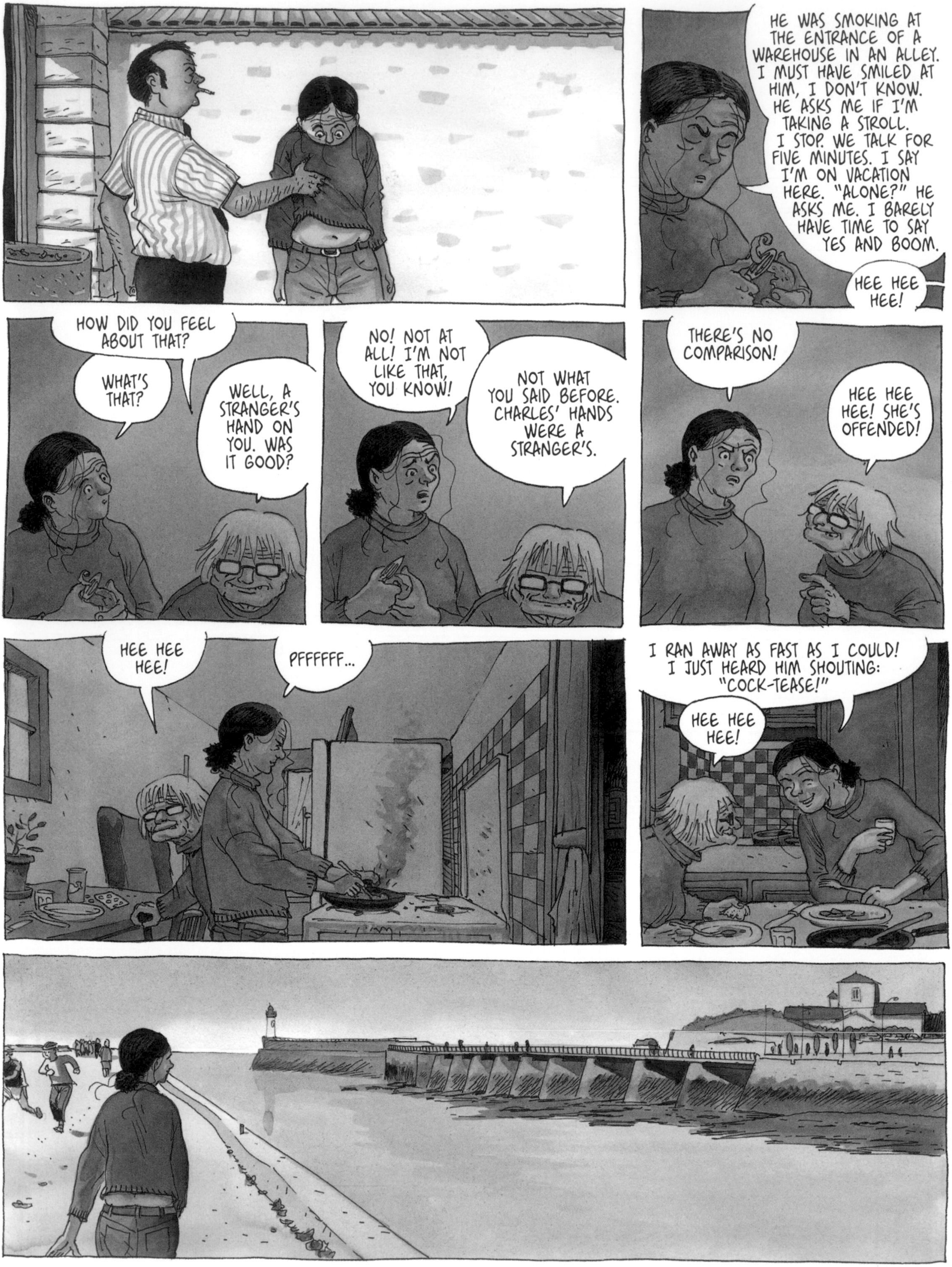
HE WAS SMOKING AT THE ENTRANCE OF A WAREHOUSE IN AN ALLEY. I MUST HAVE SMILED AT HIM, I DON'T KNOW. HE ASKS ME IF I'M TAKING A STROLL. I STOP. WE TALK FOR FIVE MINUTES. I SAY I'M ON VACATION HERE. "ALONE?" HE ASKS ME. I BARELY HAVE TIME TO SAY YES AND BOOM.
HEE HEE HEE!
HOW DID YOU FEEL ABOUT THAT?
WHAT'S THAT?
WELL, A STRANGER'S HAND ON YOU. WAS IT GOOD?
NO! NOT AT ALL! I'M NOT LIKE THAT, YOU KNOW!
NOT WHAT YOU SAID BEFORE. CHARLES' HANDS WERE A STRANGER'S.
THERE'S NO COMPARISON!
HEE HEE HEE! SHE'S OFFENDED!
HEE HEE HEE!
PFFFFFF...
I RAN AWAY AS FAST AS I COULD! I JUST HEARD HIM SHOUTING: "COCK-TEASE!"
HEE HEE HEE!

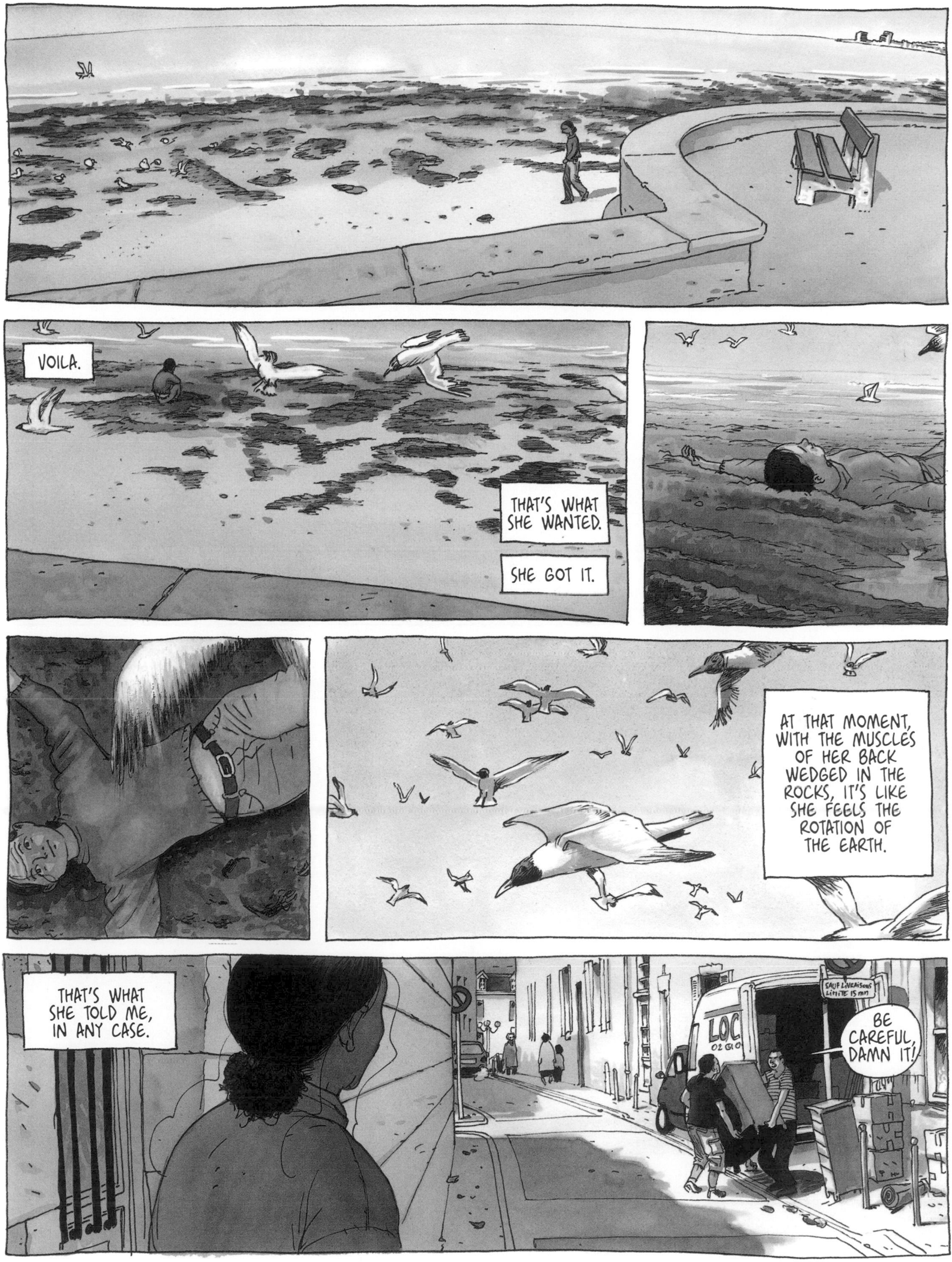
VOILA.
THAT'S WHAT SHE WANTED.
SHE GOT IT.
AT THAT MOMENT, WITH THE MUSCLES OF HER BACK WEDGED IN THE ROCKS, IT'S LIKE SHE FEELS THE ROTATION OF THE EARTH.
THAT'S WHAT SHE TOLD ME, IN ANY CASE.
LOC
BE CAREFUL, DAMN IT!

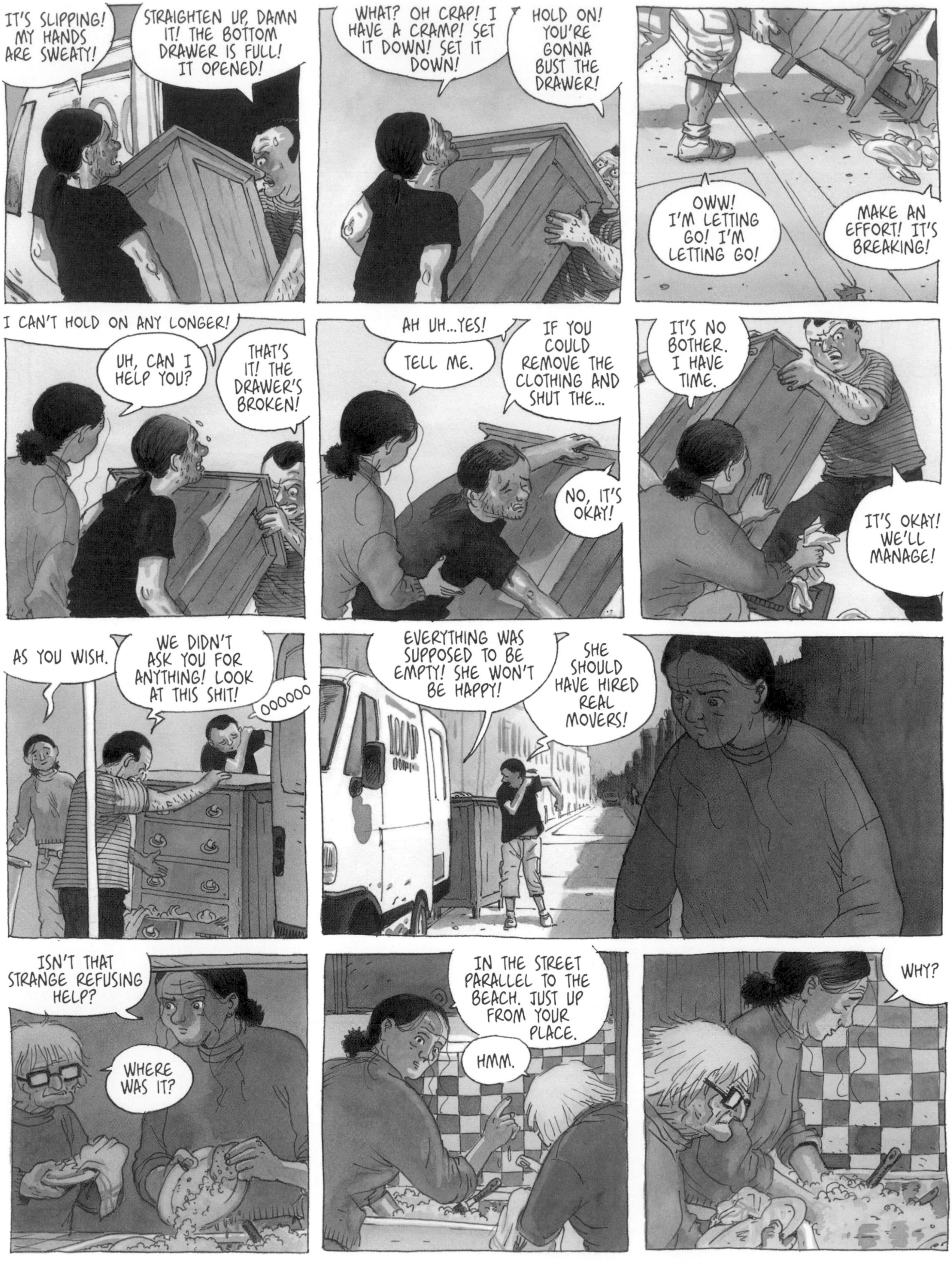
IT'S SLIPPING! MY HANDS ARE SWEATY!
STRAIGHTEN UP, DAMN IT! THE BOTTOM DRAWER IS FULL! IT OPENED!
WHAT? OH CRAP! I HAVE A CRAMP! SET IT DOWN! SET IT DOWN!
HOLD ON! YOU'RE GONNA BUST THE DRAWER!
OWW! I'M LETTING GO! I'M LETTING GO!
MAKE AN EFFORT! IT'S BREAKING!
I CAN'T HOLD ON ANY LONGER!
UH, CAN I HELP YOU?
THAT'S IT! THE DRAWER'S BROKEN!
AH UH...YES!
TELL ME.
IF YOU COULD REMOVE THE CLOTHING AND SHUT THE...
NO, IT'S OKAY!
IT'S NO BOTHER. I HAVE TIME.
IT'S OKAY! WE'LL MANAGE!
AS YOU WISH.
WE DIDN'T ASK YOU FOR ANYTHING! LOOK AT THIS SHIT!
OOOOOO
EVERYTHING WAS SUPPOSED TO BE EMPTY! SHE WON'T BE HAPPY!
SHE SHOULD HAVE HIRED REAL MOVERS!
ISN'T THAT STRANGE REFUSING HELP?
WHERE WAS IT?
IN THE STREET PARALLEL TO THE BEACH. JUST UP FROM YOUR PLACE.
HMM.
WHY?

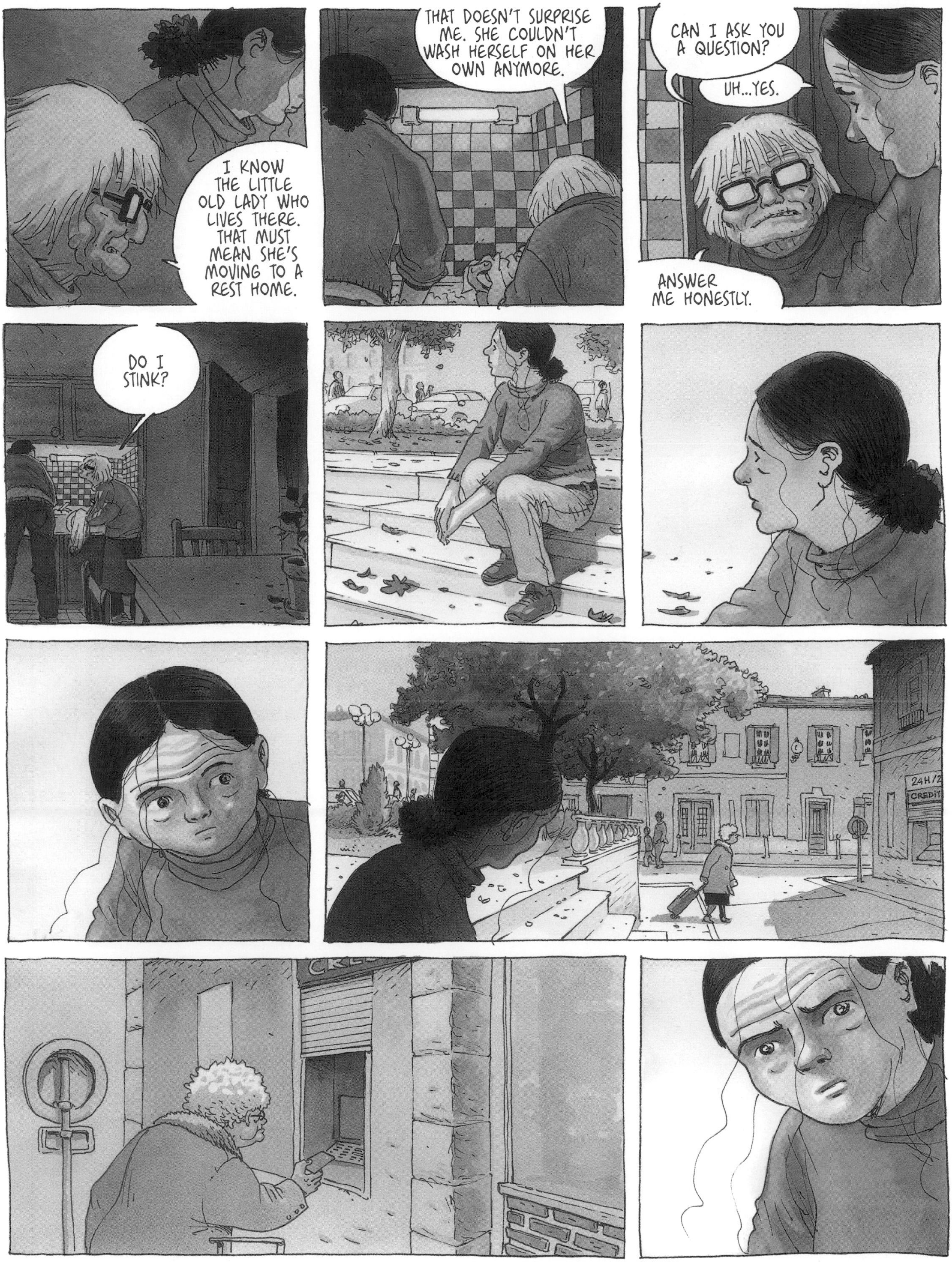

I KNOW THE LITTLE OLD LADY WHO LIVES THERE. THAT MUST MEAN SHE'S MOVING TO A REST HOME.
THAT DOESN'T SURPRISE ME. SHE COULDN'T WASH HERSELF ON HER OWN ANYMORE.
CAN I ASK YOU A QUESTION?
UH...YES.
ANSWER ME HONESTLY.
DO I STINK?
24H/2
CREDIT
CRED

WHILE OBSERVING HER, I'M WONDERING WHETHER, IN THE END, I'M CAPABLE OF IT OR NOT.

SO I APPROACH HER...

I FOLLOW HER FROM A DISTANCE FOR A FEW MINUTES.

AND LIKE WITH YOU, WHEN I'M SURE NOBODY SEES US, I RUN TOWARDS HER!

I JOSTLE HER. SHE LANDS ON HER FACE WITHOUT SAYING ANYTHING.

I..UH...GIVE HER A BIG KICK IN THE GUT.

SHE SHOUTS. I GIVE HER ANOTHER KICK, LESS HARD. SHE QUIETS DOWN.

I SNATCH HER PURSE FROM HER AND RUN AWAY.

AS SOON AS I TURN THE STREET CORNER -I SAW THIS IN MOVIES- I START WALKING CALMLY.

THEN I GO SIT BY MYSELF, ON THE BEACH. I CLOSE MY EYES. IT'S WEIRD, BUT I...I FEEL A KIND OF PRIDE IN SUCCEEDING IN FORCING MYSELF.

THAT'S NO MEAN FEAT, IS IT?

UH...

BUT HEAR THIS...

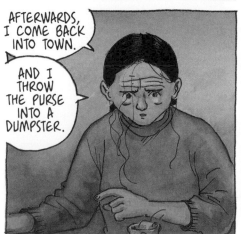

AFTERWARDS, I COME BACK INTO TOWN.

AND I THROW THE PURSE INTO A DUMPSTER.

I JUST COULDN'T STEAL.

OH?

I'M MORE THAN FORTY YEARS OLD, AND THAT'S THE FIRST TIME I'VE REALLY TRIED PHYSICAL VIOLENCE.

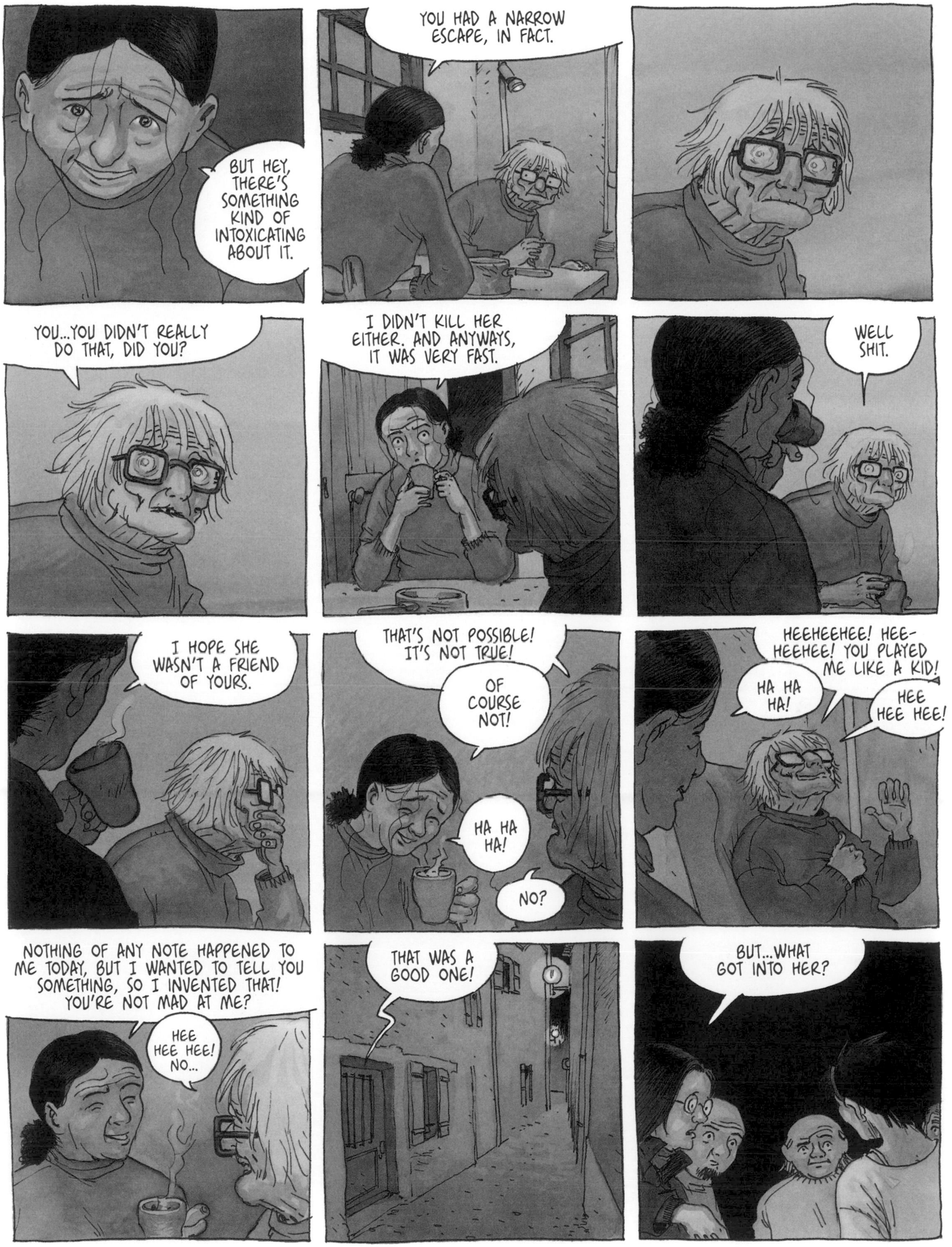
BUT HEY, THERE'S SOMETHING KIND OF INTOXICATING ABOUT IT.
YOU HAD A NARROW ESCAPE, IN FACT.
YOU...YOU DIDN'T REALLY DO THAT, DID YOU?
I DIDN'T KILL HER EITHER. AND ANYWAYS, IT WAS VERY FAST.
WELL SHIT.
I HOPE SHE WASN'T A FRIEND OF YOURS.
THAT'S NOT POSSIBLE! IT'S NOT TRUE!
OF COURSE NOT!
HA HA HA!
NO?
HEEHEEHEE! HEE-HEEHEE! YOU PLAYED ME LIKE A KID!
HA HA HA!
HEE HEE HEE!
NOTHING OF ANY NOTE HAPPENED TO ME TODAY, BUT I WANTED TO TELL YOU SOMETHING, SO I INVENTED THAT! YOU'RE NOT MAD AT ME?
HEE HEE HEE! NO...
THAT WAS A GOOD ONE!
BUT...WHAT GOT INTO HER?

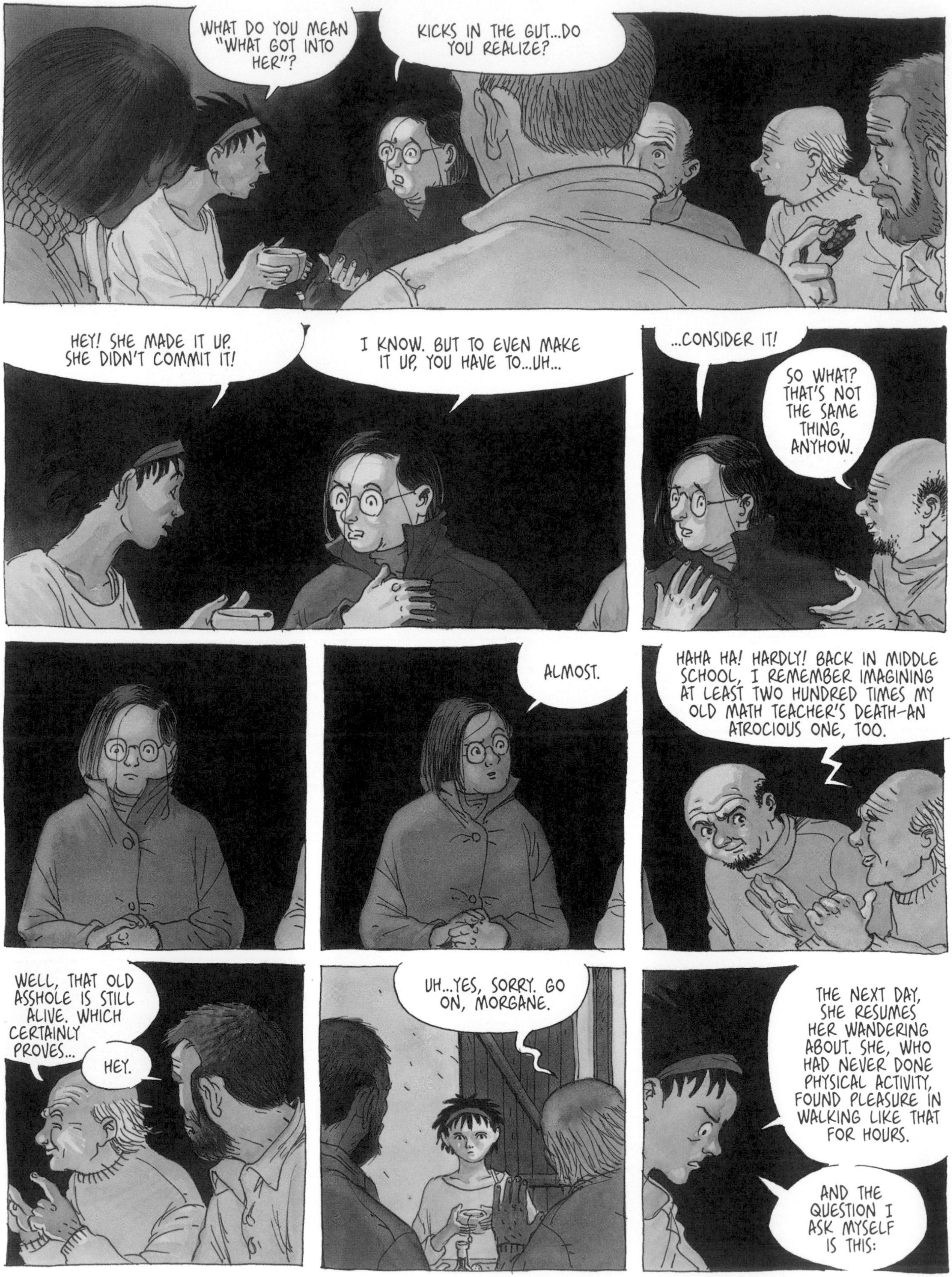
WHAT DO YOU MEAN "WHAT GOT INTO HER"?
KICKS IN THE GUT...DO YOU REALIZE?
HEY! SHE MADE IT UP. SHE DIDN'T COMMIT IT!
I KNOW. BUT TO EVEN MAKE IT UP, YOU HAVE TO...UH...
...CONSIDER IT!
SO WHAT? THAT'S NOT THE SAME THING, ANYHOW.
ALMOST.
HAHA HA! HARDLY! BACK IN MIDDLE SCHOOL, I REMEMBER IMAGINING AT LEAST TWO HUNDRED TIMES MY OLD MATH TEACHER'S DEATH—AN ATROCIOUS ONE, TOO.
WELL, THAT OLD ASSHOLE IS STILL ALIVE. WHICH CERTAINLY PROVES...
HEY.
UH...YES, SORRY. GO ON, MORGANE.
THE NEXT DAY, SHE RESUMES HER WANDERING ABOUT. SHE, WHO HAD NEVER DONE PHYSICAL ACTIVITY, FOUND PLEASURE IN WALKING LIKE THAT FOR HOURS.
AND THE QUESTION I ASK MYSELF IS THIS:

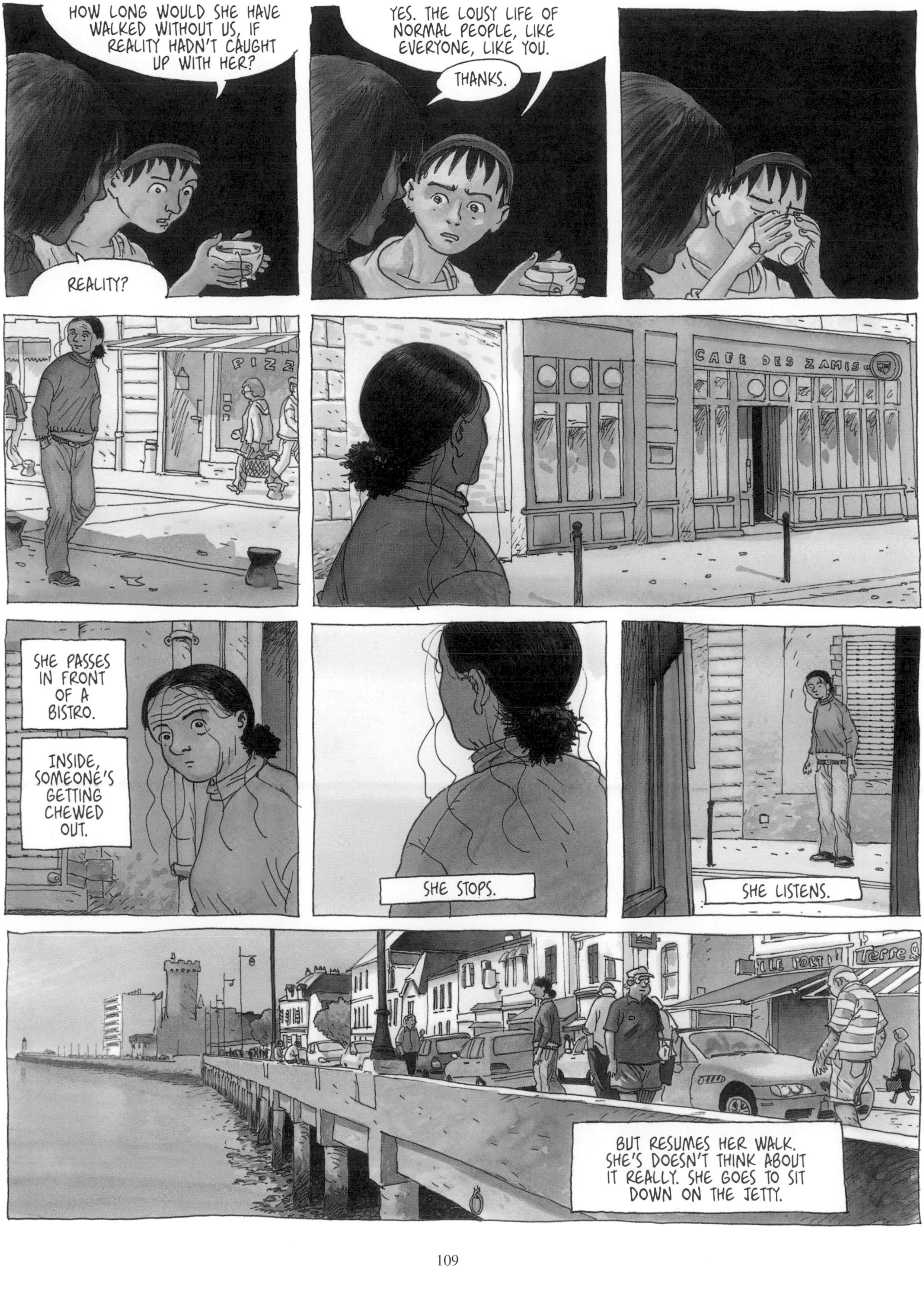
HOW LONG WOULD SHE HAVE WALKED WITHOUT US, IF REALITY HADN'T CAUGHT UP WITH HER?
REALITY?
YES. THE LOUSY LIFE OF NORMAL PEOPLE, LIKE EVERYONE, LIKE YOU.
THANKS.
PIZZ
CAFE DES ZAMIS
SHE PASSES IN FRONT OF A BISTRO.
INSIDE, SOMEONE'S GETTING CHEWED OUT.
SHE STOPS.
SHE LISTENS.
LE PORT
Terre
BUT RESUMES HER WALK. SHE'S DOESN'T THINK ABOUT IT REALLY. SHE GOES TO SIT DOWN ON THE JETTY.

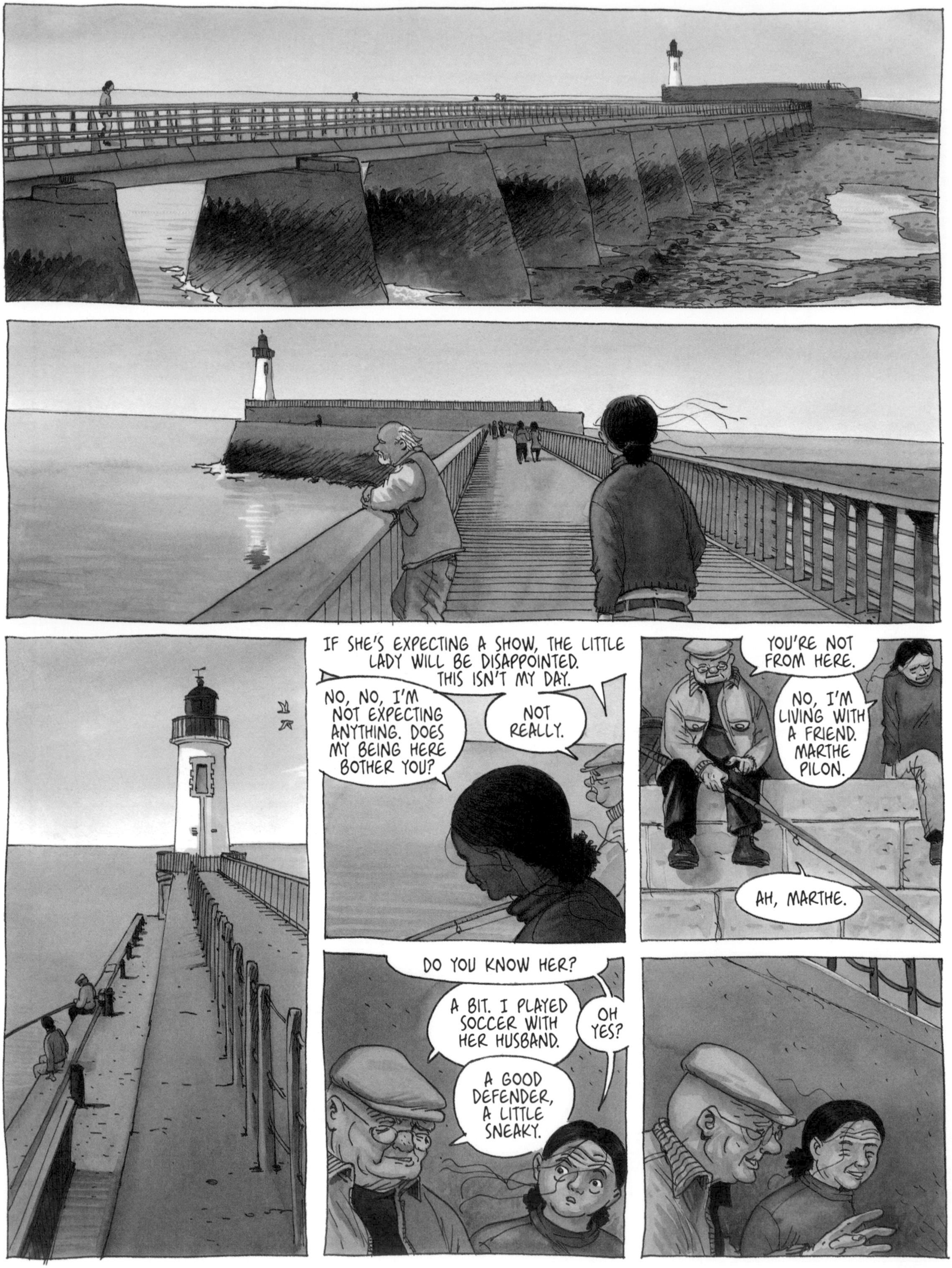

IF SHE'S EXPECTING A SHOW, THE LITTLE LADY WILL BE DISAPPOINTED. THIS ISN'T MY DAY.
NO, NO, I'M NOT EXPECTING ANYTHING. DOES MY BEING HERE BOTHER YOU?
NOT REALLY.
YOU'RE NOT FROM HERE.
NO, I'M LIVING WITH A FRIEND. MARTHE PILON.
AH, MARTHE.
DO YOU KNOW HER?
A BIT. I PLAYED SOCCER WITH HER HUSBAND.
OH YES?
A GOOD DEFENDER, A LITTLE SNEAKY.

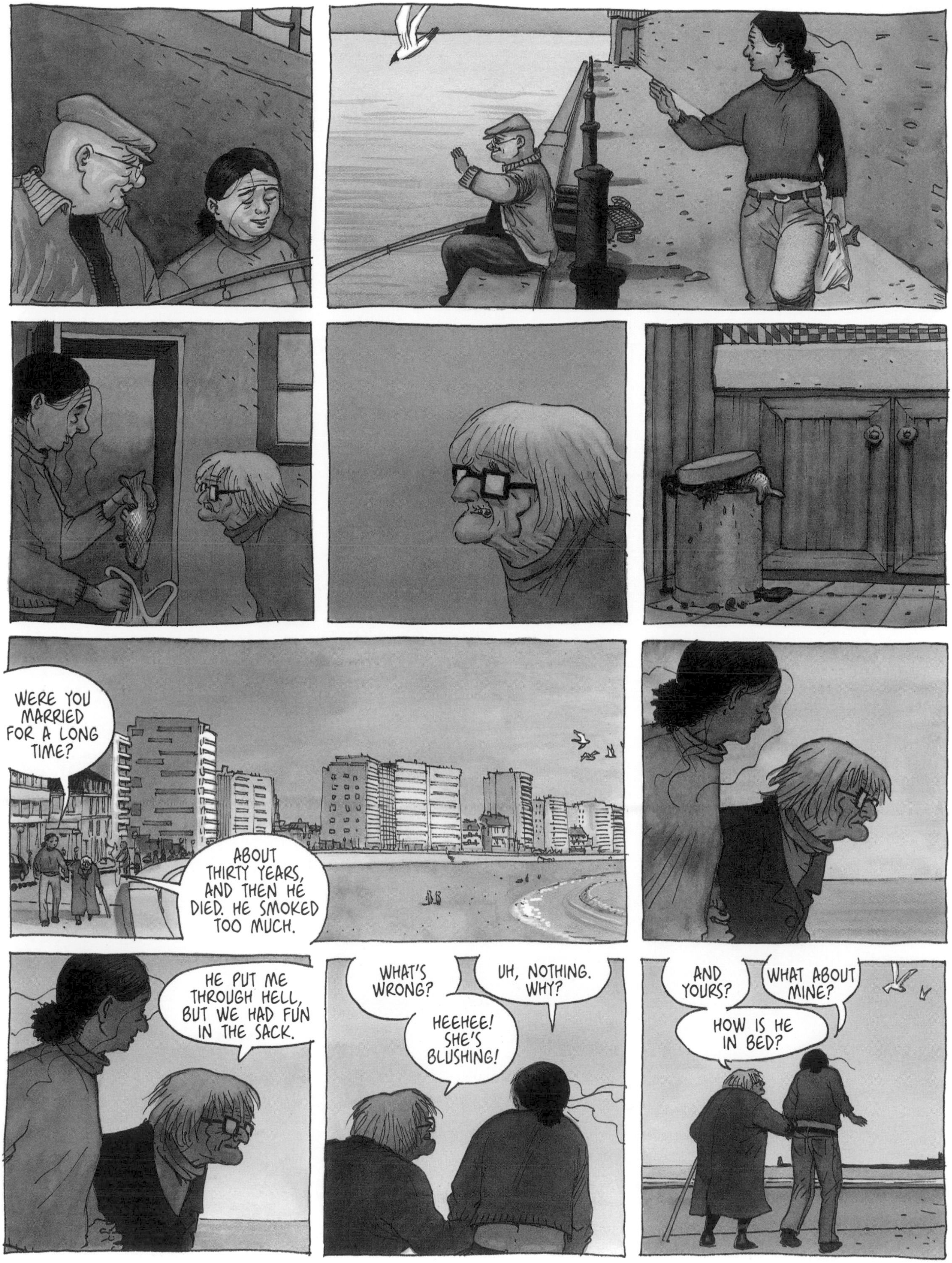

WERE YOU MARRIED FOR A LONG TIME?
ABOUT THIRTY YEARS, AND THEN HE DIED. HE SMOKED TOO MUCH.
HE PUT ME THROUGH HELL, BUT WE HAD FUN IN THE SACK.
WHAT'S WRONG?
UH, NOTHING. WHY?
HEEHEE! SHE'S BLUSHING!
AND YOURS?
WHAT ABOUT MINE?
HOW IS HE IN BED?

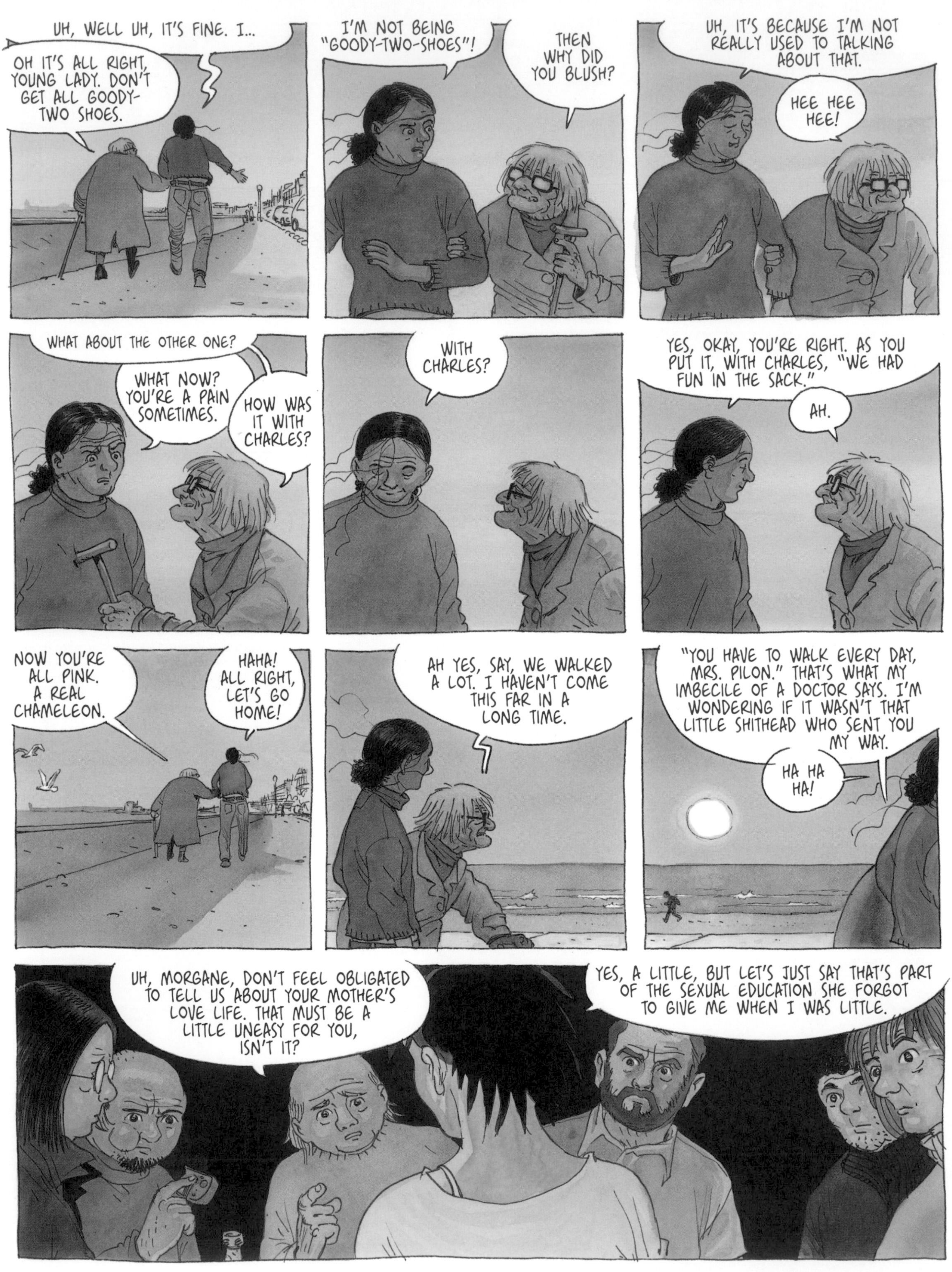
UH, WELL UH, IT'S FINE. I...
OH IT'S ALL RIGHT, YOUNG LADY. DON'T GET ALL GOODY-TWO SHOES.
I'M NOT BEING "GOODY-TWO-SHOES"!
THEN WHY DID YOU BLUSH?
UH, IT'S BECAUSE I'M NOT REALLY USED TO TALKING ABOUT THAT.
HEE HEE HEE!
WHAT ABOUT THE OTHER ONE?
WHAT NOW? YOU'RE A PAIN SOMETIMES.
HOW WAS IT WITH CHARLES?
WITH CHARLES?
YES, OKAY, YOU'RE RIGHT. AS YOU PUT IT, WITH CHARLES, "WE HAD FUN IN THE SACK."
AH.
NOW YOU'RE ALL PINK. A REAL CHAMELEON.
HAHA! ALL RIGHT, LET'S GO HOME!
AH YES, SAY, WE WALKED A LOT. I HAVEN'T COME THIS FAR IN A LONG TIME.
"YOU HAVE TO WALK EVERY DAY, MRS. PILON." THAT'S WHAT MY IMBECILE OF A DOCTOR SAYS. I'M WONDERING IF IT WASN'T THAT LITTLE SHITHEAD WHO SENT YOU MY WAY.
HA HA HA!
UH, MORGANE, DON'T FEEL OBLIGATED TO TELL US ABOUT YOUR MOTHER'S LOVE LIFE. THAT MUST BE A LITTLE UNEASY FOR YOU, ISN'T IT?
YES, A LITTLE, BUT LET'S JUST SAY THAT'S PART OF THE SEXUAL EDUCATION SHE FORGOT TO GIVE ME WHEN I WAS LITTLE.

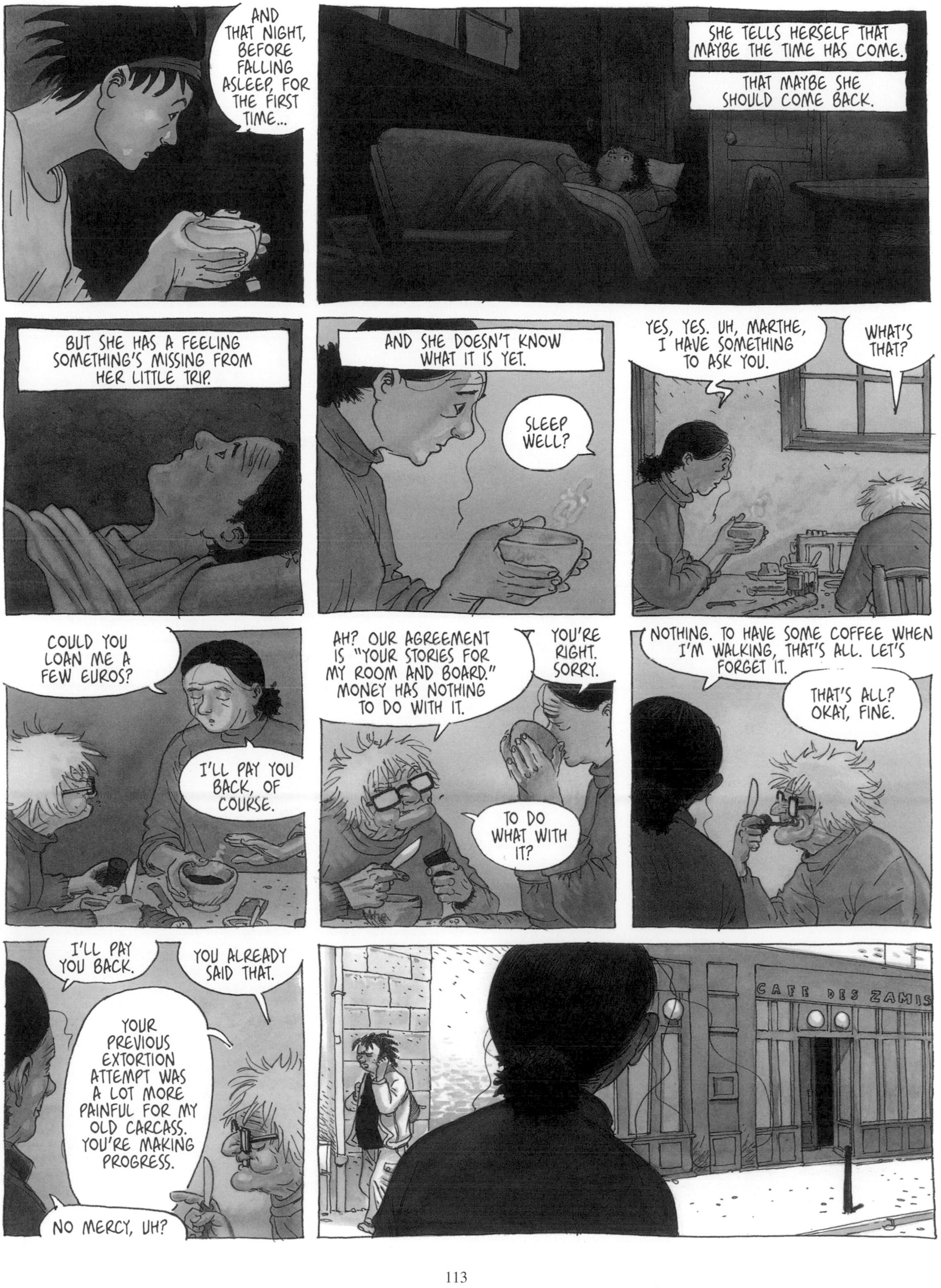
AND THAT NIGHT, BEFORE FALLING ASLEEP, FOR THE FIRST TIME...
SHE TELLS HERSELF THAT MAYBE THE TIME HAS COME.
THAT MAYBE SHE SHOULD COME BACK.
BUT SHE HAS A FEELING SOMETHING'S MISSING FROM HER LITTLE TRIP.
AND SHE DOESN'T KNOW WHAT IT IS YET.
SLEEP WELL?
YES, YES. UH, MARTHE, I HAVE SOMETHING TO ASK YOU.
WHAT'S THAT?
COULD YOU LOAN ME A FEW EUROS?
I'LL PAY YOU BACK, OF COURSE.
AH? OUR AGREEMENT IS "YOUR STORIES FOR MY ROOM AND BOARD." MONEY HAS NOTHING TO DO WITH IT.
YOU'RE RIGHT. SORRY.
TO DO WHAT WITH IT?
NOTHING. TO HAVE SOME COFFEE WHEN I'M WALKING, THAT'S ALL. LET'S FORGET IT.
THAT'S ALL? OKAY, FINE.
I'LL PAY YOU BACK.
YOU ALREADY SAID THAT.
YOUR PREVIOUS EXTORTION ATTEMPT WAS A LOT MORE PAINFUL FOR MY OLD CARCASS. YOU'RE MAKING PROGRESS.
NO MERCY, UH?
CAFE DES ZAMIS

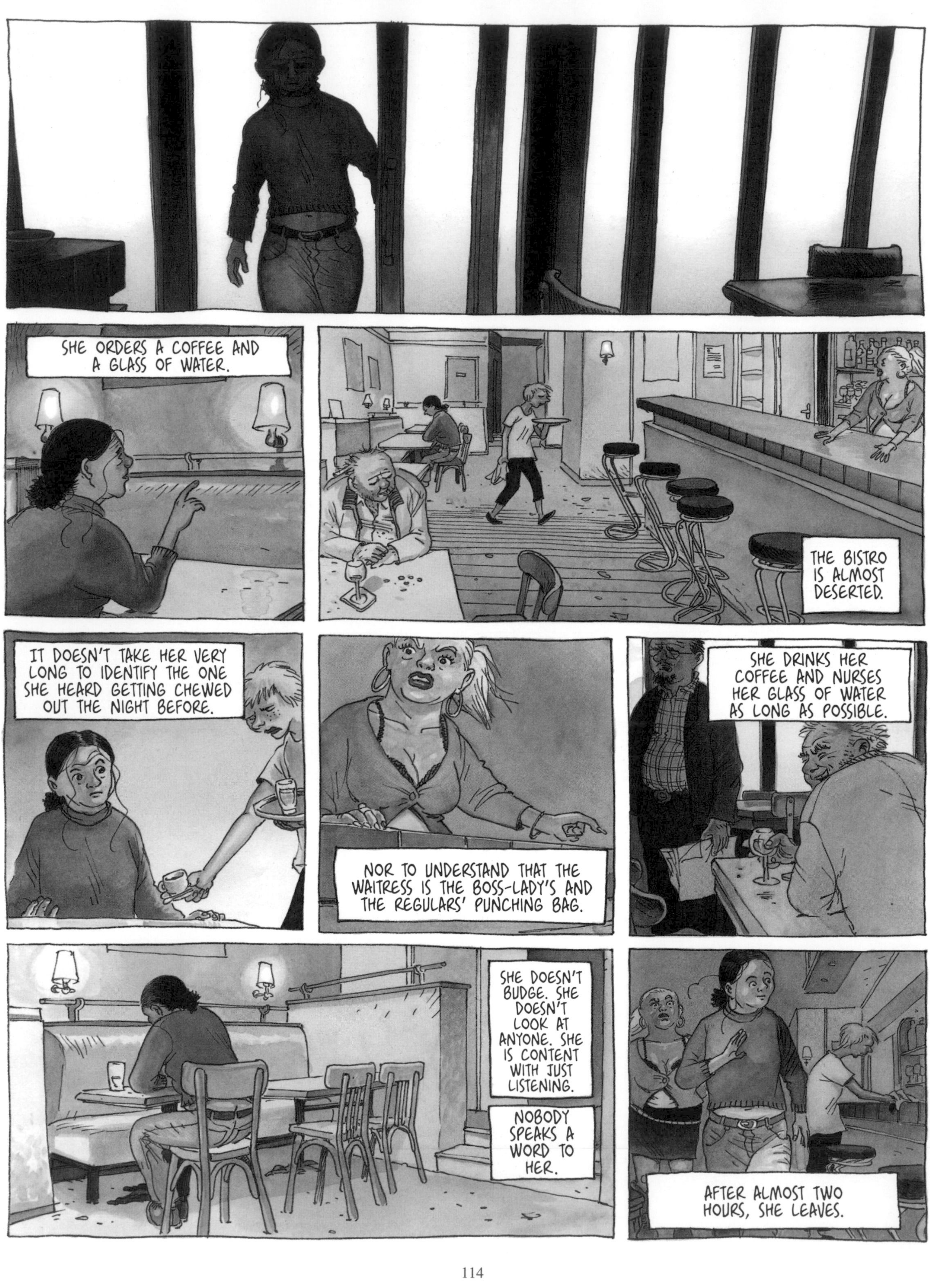
SHE ORDERS A COFFEE AND A GLASS OF WATER.
THE BISTRO IS ALMOST DESERTED.
IT DOESN'T TAKE HER VERY LONG TO IDENTIFY THE ONE SHE HEARD GETTING CHEWED OUT THE NIGHT BEFORE.
NOR TO UNDERSTAND THAT THE WAITRESS IS THE BOSS-LADY'S AND THE REGULARS' PUNCHING BAG.
SHE DRINKS HER COFFEE AND NURSES HER GLASS OF WATER AS LONG AS POSSIBLE.
SHE DOESN'T BUDGE. SHE DOESN'T LOOK AT ANYONE. SHE IS CONTENT WITH JUST LISTENING.
NOBODY SPEAKS A WORD TO HER.
AFTER ALMOST TWO HOURS, SHE LEAVES.

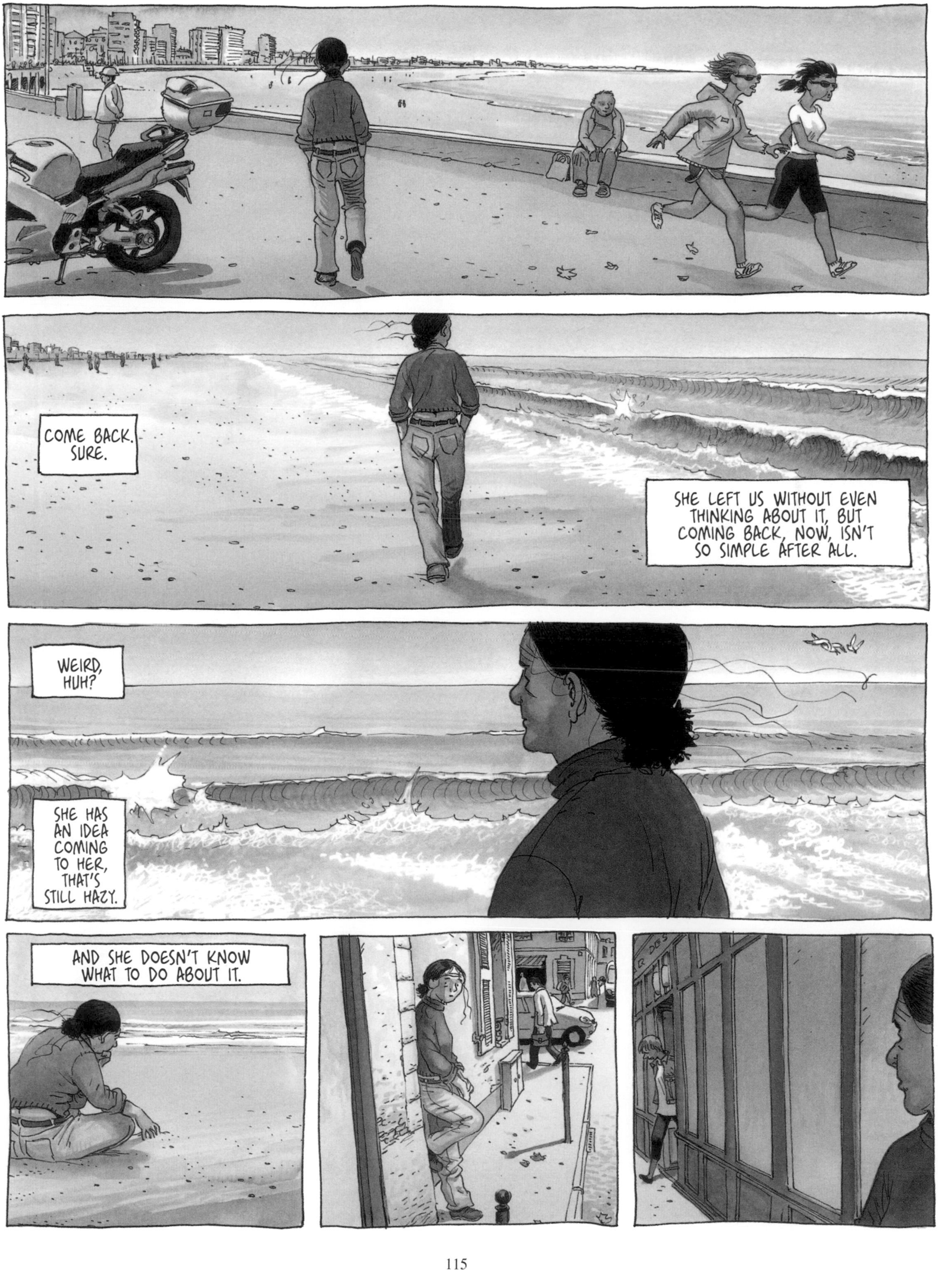
COME BACK. SURE.
SHE LEFT US WITHOUT EVEN THINKING ABOUT IT, BUT COMING BACK, NOW, ISN'T SO SIMPLE AFTER ALL.
WEIRD, HUH?
SHE HAS AN IDEA COMING TO HER, THAT'S STILL HAZY.
AND SHE DOESN'T KNOW WHAT TO DO ABOUT IT.

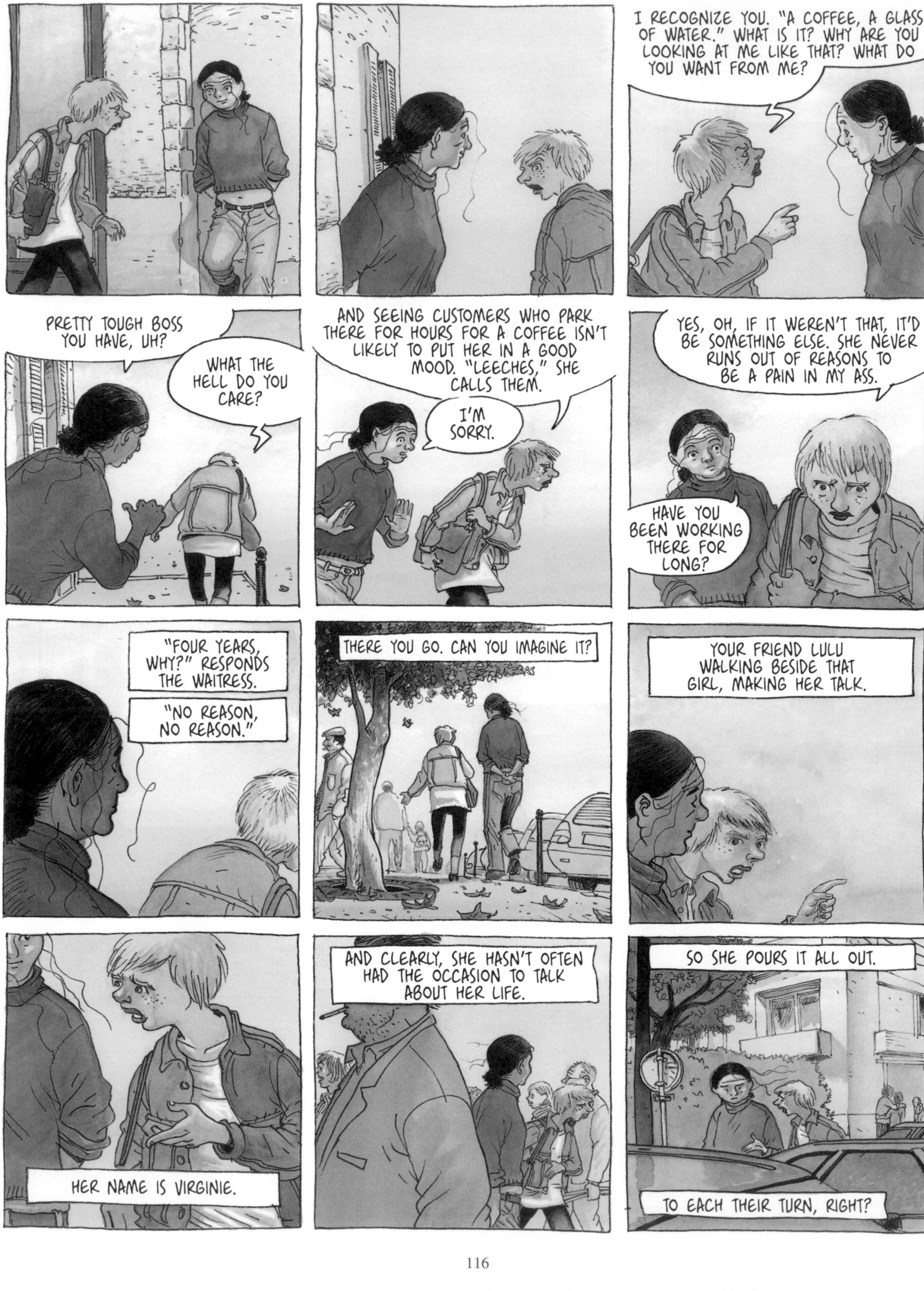
I RECOGNIZE YOU. "A COFFEE, A GLASS OF WATER." WHAT IS IT? WHY ARE YOU LOOKING AT ME LIKE THAT? WHAT DO YOU WANT FROM ME?
PRETTY TOUGH BOSS YOU HAVE, UH?
WHAT THE HELL DO YOU CARE?
AND SEEING CUSTOMERS WHO PARK THERE FOR HOURS FOR A COFFEE ISN'T LIKELY TO PUT HER IN A GOOD MOOD. "LEECHES," SHE CALLS THEM.
I'M SORRY.
YES, OH, IF IT WEREN'T THAT, IT'D BE SOMETHING ELSE. SHE NEVER RUNS OUT OF REASONS TO BE A PAIN IN MY ASS.
HAVE YOU BEEN WORKING THERE FOR LONG?
"FOUR YEARS, WHY?" RESPONDS THE WAITRESS.
"NO REASON, NO REASON."
THERE YOU GO. CAN YOU IMAGINE IT?
YOUR FRIEND LULU WALKING BESIDE THAT GIRL, MAKING HER TALK.
HER NAME IS VIRGINIE.
AND CLEARLY, SHE HASN'T OFTEN HAD THE OCCASION TO TALK ABOUT HER LIFE.
SO SHE POURS IT ALL OUT.
TO EACH THEIR TURN, RIGHT?

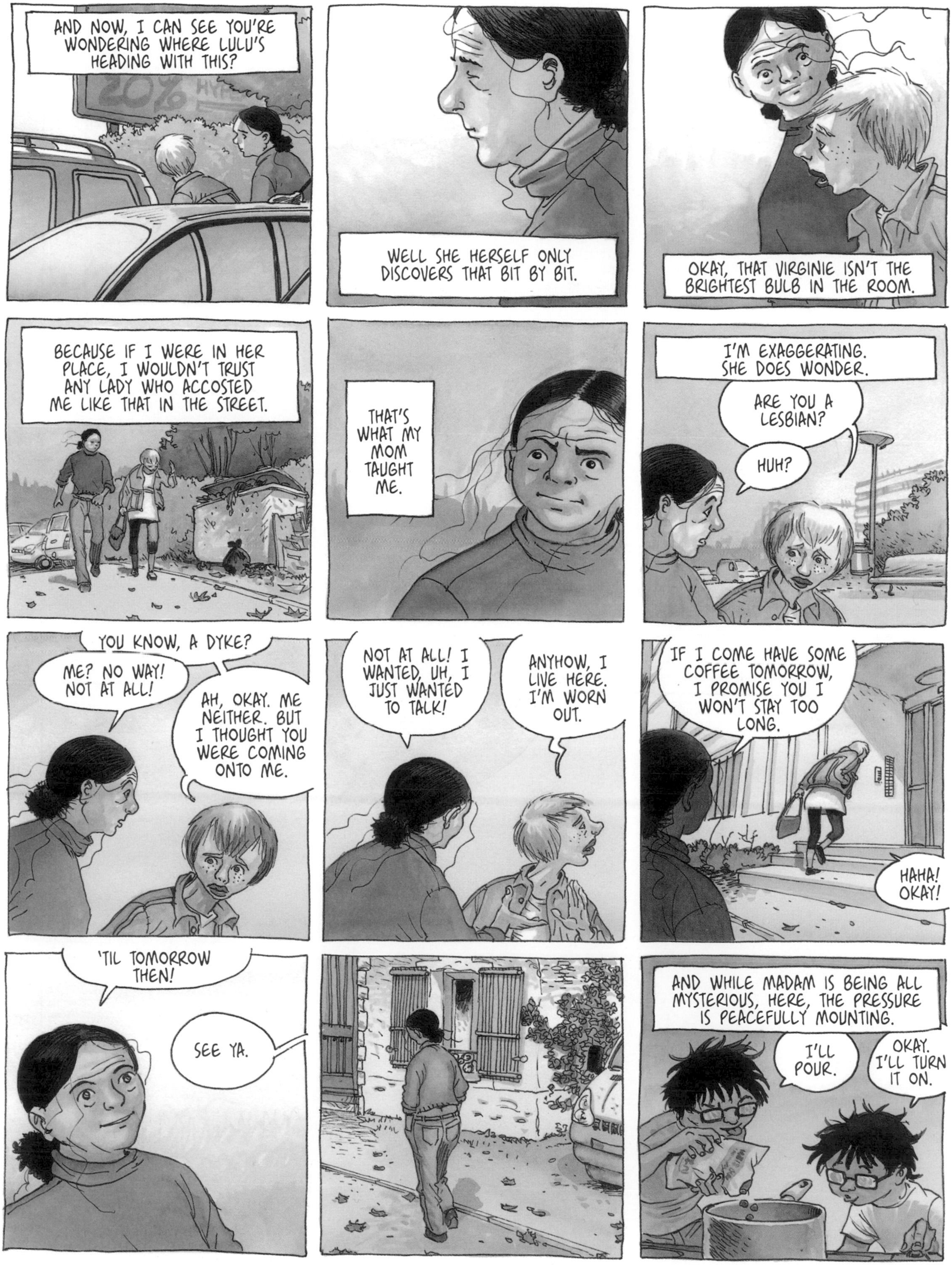
AND NOW, I CAN SEE YOU'RE WONDERING WHERE LULU'S HEADING WITH THIS?
WELL SHE HERSELF ONLY DISCOVERS THAT BIT BY BIT.
OKAY, THAT VIRGINIE ISN'T THE BRIGHTEST BULB IN THE ROOM.
BECAUSE IF I WERE IN HER PLACE, I WOULDN'T TRUST ANY LADY WHO ACCOSTED ME LIKE THAT IN THE STREET.
THAT'S WHAT MY MOM TAUGHT ME.
I'M EXAGGERATING. SHE DOES WONDER.
ARE YOU A LESBIAN?
HUH?
YOU KNOW, A DYKE?
ME? NO WAY! NOT AT ALL!
AH, OKAY. ME NEITHER. BUT I THOUGHT YOU WERE COMING ONTO ME.
NOT AT ALL! I WANTED, UH, I JUST WANTED TO TALK!
ANYHOW, I LIVE HERE. I'M WORN OUT.
IF I COME HAVE SOME COFFEE TOMORROW, I PROMISE YOU I WON'T STAY TOO LONG.
HAHA! OKAY!
'TIL TOMORROW THEN!
SEE YA.
AND WHILE MADAM IS BEING ALL MYSTERIOUS, HERE, THE PRESSURE IS PEACEFULLY MOUNTING.
I'LL POUR.
OKAY. I'LL TURN IT ON.

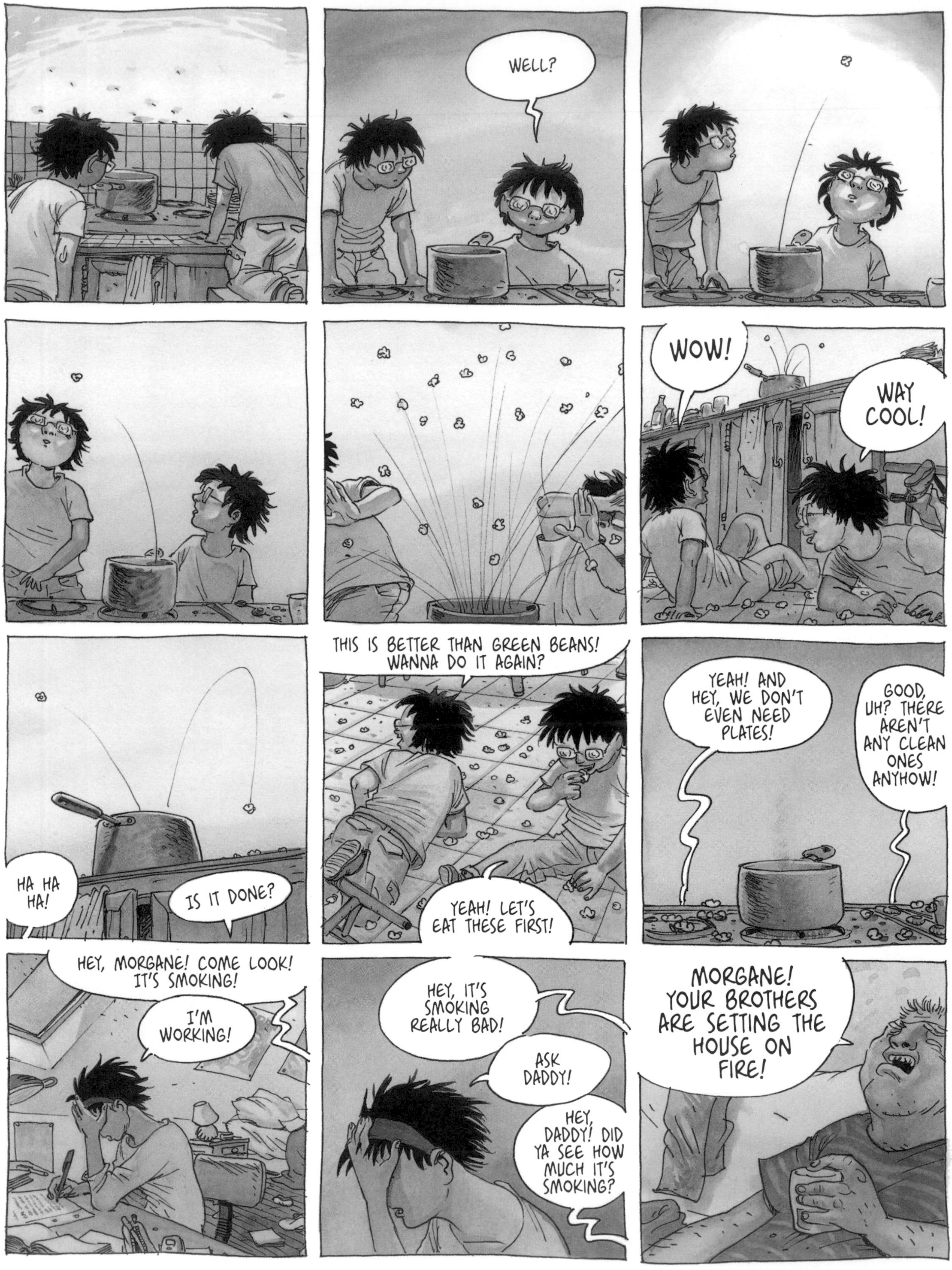
WELL?
WOW!
WAY COOL!
HA HA HA!
IS IT DONE?
THIS IS BETTER THAN GREEN BEANS! WANNA DO IT AGAIN?
YEAH! LET'S EAT THESE FIRST!
YEAH! AND HEY, WE DON'T EVEN NEED PLATES!
GOOD, UH? THERE AREN'T ANY CLEAN ONES ANYHOW!
HEY, MORGANE! COME LOOK! IT'S SMOKING!
I'M WORKING!
HEY, IT'S SMOKING REALLY BAD!
ASK DADDY!
HEY, DADDY! DID YA SEE HOW MUCH IT'S SMOKING?
MORGANE! YOUR BROTHERS ARE SETTING THE HOUSE ON FIRE!

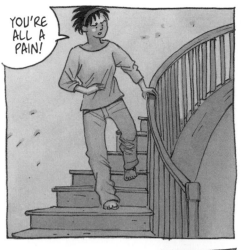

YOU'RE ALL A PAIN!

YOU CAN'T LEAVE AN EMPTY POT ON THE BURNER! WHAT DID YOU PUT IN IT? BUTTER?

YEAH!

WITH OIL, SO IT WOULDN'T STICK.

RIGHT!

YOU MAKE DINNER FOR THEM. I HAVE HOMEWORK!

MY TWO LITTLE SPEEDSTERS ARE MANAGING JUST FINE ON THEIR OWN.

IT'S CALLED "AUTONOMY." THAT'S IMPORTANT, RIGHT, BOYS?

YEAH, DADDY! WANT SOME POPCORN?

YOU FIGURE IT OUT! I HAVE ENGLISH HOMEWORK FOR TOMORROW!

"POPCORN" THAT'S ENGLISH, ISN'T IT?

VERY GOOD, BOYS, 'YOU EAT THE POPCORN'!

'YOU LOVE POPCORN? NO. I LOVE NOT...'

'...I NOT LOVE.'

YO, MORGÁNE, HOW DO YOU SAY IT?

'I LOVE WHISKEY,' VOILA.

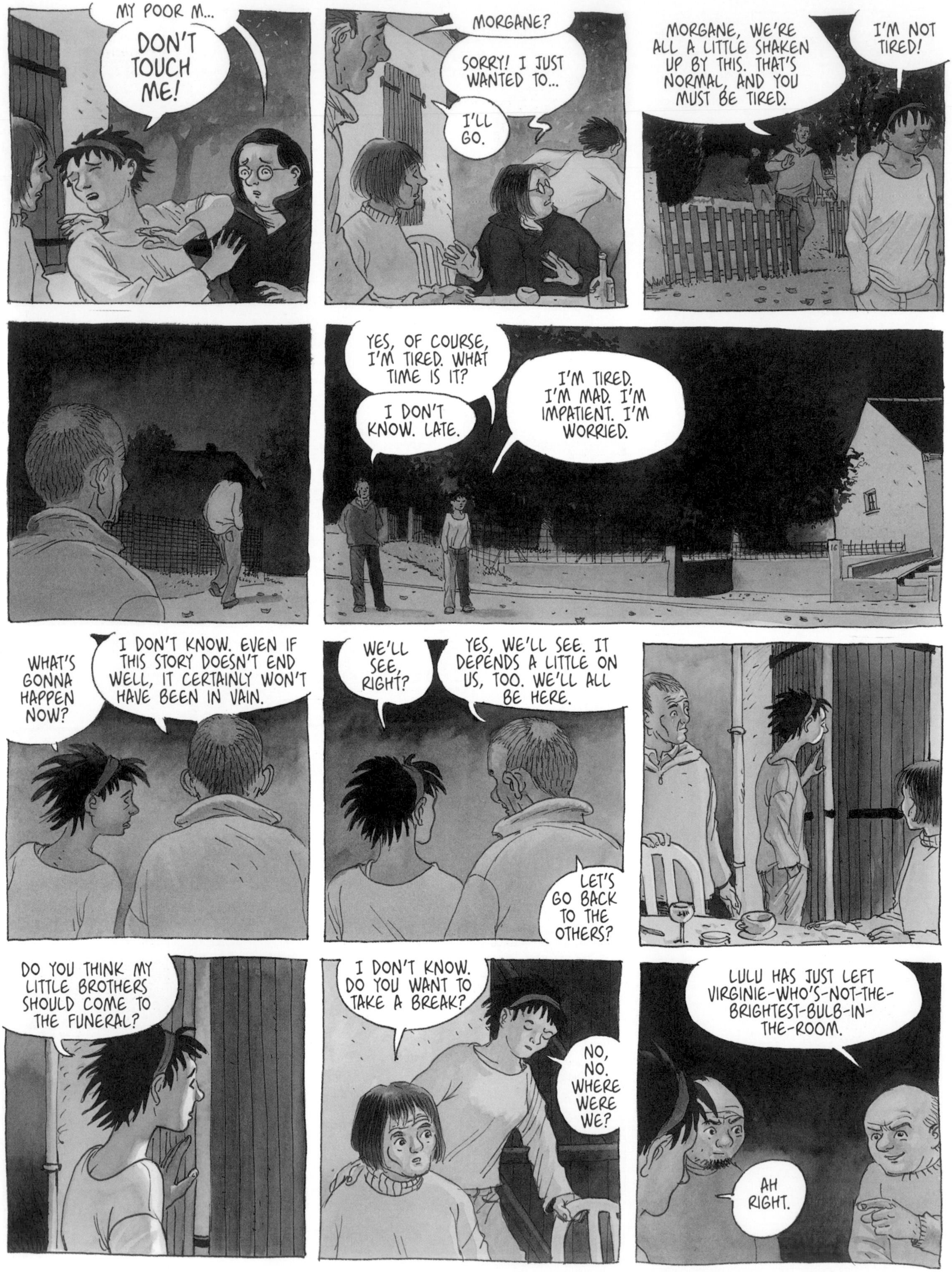
MY POOR M...
DON'T TOUCH ME!
MORGANE?
SORRY! I JUST WANTED TO...
I'LL GO.
MORGANE, WE'RE ALL A LITTLE SHAKEN UP BY THIS. THAT'S NORMAL, AND YOU MUST BE TIRED.
I'M NOT TIRED!
YES, OF COURSE, I'M TIRED. WHAT TIME IS IT?
I DON'T KNOW. LATE.
I'M TIRED. I'M MAD. I'M IMPATIENT. I'M WORRIED.
WHAT'S GONNA HAPPEN NOW?
I DON'T KNOW. EVEN IF THIS STORY DOESN'T END WELL, IT CERTAINLY WON'T HAVE BEEN IN VAIN.
WE'LL SEE, RIGHT?
YES, WE'LL SEE. IT DEPENDS A LITTLE ON US, TOO. WE'LL ALL BE HERE.
LET'S GO BACK TO THE OTHERS?
DO YOU THINK MY LITTLE BROTHERS SHOULD COME TO THE FUNERAL?
I DON'T KNOW. DO YOU WANT TO TAKE A BREAK?
NO, NO. WHERE WERE WE?
LULU HAS JUST LEFT VIRGINIE-WHO'S-NOT-THE-BRIGHTEST-BULB-IN-THE-ROOM.
AH RIGHT.

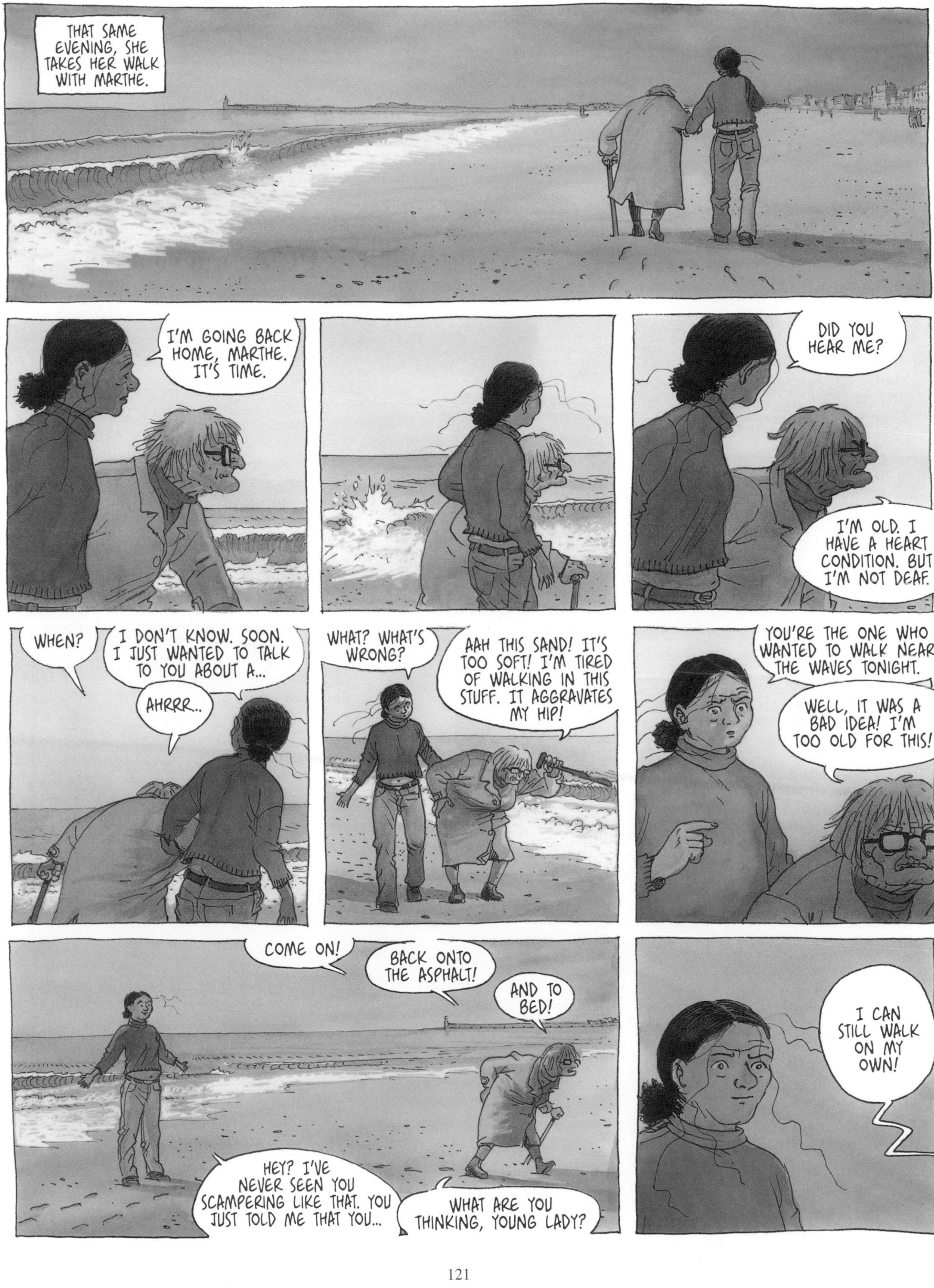
THAT SAME EVENING, SHE TAKES HER WALK WITH MARTHE.
I'M GOING BACK HOME, MARTHE. IT'S TIME.
DID YOU HEAR ME?
I'M OLD. I HAVE A HEART CONDITION. BUT I'M NOT DEAF.
WHEN?
I DON'T KNOW. SOON. I JUST WANTED TO TALK TO YOU ABOUT A...
AHRRR...
WHAT? WHAT'S WRONG?
AAH THIS SAND! IT'S TOO SOFT! I'M TIRED OF WALKING IN THIS STUFF. IT AGGRAVATES MY HIP!
YOU'RE THE ONE WHO WANTED TO WALK NEAR THE WAVES TONIGHT.
WELL, IT WAS A BAD IDEA! I'M TOO OLD FOR THIS!
COME ON!
BACK ONTO THE ASPHALT!
AND TO BED!
HEY? I'VE NEVER SEEN YOU SCAMPERING LIKE THAT. YOU JUST TOLD ME THAT YOU...
WHAT ARE YOU THINKING, YOUNG LADY?
I CAN STILL WALK ON MY OWN!

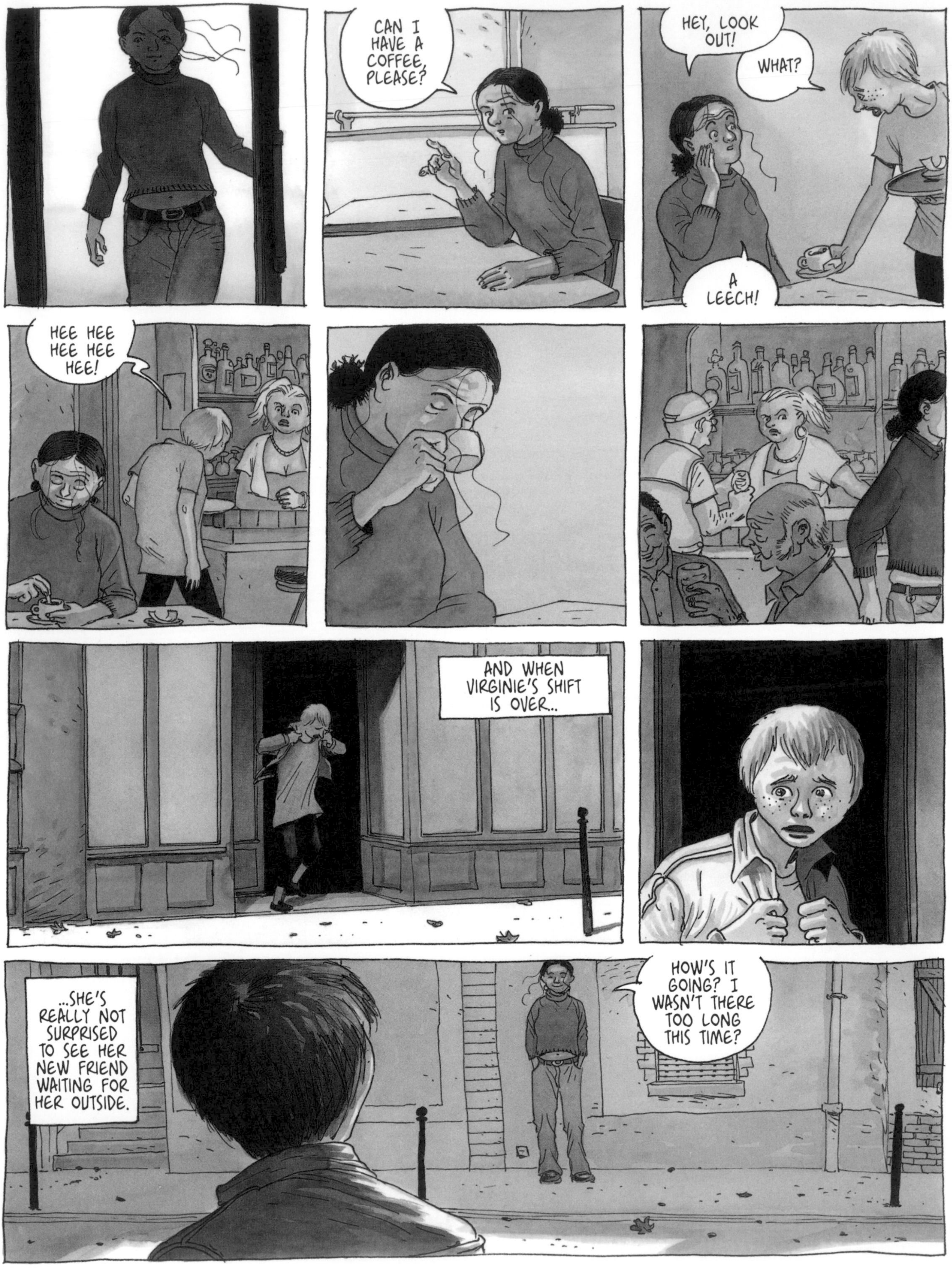
CAN I HAVE A COFFEE, PLEASE?
HEY, LOOK OUT!
WHAT?
A LEECH!
HEE HEE HEE HEE HEE!
AND WHEN VIRGINIE'S SHIFT IS OVER...
...SHE'S REALLY NOT SURPRISED TO SEE HER NEW FRIEND WAITING FOR HER OUTSIDE.
HOW'S IT GOING? I WASN'T THERE TOO LONG THIS TIME?

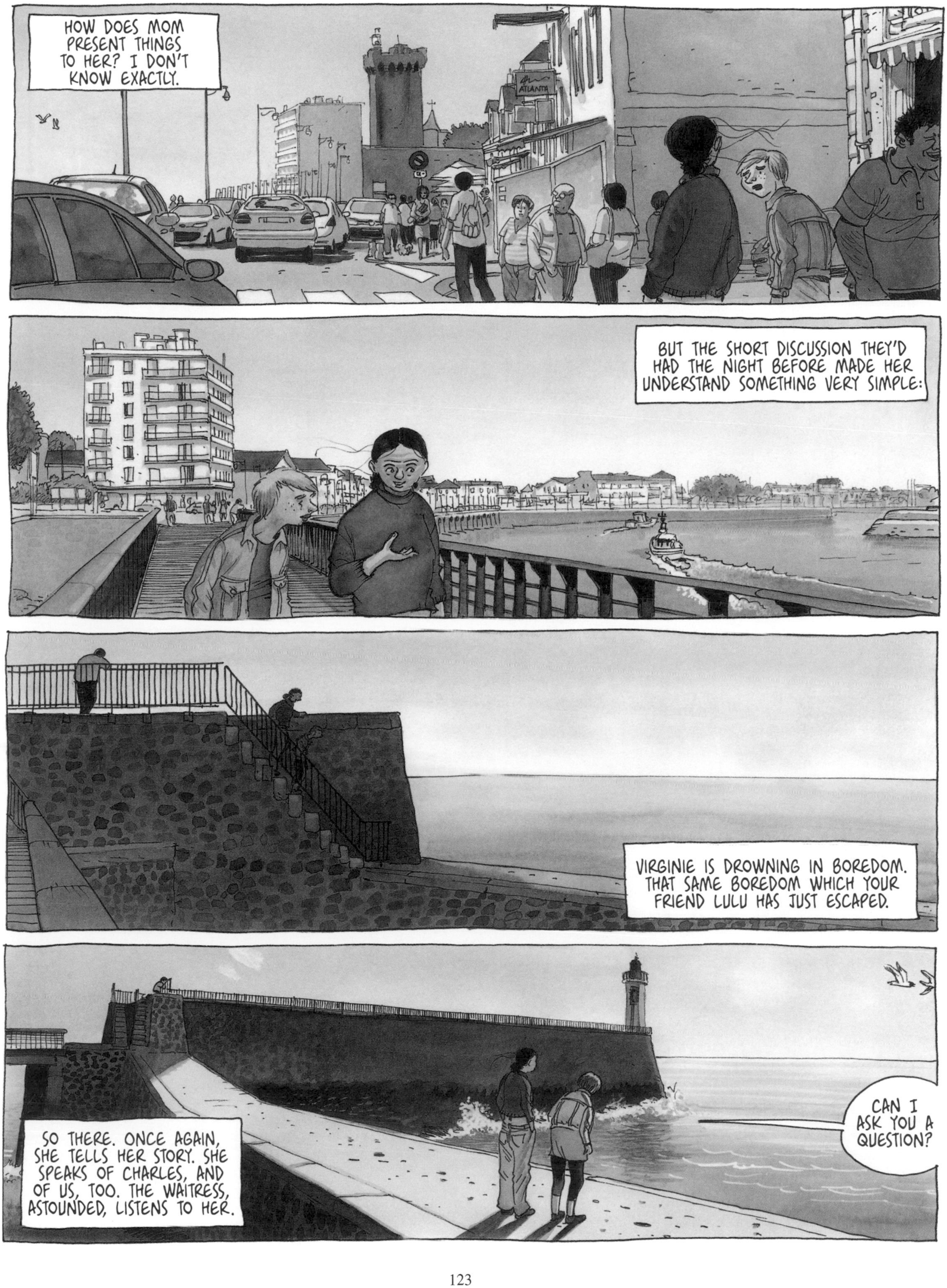
HOW DOES MOM PRESENT THINGS TO HER? I DON'T KNOW EXACTLY.
BUT THE SHORT DISCUSSION THEY'D HAD THE NIGHT BEFORE MADE HER UNDERSTAND SOMETHING VERY SIMPLE:
VIRGINIE IS DROWNING IN BOREDOM. THAT SAME BOREDOM WHICH YOUR FRIEND LULU HAS JUST ESCAPED.
SO THERE. ONCE AGAIN, SHE TELLS HER STORY. SHE SPEAKS OF CHARLES, AND OF US, TOO. THE WAITRESS, ASTOUNDED, LISTENS TO HER.
CAN I ASK YOU A QUESTION?

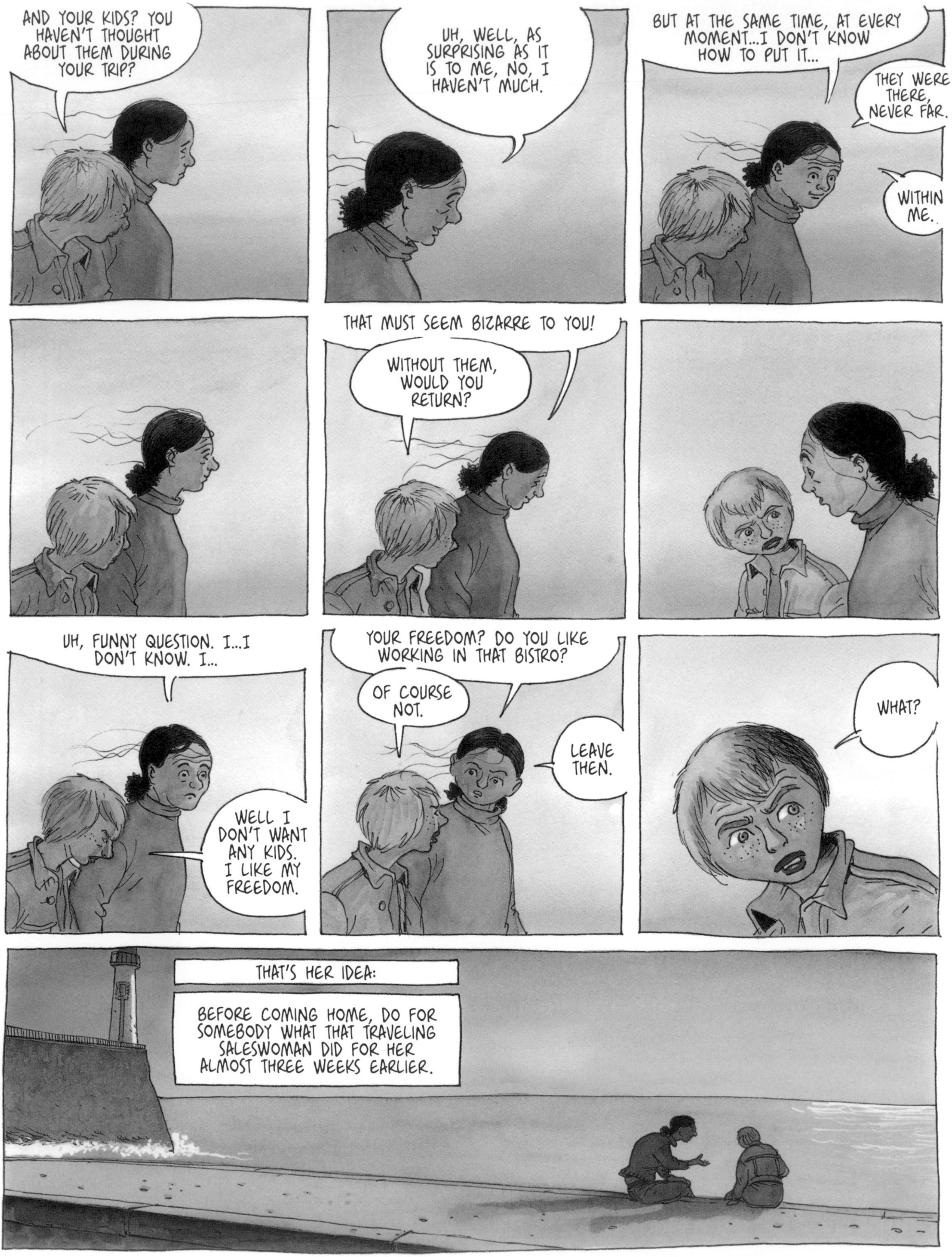
AND YOUR KIDS? YOU HAVEN'T THOUGHT ABOUT THEM DURING YOUR TRIP?
UH, WELL, AS SURPRISING AS IT IS TO ME, NO, I HAVEN'T MUCH.
BUT AT THE SAME TIME, AT EVERY MOMENT...I DON'T KNOW HOW TO PUT IT...
THEY WERE THERE, NEVER FAR.
WITHIN ME.
THAT MUST SEEM BIZARRE TO YOU!
WITHOUT THEM, WOULD YOU RETURN?
UH, FUNNY QUESTION. I...I DON'T KNOW. I...
WELL I DON'T WANT ANY KIDS. I LIKE MY FREEDOM.
YOUR FREEDOM? DO YOU LIKE WORKING IN THAT BISTRO?
OF COURSE NOT.
LEAVE THEN.
WHAT?
THAT'S HER IDEA:
BEFORE COMING HOME, DO FOR SOMEBODY WHAT THAT TRAVELING SALESWOMAN DID FOR HER ALMOST THREE WEEKS EARLIER.

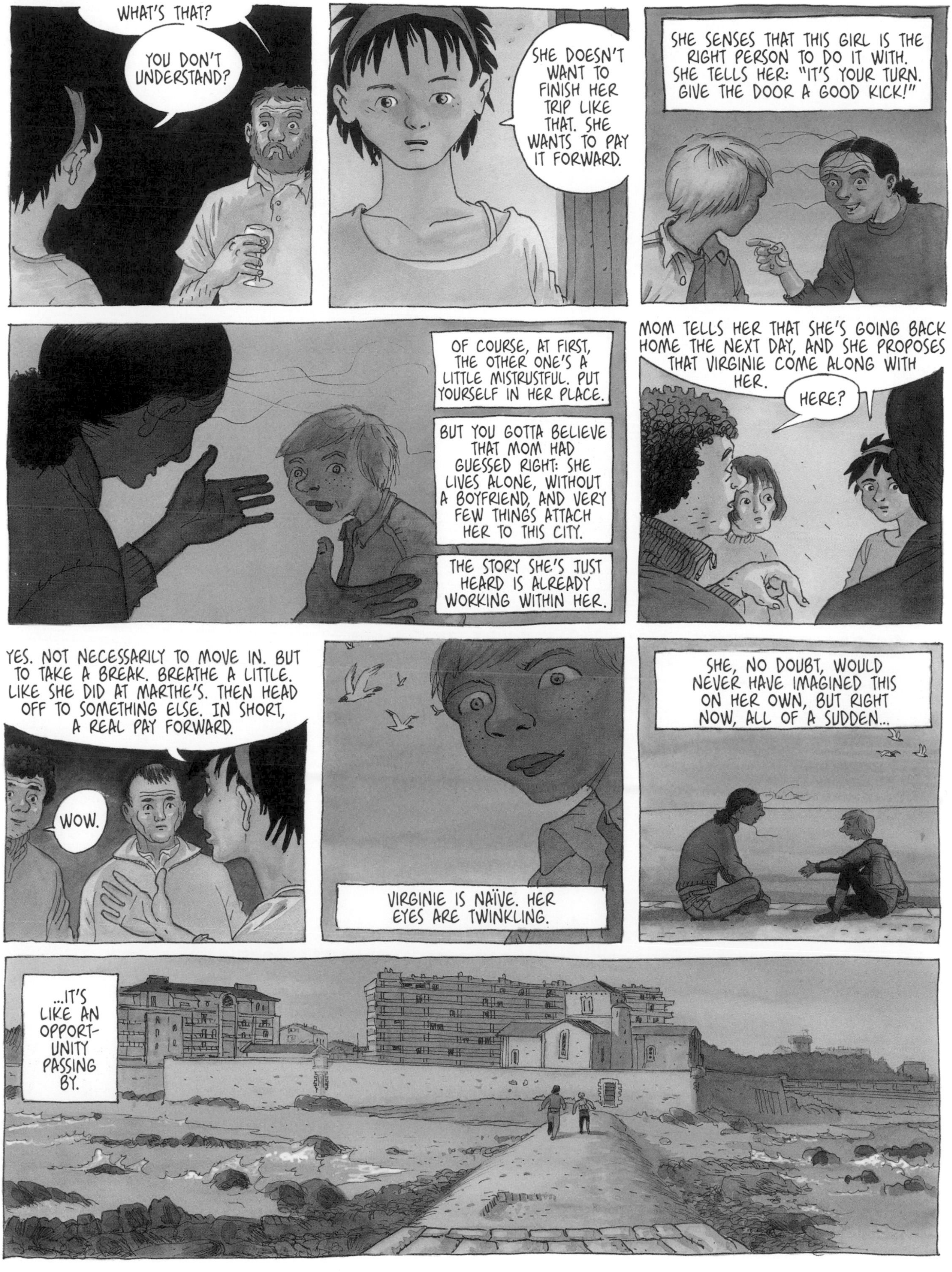
WHAT'S THAT?
YOU DON'T UNDERSTAND?
SHE DOESN'T WANT TO FINISH HER TRIP LIKE THAT. SHE WANTS TO PAY IT FORWARD.
SHE SENSES THAT THIS GIRL IS THE RIGHT PERSON TO DO IT WITH. SHE TELLS HER: "IT'S YOUR TURN. GIVE THE DOOR A GOOD KICK!"
OF COURSE, AT FIRST, THE OTHER ONE'S A LITTLE MISTRUSTFUL. PUT YOURSELF IN HER PLACE.
BUT YOU GOTTA BELIEVE THAT MOM HAD GUESSED RIGHT: SHE LIVES ALONE, WITHOUT A BOYFRIEND, AND VERY FEW THINGS ATTACH HER TO THIS CITY.
THE STORY SHE'S JUST HEARD IS ALREADY WORKING WITHIN HER.
MOM TELLS HER THAT SHE'S GOING BACK HOME THE NEXT DAY, AND SHE PROPOSES THAT VIRGINIE COME ALONG WITH HER.
HERE?
YES. NOT NECESSARILY TO MOVE IN. BUT TO TAKE A BREAK. BREATHE A LITTLE. LIKE SHE DID AT MARTHE'S. THEN HEAD OFF TO SOMETHING ELSE. IN SHORT, A REAL PAY FORWARD.
WOW.
VIRGINIE IS NAÏVE. HER EYES ARE TWINKLING.
SHE, NO DOUBT, WOULD NEVER HAVE IMAGINED THIS ON HER OWN, BUT RIGHT NOW, ALL OF A SUDDEN...
...IT'S LIKE AN OPPORT-UNITY PASSING BY.

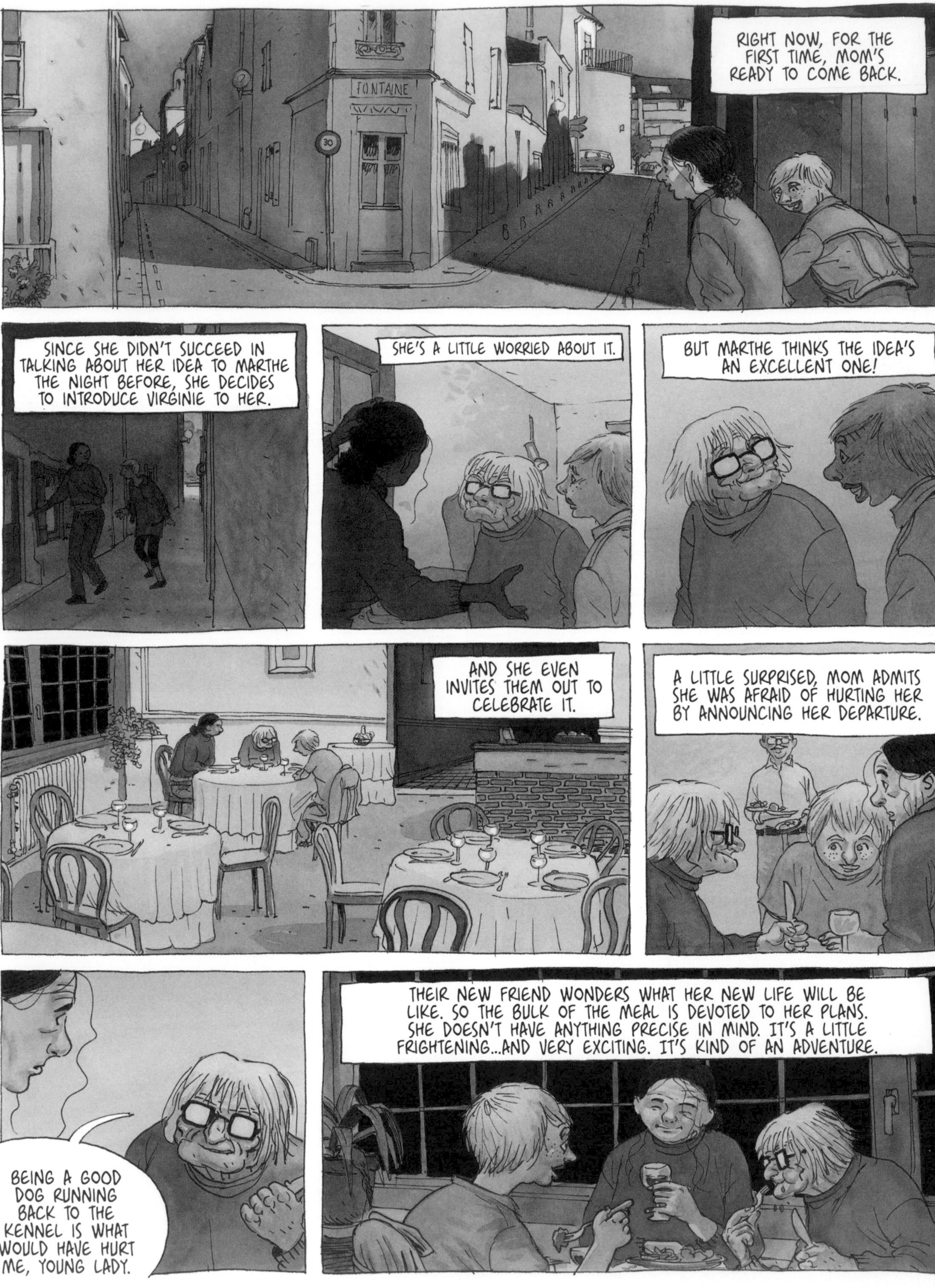
FONTAINE
30
RIGHT NOW, FOR THE FIRST TIME, MOM'S READY TO COME BACK.
SINCE SHE DIDN'T SUCCEED IN TALKING ABOUT HER IDEA TO MARTHE THE NIGHT BEFORE, SHE DECIDES TO INTRODUCE VIRGINIE TO HER.
SHE'S A LITTLE WORRIED ABOUT IT.
BUT MARTHE THINKS THE IDEA'S AN EXCELLENT ONE!
AND SHE EVEN INVITES THEM OUT TO CELEBRATE IT.
A LITTLE SURPRISED, MOM ADMITS SHE WAS AFRAID OF HURTING HER BY ANNOUNCING HER DEPARTURE.
BEING A GOOD DOG RUNNING BACK TO THE KENNEL IS WHAT WOULD HAVE HURT ME, YOUNG LADY.
THEIR NEW FRIEND WONDERS WHAT HER NEW LIFE WILL BE LIKE. SO THE BULK OF THE MEAL IS DEVOTED TO HER PLANS. SHE DOESN'T HAVE ANYTHING PRECISE IN MIND. IT'S A LITTLE FRIGHTENING...AND VERY EXCITING. IT'S KIND OF AN ADVENTURE.

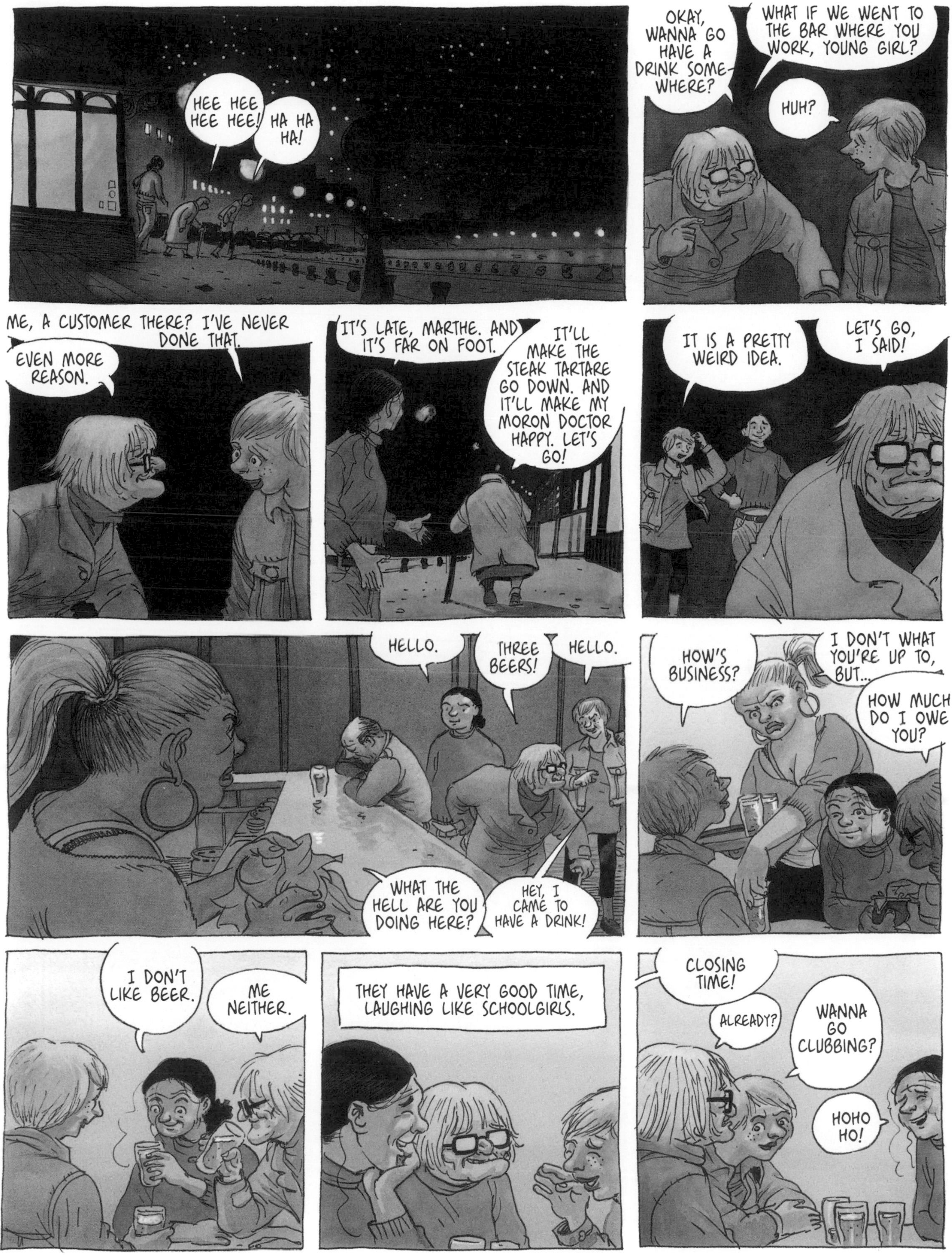
HEE HEE HEE HEE!
HA HA HA!
OKAY, WANNA GO HAVE A DRINK SOMEWHERE?
WHAT IF WE WENT TO THE BAR WHERE YOU WORK, YOUNG GIRL?
HUH?
ME, A CUSTOMER THERE? I'VE NEVER DONE THAT.
EVEN MORE REASON.
IT'S LATE, MARTHE. AND IT'S FAR ON FOOT.
IT'LL MAKE THE STEAK TARTARE GO DOWN. AND IT'LL MAKE MY MORON DOCTOR HAPPY. LET'S GO!
IT IS A PRETTY WEIRD IDEA.
LET'S GO, I SAID!
HELLO.
THREE BEERS!
HELLO.
WHAT THE HELL ARE YOU DOING HERE?
HEY, I CAME TO HAVE A DRINK!
HOW'S BUSINESS?
I DON'T WHAT YOU'RE UP TO, BUT...
HOW MUCH DO I OWE YOU?
I DON'T LIKE BEER.
ME NEITHER.
THEY HAVE A VERY GOOD TIME, LAUGHING LIKE SCHOOLGIRLS.
CLOSING TIME!
ALREADY?
WANNA GO CLUBBING?
HOHO HO!

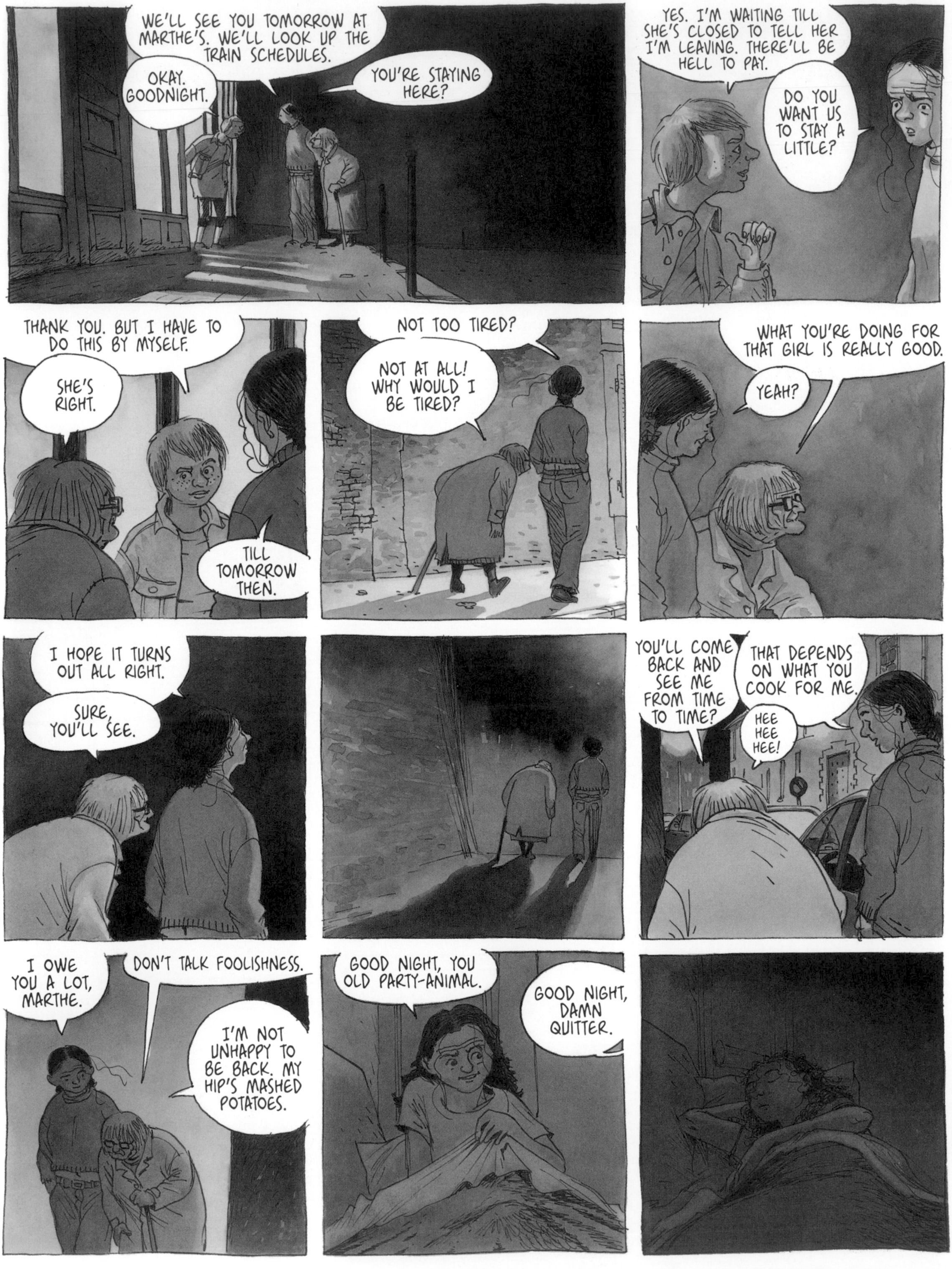
WE'LL SEE YOU TOMORROW AT MARTHE'S. WE'LL LOOK UP THE TRAIN SCHEDULES.
OKAY. GOODNIGHT.
YOU'RE STAYING HERE?
YES. I'M WAITING TILL SHE'S CLOSED TO TELL HER I'M LEAVING. THERE'LL BE HELL TO PAY.
DO YOU WANT US TO STAY A LITTLE?
THANK YOU. BUT I HAVE TO DO THIS BY MYSELF.
SHE'S RIGHT.
TILL TOMORROW THEN.
NOT TOO TIRED?
NOT AT ALL! WHY WOULD I BE TIRED?
WHAT YOU'RE DOING FOR THAT GIRL IS REALLY GOOD.
YEAH?
I HOPE IT TURNS OUT ALL RIGHT.
SURE, YOU'LL SEE.
YOU'LL COME BACK AND SEE ME FROM TIME TO TIME?
THAT DEPENDS ON WHAT YOU COOK FOR ME.
HEE HEE HEE!
I OWE YOU A LOT, MARTHE.
DON'T TALK FOOLISHNESS.
I'M NOT UNHAPPY TO BE BACK. MY HIP'S MASHED POTATOES.
GOOD NIGHT, YOU OLD PARTY-ANIMAL.
GOOD NIGHT, DAMN QUITTER.

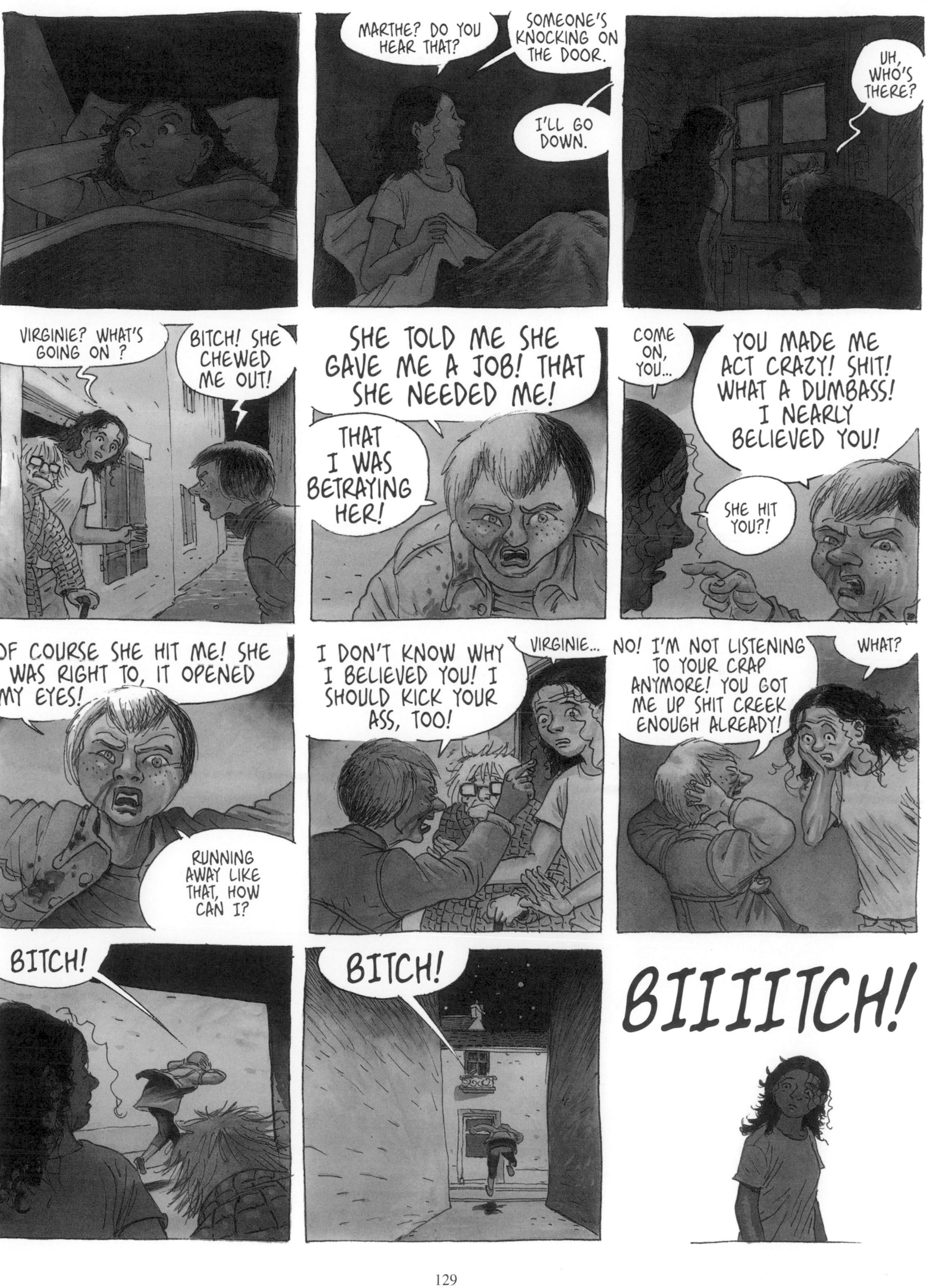
MARTHE? DO YOU HEAR THAT?
SOMEONE'S KNOCKING ON THE DOOR.
I'LL GO DOWN.
UH, WHO'S THERE?
VIRGINIE? WHAT'S GOING ON ?
BITCH! SHE CHEWED ME OUT!
SHE TOLD ME SHE GAVE ME A JOB! THAT SHE NEEDED ME!
THAT I WAS BETRAYING HER!
COME ON, YOU...
YOU MADE ME ACT CRAZY! SHIT! WHAT A DUMBASS! I NEARLY BELIEVED YOU!
SHE HIT YOU?!
OF COURSE SHE HIT ME! SHE WAS RIGHT TO, IT OPENED MY EYES!
RUNNING AWAY LIKE THAT, HOW CAN I?
I DON'T KNOW WHY I BELIEVED YOU! I SHOULD KICK YOUR ASS, TOO!
VIRGINIE...
NO! I'M NOT LISTENING TO YOUR CRAP ANYMORE! YOU GOT ME UP SHIT CREEK ENOUGH ALREADY!
WHAT?
BITCH!
BITCH!
BIIIITCH!

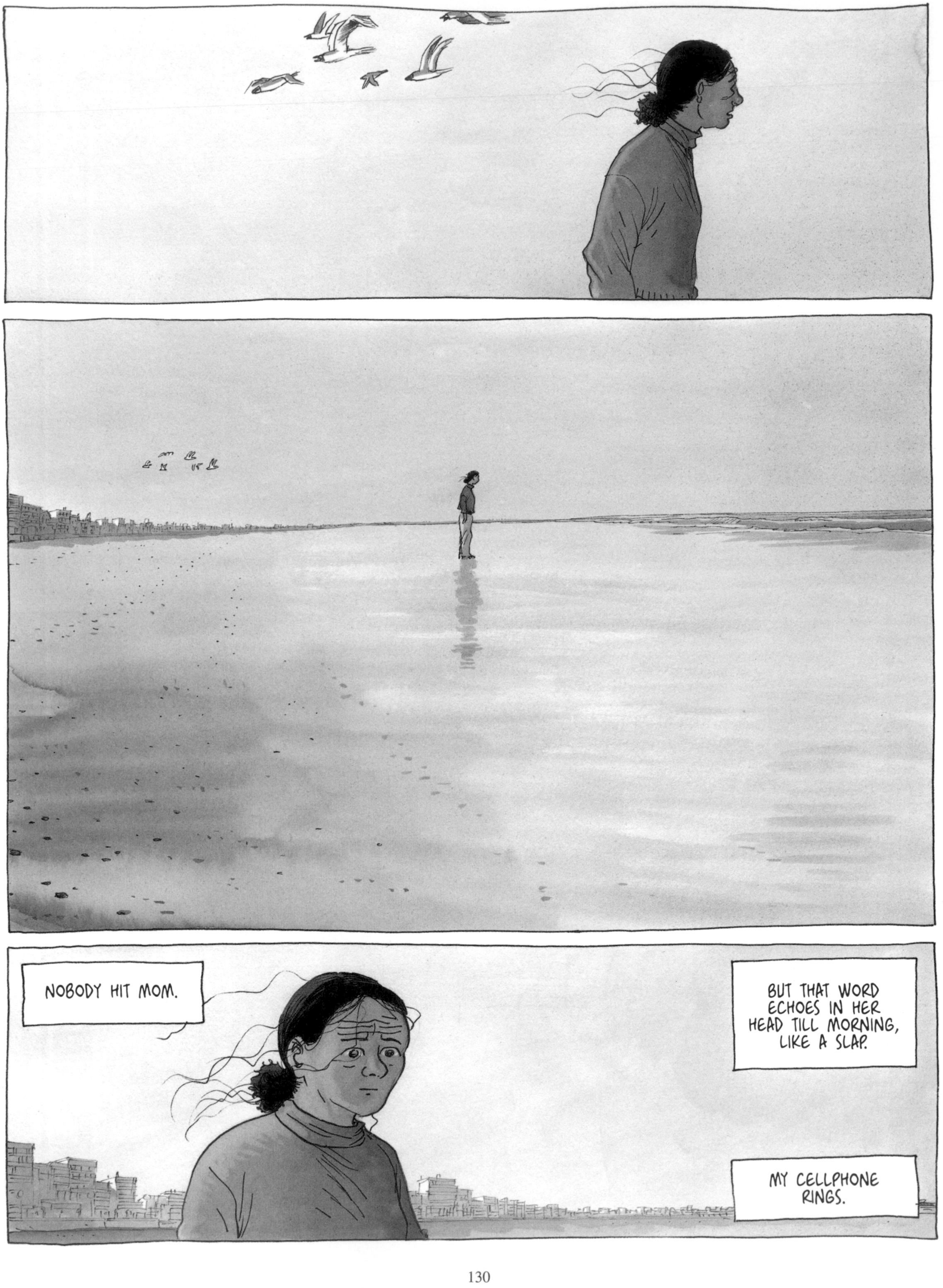
NOBODY HIT MOM.
BUT THAT WORD ECHOES IN HER HEAD TILL MORNING, LIKE A SLAP.
MY CELLPHONE RINGS.

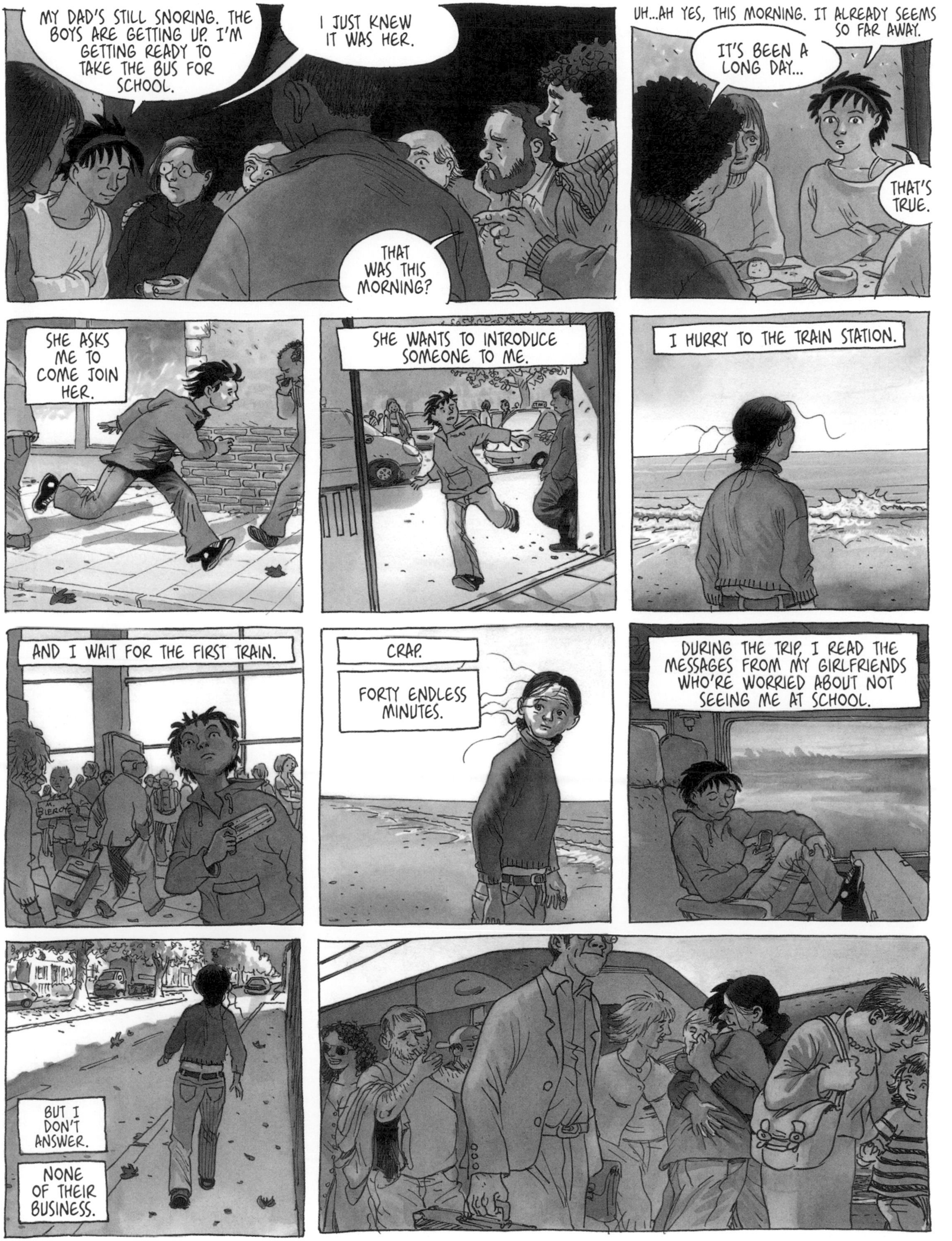
MY DAD'S STILL SNORING. THE BOYS ARE GETTING UP. I'M GETTING READY TO TAKE THE BUS FOR SCHOOL.
I JUST KNEW IT WAS HER.
THAT WAS THIS MORNING?
UH...AH YES, THIS MORNING. IT ALREADY SEEMS SO FAR AWAY.
IT'S BEEN A LONG DAY...
THAT'S TRUE.
SHE ASKS ME TO COME JOIN HER.
SHE WANTS TO INTRODUCE SOMEONE TO ME.
I HURRY TO THE TRAIN STATION.
AND I WAIT FOR THE FIRST TRAIN.
CRAP.
FORTY ENDLESS MINUTES.
DURING THE TRIP, I READ THE MESSAGES FROM MY GIRLFRIENDS WHO'RE WORRIED ABOUT NOT SEEING ME AT SCHOOL.
BUT I DON'T ANSWER.
NONE OF THEIR BUSINESS.

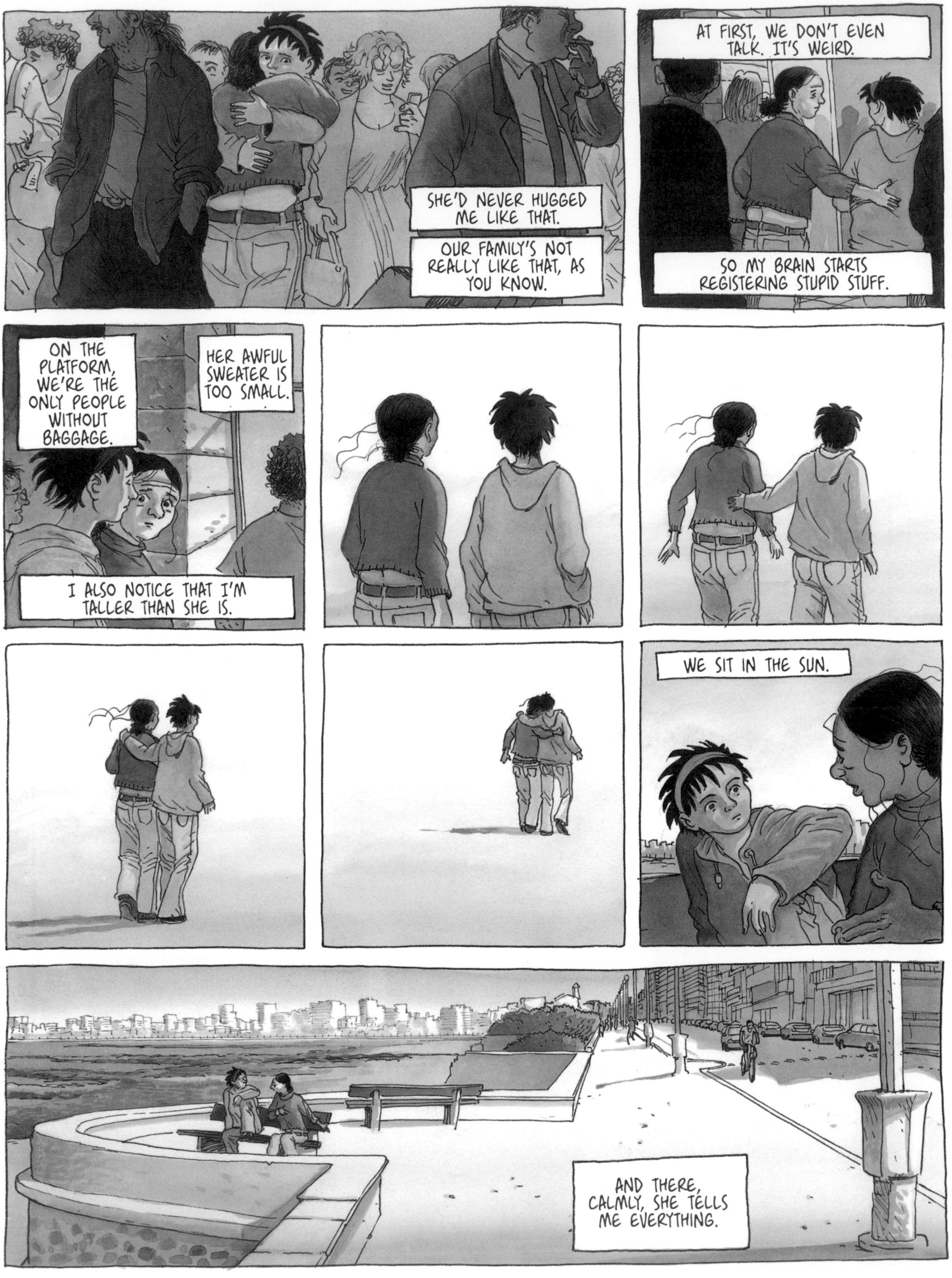
SHE'D NEVER HUGGED ME LIKE THAT.
OUR FAMILY'S NOT REALLY LIKE THAT, AS YOU KNOW.
AT FIRST, WE DON'T EVEN TALK. IT'S WEIRD.
SO MY BRAIN STARTS REGISTERING STUPID STUFF.
ON THE PLATFORM, WE'RE THE ONLY PEOPLE WITHOUT BAGGAGE.
HER AWFUL SWEATER IS TOO SMALL.
I ALSO NOTICE THAT I'M TALLER THAN SHE IS.
WE SIT IN THE SUN.
AND THERE, CALMLY, SHE TELLS ME EVERYTHING.

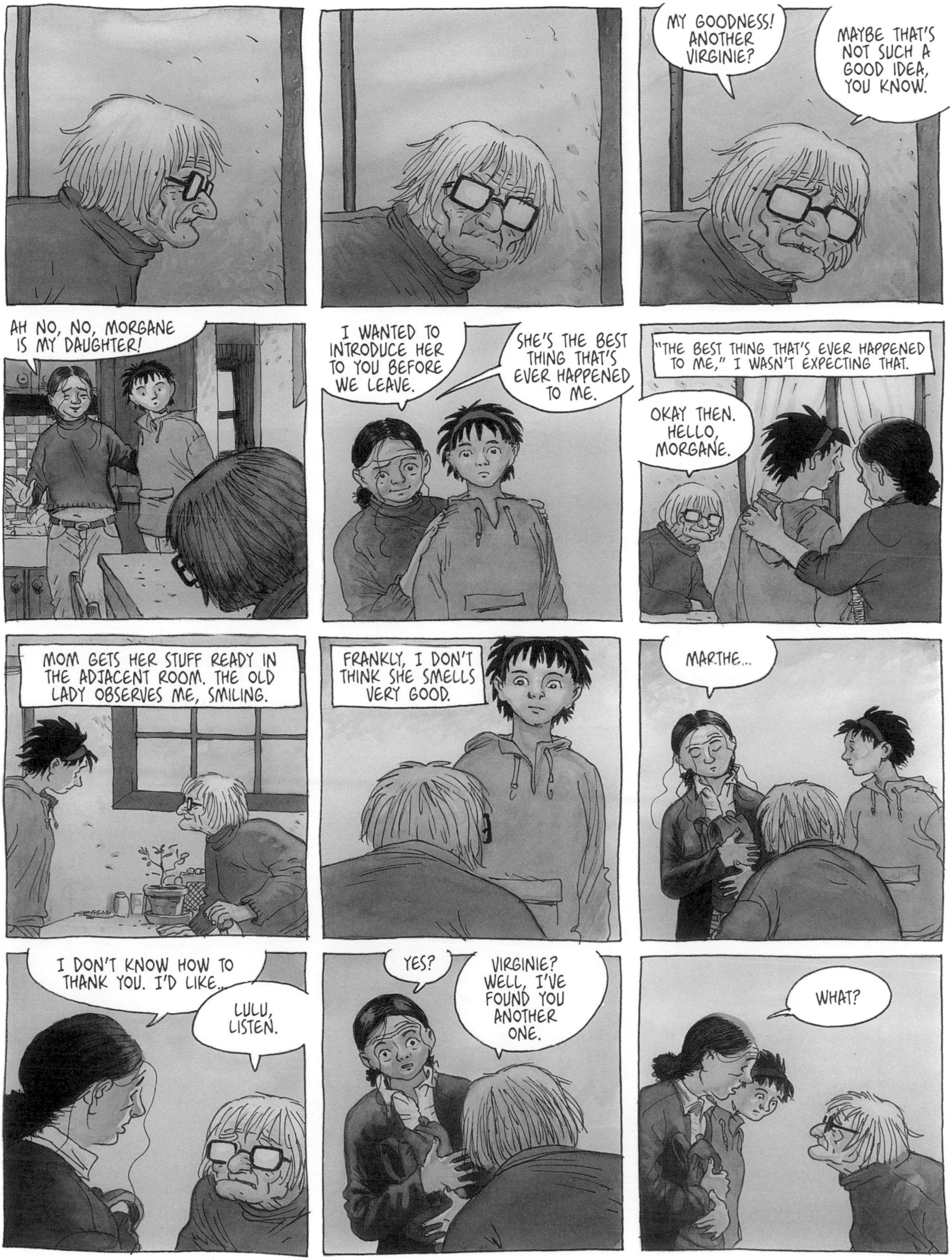
MY GOODNESS! ANOTHER VIRGINIE?
MAYBE THAT'S NOT SUCH A GOOD IDEA, YOU KNOW.
AH NO, NO, MORGANE IS MY DAUGHTER!
I WANTED TO INTRODUCE HER TO YOU BEFORE WE LEAVE.
SHE'S THE BEST THING THAT'S EVER HAPPENED TO ME.
"THE BEST THING THAT'S EVER HAPPENED TO ME," I WASN'T EXPECTING THAT.
OKAY THEN. HELLO, MORGANE.
MOM GETS HER STUFF READY IN THE ADJACENT ROOM. THE OLD LADY OBSERVES ME, SMILING.
FRANKLY, I DON'T THINK SHE SMELLS VERY GOOD.
MARTHE...
I DON'T KNOW HOW TO THANK YOU. I'D LIKE...
LULU, LISTEN.
YES?
VIRGINIE? WELL, I'VE FOUND YOU ANOTHER ONE.
WHAT?

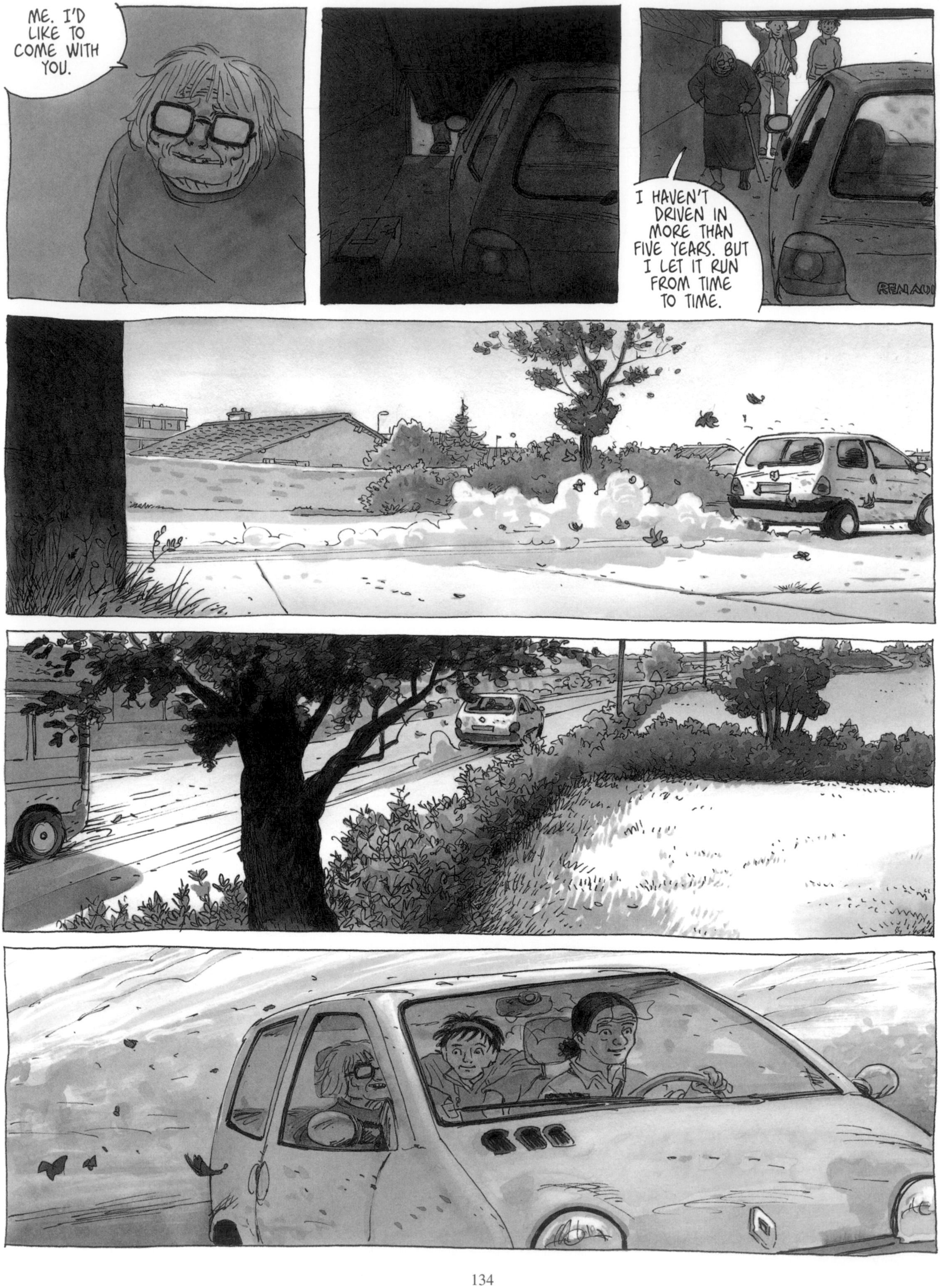
ME. I'D LIKE TO COME WITH YOU.
I HAVEN'T DRIVEN IN MORE THAN FIVE YEARS. BUT I LET IT RUN FROM TIME TO TIME.
RENAULT

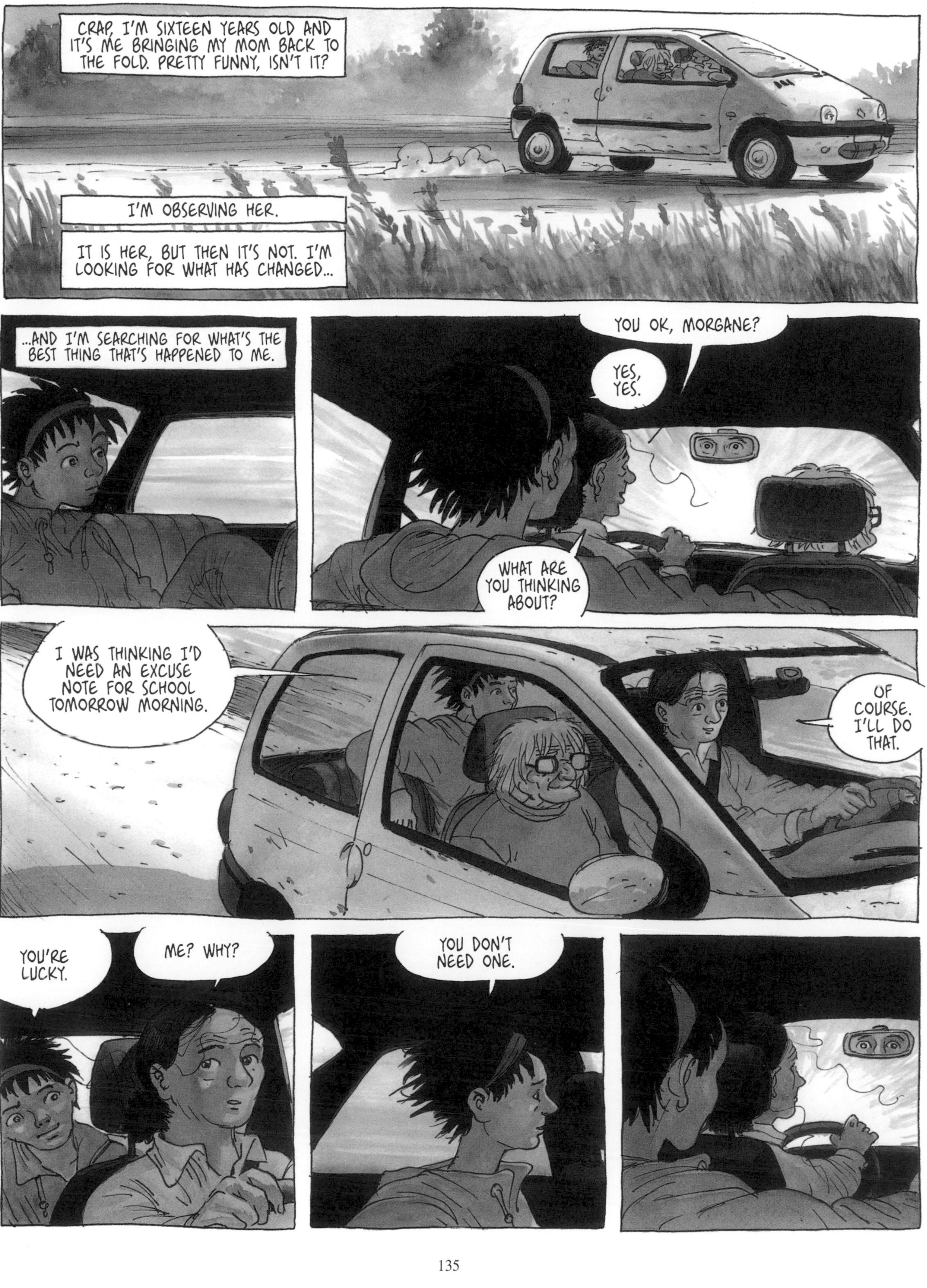
CRAP, I'M SIXTEEN YEARS OLD AND IT'S ME BRINGING MY MOM BACK TO THE FOLD. PRETTY FUNNY, ISN'T IT?
I'M OBSERVING HER.
IT IS HER, BUT THEN IT'S NOT. I'M LOOKING FOR WHAT HAS CHANGED...
...AND I'M SEARCHING FOR WHAT'S THE BEST THING THAT'S HAPPENED TO ME.
YOU OK, MORGANE?
YES, YES.
WHAT ARE YOU THINKING ABOUT?
I WAS THINKING I'D NEED AN EXCUSE NOTE FOR SCHOOL TOMORROW MORNING.
OF COURSE. I'LL DO THAT.
YOU'RE LUCKY.
ME? WHY?
YOU DON'T NEED ONE.

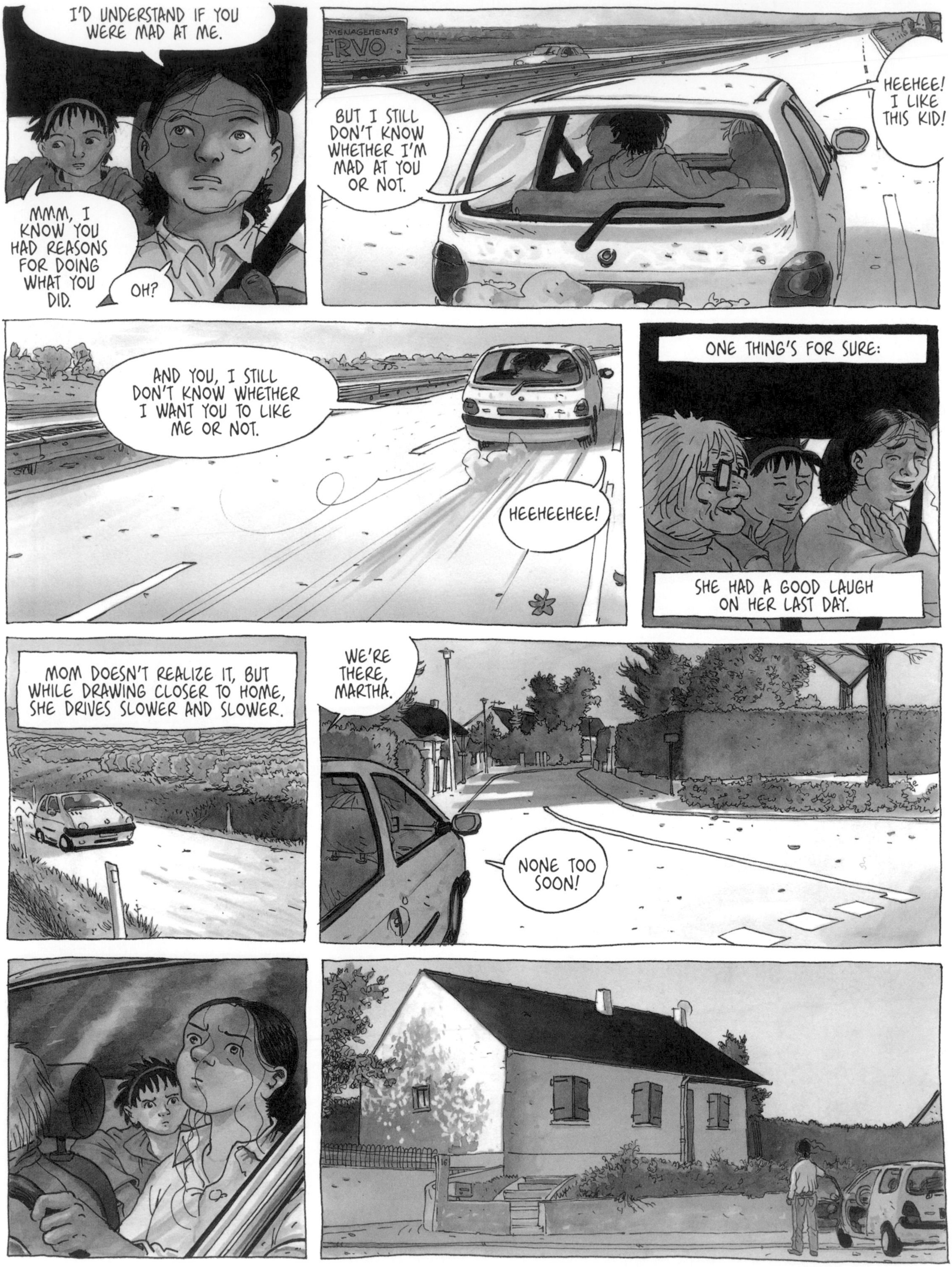

I'D UNDERSTAND IF YOU WERE MAD AT ME.
MMM, I KNOW YOU HAD REASONS FOR DOING WHAT YOU DID.
OH?
EMENAGEMENTS
ERVO
BUT I STILL DON'T KNOW WHETHER I'M MAD AT YOU OR NOT.
HEEHEE! I LIKE THIS KID!
AND YOU, I STILL DON'T KNOW WHETHER I WANT YOU TO LIKE ME OR NOT.
HEEHEEHEE!
ONE THING'S FOR SURE:
SHE HAD A GOOD LAUGH ON HER LAST DAY.
MOM DOESN'T REALIZE IT, BUT WHILE DRAWING CLOSER TO HOME, SHE DRIVES SLOWER AND SLOWER.
WE'RE THERE, MARTHA.
NONE TOO SOON!

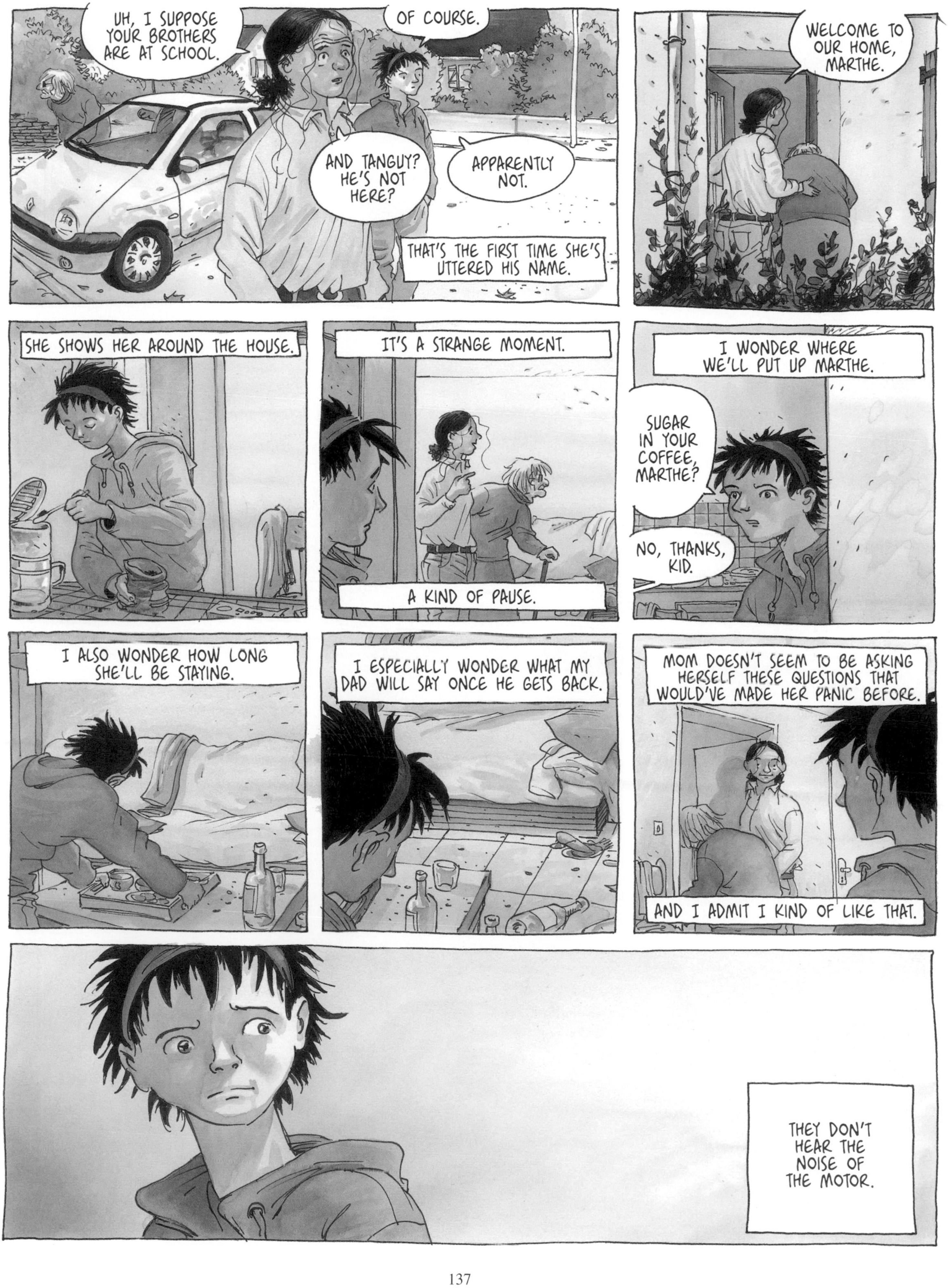

UH, I SUPPOSE YOUR BROTHERS ARE AT SCHOOL.
OF COURSE.
AND TANGUY? HE'S NOT HERE?
APPARENTLY NOT.
THAT'S THE FIRST TIME SHE'S UTTERED HIS NAME.
WELCOME TO OUR HOME, MARTHE.
SHE SHOWS HER AROUND THE HOUSE.
IT'S A STRANGE MOMENT.
A KIND OF PAUSE.
I WONDER WHERE WE'LL PUT UP MARTHE.
SUGAR IN YOUR COFFEE, MARTHE?
NO, THANKS, KID.
I ALSO WONDER HOW LONG SHE'LL BE STAYING.
I ESPECIALLY WONDER WHAT MY DAD WILL SAY ONCE HE GETS BACK.
MOM DOESN'T SEEM TO BE ASKING HERSELF THESE QUESTIONS THAT WOULD'VE MADE HER PANIC BEFORE.
AND I ADMIT I KIND OF LIKE THAT.
THEY DON'T HEAR THE NOISE OF THE MOTOR.

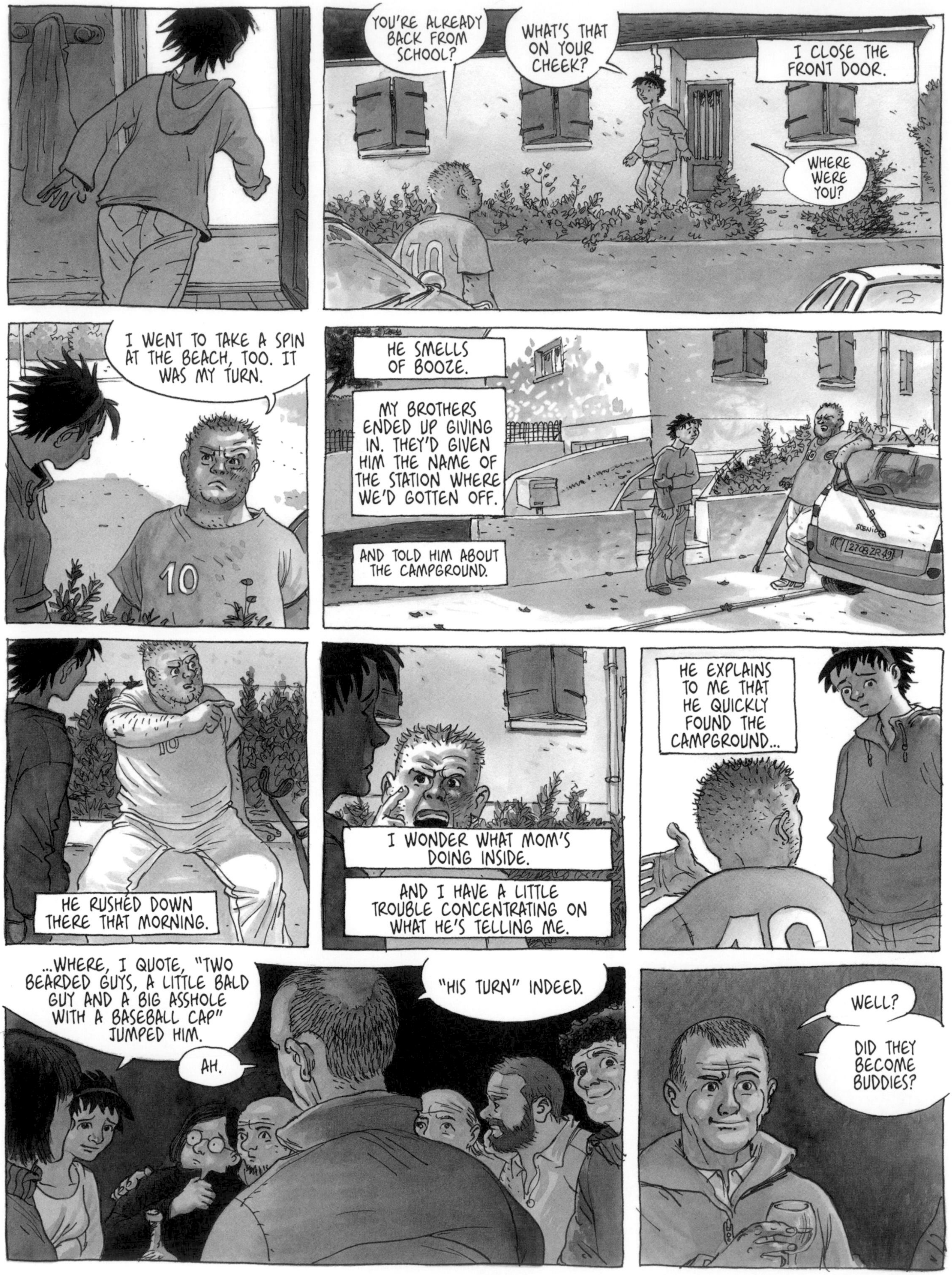
YOU'RE ALREADY BACK FROM SCHOOL?
WHAT'S THAT ON YOUR CHEEK?
I CLOSE THE FRONT DOOR.
WHERE WERE YOU?
I WENT TO TAKE A SPIN AT THE BEACH, TOO. IT WAS MY TURN.
HE SMELLS OF BOOZE.
MY BROTHERS ENDED UP GIVING IN. THEY'D GIVEN HIM THE NAME OF THE STATION WHERE WE'D GOTTEN OFF.
AND TOLD HIM ABOUT THE CAMPGROUND.
HE RUSHED DOWN THERE THAT MORNING.
I WONDER WHAT MOM'S DOING INSIDE.
AND I HAVE A LITTLE TROUBLE CONCENTRATING ON WHAT HE'S TELLING ME.
HE EXPLAINS TO ME THAT HE QUICKLY FOUND THE CAMPGROUND...
...WHERE, I QUOTE, "TWO BEARDED GUYS, A LITTLE BALD GUY AND A BIG ASSHOLE WITH A BASEBALL CAP" JUMPED HIM.
AH.
"HIS TURN" INDEED.
WELL?
DID THEY BECOME BUDDIES?

HEEHEE, THE BRUISE ON HIS CHEEK DIDN'T COME FROM A KISS, OK?

ONCE HE'D CALMED DOWN, HE STARTED DEMANDING HIS WIFE, BUT CAME TO REALIZE SHE HADN'T BEEN THERE IN A LONG TIME.

AT THAT MOMENT, CHARLES UNDERSTOOD THAT, CONTRARY TO WHAT SHE HAD TOLD THEM, LULU HAD A FAMILY.

HE ALSO LEARNED THAT WE'D BEEN CLOSE BY AND EVEN THAT HIS DEAR BROTHERS HAD SECRETLY WELCOMED US. HE TAKES IT ALL RATHER BADLY.

NO WONDER! THE POOR GUY!

AND THEN?

THEN, MY DAD GOT A WEIRD IDEA...

HE EXPLAINS TO ME THAT THE TWO OF THEM STARTED TALKING.

GETTING DUMPED BY MOM GIVES THEM SOMETHING IN COMMON, I GUESS.

DAD TRIED TO FIND OUT EVERYTHING THAT HAD HAPPENED BETWEEN HER AND CHARLES.

AND, CLEARLY, THEY TALKED A LONG TIME.

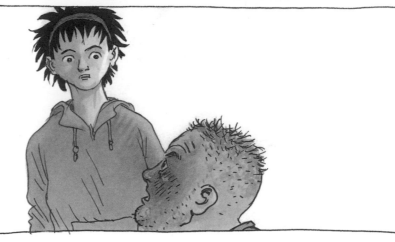

AND THEN, CARRIED AWAY BY HIS STORY, HE BEGINS TELLING ME, HIS DAUGHTER, ALL THAT, WITHOUT HIDING ANYTHING.

AND SINCE I REALLY DON'T WANT TO HEAR ABOUT MY MOTHER'S SEX LIFE, I TELL HIM:

SHE'S BACK.

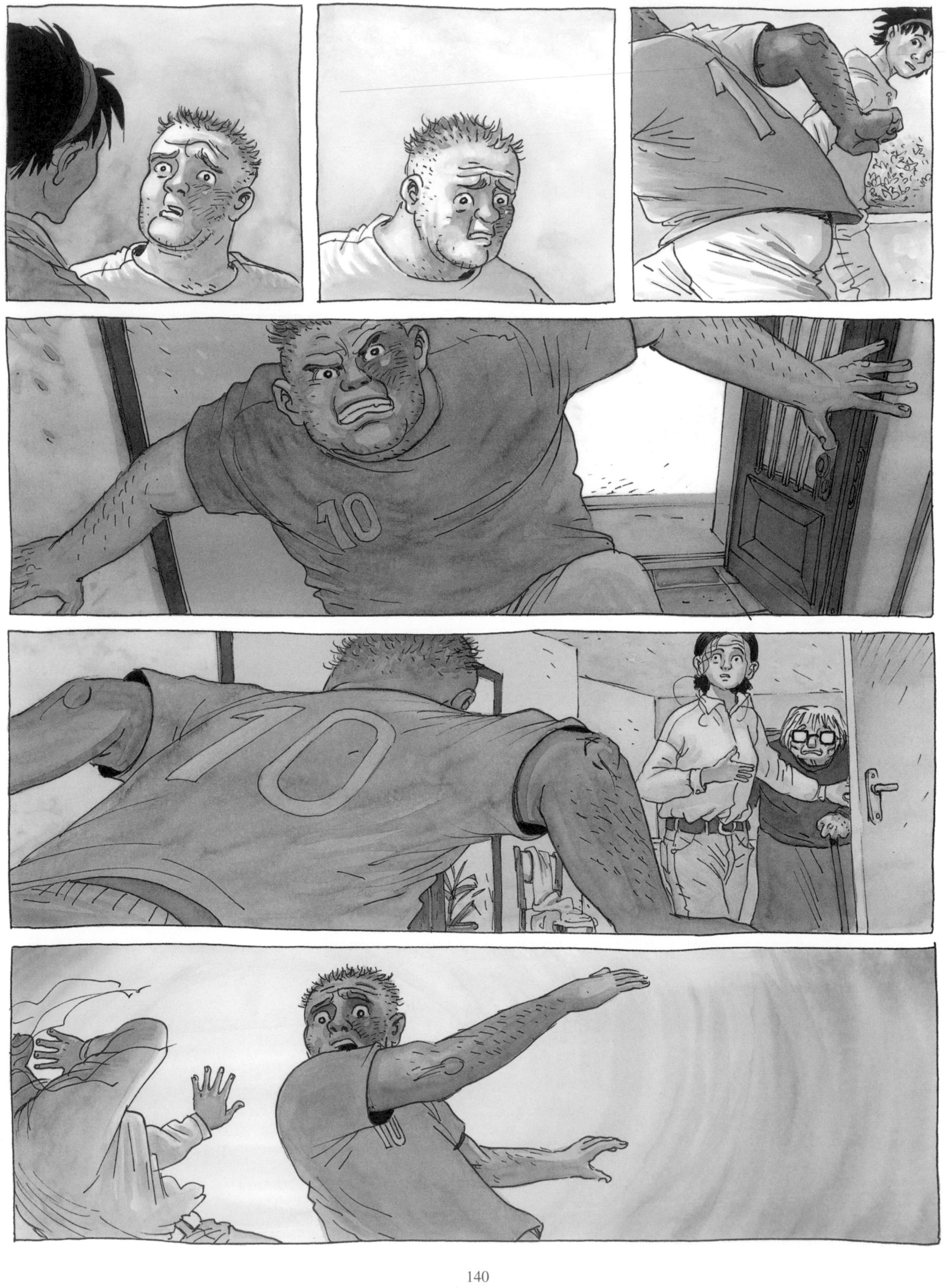

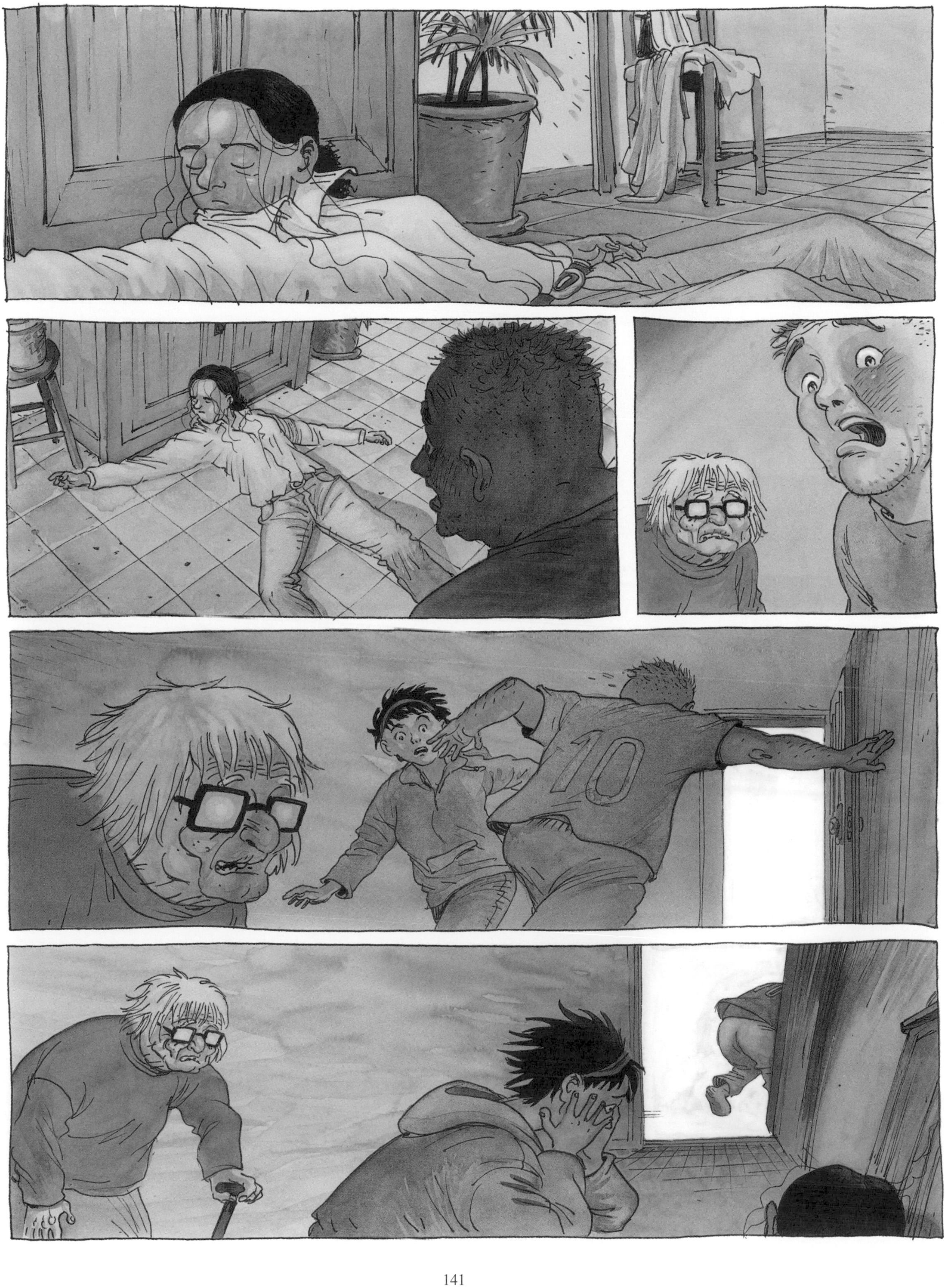
10

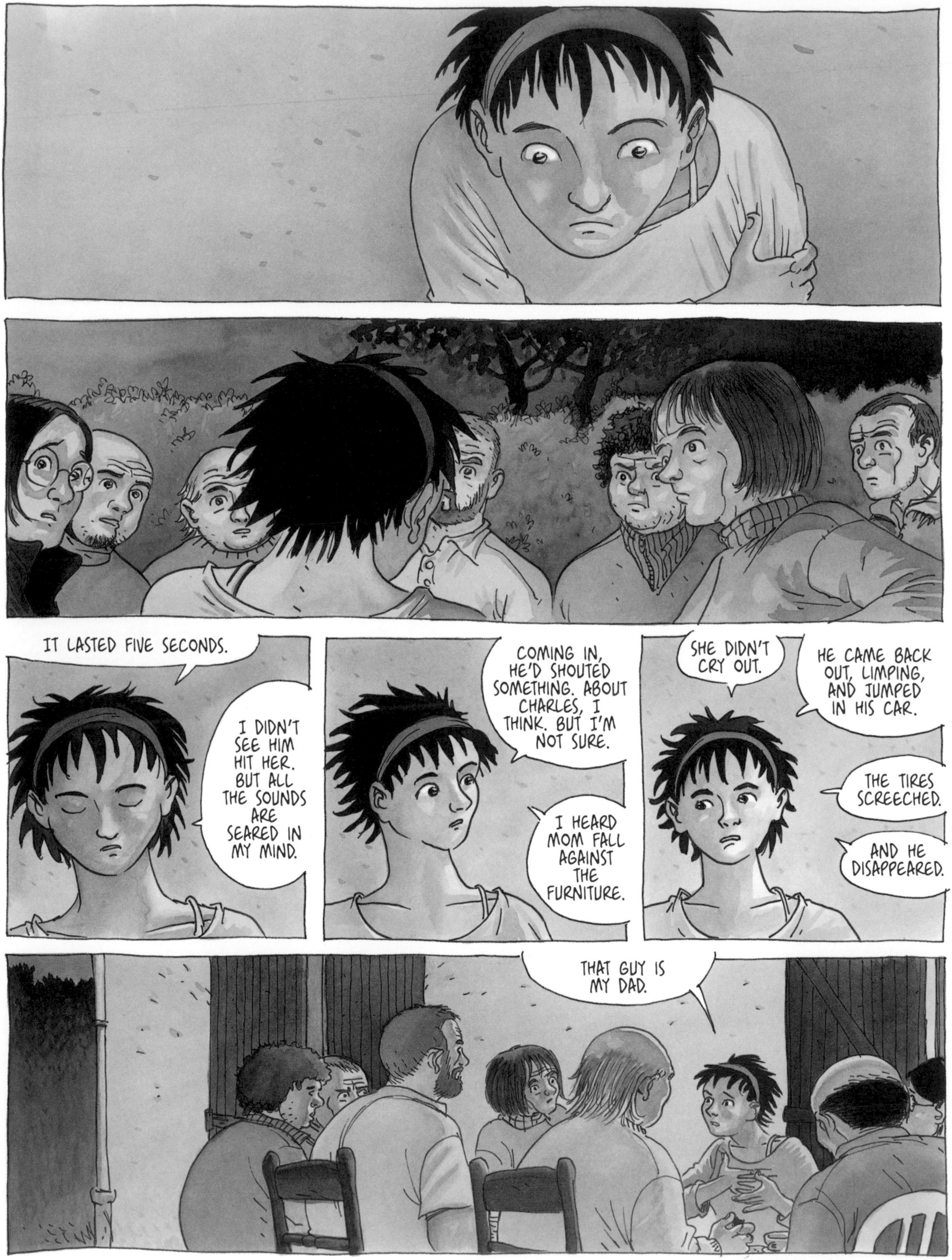
IT LASTED FIVE SECONDS.
I DIDN'T SEE HIM HIT HER. BUT ALL THE SOUNDS ARE SEARED IN MY MIND.
COMING IN, HE'D SHOUTED SOMETHING. ABOUT CHARLES, I THINK. BUT I'M NOT SURE.
I HEARD MOM FALL AGAINST THE FURNITURE.
SHE DIDN'T CRY OUT.
HE CAME BACK OUT, LIMPING, AND JUMPED IN HIS CAR.
THE TIRES SCREECHED.
AND HE DISAPPEARED.
THAT GUY IS MY DAD.

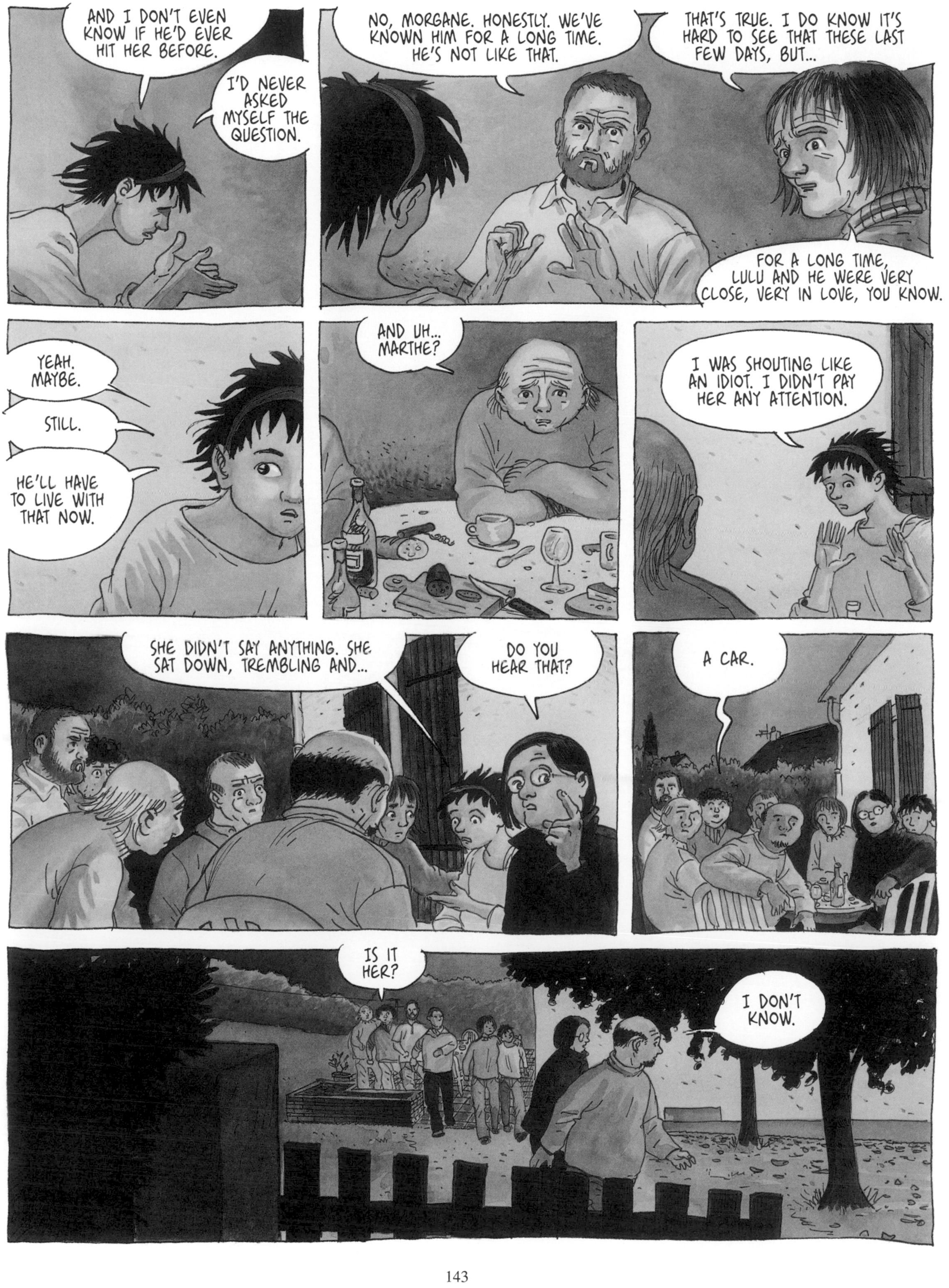
AND I DON'T EVEN KNOW IF HE'D EVER HIT HER BEFORE.
I'D NEVER ASKED MYSELF THE QUESTION.
NO, MORGANE. HONESTLY. WE'VE KNOWN HIM FOR A LONG TIME. HE'S NOT LIKE THAT.
THAT'S TRUE. I DO KNOW IT'S HARD TO SEE THAT THESE LAST FEW DAYS, BUT...
FOR A LONG TIME, LULU AND HE WERE VERY CLOSE, VERY IN LOVE, YOU KNOW.
YEAH. MAYBE.
STILL.
HE'LL HAVE TO LIVE WITH THAT NOW.
AND UH... MARTHE?
I WAS SHOUTING LIKE AN IDIOT. I DIDN'T PAY HER ANY ATTENTION.
SHE DIDN'T SAY ANYTHING. SHE SAT DOWN, TREMBLING AND...
DO YOU HEAR THAT?
A CAR.
IS IT HER?
I DON'T KNOW.

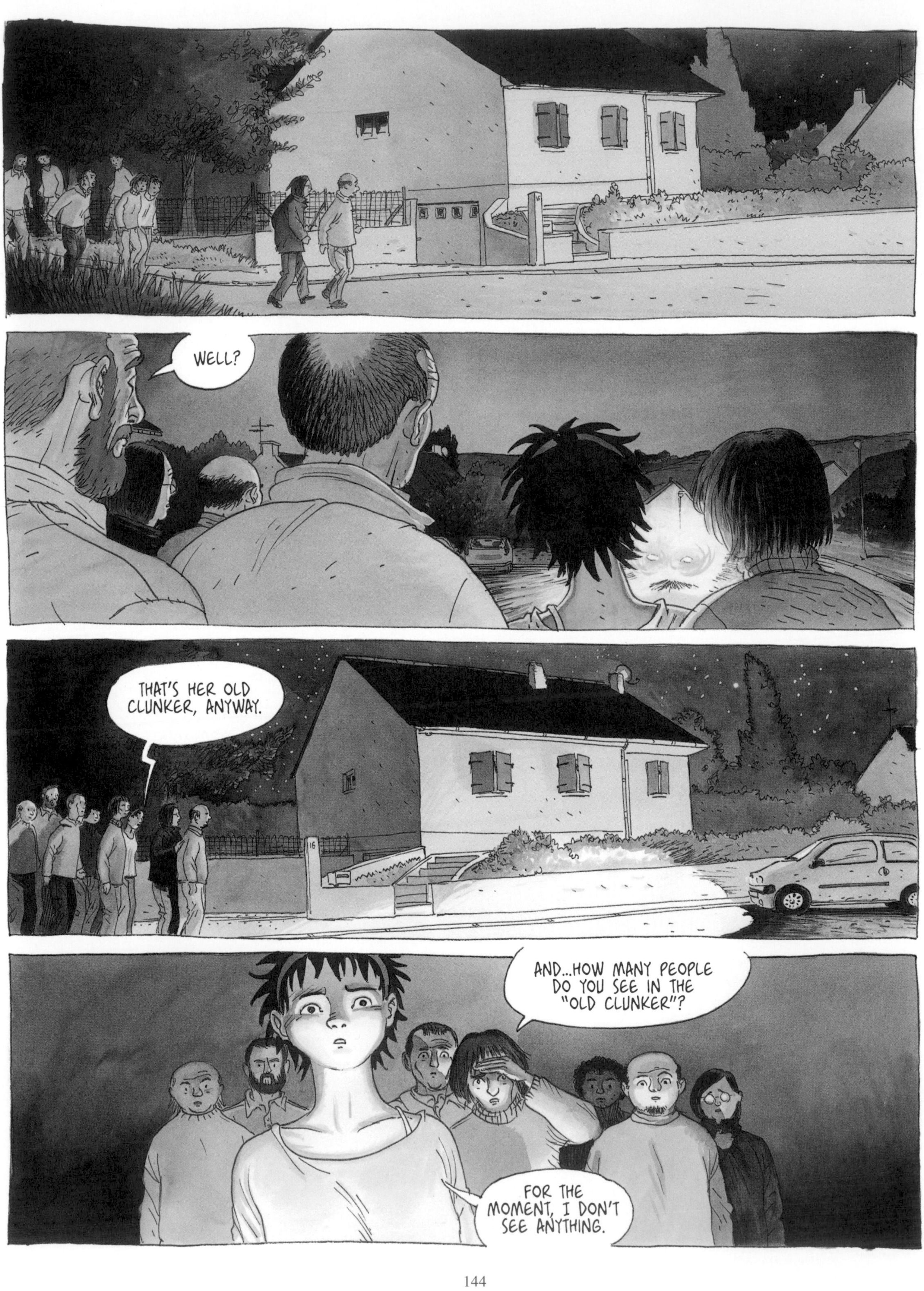
WELL?
THAT'S HER OLD CLUNKER, ANYWAY.
AND...HOW MANY PEOPLE DO YOU SEE IN THE "OLD CLUNKER"?
FOR THE MOMENT, I DON'T SEE ANYTHING.

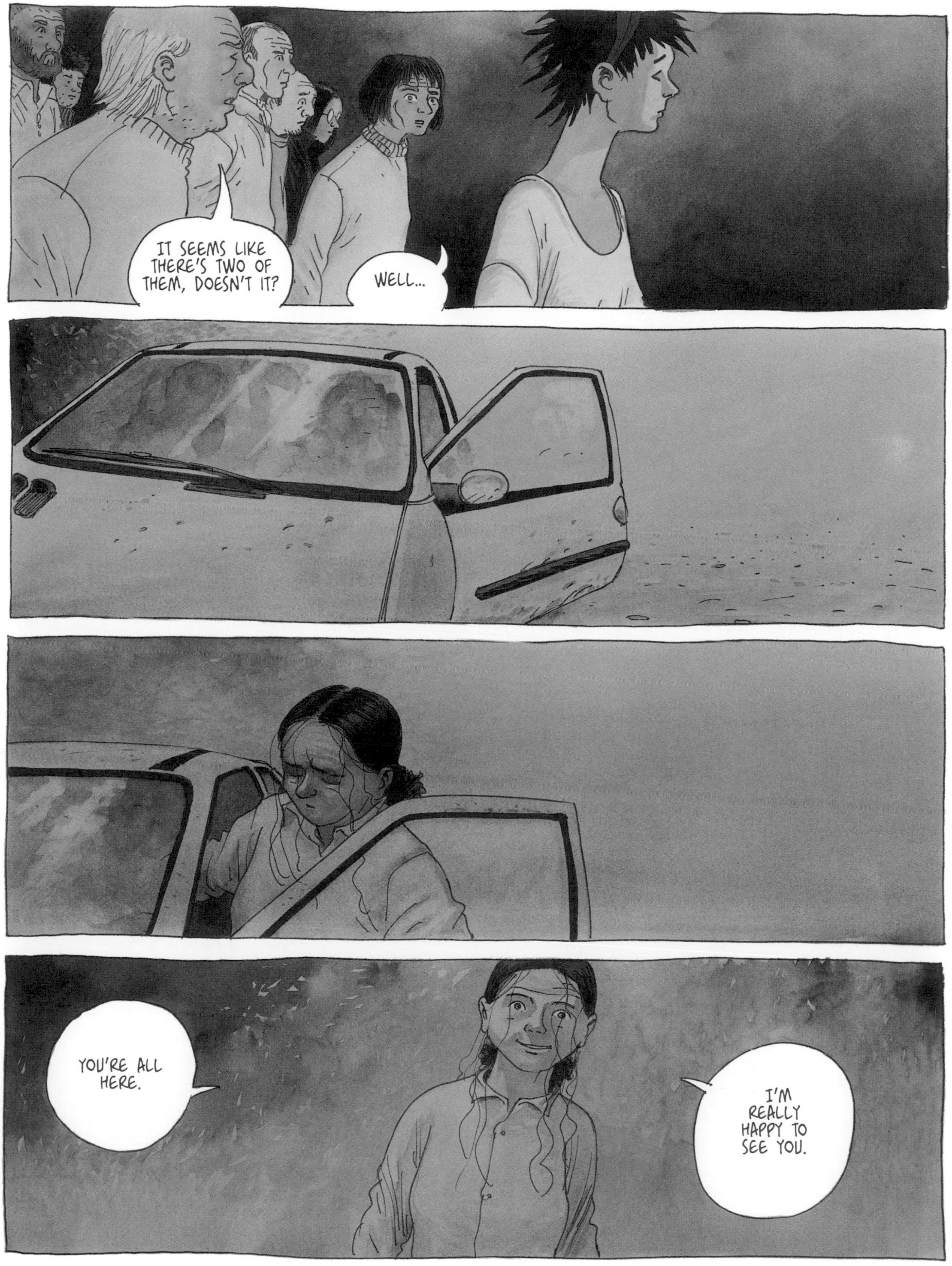
IT SEEMS LIKE THERE'S TWO OF THEM, DOESN'T IT?
WELL...
YOU'RE ALL HERE.
I'M REALLY HAPPY TO SEE YOU.

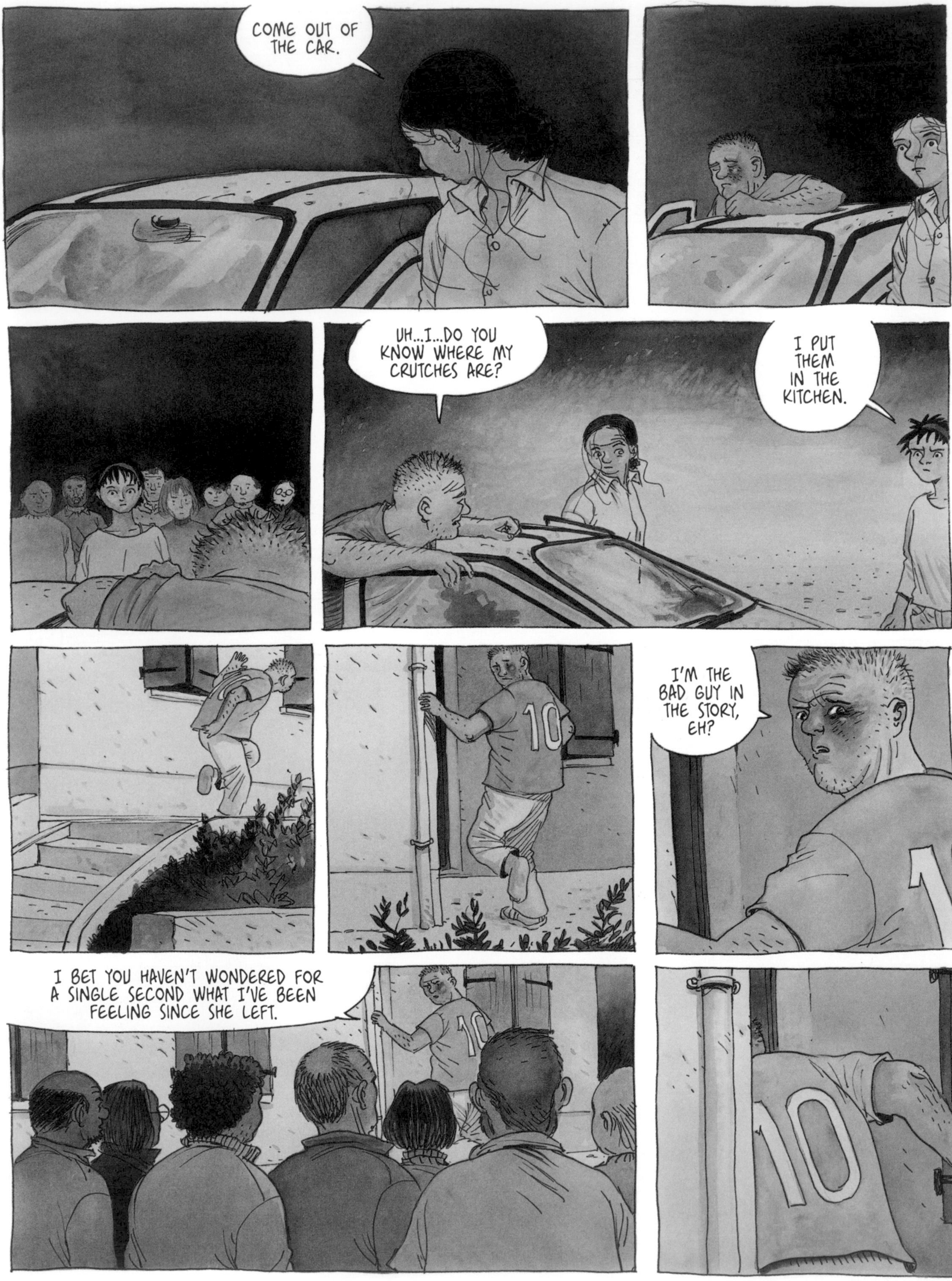
COME OUT OF THE CAR.
UH...I...DO YOU KNOW WHERE MY CRUTCHES ARE?
I PUT THEM IN THE KITCHEN.
I'M THE BAD GUY IN THE STORY, EH?
I BET YOU HAVEN'T WONDERED FOR A SINGLE SECOND WHAT I'VE BEEN FEELING SINCE SHE LEFT.
10

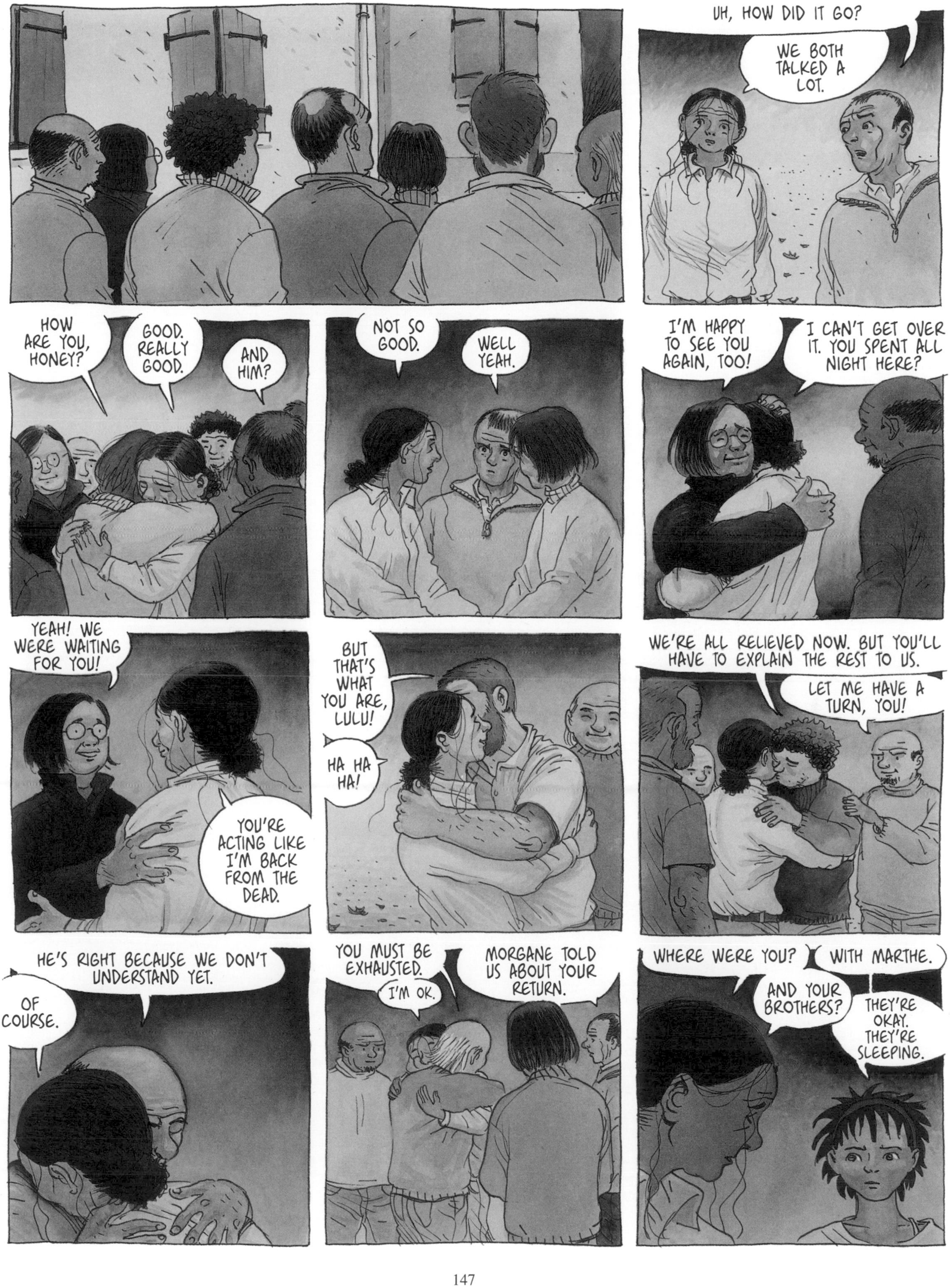
UH, HOW DID IT GO?
WE BOTH TALKED A LOT.
HOW ARE YOU, HONEY?
GOOD. REALLY GOOD.
AND HIM?
NOT SO GOOD.
WELL YEAH.
I'M HAPPY TO SEE YOU AGAIN, TOO!
I CAN'T GET OVER IT. YOU SPENT ALL NIGHT HERE?
YEAH! WE WERE WAITING FOR YOU!
YOU'RE ACTING LIKE I'M BACK FROM THE DEAD.
BUT THAT'S WHAT YOU ARE, LULU!
HA HA HA!
WE'RE ALL RELIEVED NOW. BUT YOU'LL HAVE TO EXPLAIN THE REST TO US.
LET ME HAVE A TURN, YOU!
HE'S RIGHT BECAUSE WE DON'T UNDERSTAND YET.
OF COURSE.
YOU MUST BE EXHAUSTED.
I'M OK.
MORGANE TOLD US ABOUT YOUR RETURN.
WHERE WERE YOU?
WITH MARTHE.
AND YOUR BROTHERS?
THEY'RE OKAY. THEY'RE SLEEPING.

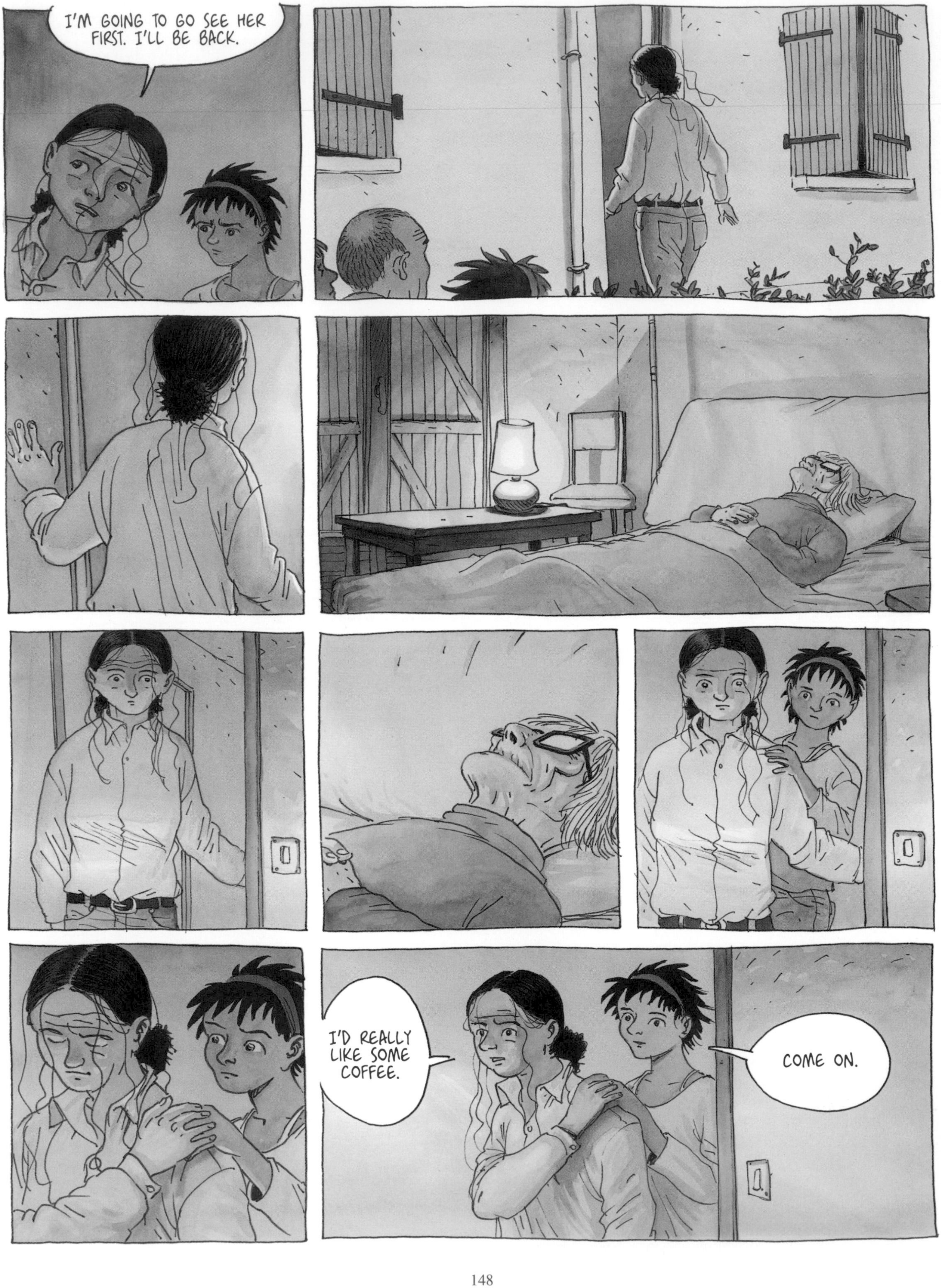
I'M GOING TO GO SEE HER FIRST. I'LL BE BACK.
I'D REALLY LIKE SOME COFFEE.
COME ON.

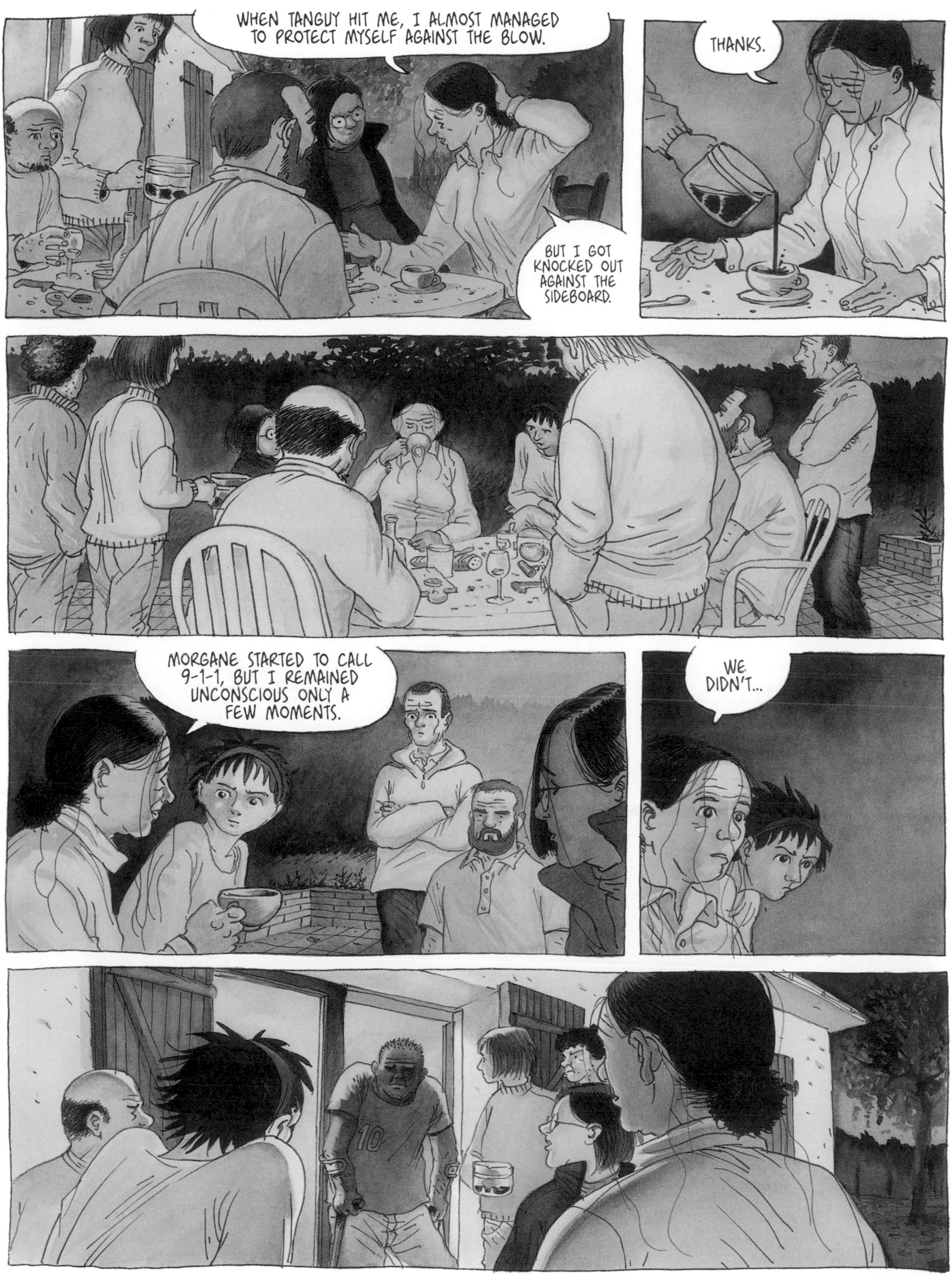
When Tanguy hit me, I almost managed to protect myself against the blow.
But I got knocked out against the sideboard.
Thanks.
Morgane started to call 9-1-1, but I remained unconscious only a few moments.
We didn't...

YOU WANT SOME COFFEE, TANGUY?

YOU CAN SIT WITH US, IF YOU LIKE.

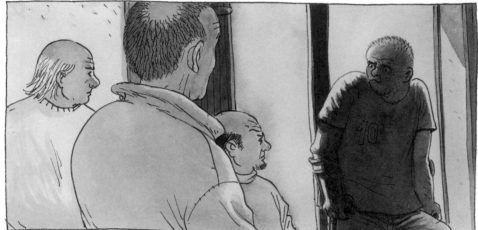

OF COURSE I CAN. THIS IS MY HOME, BUT NO, I'M GONNA TRY AND SLEEP A LITTLE.

I'LL LET YOU TELL THE STORY.

GO ON, MOM.

OKAY.

WE WEREN'T CAREFUL ABOUT MARTHE.

SHE'D LET HERSELF FALL ONTO A CHAIR.

SHE WAS ALL WHITE AND IN A SWEAT.

WE REALIZE SHE'S FEELING SERIOUSLY FAINT, SO FINALLY, WE DO CALL 9-1-1.

REANIMATION

WHEN THEY ARRIVE, SHE'S STILL ALIVE.

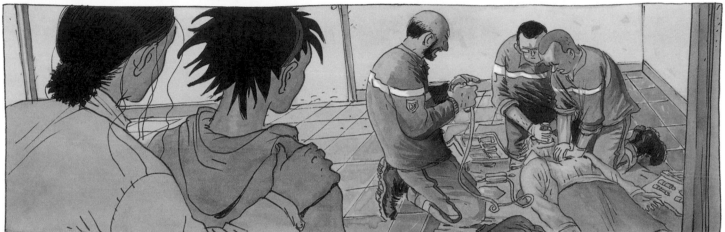

THEY STRUGGLE FOR MORE THAN A HALF-HOUR, BUT THEY CAN'T SAVE HER.

HER HEART?

YES, HER HEART, AND AGE, AND THE SHOCK.

I DON'T KNOW HOW TO TELL YOU THIS, BUT...

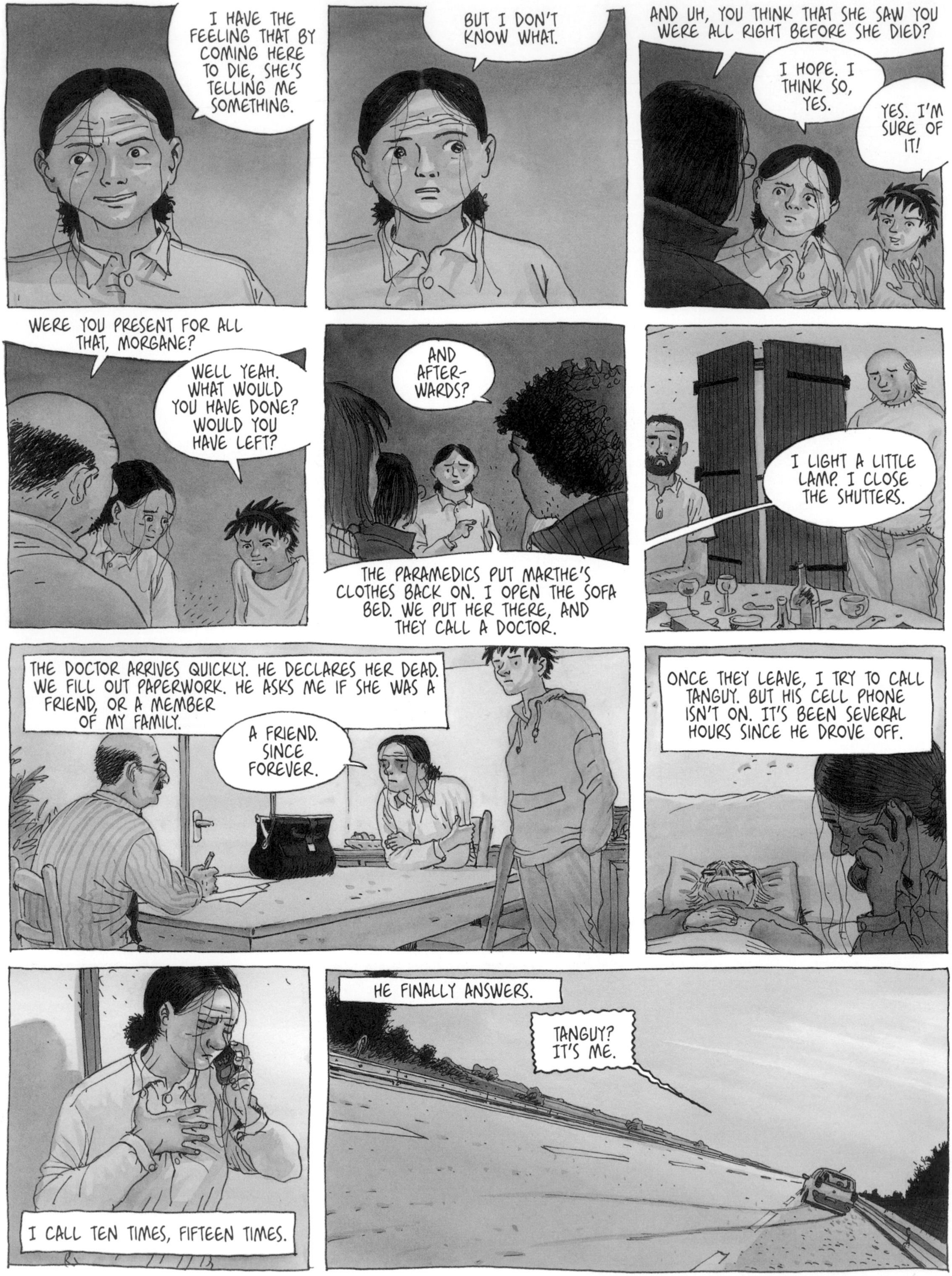
I HAVE THE FEELING THAT BY COMING HERE TO DIE, SHE'S TELLING ME SOMETHING.
BUT I DON'T KNOW WHAT.
AND UH, YOU THINK THAT SHE SAW YOU WERE ALL RIGHT BEFORE SHE DIED?
I HOPE. I THINK SO, YES.
YES. I'M SURE OF IT!
WERE YOU PRESENT FOR ALL THAT, MORGANE?
WELL YEAH. WHAT WOULD YOU HAVE DONE? WOULD YOU HAVE LEFT?
AND AFTER-WARDS?
THE PARAMEDICS PUT MARTHE'S CLOTHES BACK ON. I OPEN THE SOFA BED. WE PUT HER THERE, AND THEY CALL A DOCTOR.
I LIGHT A LITTLE LAMP. I CLOSE THE SHUTTERS.
THE DOCTOR ARRIVES QUICKLY. HE DECLARES HER DEAD. WE FILL OUT PAPERWORK. HE ASKS ME IF SHE WAS A FRIEND, OR A MEMBER OF MY FAMILY.
A FRIEND. SINCE FOREVER.
ONCE THEY LEAVE, I TRY TO CALL TANGUY. BUT HIS CELL PHONE ISN'T ON. IT'S BEEN SEVERAL HOURS SINCE HE DROVE OFF.
I CALL TEN TIMES, FIFTEEN TIMES.
HE FINALLY ANSWERS.
TANGUY? IT'S ME.

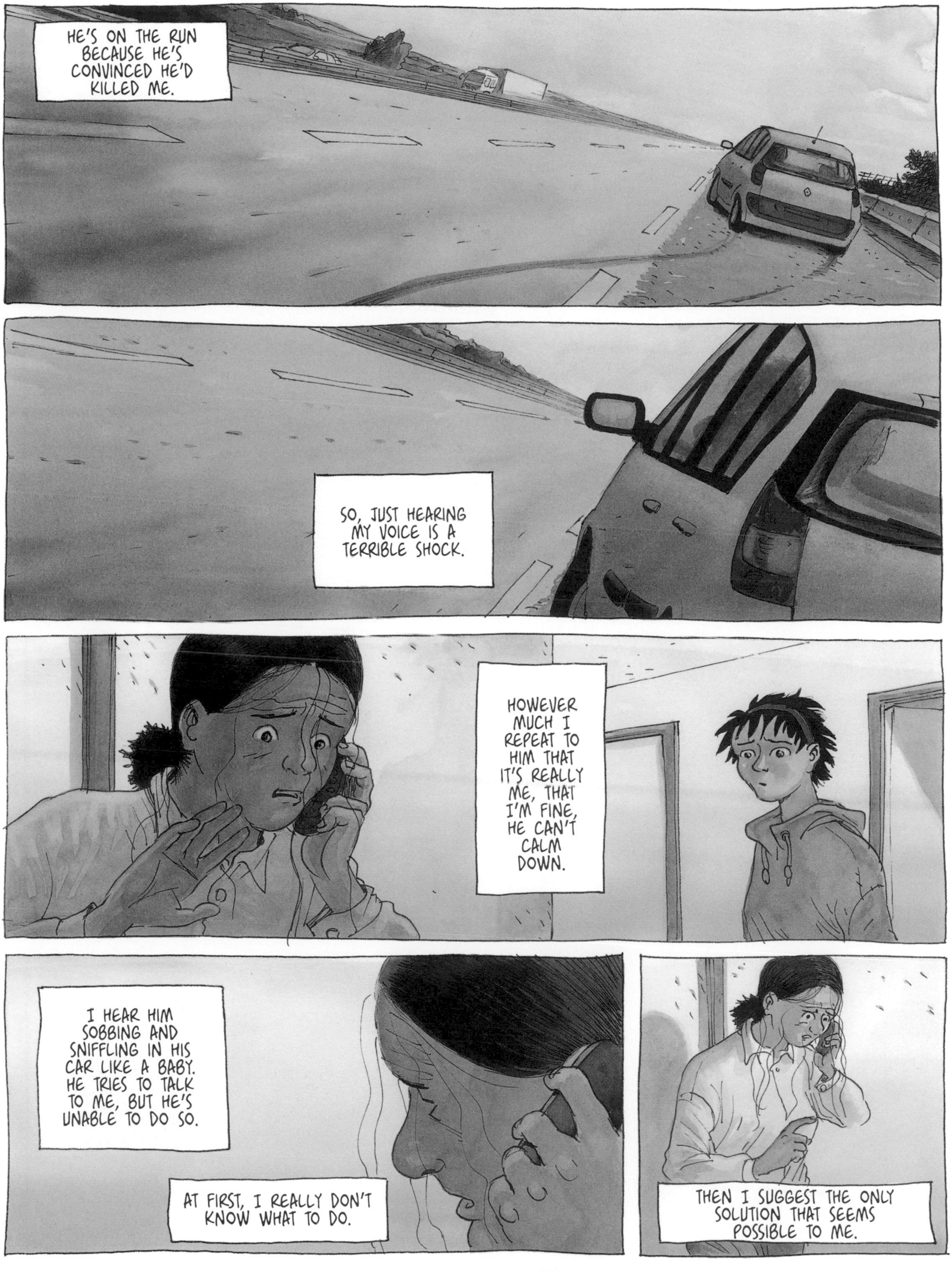
HE'S ON THE RUN BECAUSE HE'S CONVINCED HE'D KILLED ME.
SO, JUST HEARING MY VOICE IS A TERRIBLE SHOCK.
HOWEVER MUCH I REPEAT TO HIM THAT IT'S REALLY ME, THAT I'M FINE, HE CAN'T CALM DOWN.
I HEAR HIM SOBBING AND SNIFFLING IN HIS CAR LIKE A BABY. HE TRIES TO TALK TO ME, BUT HE'S UNABLE TO DO SO.
AT FIRST, I REALLY DON'T KNOW WHAT TO DO.
THEN I SUGGEST THE ONLY SOLUTION THAT SEEMS POSSIBLE TO ME.

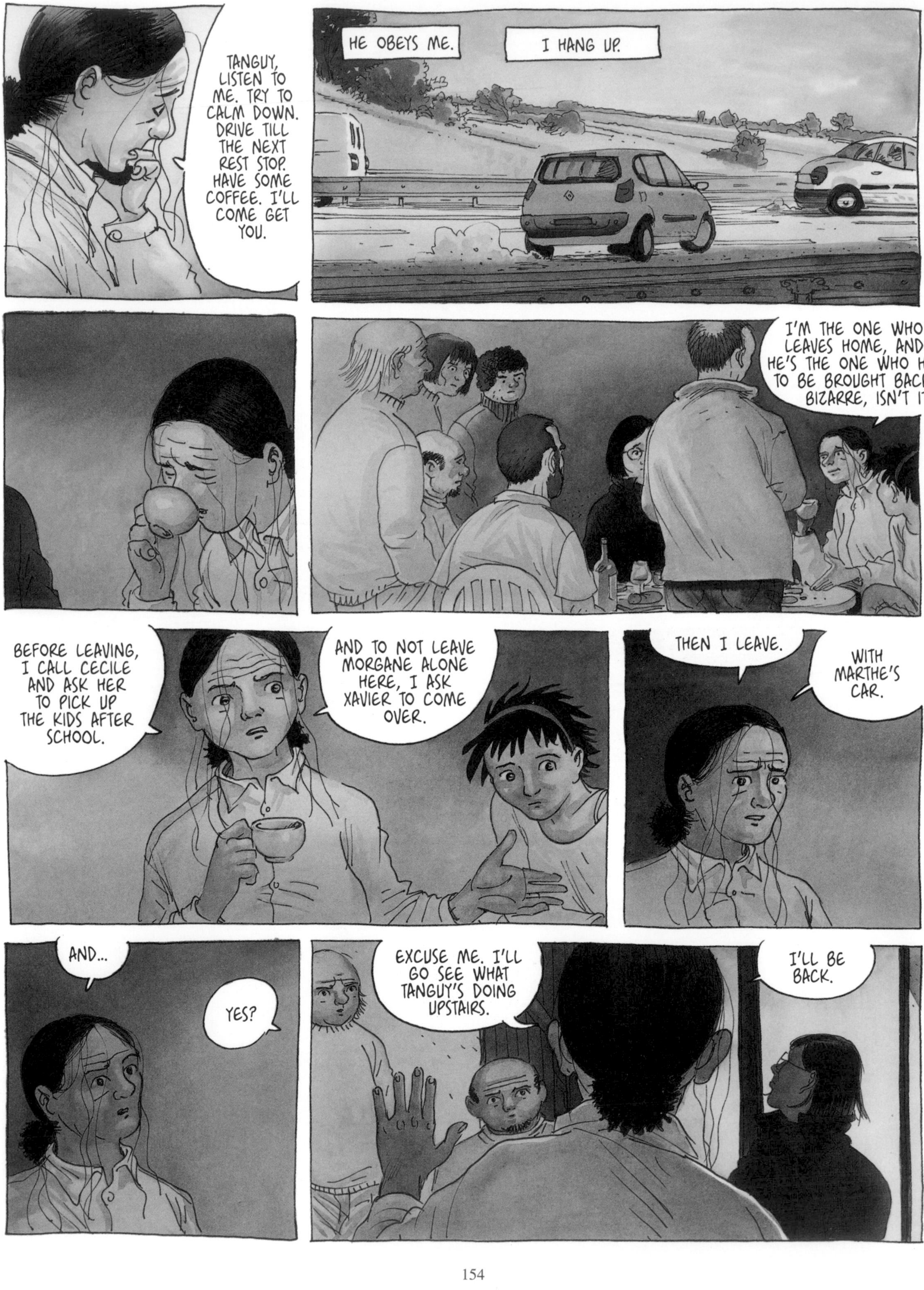
TANGUY, LISTEN TO ME. TRY TO CALM DOWN. DRIVE TILL THE NEXT REST STOP. HAVE SOME COFFEE. I'LL COME GET YOU.
HE OBEYS ME.
I HANG UP.
I'M THE ONE WHO LEAVES HOME, AND HE'S THE ONE WHO HAS TO BE BROUGHT BACK. BIZARRE, ISN'T IT?
BEFORE LEAVING, I CALL CECILE AND ASK HER TO PICK UP THE KIDS AFTER SCHOOL.
AND TO NOT LEAVE MORGANE ALONE HERE, I ASK XAVIER TO COME OVER.
THEN I LEAVE.
WITH MARTHE'S CAR.
AND...
YES?
EXCUSE ME. I'LL GO SEE WHAT TANGUY'S DOING UPSTAIRS.
I'LL BE BACK.

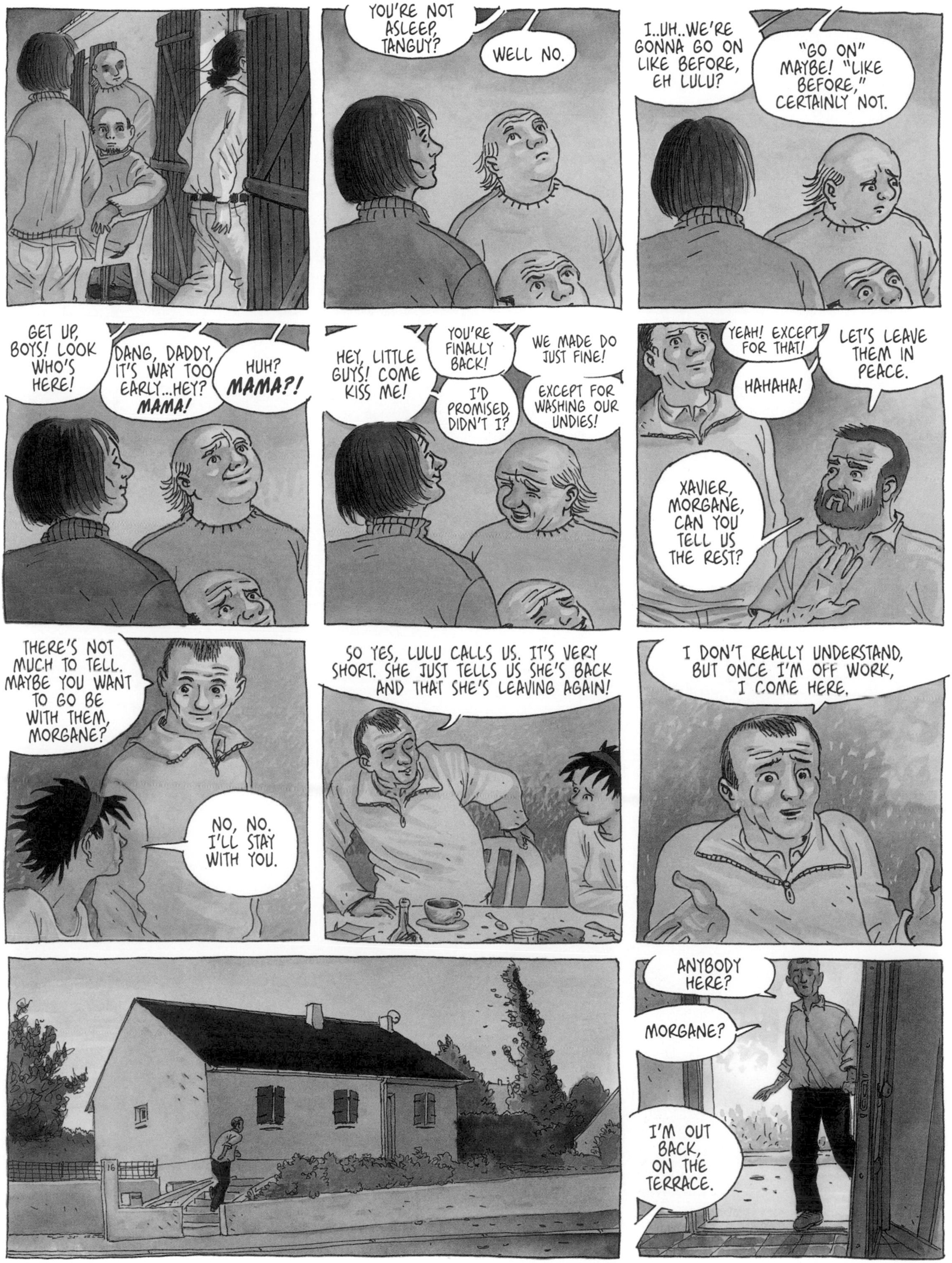
YOU'RE NOT ASLEEP, TANGUY?
WELL NO.
I..UH..WE'RE GONNA GO ON LIKE BEFORE, EH LULU?
"GO ON" MAYBE! "LIKE BEFORE," CERTAINLY NOT.
GET UP, BOYS! LOOK WHO'S HERE!
DANG, DADDY, IT'S WAY TOO EARLY...HEY? MAMA!
HUH? MAMA?!
HEY, LITTLE GUYS! COME KISS ME!
YOU'RE FINALLY BACK!
I'D PROMISED, DIDN'T I?
WE MADE DO JUST FINE!
EXCEPT FOR WASHING OUR UNDIES!
YEAH! EXCEPT FOR THAT!
HAHAHA!
LET'S LEAVE THEM IN PEACE.
XAVIER, MORGANE, CAN YOU TELL US THE REST?
THERE'S NOT MUCH TO TELL. MAYBE YOU WANT TO GO BE WITH THEM, MORGANE?
NO, NO. I'LL STAY WITH YOU.
SO YES, LULU CALLS US. IT'S VERY SHORT. SHE JUST TELLS US SHE'S BACK AND THAT SHE'S LEAVING AGAIN!
I DON'T REALLY UNDERSTAND, BUT ONCE I'M OFF WORK, I COME HERE.
16
ANYBODY HERE?
MORGANE?
I'M OUT BACK, ON THE TERRACE.

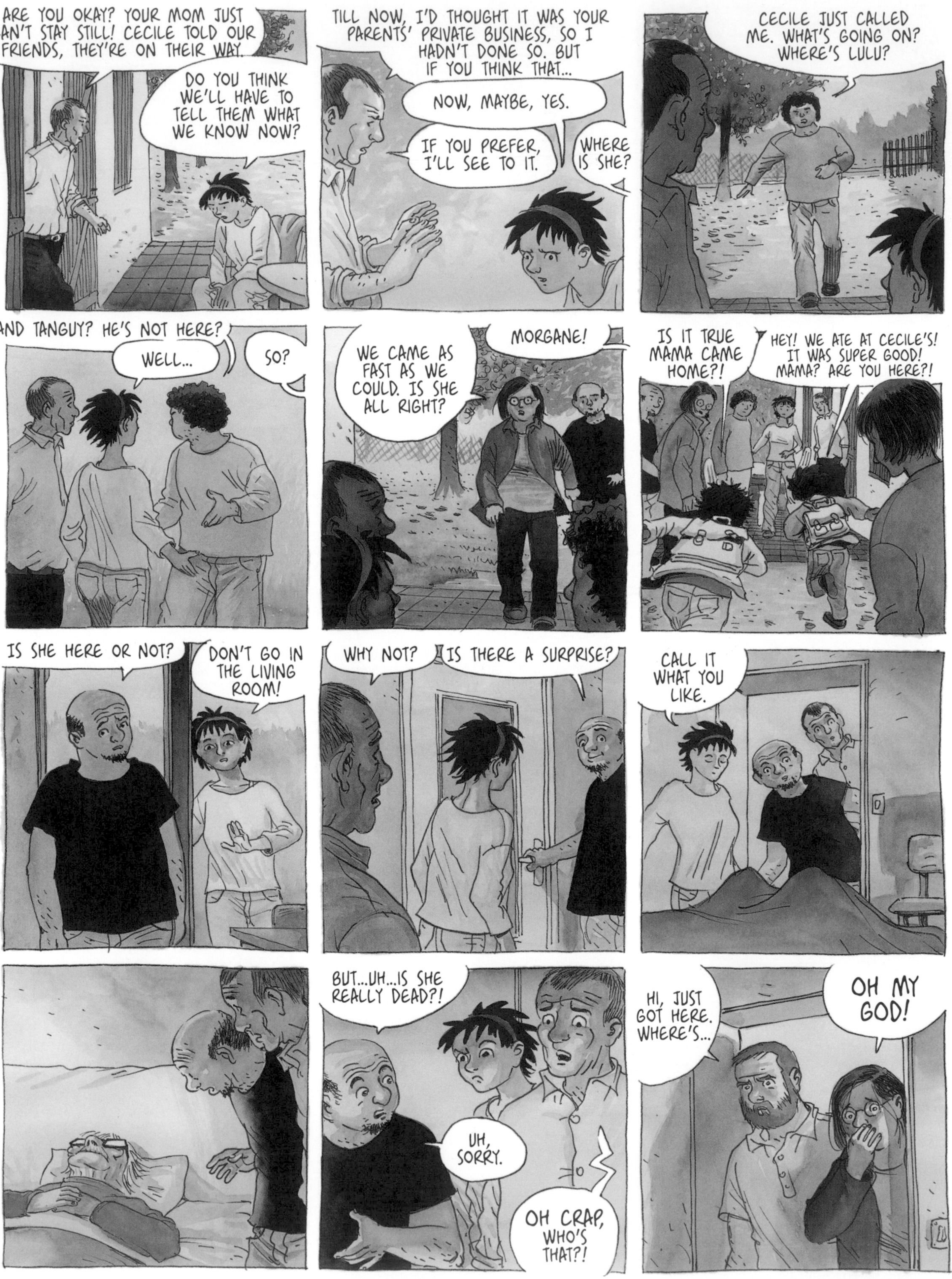
ARE YOU OKAY? YOUR MOM JUST CAN'T STAY STILL! CECILE TOLD OUR FRIENDS, THEY'RE ON THEIR WAY.
DO YOU THINK WE'LL HAVE TO TELL THEM WHAT WE KNOW NOW?
TILL NOW, I'D THOUGHT IT WAS YOUR PARENTS' PRIVATE BUSINESS, SO I HADN'T DONE SO. BUT IF YOU THINK THAT...
NOW, MAYBE, YES.
IF YOU PREFER, I'LL SEE TO IT.
WHERE IS SHE?
CECILE JUST CALLED ME. WHAT'S GOING ON? WHERE'S LULU?
AND TANGUY? HE'S NOT HERE?
WELL...
SO?
WE CAME AS FAST AS WE COULD. IS SHE ALL RIGHT?
MORGANE!
IS IT TRUE MAMA CAME HOME?!
HEY! WE ATE AT CECILE'S! IT WAS SUPER GOOD! MAMA? ARE YOU HERE?!
IS SHE HERE OR NOT?
DON'T GO IN THE LIVING ROOM!
WHY NOT?
IS THERE A SURPRISE?
CALL IT WHAT YOU LIKE.
BUT...UH...IS SHE REALLY DEAD?!
UH, SORRY.
OH CRAP, WHO'S THAT?!
HI, JUST GOT HERE. WHERE'S...
OH MY GOD!

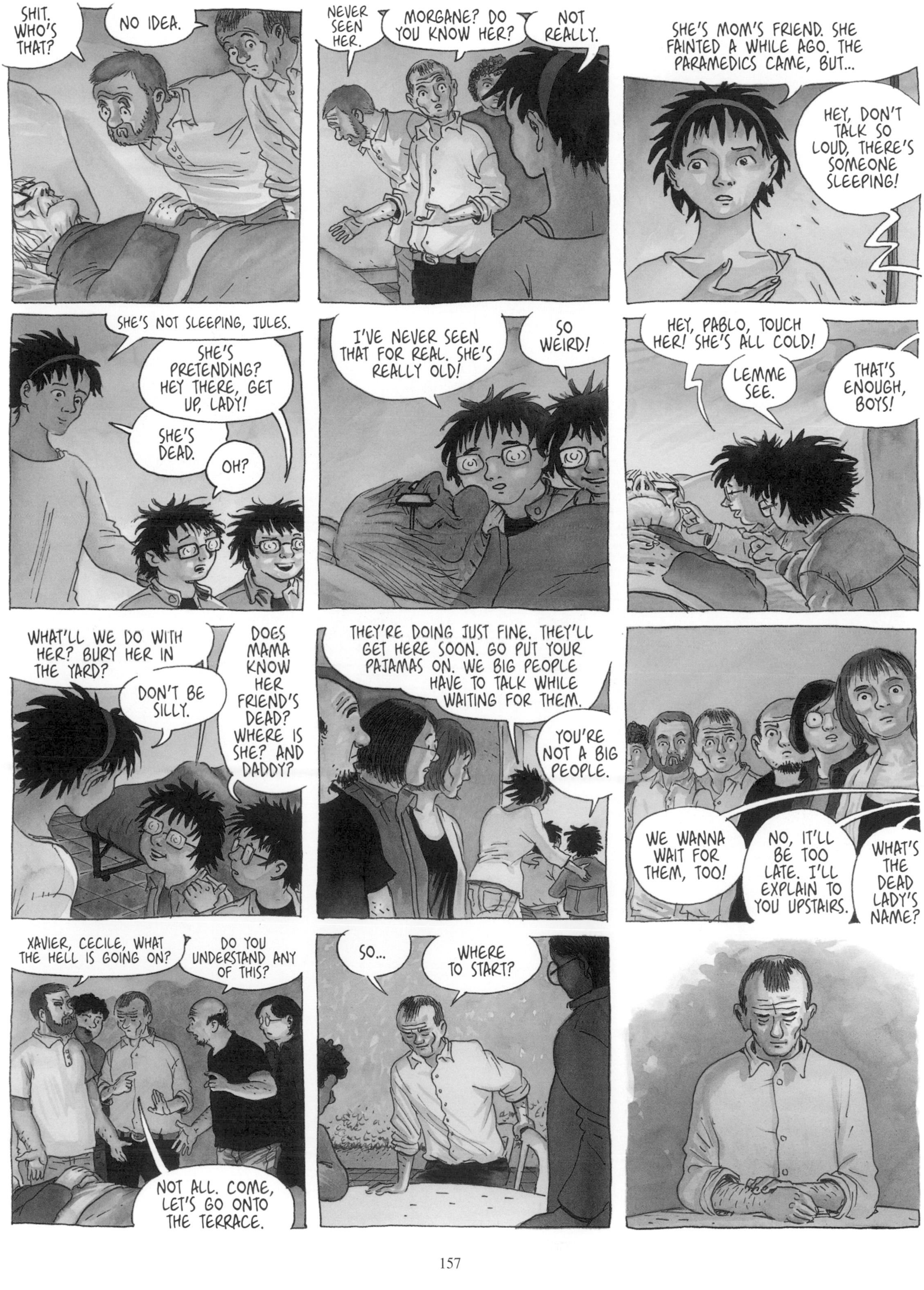

SHIT. WHO'S THAT?
NO IDEA.
NEVER SEEN HER.
MORGANE? DO YOU KNOW HER?
NOT REALLY.
SHE'S MOM'S FRIEND. SHE FAINTED A WHILE AGO. THE PARAMEDICS CAME, BUT...
HEY, DON'T TALK SO LOUD, THERE'S SOMEONE SLEEPING!
SHE'S NOT SLEEPING, JULES.
SHE'S PRETENDING? HEY THERE, GET UP, LADY!
SHE'S DEAD.
OH?
I'VE NEVER SEEN THAT FOR REAL. SHE'S REALLY OLD!
SO WEIRD!
HEY, PABLO, TOUCH HER! SHE'S ALL COLD!
LEMME SEE.
THAT'S ENOUGH, BOYS!
WHAT'LL WE DO WITH HER? BURY HER IN THE YARD?
DON'T BE SILLY.
DOES MAMA KNOW HER FRIEND'S DEAD? WHERE IS SHE? AND DADDY?
THEY'RE DOING JUST FINE. THEY'LL GET HERE SOON. GO PUT YOUR PAJAMAS ON. WE BIG PEOPLE HAVE TO TALK WHILE WAITING FOR THEM.
YOU'RE NOT A BIG PEOPLE.
WE WANNA WAIT FOR THEM, TOO!
NO, IT'LL BE TOO LATE. I'LL EXPLAIN TO YOU UPSTAIRS.
WHAT'S THE DEAD LADY'S NAME?
XAVIER, CECILE, WHAT THE HELL IS GOING ON?
DO YOU UNDERSTAND ANY OF THIS?
NOT ALL. COME, LET'S GO ONTO THE TERRACE.
SO...
WHERE TO START?

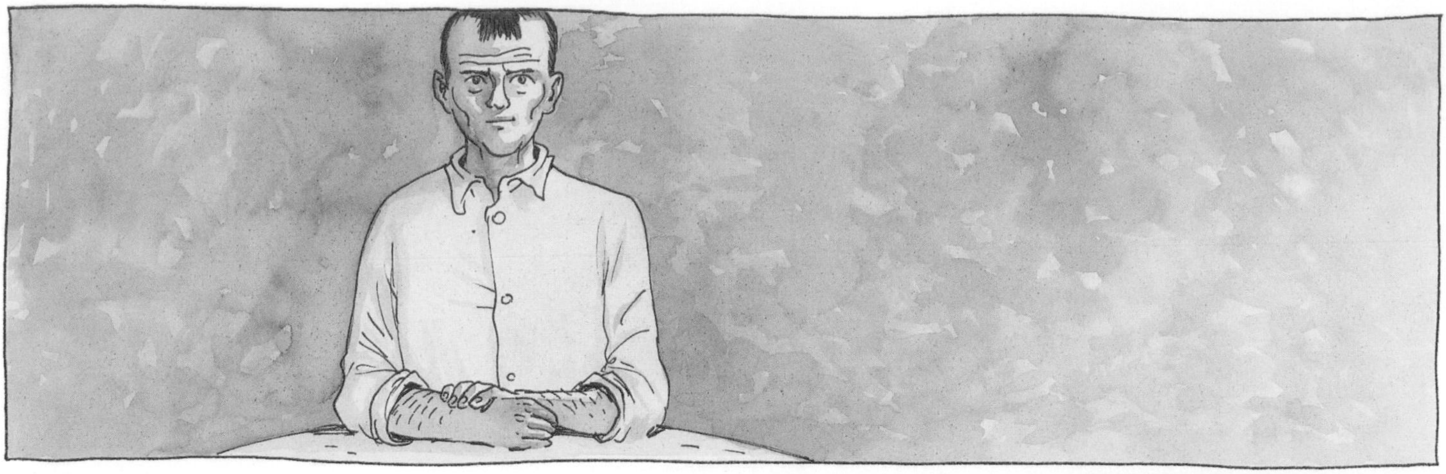

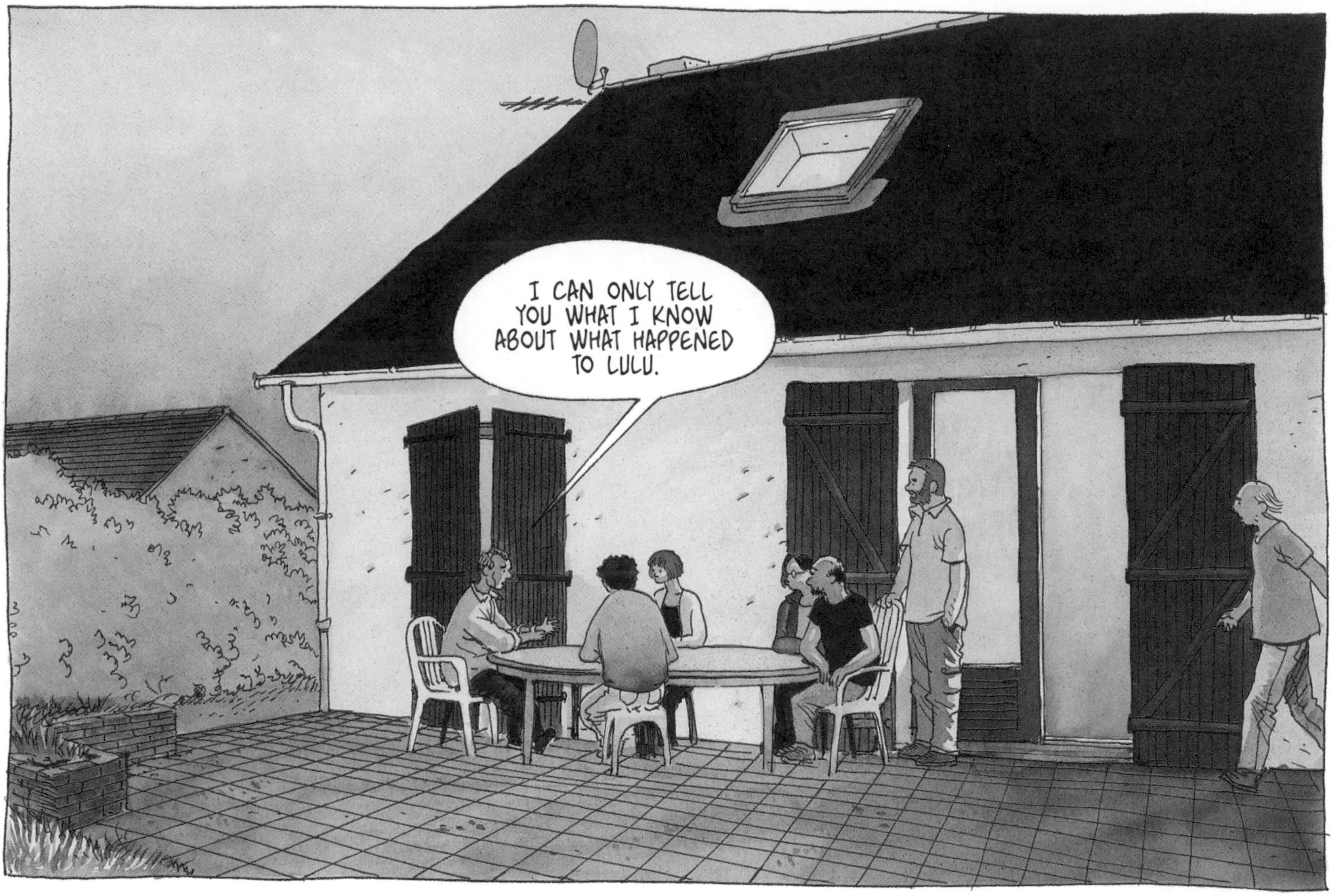
I CAN ONLY TELL YOU WHAT I KNOW ABOUT WHAT HAPPENED TO LULU.

Etienne DAVODEAU

Étienne Davodeau
THE INITIATES
A Comic Artist and a Wine Artisan Exchange Jobs

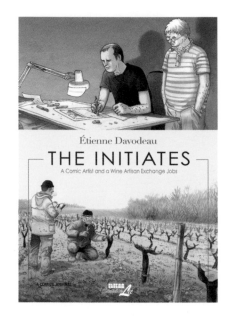

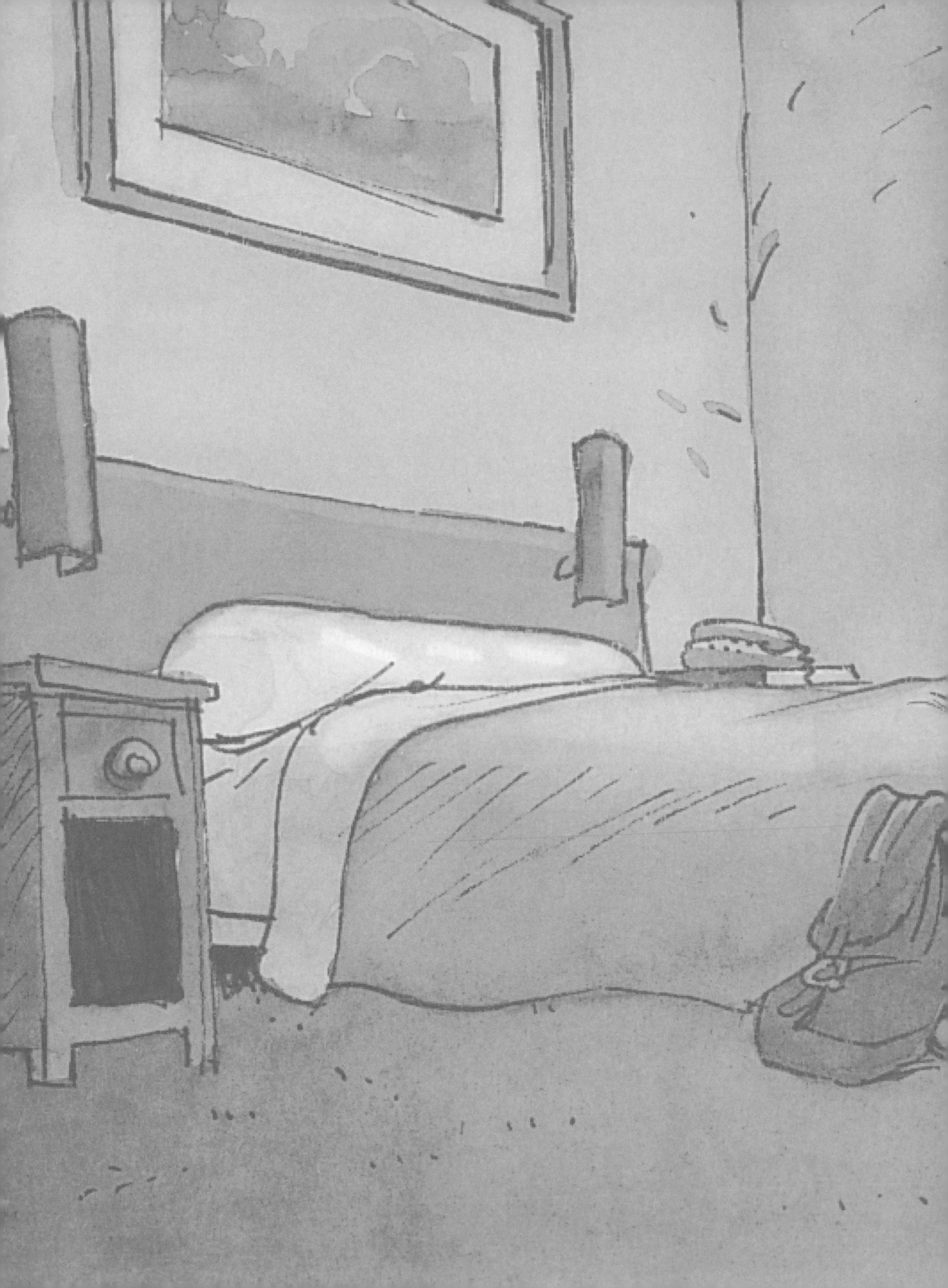